learning
as a
political act

*struggles for learning and
learning from struggles*

JOSÉ A. SEGARRA
RICARDO DOBLES

Editors

Harvard Educational Review
Reprint Series No. 33

Library of Congress Catalog Card Number 99-72060

ISBN 0-916690-35-0

Harvard Educational Review
Gutman Library Suite 349
6 Appian Way
Cambridge, MA 02138
http://gseweb.harvard.edu/~hepg/her.html

Cover Design: Alyssa Morris
Cover Artwork: Gamaal Tyrone "Willie" Wilson
Editorial Production: Dody Riggs
Typography: Sheila Walsh

First, education is a political act, whether at the university, high school, primary school, or adult literacy classroom. Why? Because the very nature of education has the inherent qualities to be political, as indeed politics has educational aspects. In other words, an educational act has a political nature and a political act has an educational nature. If this is generally so, it would be incorrect to say that Latin American education alone has a political nature. Education worldwide is political by nature.

Paulo Freire
The Politics of Education

DEDICATION

*We would like to dedicate our book to the memory of
Felicita Escobar Valentín, a Puerto Rican woman who made us
better people through her love, her courage, and her sacrifice;
and to Bonnie Resto, a young Puerto Rican woman who
brightened the lives of all those around her with her
humor, intelligence, and love of life.*

Contents

Foreword

MAXINE GREENE

At the end of his book, *Culture and Imperialism,* Edward Said writes:

> No one today is purely one thing. Labels like Indian, or woman, or Muslim, or American are not more than starting points, which if followed into actual experience for a moment are quickly left behind. Imperialism consolidated the mixture of cultures and identities on a global scale. But its worst and most paradoxical gift was to allow people to believe that they were only, mainly, exclusively white or Black or Western or Oriental. Yet just as human beings make their own history, they also make their cultures and their ethnic identities.[1]

We need to think about the connections between things, not the separation. "But this also means," says Said, "not trying to rule others, not trying to classify them or put them in hierarchies, above all, not constantly reiterating how 'our' culture or country is number one."

In this remarkable book, which allows us to listen to voices long silenced and to confront struggles long unseen, we are challenged to think about how learning can create what Said calls "starting points." But this can only happen, we are soon reminded, if languages and cultures are no longer demeaned, if timeworn exclusions are no longer maintained. Gender, ethnic identity, class, national allegiances, age, sexuality: all these are dealt with in the chapters that follow, all of which were originally published in the *Harvard Educational Review.* Most significantly, they are dealt with from the vantage points of people who have suffered what is being described, people engaged in struggles to learn and, through learning, to reach beyond where they are.

It is not only that readers are introduced to a rich variety of human beings — Native women, Chicana women, Puerto Rican schoolchildren, Eritrean women, Palestinian liberation fighters, Hmong college women. We also engage with them in moments of struggle, moments of reflective action. Going beyond familiar "multicultural" distinctions, writers here (including a quietly eloquent Cornel West) share experiences that other minorities and marginalized people also undergo. The interview with Dr. West, like the stories the book's young people tell, underlines the political dimension of learning. Not incidentally, a concern for the erotic (which can be "empowering and ennobling" and become a source of hope) summons up some of the ideas infusing what is thought of as "educational renewal," a movement at odds with the technicist, the monocultural, the manipulative.

---

[1] Edward Said, *Culture and Imperialism* (New York: Vintage Press, 1993), p. 336.

There is hope, too, embodied in the brave and brilliant lifework of Antonia Pantoja, a leader of New York City's Puerto Rican community, founder of ASPIRA, a proudly political educator. There is the civil rights activist, Robert Moses, working in the spirit of Ella Baker, developing the emancipatory "Algebra Project" to give deprived children access to programs teaching skills that are required in our advanced technological economy/society. Underlying what is presented in this book is a commitment to social justice linked to a realization that schooling and struggle mean different things in different cultures, and that there are distinctive modes of liberatory action.

The reader cannot but be challenged by the images of control and ideological unfairness, by the starkness of the oppression lived in some communities day after day. There is, however, a continuous reminder of what human agency can signify, what courage can mean in the struggle for freedom and justice, wherever it takes place. Editors José Segarra and Ricardo Dobles have, through their sensitive selection of contributors, opened windows of possibility. Glimpses of what Paulo Freire called "a lovelier world" appear in the midst of campaigns and struggles in neighborhoods and communities throughout the country. Learning can indeed be a political act involving a rediscovery of old legacies and a confrontation of new stories. And always, always a turn toward *praxis* in ongoing efforts to explore, to understand, to transform.

Introduction

Where should a book like ours begin? Perhaps it is best if we begin where we ourselves work and study, deciphering what is around us, what we see and hear beyond the classroom and in the larger context of our world. What better place to examine a ubiquitous pedagogy that penetrates the classroom and, like white noise, invades all dimensions of everyday life than at Harvard University — a place many have come to regard as a center of capitalist production (Freire & Faundez, 1992). As students at one of this nation's intellectual centers of power and privilege, we often marvel at the overabundance of hypocrisy and "false generosity" (Freire, 1970) we find here. For instance, while countless hours are spent by well-meaning liberal students and faculty alike on "community service" (a euphemism for helping those we deem helpless), we rarely speak of our role in producing the very conditions that create human beings "in need" or "at risk." The authors in this book, however, are not silent on the subject of power and privilege. Through their writings, we come to understand that it is precisely an education that dares to examine the unexamined and to unearth the underlying contradictions in the lessons we are taught on a daily basis that makes learning political.

The reader may ask, and rightly so, what do we mean by "underlying contradictions" or "ubiquitous pedagogy"? Indeed, lacking a proper context, these are abstract and fairly meaningless phrases. We can only offer in response our everyday experiences as Puerto Rican students at Harvard University. Our journey into learning as a political act, into understanding the power of struggle, begins here. In fact, a short walk from the Harvard Square subway stop to the Harvard Graduate School of Education can be an extraordinary introduction to the dual concepts of struggling to learn and learning from struggle. We ask the reader to indulge us as we take you along that walk and reflect upon aspects of a short and seemingly innocent trip that is in fact filled with irony, ideology, politics, privilege, and, yes, education.

As we move past the open doors of the subway, it is impossible to miss the advertisements for the *Wall Street Journal* that line the walls of the station. In the lower right-hand corner of these large billboards we are told that if we buy the *Journal* we will enter into a world filled with "Adventures in Capitalism." According to the *Boston Phoenix*, this type of advertising is called "station domination" — a fitting description. It is fair to say that the *Wall Street Journal* has indeed dominated the station and set our minds on the notion of capitalism as an adventure; we wonder, as we move past these ads, up the escalators, and into the heart of Harvard Square, just what type of adventure that will be. In the square, we are immediately approached by young men and women asking for money. The *Boston Globe* has called these youth our "new homeless." Infused with the notion of adventure, however, we wonder whether it might be more fitting to call these young people "officeless free-market entrepreneurs." One young White man asks for fare money, while above his head lies an image of physicist Richard Feynman surrounded by mathematical equations. This is another media campaign, this time for the Macintosh iMac computer, that reads, "Think Different." We try.

We cross the street for a cup of coffee and walk into Au Bon Pain, a coffee-sandwich franchise chain. Once inside, we see older homeless men and women who perhaps are looking for shelter, want to use the bathroom, or maybe even buy an overpriced cup of coffee. But, this being a private establishment, the police are never far behind, asking them to leave and find another place if they are not going to buy anything. As most of the "paying" customers look away from this adventure in homelessness and humiliation, we experience our present-day American urban nomadism, the invisible homeless, right before our eyes.

As we leave Au Bon Pain, and the invisible hungry homeless people in it, we are still trying to "think different," to think about the "adventure of capitalism," but it is becoming increasingly difficult. We cross the street toward BankBoston, where ten automated teller machines are filled with rows of people eagerly awaiting their undoubtedly hard-earned money. Another homeless man, this time an older African American man, stands outside of the bank and says, "Please help the homeless, buy your copy of *Spare Change!* Just one dollar." Perhaps this is what the *Wall Street Journal* was referring to when they asked us to take an "Adventure in Capitalism." He smiles at the passersby, trying to catch their attention as they change the trajectory of their gaze, or as they look directly at the man but assume a learned and practiced glazed look which effectively renders the man invisible. Thus we see and understand at a concrete visceral level how the layers of invisibility of this African American homeless man and his poverty are intrinsically connected to the unearned privileges of those studying behind the insulated ivy-covered walls of Harvard University.

On this particular day, we buy a copy of *Spare Change.* On the cover of this "homeless" weekly newspaper one usually finds interviews with the homeless, with politicians, or with scholars and intellectuals. During the past few weeks there have been intellectuals on the cover, people like Cornel West, Noam Chomsky, and Howard Zinn, who have committed their words and their work to laying bare the relationships of injustice and oppression to power and privilege. However, on this particular day there is a highly regarded Harvard intellectual on the cover who speaks about being an intellectual entrepreneur (read "intellectual profiteer") and says that one of the paths to liberation in this country is the attempt to "humanize capitalism." In a day already filled with ample contradictions, this oxymoron is almost beyond comprehension. This highly regarded scholar in essence believes we should consider humanizing a system that only functions through its dehumanization and oppression — a rather difficult if not impossible task. But for many of Harvard's intellectual elite, accustomed to neither being questioned nor questioning themselves, perhaps absurd notions of liberation and justice are possible. Our walk is not over.

On our short walk to the Harvard Graduate School of Education, we pass Christ Church of Cambridge, founded in 1759, where we notice a conspicuous plaque on the side of the church:

George and Martha Washington worshipped here December 31, 1775.
While a student at Harvard College President Theodore Roosevelt served as a
Sunday school instructor.

One of Harvard's libraries currently has a display case filled with pictures and
booklets chronicling and commemorating the exploits of Teddy Roosevelt, president of the United States, Nobel Peace Prize recipient, and Harvard graduate, and
his adventures in the United States, in the Caribbean, and in the Philippines as a
Rough Rider. What is not seen in the display case are some of Roosevelt's ideas,
which would not be as popularly regarded today. For example, regarding indigenous peoples, this American hero stated:

> I don't go so far as to think that the only good Indians are dead Indians, but I
> believe that nine out of ten are and I shouldn't like to inquire too closely into
> the case of the tenth. (Stannard, 1992, p. 245)

Among his many adventures in colonization, during the Spanish American War,
Roosevelt romantically rode up such places as San Juan Hill to liberate the
Cubans, the Puerto Ricans, and the Filipinos from the clutches of the cruel and
malevolent Spanish Empire. What the library display and most literature on this
national hero fail to mention is that the Spanish Empire he fought to remove in
these areas was quickly replaced by the American Empire.

What we never see on our walks around campus is any plaque or display case
honoring another Harvard alumnus, Pedro Albizu Campos, a Puerto Rican who
received both a doctor of philosophy and letters and a doctor of laws by the age of
thirty and spent the last twenty-five years of his life in prison for acts of seditious
conspiracy against the New World Empire that Roosevelt helped to create. Speaking about the impact this one great man had on national liberation struggles
across Africa, Asia, and Latin America in the 1960s, Dr. Ernesto "Che" Guevara
said:

> We express our solidarity with the people of Puerto Rico and their great leader,
> Pedro Albizu Campos, who, in another act of hypocrisy, has been set free at the
> age of 72, almost unable to speak, paralyzed, after spending a lifetime in jail.
> Albizu Campos is a symbol of the as yet unfree but indomitable Latin America.
> Years and years of solitude, total isolation from his people and his family, the in-
> solence of the conqueror and its lackeys in the land of his birth; nothing broke
> his will. The delegation of Cuba, on behalf of its people, pays a tribute of admi-
> ration and gratitude to a patriot who confers honor upon our America.
> (Deutschmann, 1997, p. 285)

The paths of these two Harvard graduates in fact crossed in Puerto Rico. Roosevelt, as colonial governor of Puerto Rico in the late 1920s, was overseeing all aspects of governance. At that time, Dr. Pedro Albizu Campos became the leader of
the Nationalist Party, advocated for the independence of the island from the tyr-
anny of U.S. colonialism. One man utilized his privileged educational training for
domination and colonization, while the other utilized his privileged educational
training to resist domination and colonization, to attempt to liberate his people
from the bondage of U.S. imperialism. Both a colonizer and a liberator were edu-

cated in the same elite institution. And yet, only one of these men is revered and celebrated — another example of the age-old adage, "to the victor (i.e., colonizer) go the spoils."

We, two privileged Puerto Rican educators and scholars, buffeted by the reality of our unearned privileges every time we take a short walk through our surroundings, finally come to our destination: the Harvard Graduate School of Education, where we study. As if we needed to be reminded of our stature, the school is located on Appian Way, named after the Roman la Via Appia, a prominent road of the Roman Empire that was also infamous for the prisoners of war and disobedient slaves who were crucified along it and made examples for all to see. Here at the Harvard Graduate School of Education we speak of excellence, equity, and social justice for all students. And here, with the same breath, we advocate for standards and standards-based reform, which keep our students and faculty employed and ensures that excellence and equity will never meet with social justice.

Along our journey from the subway to Appian Way, we have no doubt that there is indeed an education being provided, that there is a curriculum that is not at all hidden. We are compelled to ask ourselves, however: An education for whom and for what? An education for liberation or for domination? We read the messages on our journey and interpret the curriculum in a manner that admittedly could differ greatly from another person's reading. Part of the message of this book is that there are many avenues to learning, but too often in our schools and in our everyday lives we are privy to only a very narrow road. One of the most important avenues to learning often denied to our students is the opportunity to place themselves and others within, between, and outside of our historical, cultural, national, and political boundaries. In *learning as a political act,* all the authors understand learning as an activity that seeks to enrich rather than impoverish. Our learning comes from what we see or choose not to see and how we are seen or not seen. How we see or don't see ourselves implicated in the struggles of others and what circumstances compel us to act or not act forms an integral part of our learning process.

We hope that our book is a first step on a path toward looking at the educational journeys others have taken toward learning and liberation. To that end, *learning as a political act* brings together the work of students, scholars, and activists. As we have discussed above, our own experiences in both public and private educational arenas have revealed that our present systems of education and scholarship highlight some peoples' histories, cultures, and work, while at the same time casting shadows on other groups of people and their work, thus rendering them invisible. Our book is intended to be an invitation to challenge ourselves and others to illuminate those people whose words, works, and acts have been made anonymous.

LEARNING AS A POLITICAL ACT

learning as a political act is organized into two parts: "struggles for learning" and "learning from struggles," which are meant to be seen as two parts of one whole. What holds these essays together? you may ask. For this we refer to Paulo Freire, who speaks of an "intellectual kinship" of work involving similarity "in the manner in which facts are assessed, comprehended and valued that is also comprised of dissimilarities and incongruencies" (Freire, cited in McLaren, 1995, p. ix). We would like to extend Freire's conception and say further that there is an intellectual solidarity that unites the words and the ideas of the authors in our book, an intellectual solidarity that seeks to lay bare the ideas and histories of groups that have been silenced in mainstream educational arenas.

We underscore the fact that we see ourselves as being intimately implicated in a never-ending struggle for learning and learning from struggle. We want you, our readers, to begin to analyze and reflect on what you see, read, and hear, and to challenge your taken-for-granted assumptions about learning. We contend that what we refer to as political learning allows you to see yourself as being intimately implicated and inextricably linked with us in our struggles for learning and learning from struggles.

One final point about the book. You may have noticed that the words "learning," "political," and "struggle" are all in lower case. We did this deliberately. Since there are many ways that people come to learn and many ways that individuals or groups come to be political, we wish to shy away from advocating any monolithic concept of either idea. Instead, we have lowercased these and other words in order to ground, to bring to the messy earth, the many expressions and interpretations that they conjure up. We hope that you the reader will formulate your own concrete conceptions of what the words in the text mean in the lives of the writers and in your own lives. It is only in so doing that we come to envision and, if need be, resist the power of the multiple texts and curricula of domination and oppression that we encounter on a daily basis.

José A. Segarra
Ricardo Dobles

REFERENCES

Deutschmann, D. (1997). *Che Guevara reader.* New York: Ocean Press.
Freire, P. (1970). *Pedagogy of the oppressed.* New York: Continuum.
Freire, P., & Faundez, A. (1992). *Learning to question.* New York: Continuum.
McLaren, P. (1995). *Critical pedagogy and predatory culture.* New York: Routledge.
Stannard, D. E. (1992). *American holocaust.* New York: Oxford University Press.

Acknowledgments

We hope that the words and ideas of the authors in this book act as a provocation and a stimulus for the reader to grapple with concrete issues in education. We also hope that this work will move the reader to become engaged in struggle itself. We wish to thank all those whose engaged "political" work in pedagogy guides and fuels us. Without their acts of kindness, compassion, reciprocity, and love, freedom and transformation are impossible.

We would like to thank our colleagues and the staff of the *Harvard Educational Review* for their patience, support, and work in making this book a reality. We would also like to acknowledge the powerful cover artwork of Gamaal Tyrone "Willie" Wilson, a third-year student at the Cambridge School of Weston in Massachusetts. He would like to dedicate his artwork to the memory of his grandfather, Willie Lindsay, for whom he is named.

We would also like to thank Maxine Greene for her ever-inspiring vision and her contribution to our text.

Part One

struggles for learning

struggles for learning

Part One of our book contains two sections: *cultural and historical action* and *community and popular education*. In the first section we look at the stories of people excluded from and made invisible in mainstream educational histories, who have taken action to make themselves present in the histories of education. The second section looks at educational campaigns that have emerged from people and communities to develop numeracy (mathematical literacy) and literacy, and the fight for language (bilingual) rights.

CULTURAL AND HISTORICAL ACTION

Again we begin at Harvard University. Winona LaDuke, a well-known and respected Native American woman activist and scholar, asserts that the history of the United States is founded on the denial of the Native. Native American students at Harvard have asserted for years that more Natives are buried under Harvard University than are actually being admitted or attending the school. They are absolutely right.

In May 1999, approximately one thousand members of the Jemez Pueblo community awaited the repatriation of their ancestors' remains from the bowels of Harvard University. The remains of over 1,912 Pueblo bodies that were excavated from Pecos Pueblo, New Mexico, between 1915 and 1929 by archaeologist Alfred V. Kidder, were finally going home to the lands from which their bodies were stolen. This is concrete evidence of the historical "denial of the native," and the persistent disrespect for the beliefs, culture, and bodies of Native peoples. The repatriation of these ancestral remains gives testimony to the very real and ongoing struggles of Native peoples who refuse to be excluded and erased or to have their histories written by others. Through their scholarship, cultures and peoples erased from mainstream educational history have worked and continue to work to counteract the distortions, misrepresentations, and omissions by struggling to portray their own histories and cultures as authentically as possible.

In mainstream educational research, Native women's scholarship, like that conducted by men and women "of color," has been considered non-intellectual — when it even exists. This belief in the non-intellectual nature of their work reflects deeper ideological and political issues in education. As Paulo Freire states:

> The intellectual activity of those without power is always characterized as non-intellectual. I think this issue should be underscored, not just as a dimension of pedagogy, but a dimension of politics, as well. This is difficult to do in a society like that of the United States, where the political nature of pedagogy is negated

3

ideologically. It is necessary to negate the political nature of pedagogy to give the superficial appearance that education serves everyone, thus assuring that it continues to function in the interest of the dominant class.[1]

In *The Hidden Half: A History of Native American Women's Education*, Deirdre Almeida, a Native American woman scholar, presents a general account of Native American education since the Europeans' arrival in the Americas. She writes about the effect the Europeans had on Native American women in the United States starting from the late nineteenth century. Almeida studies the educational experiences of Native American women, especially focusing on the boarding school program for Natives from 1878 to 1928. Her work looks to the future of Native American women's scholarship that works to reclaim, generate, and sustain traditional modes of political standing through education.

In *The Road to College: Hmong American Women's Pursuit of Higher Education*, Stacy Lee sees the complex issues affecting low-income and working-class Hmong American women as they strive for a college education as being "fraught with tension and struggle." Lee moves the conversation of Hmong American women's educational participation beyond the typical monolithic attribution of cultural differences as the sole explanation for low educational persistence among Hmong American women. She argues that other barriers to educational attainment for these women include economics, race, and membership in a national minority group. In Lee's work, Hmong American women tell their stories in their own words. They speak out about the various factors that helped or hindered them in their pursuit of higher education and their process of cultural and personal transformation.

Dealing with the complexities of another national minority group, Sonia Nieto, in *Fact and Fiction: Stories of Puerto Ricans in U.S. Schools*, states that the history of Puerto Ricans in U.S. schools is unknown to the general public, including educators at every level, although much research has been done in this area. Fictional accounts in English are providing another avenue from which to understand the continuous struggles that Puerto Ricans experience in schools in the United States. In this chapter, Nieto creates a comprehensive portrait of Puerto Rican students by combining the research on this group with the body of fiction written by Puerto Ricans. Nieto identifies four themes that have emerged through stories about Puerto Ricans in U.S. schools: colonialism/resistance, cultural deficit/cultural acceptance, assimilation/identity, and marginalization/belonging. After analyzing these themes, Nieto concludes that care is the one factor that is missing in the education of Puerto Ricans in the United States.

We end this section with the contributions of youth who write of their life experiences from a variety of perspectives. In *Youth Speak Out*, the words of young women and men speak to us about the real-life complexities and issues that youth contend with day to day. A vivid example comes from Mohamad Bazzi, writing about the Los Angeles uprising, as he reflects on his experiences in the inner-city Lebanese neighborhood of his youth, Al-Shayah. Mohamad sees and articulates the commonalities and solidarity he shares with the struggles of the youth in South Central Los Angeles:

[1] Paulo Freire and Donaldo Macedo, *Literacy* (New York: Bergin & Garvey, 1987), p. 122.

The people of South-Central Los Angeles and the people of West Beirut have a great deal in common. Both are minorities, both are alienated. The Muslims of West Beirut, like L.A.'s Blacks and Latinos, have long been excluded from the national political and economic life. In both places the inequities were built into the system from the beginning.

COMMUNITY AND POPULAR EDUCATION

This section of the book opens with the organizing efforts around developing a mathematics literacy program in the 1980s that is still active today. In *The Algebra Project: Organizing in the Spirit of Ella*, mathematician and activist Robert Moses, together with Mieko Kamii, Susan McAllister Swap, and Jeff Howard, describes the project, which he founded as a way for students to begin demystifying and making accessible the language of mathematics in order to use it as an instrument to decode and interpret the world where they live. Ella Baker, an African American woman whose wisdom derived from her social and political consciousness as a community organizer and human rights activist during the civil rights movement and up to her death in 1986, inspired the organizing spirit of this innovative and socially conscious mathematics and science project of the people.

Writing against the backdrop of Israel's occupation of Palestine and the Palestinian people living on the West Bank and the Gaza Strip, Munir Fasheh discusses some of the positive changes affecting Palestinian teachers, parents, and students due to the work generated by a community-generated reading campaign. In *The Reading Campaign Experience within Palestinian Society: Innovative Strategies for Learning and Building Community*, Fasheh explains how the Tamer Institute understood learning and community building as being inseparably linked to the building of learning environments within Palestinian society. This project brought together the invaluable and immeasurable human, cultural, intellectual, and spiritual resources that the Palestinian community has in abundance in order to transform their education. This in turn strengthened the community, as participants coalesced their efforts to work and solve problems collectively and learned to apply their skills to future endeavors.

The struggle for language rights and bilingual education for working-class and low-income immigrant populations and other national minority groups in U.S. public schools goes to the very heart of resisting cultural, linguistic, and historical subordination in the United States. In *Bilingual Education for Puerto Ricans in New York City: From Hope to Compromise*, Sandra Del Valle focuses on the role that lawyers and litigation have played in the struggle for bilingual education by examining the role of Puerto Ricans in education in New York City. Del Valle analyzes and explains two visions of bilingual education — that of the grassroots Puerto Rican community that believed in the value of bilingual education, and the remedial model adopted and advanced by lawyers and other professionals in the courts. Del Valle discusses how education advocates, policymakers, and the courts must come up with different ways to work together with students, parents, and local grassroots organizations in order to amend and improve bilingual education, which is now under increasing scrutiny and attack from monolingual language policy advocates, such as those involved in the English-only movement.

The last chapter in Part One presents the wisdom of Antonia Pantoja, a Puerto Rican activist and educator who was interviewed for the *Harvard Educational Review* by Wilhelmina Perry, an African American educator who has known Pantoja for the last twenty years as a colleague, friend, and coworker. This interview focuses on the significant issues that reflect Pantoja's lifework in resisting the colonization of the Puerto Rican community, both in the United States and on the island of Puerto Rico. Pantoja's contribution to this book brings the unique voice of a Puerto Rican woman who has committed her life to her people. Her ideas on the political role that education plays in our society is illuminating, and sets the tone for this part of the book:

> Education is always political in its methodology, its curriculum, and the arrangements it uses to administer its product. One need only read the history of the development of education in the schools of Puerto Rico. From this experience, as well as the experiences of other countries, including the United States, we know that education is used by the ruling classes or ruling power to promote certain ideas and create a body of workers and professionals who respond to a vision of society that those in power hold.

Section One

cultural and historical action

The Hidden Half:
A History of Native American
Women's Education

DEIRDRE A. ALMEIDA

In their roles as missionaries, Indian agents, folklorists, and ethnographers, European and European American males have throughout history been the ones to collect and interpret Native American narratives and have established themselves as the "leading experts" on Native Americans, including Native American women.[1] Even as we near the end of the twentieth century, many European American students of Native American cultures still continue to present Native women as drudges of men and Native men as hardly distinguishable from lower animals. However, Native American scholars such as Paula Gunn Allen (1989), Rayna Green (1992), M. Annette Jaimes (1992), Haunani Kay Trask (1993), and Ward Churchill (1994) have developed a body of academic research that attacks the appropriation and exploitation of Native American and indigenous intellectual property rights.[2] The scholarship of these writers provides a critical historical and political analysis of the European American ownership of research focused on Native Americans. As Margo Thunderbird, an activist of the Shinnecock Nation of Long Island, New York, explains:

> They've [European Americans] come for the very last of our possessions; now they want our pride, our history, our spiritual traditions. They want to rewrite and remake these things, to claim them for themselves. The lies and thefts just never end. (Churchill, 1994, p. 216)

Oneida scholar Pam Colorado frames the issue this way:

> The process is ultimately intended to supplant Indians, even in areas of their own culture and spirituality. In the end, non-Indians will have complete power to define what is and what is not Indian, even for Indians. We are talking here about a complete ideological/conceptual subordination of Indian people in addition to the total physical subordination they already experience. When this happens, the last vestiges of real Indian society and Indian rights will disappear. Non-Natives will then claim to "own" our heritage and ideas as thoroughly as they now claim to own our land and resources. (Churchill, 1994, p. 216)

Harvard Educational Review Vol. 67 No. 4 Winter 1997, 757–771

As a Native American educator, I embrace the views expressed by other indigenous scholars concerning ownership of our cultural research. As a Native American woman, I believe it is our responsibility and right to produce research that specifically relates to us as Native women. In their research, European Americans have continually portrayed Native Americans as a vanishing race. In addition, Native American women are virtually nonexistent in their writings. Allen (1989) states that there are a number of reasons why Native women's voices and stories have not always been heard, not all of which can be blamed on European American male chauvinism. Allen explains that, bolstered by the authority of long-standing customs, Native American men believe that Native women have their own mouths and can tell their own stories and should be allowed to do so. They simply do not feel qualified to tell about women's lives or activities, particularly to other men.

Native American women scholars are beginning to create our own research. Native American women activists and scholars, such as Zitkala-Sa (1921/1993), Beverly Hungry Wolf (1981), Ella Deloria (1988), Mary Crow Dog (1990), Winona LaDuke (Churchill & LaDuke, 1992), and Lilikala Kame' eleihiwa (1992) have all contributed to the development of a history of Native American women from a woman's perspective. This is a continuation of the practice of many Native American nations in which the women are responsible for keeping the oral traditions alive and passing them on to the future generations (Billson, 1995).

In this article I focus on the history of Native American women and education. Education has been a key factor in making Native women invisible and silencing our voices. A Native epistemology is needed, according to Hawaiian educator and scholar Manu Meyer (1997), because of the vast inequality between the diversity of knowledge structures and what is respected, assessed, and upheld in Native schools and society. Meyer describes cultural epistemology as a study of difference for its appeal to non-universal principles and because it challenges mainstream philosophical assumptions. This article contributes to the development of this epistemology by tracing both the positive and negative influences of education on the lives of Native American women.

NATIVE WOMEN'S MARKING OF TIME

Institutional racism was rampant in North American colonists' effort to educate Native Americans (Wright, 1992, p. 93). Educational institutions established by European colonists attempted to impose their beliefs and values on Native students, and their social, economic, and political structures onto Native American cultures and civilizations (Almeida, 1992, p. 2). Over the centuries, education has been misused to appropriate land, to destroy Native American languages and cultures, and to enslave nations of Indigenous peoples (Crow Dog, 1990; Trask, 1993). Spanish, French, and British missionary schools used education to disguise their efforts to eliminate Native American society. The U.S. government later established boarding schools that continued these efforts. Most importantly, education has been used to both justify and minimize first colonists' and later the federal government's involvement in these acts of genocide (Churchill, 1994, p. 45). This has been accomplished by eliminating any discussions of these facts from the U.S. history textbooks and from the U.S. educational system in general.

Immediately upon arrival, the first European explorers of Turtle Island in North America began recording their opinions of the "New World" (Jaimes & Halsey, 1992, p. 311) through written descriptions and drawings of the land and the Indigenous peoples encountered. These early records were often heavily influenced by European mythology and imagination rather than based on what the early explorers were actually observing. Prior to the mid-eighteenth century there was little research and scholarship that focused on Native American women; the non-Natives who documented history were usually male, and were primarily interested in war and diplomatic transactions (Green, 1992; Jaimes & Halsey, 1992). Today, European Americans continue to have a poor understanding of the historical significance of Native women. History highlights the accomplishments of Native American war heroes such as Geronimo, Sitting Bull, and Red Cloud, while the history of Native American women of significant importance is rarely acknowledged. Green's (1992) research shows that Native American women have primarily been represented as anonymous figures who prepare food, haul wood, tan hides, and take care of children.

Historical texts focus mainly on Native American men, especially those having a formal role such as chief, warrior, spiritual leader, or diplomat (Jaimes & Halsey, 1992, p. 315) even though Native American women held equally important roles in determining the sovereignty of their nations (Almeida, 1995, p. 2). Some examples include the clan mothers of many northeastern and southeastern Native American nations, and Native American women's societies of the Western Plains nations, such as the Cheyenne and Piegans (Billson, 1995, p. 14). The following observations reflect the leadership roles of Native American women:

> Though some observers saw women as drudges, LeJeune (Jesuit Priest) saw women as holding great power and having in every instance . . . the choice of plans. . . . The idea of Native American women actively participating in the decisions pertaining to the use of land and the governing of their community was widely accepted by Native American nations, however it would be an aspect of native cultures which European colonists could not comprehend and accept. (Jaimes & Halsey, 1992, p. 320)

Because it went against their cultural beliefs, as described by Jaimes and Halsey, European colonizers made it a priority to reduce the status of Native women within their nations. As a result, the economic, political, and social status of Native women suffered immeasurably (Green, 1992).

Education became a key component in the plan to eliminate Native American sovereignty (Churchill, 1994, p. 139). Some of the most prestigious and enduring educational institutions, such as Harvard University and Dartmouth College, included the education of Native Americans in their charters (Wright, 1992, p. 93). Despite this history, Native American education still remains an overlooked and under-researched topic in education. The limited research that has been conducted on the history of Native American education has primarily been from non-Native scholars, the majority of whom are men (Allen, 1989; Green, 1989). Their focus has been on the development of educational systems for Native Americans and its impact on Native Americans in general, with emphasis on Native men.[3]

Over the past ten years, Native women historians and educators have begun to draw public attention to the history of Native American women, including the influence of education on their lives and their roles within their nations. Scholars such as Rayna Green (1992), Ardy Bowker (1993), Paulette Molin (Hultgren & Molin, 1989), and K. Tsiania Lomawaima (1994) have provided a forum where Native American women — whom I call "the hidden half" — can be heard. Native American women scholars and other women seeking to preserve their Native culture have begun to document their lives and achievements in text, on film, and through oral histories.

Oral traditions and histories are an important source of information for and about Native Americans. These reflect how Native American women see themselves and how they are viewed and understood within their own culture by their own community, and must be valued as legitimate, relevant perspectives on Native women's history. However, non-Native scholars view Native American oral traditions as folklore and myths. Some examples would be the Haudenosaunnee and other nations of the Northeast who believe that the world rests on the back of a giant turtle and the first person to dwell on it was Sky Woman (Billson, 1995, p. 13). The Shawnee honor a spiritual holy woman named "Our grandmother," who received assistance from the "Great Spirit" in creating humankind; she gave the Shawnee life, as well as their code of ethics and most of their religious ceremonies (Allen, 1989, p. 7). Native scholars who utilize their oral traditions and indigenous knowledge find their research being labeled as nothing but a generalization and dismissed by self-appointed non-Native "experts" (Almeida, 1992, p. 4). Value and legitimacy has to be given to research and history from a Native American woman's perspective. Also, it is important when writing from a Native American point of view to present history in time frames more relevant to Native American experiences.

Native American historians have identified five distinct periods since the Europeans' arrival in the Americas: Creation (the beginning of time established in Native American stories of origin, prior to European contact in 1492); Contact with Europeans (1492–1800); The Removal Era (1800–1830); The Reservation Era (1830–1929); The Reform Era (1930–1969); and Contemporary Resistance (1970–1997). This article looks at the off-reservation boarding school education of young Native American women, with a focus on the Hampton Institute of Virginia during the mid-to-late Reservation Era, 1878–1929, and includes a brief discussion of the influence of off-reservation boarding schools on the lives of Native American women and their communities during the eras of Reform and Contemporary Resistance.

NATIVE AMERICAN WOMEN'S EDUCATION UNDER THE INDIAN EDUCATIONAL REFORM MOVEMENT

The Native Americans' struggle to maintain our traditional lifestyles was increased with the Western invasion by European Americans onto Native American lands from the mid-1800s to the early 1900s. The eventual reduction of Native societies through systematic genocide,[4] warfare, broken treaties, and the destruction of natural and food resources resulted in U.S. government control over Native American nations and the establishment of the reservation system (Bowker, 1993; Green, 1992).

Confinement to reservations made Native American men unable to hunt to supply their communities not only with food, but also with the materials needed for ˙clothing, housing, and other tools and implements. For Native American women and men, the honor and respect that the hunt brought them was also lost. Also at jeopardy was the traditional form of education for Native American children. The tanning and quilling societies of the women disappeared because clothing made of hides was replaced by government-distributed trade cloth. The training young Native American women had traditionally received from their female elders was altered greatly; in time they were forced to turn to another source for their education — the U.S. government (Green, 1992; Standing Bear, 1975).

The reservation system thus led to the development of a major institution of Native education, whose impact is still felt within contemporary times — the off-reservation boarding school. These schools were viewed as a means to speed up the assimilation process (Bowker, 1993, p. 24) in order to force Native Americans into a European American lifestyle (Hultgren & Molin, 1989; Standing Bear, 1975). Non-Native educators won federal support and funding by promoting the idea that the best way to educate Native American children was to remove them as soon as possible from their families and communities and to place them where they only had contact with European Americans.

Native children, young adults, and, in some cases, entire families were transported from their communities to boarding schools, first in the East and later to regional federal schools in the West. This formal education system contributed enormously to the breakdown of Native families, including women's traditional roles, and led to the development of many of the social ills that still affect Native nations today, such as dysfunctional families and substance abuse (Almeida, 1992; Bowker, 1993; Green, 1989; Lomawaima, 1994; Reyhner & Eder, 1994).[5] However, the off-reservation boarding school was not a new concept in 1878. The idea that the best way to educate Native American youth was by removing them as far as possible from their home environment dates back to colonial times and Eleazer Wheelock Moor's Charity school.[6] These boarding schools flourished during the late nineteenth century, due to the increasing conflict over land and the U.S. government's misguided policies for "handling" Native Americans.

After the Civil War, many European Americans who had actively participated in the abolitionist movement sought a new cause to champion (Hultgren & Molin, 1989, p. 18). Those who chose the issue of Indian reform dedicated themselves to achieving the Americanization of Native Americans. With the end of the Native American wars at the close of the nineteenth century, new versions of containment policies for Native Americans sprang up in the belief that the United States would best serve Native Americans by assimilating them into European American society (Hultgren & Molin, 1989; Robbins, 1992; Standing Bear, 1975).

This Indian Reform movement was made up of politicians, ministers, educators, and lawyers. Most were men, but some of their wives were among the most active reformists. They established organizations such as the Friends of the American Indian and held conferences to discuss how they could assist with the reforms needed to help Native Americans become more assimilated or, in their words, "Americanized" (Reyhner & Eder, 1994, p. 46). The Indian reformists lobbied for the General Allotment Act, a bill sponsored by Senator Henry Dawes of Massachusetts. The Dawes Act, as it is also known, advocated for the breakup of Native American communal lands, to be replaced by allotted plots of land separately owned by Native families and individuals. Private ownership of land was one of the first strategies used to force Native Americans to assimilate into a European American value system (Noriega, 1992, p. 382). The other component of the Dawes Act dealt with providing educational training for both males and females so that Native Americans could be educated into becoming good, civilized Christians (Lomawaima, 1994, p. 2). The Indian Reform Movement also became known as the Indian Educational Reform Movement; the establishment of off-reservation boarding schools was one of its main projects (Reyhner & Eder, 1994, p. 46).

The first school to attempt to educate adult Native American students in the East was the Hampton Normal and Agricultural Institute in Virginia. Established in 1868 to educate African Americans following the Civil War, Hampton became the first boarding school to establish an Indian education program when, in April 1878, fifteen Native American adult male war hostages were admitted at the request of Captain Richard Pratt. Hampton's founder, General Samuel Armstrong, recognized the benefits to be gained from educating Native Americans (Almeida, 1992; Hultgren & Molin, 1989). He expressed his reaction to the arrival at Hampton of the Native Americans in a letter to his wife:

> They are a new step ahead and make the school very strong and really, Kitty, they are a big card for the school and will diminish my gray hairs. There's money in them I tell you. (Samuel Chapman Armstrong to Emma Armstrong, April 19, 1878, in Williamsiana Collection)

In the late fall of 1878, Captain Pratt returned from the Dakota territories with the first group of Native American children to be educated in the off-reservation system. Included in this first group were nine girls, the first Native American females to undergo the "Americanization" process in an educational setting (Hultgren & Molin, 1989, p. 18). Pratt would eventually leave Hampton to establish the first government-sponsored, all-Native American boarding school, the Carlisle Indian Industrial School in Carlisle, Pennsylvania. By 1885, Hampton and Carlisle had served as models for 106 Native American boarding schools, many of which were established on abandoned military installations (Green, 1989, p. 12).

Native children were accustomed to being educated and taken care of by people other than their natural parents, but little had prepared them for the sheer strangeness of the boarding school, with its echoing halls and electric lighting, and a staff speaking an unintelligible language and taking unacceptable familiarities with them (Coleman, 1993, p. 79). In 1884, a Yankton female student named Gertrude Simmons, who would later become famous under her tribal name of Zitkala-Sa, entered the White's Manual Labor Institute in Wabash, Indiana. She later described her fearful arrival:

> Entering the house, I stood close against the wall. The strong glaring light in the whitewashed room dazzled my eyes. The noisy hurrying of hard shoes upon a bare wooded floor increased the whirring in my ears. My only safety seemed to be in keeping next to the wall. As I was wondering in which direction to escape from all this confusion, two warm hands grasped me firmly, and in the

same motion I was tossed high in midair. A rosy-cheeked paleface woman caught me in her arms. I was both frightened and insulted by such trifling. I stared into her eyes, wishing her to let me stand on my own feet, but she jumped me up and down with increasing enthusiasm. My mother had never made a plaything of her wee daughter. Remembering this I began to cry aloud. (Zitkala-Sa, 1921/1993, p. 225)

It was not unusual for Native children to be sent away to boarding school at the age of six or seven, and not to see their homes and families again until the age of seventeen or eighteen (Noriega, 1992, p. 381). The goals of these boarding schools were to teach Native American students how to speak English, to teach them basic academics, and to turn them into good, hard-working Christians. The education of female students at Hampton Institute was very general compared to the technical education of the male students. The girls' industrial curriculum included making and mending garments, crocheting and knitting, as well as learning to sew by hand and machine. Household training involved washing, ironing, cooking, and table duty, plus care of their own dormitories. Beginning in 1886, female students also participated in the "Technical Round" established for male students, where they learned skills like framing a window or building a set of shelves, which the school administrators felt would be useful to them on the reservation (Hultgren & Molin, 1989, p. 28).

Another key component of the boarding schools was a work-study program known as the "outing system," which placed Native American students in the homes of European Americans during the summer months so they could be exposed to European American morals and manners and develop their English-language skills. Hampton Institute placed its students on farms and in households in western Massachusetts, where they provided cheap labor, with the males working as farmhands and the females responsible for domestic work.

Some of the female students wrote favorably of their placement, saying that they were treated as a member of the family and provided opportunities to expand their knowledge and coping skills needed for survival in European American society. Lizzie Young, a Wyandotte from Oklahoma, was placed with the Bryant family of Northampton, Massachusetts, in 1891. She shared her experiences with her teachers back at Hampton Institute:

I like my home very much, only once in awhile I get lonesome when it rains, for I do not know what to do with myself. Yesterday Mr. b. invited us down to see him play a scientific game of croquet. That was the first time I ever did see a game of that kind. . . . They are kind to me. There are just three of us in the family. . . . I do not do anything but the cooking. Another woman across the street does the washing. . . . I am learning to use the typewriter. Please excuse mistakes this time, for I am not an expert yet, but I hope I may be some day. (Letter from Lizzie Young published in *Southern Workman*, August 1891, Indian Student files, Hampton University Archives)

However, most of the female students who went through the outing system were not as fortunate as Lizzie Young. Their placements meant long days of hard work with little time for themselves. One unidentified student wrote to her friends at Hampton of her outing experience:

I spent my summer in Westfield, Massachusetts. . . . I used to wash, iron, make beds and sweep the parlor and sitting room once a week, and keep the house when they all go away. When I came away they gave me $10.50. I never had a regular holiday, but once that was when we went to Sunday School picnic. I never went to visit any city or interesting place. (Letter from student published in *Southern Workman,* January 1890, Indian Student files, Hampton University Archives)

The boarding school further destroyed the traditional roles of Native American women, as the girls were expected to learn European American techniques of childrearing, household maintenance, and food preparation. The rationale for this instruction was not only to assist Native American women in assimilating into mainstream culture, but also to limit their work skills so that the only choices of work they had when they returned to the reservation was to be a servant in a European American home. A few of those who returned to the reservation would be hired as maids in the federal Indian agent's home (Lomawaima, 1994, p. 81).

Native American women were discouraged by their teachers and school administrators from maintaining any knowledge of their traditional Native American lifestyle and brainwashed into looking down on anyone who still lived in a traditional manner. Except for the few Native women who integrated into mainstream European American society, the majority of the female boarding school students returned to their reservations and the same lifestyle they had left. However, they found that they had become disconnected from their traditional gender roles and from their communities. It was not always easy for them, as they had to prove themselves to regain the trust of their community members, many of whom were skeptical of returning students and viewed them as the new oppressor:

The educated Indian does not hold the respect and admiration of the old people. . . . Instead, Indian alumni had to struggle to re-establish themselves in native communities, trying to gain acceptance while introducing changes resisted by family and friends. (*Indians' Education at Hampton Institute,* p. 19)

Returning students often accepted employment with federal Indian agencies, and many found employment as domestics in the same boarding schools that had trained them (Lomawaima, 1994, p. 81). Those who chose to assimilate into European American life changed not only their own lives, but also those of future generations, as it meant they would not pass on the traditional skills, culture, and social connections of their Native community. Attending boarding schools led many Native American women into situations of extreme isolation, and increased their dependency on the U.S. government.

In contrast, some Native American women used their boarding school education to help them lead their people to resist extinction. Armed with knowledge of European American ways and values, these women were among the central figures in the reform and resistance movements through which many Native nations, though virtual captives of the United States, would resist non-Native efforts to destroy their culture (Green, 1992, p. 69).

The boarding schools operated along these lines until 1928, when the U.S. government released the Meriam Report, which condemned the poor quality of services provided by the Bureau of Indian Affairs. It pointed out shocking conditions of boarding schools, recommended that elementary age children not be sent to boarding schools at all, and urged an increase in the number of day schools on the reservations (Reyhner & Eder, 1994, p. 50). The Meriam Report focused on educational reform within Western boarding schools, and called for improved nutrition and health care standards for Native American children attending these schools. It noted that "discipline of the schools were merely restrictive, not developmental, and did not encourage individual expression or responsibility" (Meriam, 1928, p. 11). It further suggested that Indian Services should devote its energies to social and economic advancements that would help Native Americans adapt to mainstream European American society, or to live on their own terms with at least a minimum standard of health and decency (Lomawaima, 1994, p. 31).

This policy of educational reform eventually lead to the Indian New Deal of 1934 and a reorganization of Native American government systems. Federal programs under the 1934 Johnson-O'Malley Act (JOM) were established to fund Native American educational programs. The Act allowed the federal government to pay states for educating Native American children in public schools (Reyhner & Eder, 1994, p. 50), and established two important concepts. First, it made it theoretically possible for Native American nations or organizations to contract for educational services with the Department of the Interior. Second, the Act reaffirmed the continuing legal responsibility of both the federal government and the states to provide education for Native Americans. These policies served to further support the boarding school approach, and during the period 1950–1975 the number of students attending off-reservation boarding schools increased. The Bureau of Indian Affairs maintained direct responsibility for the education of 52,000 Native American children. Of these, more than 35,000 were enrolled in boarding schools (Noriega, 1992, p. 385). Many of the older boarding schools were completely dilapidated and functioned more as holding pens than as schools, although a few, such as the Institute of American Indian Art in New Mexico, were very modern, having been recently constructed or refurbished (Bowker, 1993; Noriega, 1992). Despite continuous indications that the relocation experience was a disaster, for both the Native American individuals involved and their respective Native American nations, relocation programs were maintained up until 1980.

By 1980, ongoing federal pressure had resulted in the relocation to cities of slightly over half of all Native Americans, approximately 880,000 of the 1.6 million reflected in the 1980 census (Robbins, 1992, p. 99). Adjustment to urban living was often difficult for relocated Native Americans and their families, and created great pressures on women to deny their Native American identity. Many became alienated from their traditions and were rejected by Native Americans who remained on the reservation. Those who maintained contact with their relatives, both on reservations and those living in urban areas, were more successful in adjusting to a new way of life. Moreover, access to education and jobs meant that Native American women developed skills and independence that might have eluded them in the reservations' economic and social structures (Green, 1992, p. 87).

These relocation policies backfired on the U.S. government. Instead of creating a better atmosphere for assimilation, they produced a new population of educated Native American women who turned their newfound skills into tools for political and cultural activism (Green, 1992, p. 18). Nevertheless, the relocation presented Native American nations with new battles for survival. Native women met the challenge both on and off the reservations (Green, 1992; Jaimes & Halsey, p. 1992), though they had to make many personal sacrifices. For example, Menominee activist Ada Deer, who helped restore federal recognition to her nation, describes her experience:

> As a teenager, I saw the poverty of the people — poor housing, poor education, poor health. I thought, this isn't the way it should be. . . . I wanted to help the tribe in some way. . . . People said I was too young, too naive . . . so I dropped out of law school. That was the price I had to pay to get involved. . . . I spent six months in Washington influencing legislation and mobilizing the support of our people throughout the country. . . . The land was restored to trust status. . . . Where did the manpower and the woman power come to accomplish this? It came from the people. (Green, 1992, p. 88)

COMING FULL CIRCLE AND LOOKING TO THE GRANDMOTHERS: CONTEMPORARY NATIVE AMERICAN WOMEN AND EDUCATION

During the late 1960s and the 1970s, Native American educators, along with Native political activists, became increasingly active in promoting the rights of Native Americans and calling for national attention to their plight (Bowker, 1993, p. 23). Native American activist groups such as the American Indian Movement (AIM) and Women of All Red Nations (WARN) grew out of the urban Native communities created by the relocation programs. These organizations and others encouraged Native Americans to stand up for their rights and to resist any further destruction of their cultures and land. AIM staged sit-ins and walk-outs in secondary and some elementary schools, where parents and students demanded greater curriculum relevance and increased Native involvement in school affairs. During this period of "Indian activism," a number of Native American educational organizations were established, including the National Indian Education Association and the Coalition of Indian Controlled School Boards (Bowker, 1993, p. 23).

The U.S. government, in another attempt to assimilate Native Americans through education, passed the 1975 Educational Assistance Act. This was the educational component of the Self-Determination Act, which was designed to provide Native American nations with more control over their reservations, including schools. The act was much criticized, especially by Native women connected to the alternative schools called "Survival Schools," who felt that the act was no more than another form of colonial domination. Through their work with the Survival Schools, this group of Native American women had come to believe the U.S. government wanted to train a selected group of Native American educators who would see themselves and their Native nations through the eyes of the colonizer. This would be the group from which the U.S. government would select Native American educators, place them in charge of Indian education, and have them carry out the 1975 Education and Self-Determination Acts (Bowker, 1993, p. 25). As Phyllis Young, an American Indian movement activist, explains:

> Aside from some cosmetic alterations like the inclusion of beadwork, traditional dance, basket weaving and some language classes, the curriculum taught in Indian schools remained exactly the same, reaching the same conclusions,

indoctrinating children with exactly the same values as when the schools were staffed entirely by white people. . . . You've got to hand it to them in a way. It's really a perfect system of colonization, convincing the colonized to colonize each other in the name of "self-determination" and "liberation." (Noriega, 1992, p. 387)

Government policies under the Reagan and Bush administrations proposed that Native American students would succeed more if they attended mainstream public schools. This led to a government effort to close all Bureau of Indian Affairs boarding schools and eventually reservation day schools, regardless of their success rates, and mainstream Native American students into public schools. Public schools have been a source of much conflict and tension for both female and male Native American students. Teachers, textbooks, and curriculum in public schools have been programmed to bring about the adoption of values such as competitiveness and individualism. Native American students come from homes and communities that value cooperation and positive interpersonal relationships. The results of this conflict, especially for female Native American students, have been high dropout rates, low achievement levels, and poor self-esteem. Public schools have often become places of discomfort for Native American youth (Bowker, 1993; DeJong, 1993).

Native American education has not been a major priority of the presidential administrations of the past two decades. Currently the majority of Native American students are enrolled in public schools (Bowker, 1993, p. 28), while federal funding for Native American education continues to suffer a steady decline. At present there are 100 Bureau of Indian Affairs elementary and secondary schools and sixty tribally controlled schools.

Native American women continue to play an important role in the education of their people. Many have come to understand and seek to preserve the traditional roles women held in the past, and have sought out women elders from their families and communities to instruct them in maintaining that knowledge. Some, such as Beverly Hungry Wolf (Blackfeet) and Navajo Ruth Roessel (1981) have become authors, thereby sharing their knowledge of Native American women's traditions. Native American women have become involved with their nation's political affairs and have been elected to leadership positions. Currently, approximately 12 percent of the five hundred or so federally recognized Native American and Alaskan Native nations have female leadership (Green, 1992, p. 97).

Despite the changes in government education policy from the reservation era to contemporary times, Native American women maintain their responsibilities as the keepers of their culture, working for the revitalization of the languages, arts, and religious practices of their people, with the focus always on future generations: "It was our grandmothers who held on to what they could of our identity as a People. . . . Oftentimes the fire grew dim, but still our grandmothers persisted. We were taught that the time we are in is only borrowed from future generations" (Green, 1992, p. 93). Native women today draw on the same inner strength that sustained female Native students attending the off-reservation boarding schools of the late nineteenth and early twentieth centuries. A traditional Cheyenne saying reflects the reality of Native American women: "A people are not defeated until the hearts of its women are on the ground." As long as Native American women assert their traditional rights and assume their traditional responsibility of being the central voices of their communities, Native American nations will survive and their women's voices will remain loud and strong.

NOTES

1. The term "Native American" is used throughout this article instead of "American Indian" as it has become the common term used in the northeastern region of the United States. The terms "Native" and "American Indian" will also appear, with the latter being used primarily in quoted text.
2. "Indigenous intellectual property rights" refers to the rights claimed by an indigenous people over their traditional cultural knowledge (see Greaves, 1994).
3. Examples of scholarship that has been produced with a focus on Native American men include La Flesche (1963), Alford (1936), and Rideout (1912).
4. Systematic genocide is the deliberate destruction, in whole or in part, by a government or its agents, of a racial, sexual, religious, tribal, ethnic, or political minority. It can involve not only mass murder, but also starvation, forced deportation or removal, and political, economic, and biological subjugation. For more information on genocide and systematic genocide, see Gioseffi (1993).
5. Native American children were removed from their families and communities at very young ages. Instead of being raised with their parents and extended family members, they grew up in an institutional setting. This resulted in the students' loss of knowledge of traditional parenting skills. Native American students attending boarding schools were subjected to corporal punishment, and were instructed to focus on the nuclear family instead of the extended family. When they became adults and had families of their own, these boarding school students relied on the style of childrearing they had experienced at boarding school, and passed it on to their children. Returning students also experienced issues of trying to fit back into their communities, often with much difficulty and internal conflicts. To cope with the frustration of a loss of identity, returning boarding school students often turned to alcohol as a means of escape. The result was generations of substances abusers and domestic violence. For more information on this, see Bowker (1993).
6. The Moor's Charity School for Indians was established in 1760 by Eleazer Wheelock in Lebanon, Connecticut. Between 1761 and 1769, Wheelock enrolled approximately sixteen Native American girls at Moor's School. See Szasz (1988).

REFERENCES

Alford, T. W. (1936). *Civilization*. Norman: University of Oklahoma Press.

Allen, P. G. (1989). Introduction. In P. G. Allen (Ed.), *Spider Woman's granddaughters* (pp. 1–21). Boston: Beacon Press.

Almeida, D. A. (1992). *The role of western Massachusetts in development of American Indian education reform through the Hampton Institute's summer outing program (1878–1921)*. Unpublished doctoral dissertation, University of Massachusetts, Amherst.

Almeida, D. A. (1995). *An Indian summer: Surviving Disney's Pocahontas*. Unpublished manuscript.

Billson, J. M. (1995). *Keepers of the culture: The power of tradition in women's lives*. New York: Lexington Books.

Bowker, A. (1993). *Sisters in the blood: The education of women in Native America*. Newton, MA: WEEA.

Churchill, W. (1994). *Indians are us? Culture and genocide in Native North America.* Monroe, ME: Common Courage Press.

Churchill, W., & LaDuke, W. (1992). Native North America: The political economy of radioactive America. In M. A. Jaimes (Ed.), *The state of Native America: Genocide, colonization, and resistance* (pp. 241–266). Boston: South End Press.

Coleman, M. (1993). *American Indian children at school, 1850–1930.* Jackson: University Press of Mississippi.

Crow Dog, M. (1990). *Lakota woman.* New York: Harper Collins.

DeJong, D. H. (1993). *Promise of the past: A history of Indian education in the United States.* Golden, CO: North American Press.

Deloria, E. C. (1988). *Waterlily.* Lincoln: University of Nebraska Press.

Gioseffi, D. (Ed.) (1993). *On prejudice: A global perspective.* New York: Anchor Books.

Greaves, T. (Ed.) (1994). *Intellectual property rights for indigenous peoples: A source book.* Oklahoma City: Society for Applied Anthropology.

Green, R. (1989). "Kill the Indian and save the man": Indian education in the United States. In P. F. Molin & M. L. Hultgren (Eds.), *To lead and to serve: American Indian education at Hampton Institute 1878–1923* (pp. 9–13). Virginia Beach, VA: Virginia Foundation for the Humanities and Public Policy.

Green, R. (1992). *Women in American Indian society.* New York: Chelsea House.

Hampton University Archives, Special Collections, Hampton Normal and Agricultural Institute, Indian Education Collection, Administration and Indian Student Files (1878–1928). Hampton, VA: Hampton University.

Hultgren, M. L., & Molin, P. F. (1989). *To lead and to serve: American Indian education at Hampton Institute, 1878–1923.* Virginia Beach, VA: Virginia Foundation for the Humanities and Public Policy.

Hungry Wolf, B. (1981). *The ways of my grandmothers.* New York: Morrow.

Indians' Education at Hampton Institute: Report of the Principal to Virginia Superintendent of Public Instruction. Hampton University Archives, Special Collections, Hampton Normal and Agricultural Institute, Indian Education Collection, Administration and Indian Student Files (1878–1928). Hampton, VA: Hampton University

Jaimes, M. A., & Halsey, T. (1992). American Indian women: At the center of indigenous resistance in North America. In M. A. Jaimes (Ed.), *The state of Native America: Genocide, colonization, and resistance* (pp. 311–344). Boston: South End Press.

Kame' eleihiwa, L. (1992). *Native lands, foreign desires.* Honolulu: Bishop Museum Press.

La Flesche, F. (1963). *The middle five: Indian school boys of the Omaha tribe.* Lincoln: University of Nebraska Press.

Lomawaima, K. T. (1994). *They call it prairie light: The story of Chilocco Indian School.* Lincoln: University of Nebraska Press.

Meriam, L. (1928). *The problem of Indian administration: Institute for Government Research.* Baltimore: Johns Hopkins University Press.

Meyer, M. (1997). *Native Hawaiian epistemology: A case study of other intellectualism.* Unpublished manuscript.

Noriega, J. (1992). American Indian education in the United States: Indoctrination for subordination to colonization. In M. A. Jaimes (Ed.), *The state of Native America: Genocide, colonization and resistance* (pp. 371–402). Boston: South End Press.

Reyhner, J., & Eder, J. E. (1994). A history of Indian education. In J. Reyhner (Ed.), *Teaching American Indian students* (pp. 33–58). Norman: University of Oklahoma Press.

Rideout, H. M. (1912). *Williams Jones: Indian cowboy, American scholar, and anthropologist in the field.* New York: Frederick A. Stokes.

Robbins, R. L. (1992). Self-determination and subordination: The past, present, and future of American Indian governance. In M. A. Jaimes (Ed.), *The state of Native America: Genocide, colonization, and resistance* (pp. 87–121). Boston: South End Press.

Roessel, R. (1981). *Women in Navajo society.* Rough Rock, AZ: Navajo Resource Center.

Standing Bear, L. (1975). *My people the Sioux.* Lincoln: University of Nebraska Press. (Original work published 1933)

Szasz, M. C. (1988). *Indian education in the American colonies, 1607–1783.* Albuquerque: University of New Mexico Press.

Trask, H. K. (1993). *From a native daughter: Colonialism and sovereignty in Hawaii.* Monroe, ME: Common Courage Press.

Williamsiana Collection, Williams College Archives and Special Collections. Williams, MA: Williams College.

Wright, B. (1992). American Indian and Alaska Native higher education: Towards a new century of academic achievement and cultural integrity. In P. Cahape & C. B. Howley (Eds.), *Indian nations at risk: Listening to the people* (pp. 93–96). Charleston, WV: ERIC Clearinghouse on Rural Education and Small Schools.

Zitkala-Sa (Bonnin, G.). (1993). American Indian stories. In W. G. Regier (Ed.), *Masterpieces of American Indian literature* (pp. 193–238). New York: MJF Books. (Original work published 1921)

The Road to College:
Hmong American Women's Pursuit
of Higher Education

STACEY J. LEE

Since the first Hmong refugees arrived in the United States from Southeast Asia more than twenty years ago, journalists and scholars have written extensively on this Asian American ethnic group's adjustment experiences. Many of these works have stressed the differences between Hmong culture — described as rural, clan-based, preliterate, and traditional — and mainstream American culture. In describing the Hmong, one U.S. policy analyst wrote, "This country has rarely, if ever, welcomed a group of immigrants so culturally distant from the native social and economic mainstream" (Fass, 1991, p. 1).

The differences between Hmong and American culture are often described as differences between a premodern and a modern society. In an article in *National Geographic,* for example, the Hmong's adjustment difficulties are portrayed as almost inevitable, given that they are "unfamiliar with locked doors, light switches, [and] modern plumbing" (Sherman, 1988, p. 592). Journalists and scholars have suggested that the social and economic problems faced by the Hmong (e.g., welfare dependence, gang involvement, intergenerational conflict, high school dropout rates, depression, etc.) are due entirely to these enormous cultural differences (Hirayama & Hirayama, 1988; Sherman, 1988; Tapp, 1988).

Several scholars have noted the particularly stark contrast between the roles of women and girls in U.S. and Hmong culture (Donnelly, 1994; Goldstein, 1985; Scott, 1988; Walker-Moffat, 1995). Stories of bride theft and early marriage, for instance, provide vivid examples of how Hmong attitudes towards women's roles clash with mainstream U.S. ideas (Goldstein, 1986; Scott, 1988). These and other cultural traditions that Hmong girls and women face are of particular interest to researchers in the field of education (Goldstein, 1985; Rumbaut & Ima, 1988; Walker-Moffat, 1995). These researchers link Hmong values regarding women's roles to the relatively high dropout rates among Hmong female students. In her research on Hmong American adolescents, Goldstein discovered that "girls who dropped out for domestic reasons won community approval by moving into valued gender roles" (1985, p. 276). Rumbaut and Ima assert that the high dropout rates and low achievement levels of Hmong girls are connected to the "patrilineal

Harvard Educational Review   Vol. 67 No. 4 Winter 1997, 803–827

and patriarchal norms that tend to devalue females among the Hmong" (1988, p. xiv).

Anthropological research on the Hmong has done a great deal to illuminate the culture that Hmong refugees bring with them to the United States. Educational research on cultural differences has revealed the particular pressure that Hmong American girls face within their communities to marry and begin having children during their teens. Cultural differences, and issues that arise out of these differences, are often characterized as private concerns. For example, in their study on the relationship between stress and the social support systems of Hmong refugees, Hirayama and Hirayama labeled problems such as "homesickness, child rearing, automobile breakdowns, and family finance" as "private matters" (1988, p. 104).

The sole focus on cultural obstacles, however, has in effect ignored the existence of economic, racial, and other structural barriers to Hmong American women's educational achievement and persistence. By relegating cultural and family issues to the "private" sphere, the "public" sphere is freed from any responsibility (Fine, 1991). According to this position, if Hmong American girls drop out of school to get married and have children, or if few Hmong American women pursue higher education, the reasons lie entirely within the Hmong community. Although an understanding of culture is important, an exclusive focus on culture conceals the impact of racism on Hmong American women's opportunities and on their self-perceptions. In short, by focusing solely on cultural differences, the inequalities in power and interests are silenced (Lutz & Collins, 1993).

The implicit assumption behind much of the focus on cultural differences is that Hmong culture is static and unchanging, which fails to recognize that all cultures are dynamic, constantly in the process of being created and re-created. Cultures are not only transmitted from generation to generation, they are also created within current history (Erickson, 1997). The assumption of a static Hmong culture ignores the history of accommodation, resistance, and transformation that the Hmong have undergone as an ethnic minority, first in China, then in Laos, and now in the United States (Dunnigan, 1986; Fish, 1991; Hendricks, 1986). In recent history alone, Hmong culture has been transformed by war, migration, life in refugee camps, and resettlement in the United States. Despite these historical realities, the Hmong are often portrayed as people without a history who arrived in the United States in a natural and unchanged state (Wolf, 1982). Within this framework, Europeans and European Americans depict non-Europeans as timeless and primitive peoples who are the passive victims of the changes imposed on them by modern, dynamic, and postcultural European societies. With respect to the Hmong, Hendricks asserts that this type of thinking "leads some to think in terms of before and after, that there was a traditional almost unchanging way of Hmong living that has been severely altered by the events of the period of flight and subsequent resettlement" (1986, p. 3). Thus the Hmong, like other non-European cultures, are exoticized and essentialized at the same time that European cultures are normalized and often made invisible.

During this current historical period, the practice of focusing solely on cultural differences supports existing political, economic, and social inequalities (Balibar, 1991; Harrison, 1995; Razack, 1995). Citing Said's (1978) work on orientalism, Erickson observes that "when more powerful nations or interest groups identify some Other as exotic and different there can be a tendency for the more powerful to project their own flaws, contradictions, and hostilities on the constructed Other" (1997, p. 45). Within today's anti-immigrant rhetoric in the United States, cultural differences are used as evidence of immigrants' unfitness to be "real Americans" (Suarez-Orozco, 1996). In this discourse and associated public policy, the exclusive focus on cultural difference and the concomitant denial of the mainstream group's relative power leads to victim blaming. In describing the current anti-immigrant sentiment, Suarez-Orozco writes:

> Discourse on immigration has taken a decidedly post-utopian tone. Gone are the romantic fantasies of poor immigrant peasants pulling themselves up by their bootstraps to become proud and loyal Americans. The dominant image in the public space now is that of unstoppable waves of parasitic "aliens" set on (ab)using our social services, refusing to "assimilate," and adding to the crime and social pathologies of the American urban landscape. (1996, p. 153)

In this article, I examine the cultural, economic, and racial factors that affect Hmong American women's pursuit of higher education, with a focus on the experiences of those who are pursuing or have completed higher education in the United States. I chose to focus on Hmong women who pursued higher education because I was interested in the experiences of women who actively challenged existing cultural norms. Attention to the experiences of these pioneer women will contribute to an understanding of minority student achievement, and of cultural transformation among refugee groups in the United States. The overarching questions considered in this article include: What motivates some Hmong American women to pursue higher education? What obstacles do they face in this pursuit? How are these women transforming Hmong culture? How are their families responding to their changing roles and expectations of women?

The twenty-one women in my study range in age from eighteen to thirty-two. All are first generation in the United States, and all are either pursuing or have completed four-year college degrees. Far from being a monolithic group of traditional, subservient, and docile women, as often described by the popular press, the Hmong women in my study vary in their personal experiences and in their social and political perspectives. Some of the women identify as feminists, while others shun the term. Some of the women live at home while attending college, others attend colleges halfway across the country from their families. Some of the women are more comfortable speaking English, and others are more comfortable with Hmong. Some of the women married and had children as teenagers and are now returning to school, while others have postponed marriage in order to pursue their education.

I selected my participants from a variety of sources. I met my first informant by chance when she called to find out more about my research on Asian American students. During our conversation she spoke about her own experiences as an educated Hmong woman, and thus the seeds for this study were sown. I met a few informants at a national Hmong American student conference, some I met through Hmong American student organizations, and others I recruited through referrals.

My primary means of data collection was in-depth, open-ended interviews. Throughout the research process I made efforts to be sensitive to issues of power and identity raised by feminist researchers (Fine, 1994; Oakley, 1981; Reinharz,

1992). Based on my belief that women are the experts on their own lives, and in the spirit of collaboration, I solicited each informant's help in locating other potential informants and asked them to suggest additional interview questions and topics. I also encouraged the women to ask me questions about myself and my research. Although only a few of the women asked about the research, many expressed interest in my ethnic background. The women asked questions such as "What is your ethnicity?" and "Where were you born?" As a third-generation Chinese American who conducts research in Asian American communities, I have come to expect and welcome such questions (Lee, 1996). Researchers who share ethnic, racial, cultural, or other similarities with their informants are often scrutinized for signs of authenticity (Aguilar, 1981; Foster, 1994; Kondo, 1990). Upon meeting me, the women immediately recognized that I was not a Hmong woman (i.e., not one of them), but they were interested in whether or not we shared any cultural similarities. They were particularly interested in my relationship with my family. When I told them, for example, that my ninety-year-old grandmother, who has lived in the United States for nearly seventy years, insists that I speak Chinese to her, the women nodded in understanding. When I recalled my mother's strict rules regarding dating when I was a teenager, the women and I shared a laugh. I even commiserated with one of the women about feeling "short" in the company of non-Asians. Most of the women determined that although I am not an "insider," the fact that I share race, gender, and certain cultural characteristics with them means that I am not completely an "outsider" either. This "in-between" status, sometimes called the "halfie" status, enabled me to use my experiences to invite more open and honest conversation (Abu-Lughod, 1991).

The interviews were one-and-a-half to seven hours long and took place in one to three sessions. During the initial phase of the interview, I invited the women to tell me their life histories. My approach was purposely nondirective in this phase in order to encourage the women to tell the stories that they deemed important. In subsequent phases of the interview, I asked more focused questions with an eye to uncovering information about the women's educational histories, the nature of their family life, the nature of their relationship with the larger Hmong community, their reasons for pursuing higher education, and their experiences in college. Their stories communicate what they face at home, in school, and in the larger society in their struggle to pursue higher education, as well as how their aspirations are transforming Hmong culture. The women's words reveal some of the ways in which culture, intergenerational relationships, racism, and economic conditions affect their choices and options.

In addition to the interviews, I reviewed a number of Asian American and Hmong American community newspapers and newsletters, and conducted limited participant observation in some of the women's homes and at Hmong American college student events, including a national Hmong American student conference.[1] In order to preserve the spirit of the women's voices, the quotations used in this article are verbatim transcriptions. All names are pseudonyms.

The next section focuses on cultural issues, both the cultural obstacles that Hmong women face and the ways in which they are reinventing Hmong culture through their hopes, dreams, and actions. I then focus on how the current political, economic, and social climate in the United States is affecting Hmong American women's ability to achieve their dreams. I look at how economic issues, including current proposals for welfare reform, may affect Hmong American women's pursuit of higher education, and consider how racial and ethnic stereotypes affect these women's self-perceptions.

HMONG AMERICAN COLLEGE WOMEN:
AGENTS OF CULTURAL TRANSFORMATION

As noted earlier, researchers and journalists have written a great deal about the ways in which Hmong cultural ideas clash with mainstream American ideas regarding appropriate gender roles for girls and women. As newcomers to the United States in the late 1970s and 1980s, Hmong families often found themselves in conflict with the U.S. legal system over their marriage customs (Scott, 1988). Researchers interested in gender issues singled out the practices of early marriage and childbearing as the biggest obstacles to school achievement and persistence among Hmong adolescent girls (Donnelly, 1994; Rumbaut & Ima, 1988; Walker-Moffat, 1995). Walker-Moffat, for example, notes that due to cultural practices, "Hmong girls who continue to study beyond puberty are exceptional" (1995, p. xiv). The assumption behind much of this work is that the practice of early marriage is simply a reflection of Hmong cultural traditions, as opposed to an adaptation to being in the United States.

Some research, however, suggests that the push for early marriage in Hmong communities may be a response to the perceived threat of the dominant U.S. culture. For example, Rumbaut and Ima (1988) argue that early marriage among Hmong girls is less a cultural expression than a reflection of parents' attempts to prevent their daughters from assimilating into the dominant culture. Hmong elders are particularly fearful about American pressure to assimilate. They fear the loss of a distinct Hmong identity, and have responded by reasserting gender and age hierarchies (Donnelly, 1994; Walker-Moffat, 1995). This research suggests that contact with outsiders (i.e., non-Hmongs) forces the Hmong to reevaluate their cultural practices and identities. As active makers of their culture, the Hmong do not simply passively accept imposed change, but evaluate their situations and respond according to what they believe is in their best interest. Thus young Hmong American women, for example, are likely to respond to life in the United States differently from elderly Hmong men.

Economic forces and conditions in the United States and the Hmong's evaluation of these forces have also altered their culture. Adult Hmong males who were once the unquestioned center of family authority have found themselves economically dependent on their wives, children, and the government (Donnelly, 1994). One response to these economic conditions has been an increased emphasis on formal education for the younger generation. Goldstein (1985), for example, found that Hmong parents encourage both their sons and daughters to work hard in school in order to achieve economic security. However, despite their belief in the instrumental purposes of education, Hmong parents continue to hold higher expectations for their sons than for their daughters (Goldstein, 1985; Walker-Moffat, 1995).

For their part, the women in my study are motivated by economic forces to pursue higher education. Economic conditions have also led Hmong women to transform *paj ndau* (i.e., the art of Hmong needlework) from a folk art to a source of income. In Laos, subgroups of Hmong differentiated by dialect wore clothes decorated with distinct needlework patterns that served as ethnic markers (Koltyk, 1993; Peterson, 1988). In the United States, many Hmong women make these needlework pieces for the consumer market. They have formed needlework cooperatives, and the profits from sales help to support their families (Donnelly, 1994). The actual style of needlework produced here has also changed. While the needlework was previously based largely on geometric designs, pictorial narratives in the form of story clothes now dominate (Koltyk, 1993). Peterson (1988) argues that Hmong women are aware that the story clothes represent their culture to non-Hmongs, and they purposely control the content of the story clothes in an attempt to control the image of their people. Thus, subjects such as the cultivation of opium poppy are excluded from the story clothes.

The Hmong American college women in my study understand that Hmong culture is in the process of significant change, and they see themselves as central agents of that change. They identify themselves as pioneers who are leading the Hmong people into the next generation. In the interviews, several women proudly asserted that they were among the "first" new generation of Hmong American college women. As pioneers, these women hope to affect their own lives and the lives of other Hmong women. They are motivated to pursue higher education by economic interests and by a desire for increased independence. A number of them stressed the importance of postponing marriage in order to pursue higher education; some of them also asserted that Hmong women should have smaller families. It is critical to point out that while these women are re-creating and transforming their role within their culture, they continue to assert a distinct ethnic identity as Hmong people. That is, while they describe themselves as "less traditional," they do not see themselves as being "less Hmong" than their elders.

Although proud and excited, the women are quick to point out that it is often difficult to be pioneers. Because different members of a culture may have different interests and goals, the possibility for internal struggle is endless. These women's struggles are evidence that cultural transformation is neither a linear nor a smooth process. Their ideas of cultural transformation are often at odds with those of their elders, who emphasize the importance of a strict gender hierarchy in which men are on top. Some of the women say that while the older males mourn what they believe is the loss of male power, many Hmong women of all ages embrace what they perceive to be the increased opportunities for freedom offered by life in the United States. Donnelly (1994) found that middle-aged Hmong American men often joked that if they had the opportunity to return to Laos, the first thing they would do upon their return would be to beat up on the women. By contrast, Donnelly notes that "no Hmong woman has ever told me she wanted to live in Laos again" (p. 74). The women in Donnelly's study and in mine see greater gender equality and freedom in the United States. My informants cited both U.S. cultural norms and laws as being favorable to women.

My informants assert that internal cultural struggles often center around whether women should marry early or postpone marriage in favor of pursuing higher education. They report that early marriage and childbearing continue to be the biggest obstacles to Hmong women's pursuit of higher education. All of the women who are over twenty-five years old report that their families pressured them to get married when they were adolescents. Some of these women married and remain married, some married and divorced, and a few were successfully able to resist family pressures to marry. It should be noted that while divorce is becoming more common in Hmong American communities, it is still viewed as a last resort (Donnelly, 1994; Vang, 1981). Although most of my younger informants have postponed marriage in order to pursue their education, they still cite early marriage as one of the biggest obstacles to Hmong American women's pursuit of higher education.

PIONEERS

The first time I met Joua she referred to herself as a pioneer. At thirty-one, Joua has never been married. She works for the state government, is a leader in the Hmong American community at local and national levels, and is a part-time graduate student in social work. Active in women's issues, she attended the 1996 International Women's Conference in Beijing with the Hmong women's delegation. As a pioneer, Joua is committed to encouraging Hmong women to stay in school. Reflecting on her role in the transformation of Hmong culture, Joua says:

> Culture changes every day, and I look at myself as changing the culture in my family and in my community. When you decide to stick with education and realize that education is important and really decide to go forward, that's when you . . . you change it.

Although Joua sees herself as an agent of Hmong cultural transformation, she is against cultural assimilation. Her deep commitment to maintaining a distinct Hmong identity is reflected in her interest in Hmong folk arts, the Hmong language, and her continuing work on behalf of the Hmong community.

Several of my younger (i.e., twenty-four and under) informants mention that they looked up to Joua as a role model. Blia, a twenty-one-year-old in her second year at a large midwestern university, describes Joua as a mentor who encouraged her to pursue education while reminding her that she should be proud of her Hmong background. Blia speaks of Joua's influence on her life and about Joua's status within the Hmong community:

> All of the Hmong adults in the Hmong community, they trust her and they respected her, and if she wanted to take us places, like for [Hmong] dance competitions, our parents were very okay with it. She always stressed individuality, and to pursue whatever you wanted without a spouse. And I think part of, part of my dreams and goals came from her, too, 'cause I saw what she was doing and I thought that, that's something that, that I would want to do, too.

Joua's success in gaining the confidence of Hmong elders has likely been because she fosters the preservation of certain cultural traditions (e.g., Hmong folk dancing), and encourages young people to maintain a separate Hmong identity. Blia recalls that, as an adolescent, she and some of her Hmong peers considered changing their names to "American" names, and that Joua lectured them about the importance of keeping their ethnic identities.

Reflecting on her life history, Joua notes that she has always been "different," and that this has not always made her life easy. She remembers that when she was an adolescent, Hmong girls were expected to get married and leave school. Most of the Hmong girls she knew followed this pattern. During the time Joua and her family were in the Thai refugee camps, her family arranged for her to marry a Hmong man who was living in the United States. Joua was thirteen years old and had no interest in marriage: "That time I was young. I didn't know what to say or to really argue the point, but I did just cry and say, 'I don't want to marry him.'" After she had cried for three days, one of her male relatives interceded and the marriage was called off:

> And so, finally, one of our relatives came. He was a key man, and he said [to my father], "Let me see your girl. Why do you make such a big deal out of this thing? Let me go and talk to her and see your girl." And so he came in and he said, "My gosh! Your daughter is such a little kid. She is just a girl. Why do you make such a big deal out of this arranged marriage? Why don't you just say to them [the prospective groom's family] that we'll wait until [we] get to the U.S. Then if the girl and the boy like each other, then they can initiate their own and go on with the marriage." . . . So that was that. But, I mean, that experience has, I think, taught me to be, has taught me to stick with what I believe.

As a high school student, Joua faced the skepticism of Hmong adults who questioned whether any girl had the ability or disposition to persist in school. She recalls that one of her male relatives bet her and her female cousin that they would not be able to finish high school:

> And so we were talking about the subject of education versus marriage. And so he said, "Well, if you think, if you think that you're tough, and you really want me to believe, then I make a bet that if you finish high school, then I give you both a hundred dollars each. But if you don't finish high school, then you pay back those two hundred dollars to me."

Joua laughs when she recalls this, and asserts that although her male relative never did pay her the hundred dollars he owes her, he has also never again questioned her abilities.

After graduating from high school in 1984, Joua and her female cousin attended the local community college. Joua studied secretarial science and her cousin pursued food management. During this time she and her cousin were the only two Hmong women she knew of who were pursuing postsecondary educations. After earning her associate's degree, Joua worked as a secretary, but she wanted to go back to school because she believed that more education would offer her more opportunities. Joua enrolled at a small liberal arts college where she was the first Hmong student. As a college student, Joua once again faced the criticism of the larger Hmong community. She recalls what some of her relatives said about her during this period:

> "God, why doesn't she get married? What's wrong with her?" And the general feeling is that girls go to school only because they want a husband, you know, to attract husband. They won't have a career. They won't go through with it. They won't succeed.

Since the college was a long drive from her family's home, Joua lived in the dorms. She explains that living away from home was yet another departure from Hmong tradition that brought her further criticism from the Hmong community.

Moua, a twenty-seven-year-old bilingual education teacher, is another pioneer. As one of the first Hmong public school teachers in her state, Moua believes that it is her obligation to help Hmong students. In addition to her teaching job, Moua is active in the Hmong community in her city. She and her husband chaperoned a group of students to the Hmong Youth Conference in Washington, DC, where I met her. Reflecting on her role in the Hmong community, Moua states proudly:

> I am the only lady, Hmong lady, on the executive board for the Hmong community in my city. Parents, community leaders respect me and see that I have potential to lead the Hmong into better things in the future.

Although Moua's parents are very proud of her now, they were ambivalent about her educational aspirations when she began college. As a high school student she was pressured by them into marrying a relative, and was divorced less than three months later. Moua talks about her experience with early marriage:

> I guess I'm one of those statistic cases. I was pressured into an early marriage to my Aunt and Uncle's son when I just finished my junior year in high school. We were together for two-and-a-half months. It didn't last because we didn't love each other and had never been with each other since we were in Laos. And that was twelve years ago.

After her divorce, Moua finished high school and went on to pursue a bachelor's degree at a small four-year college. Like Joua, Moua talks about the discouragement and ridicule she faced as one of the first Hmong American women to go to college in her family's network:

> When I went away to college and stayed in the dorms and hardly came home, there was a lot of rumors about me . . . [that] I was dating American (White) guys, [that] that's why I hardly came home, [that] I would never make it or finish because I'll probably get pregnant and drop out soon, and that I was too old and had wanted to wear the pants in the family.

Moua got married a few months after her college graduation. Although this time she was able to marry the man of her choice, she still feels that she married sooner than she would have liked because of community pressures.

"GETTING AHEAD IN THE UNITED STATES": ECONOMIC MOTIVATIONS FOR PURSUING HIGHER EDUCATION

Despite all of the intergenerational conflicts, Joua and Moua persisted in school because they believed that a college education would lead to economic security and independence. These women's faith in the power of education is so strong, in fact, that they maintain it is difficult, if not impossible, to get ahead in the United States without an education. Moua's and Joua's ideas regarding the connection between education and economic self-sufficiency reflect the dominant society's philosophy regarding the purpose of education. Their ideas were confirmed by their experiences growing up in families that struggled to make ends meet in their new country. When I asked Moua about her motivation for pursuing higher education, she reflected on her childhood:

> I think [I was motivated] by seeing my parents suffering and their lack of education. It was hard for my parents to make a living in the U.S. without an education and having to wait for the welfare check or getting minimum wage at $3.50 per hour and hardly make ends meet.

Moua's belief in the importance of education has led her to pursue her master's degree. Although she is often overwhelmed by her various responsibilities as a mother, wife, graduate student, and full-time teacher, she continues to go to school because she believes that further education will translate into greater financial security for her family, and will also make her a better teacher.

The belief that education will lead to financial security was echoed by all of my informants. They all maintain that one of the primary reasons they pursued higher education was to achieve social mobility and financial security. They consider access to free public education and the opportunities associated with education to be among the greatest advantages of life in the United States. Thus, like the voluntary immigrant minorities described by Ogbu (1987, 1991), my informants are motivated by folk theories of achievement that link education to success. According to Ogbu, voluntary immigrants hold a folk theory of getting ahead that leads them "to believe that in the United States they, too, can get ahead through hard work, school success, and individual ability" (1987, p. 325).

Like Moua and Joua, the younger women's ideas regarding the purpose of education are based on their family experiences. Many speak at length about their parents' struggles to survive in the United States without formal education and/or skills that could be translated into jobs. Public assistance and low-paying jobs were often the only options open to their parents, and memories of financial hardships motivated the women to persist in school. May, a nineteen-year-old in her third year at a large midwestern university, describes the impact of her family's experiences on her attitudes towards schooling:

> Well, I guess, my family, we weren't too rich. We didn't have a lot of money. So, I mean, I want money. I want to be success — successful. And I wanted to support, like have enough money to have children and take care of them, too, you know. So I mean, well you know in this society you really need money if you want to go anywhere. We knew that we can get money through you know, good education.

The women's belief in the connection between education and economic self-sufficiency is often shared by their parents. Some of their parents impressed upon them, as children, the importance of getting an education for economic survival in the United States. Since childhood, Mai, a twenty-year-old in her second year at a large midwestern university, was encouraged by her mother to go to college. Discussing her mother's interest in her education, Mai explains:

[Getting an education,] that's the only way to survive here in America. And, she [Mai's mother] wants to see us [Mai and her siblings] succeed, you know? She doesn't want us — to see us struggle like, the way she had to, you know, to raise us in America.

"BECOMING MORE EQUAL":
BREAKING FREE OF HMONG GENDER NORMS

In addition to a belief in the link between education and economic security, all of the women speak about the link between education and freedom from male domination. Their talk centers around the idea that education leads to independence and self-empowerment. Although the women vary in their attitudes towards feminism, they all agree that men and women should be, in their own words, "more equal" than in "traditional" Hmong families. The women point to the fact that male children are more valued than female children and the fact that men have more power than women within marriages as examples of the gender inequality in Hmong families. They believe that through education they will be able to achieve the gender equality within their families that their mothers and grandmothers did not have. The women reason that college degrees will lead them to good jobs, which in turn will make them equal economic partners in their marriages. Reflecting on her motivation for pursuing an education, one woman simply states: "I don't wanna ever be in [a situation] to be so dependent on a guy, on a man." They also believe that the process of education will empower them to speak up for their own interests.

Several of the younger women assert that Hmong women are better, more assertive, and more active college students than Hmong men. My observations of Hmong college student events and my reviews of Hmong American community newspapers support the women's perceptions of themselves as being more active students than Hmong men. For example, I learned that Hmong women, and not Hmong men, were the organizers of the two national conferences directed at young Hmong adults during the 1995–1996 academic year.

The women in my study explain that Hmong college women are motivated to do well in college by their desire to break free of the traditional Hmong gender norms. They maintain that while Hmong men have power and get respect with or without an education, Hmong women need to get educated in order to gain freedom. They suggest that their experiences in and out of school have taught them that they have to be assertive if they want to succeed. Ploa, a twenty-two-year-old recent graduate of an Ivy League university, states that she and her Hmong female college friends work hard in school because they have a lot to gain by getting a college education, and a lot to lose if they don't succeed in college. In the following passage, Ploa compares Hmong men's experiences with those of Hmong women:

We are in a patriarchal culture and men get the support, men get the respect, just, they get a lot more of things upon birth than the women, the women do. And I think a lot of us feel that, many of us have to sort of prove ourselves in a lot of ways in that . . . a lot of us have to speak up because if we don't speak up for ourselves, no one's gonna speak up for us.

Although Ploa and other Hmong women are proud of their own academic accomplishments, they argue that they are the exceptions within the Hmong community. All the women relate stories of Hmong girls who never made it to college because they dropped out of high school to get married, and several women tell stories of Hmong women who matriculated in college and then dropped out.

The women's understanding of gender roles within Hmong families and their hopes for their own futures come from what their own mothers taught them and from what they have observed. The women state explicitly that they do not want to live their mothers' lives. Several women report that their mothers and/or older sisters warned them about how hard it is to be a woman within Hmong families and said that life in the United States offers greater gender equality than life in Laos. Their mothers and sisters taught them that they could escape male domination by obtaining a college education. Joua explains that her older sister encouraged her to go to school and take advantage of the educational opportunities in the United States, reminding her of the lack of educational opportunities for women in Laos. Remembering her sister's influence, Joua says:

> My oldest sister is, I think, the key person who really has, I mean, deserve[s] all the credits for getting me through school. Because she['s] older and my mom and dad didn't let her go to school. They let my brother go to school but they needed her help in the house. So she always regret[ted] that she never got a chance to go to school. So when we got here, she wanted to make sure that I get educated and all that. And so she would be the one that really keep a close eye on me.

Joua recalls that her older sister made it clear that she did not want Joua to "live a life like hers." Joua laughs and adds that this has meant that she has had the pressure of living both her own life and her older sister's dream life.

Lia, a twenty-one-year-old undergraduate at a large midwestern university, says that her mother always encouraged her to go to school in order to ensure her independence:

> My mother has always told me — she says it's hard being a Hmong wife because you always have to feel like . . . you always depend on someone else and you don't have your own identity. She would never want us to feel that way. She wants us to be our own individual. The only way to do that is that you go to college, you get a good job. She has always said to me to go.

Lia asserts that because of her mother's support she "can't imagine not going to college."

The mothers who seem most straightforward in their discussions about the difficulties faced by women in traditional Hmong families are often those who have experienced marital difficulties or are widowed. The fact that some Hmong mothers encourage their daughters to go to college in order to change the nature of gender relations within their families suggests that cultural transformation is not solely the purview of the younger generation. At times these women went against their husbands in encouraging their daughters to be more independent. This intragenerational disagreement between fathers and mothers over appropriate gender roles for their daughters further demonstrates that cultures are not monolithic and static. In this case, people within the same generation are viewing their culture from gendered positions.

Other women assert that, while their mothers never spoke about the difficulties of being Hmong women, they reached this conclusion by observing gender roles within their own families. Ploa reports that her ideas about being an independent and self-sufficient woman are based on witnessing her mother's marital problems. During Ploa's senior year in high school, her father had an affair with a woman he planned to take as a second wife, a plan rooted in his desire to have more sons. Although Ploa's maternal grandfather was able to put a stop to these plans, Ploa has not forgiven her father. Furthermore, Ploa is angered by the Hmong tradition that makes Hmong women dependent upon men for support. Within traditional Hmong practices, marriage represents the union of two men's families, and thus the negotiation of marital problems must be done by men (Donnelly, 1994). Reflecting on how her father's actions have influenced her ideas, Ploa says:

> That's exactly like what I don't wanna ever be in, is to be so dependent on a guy, on a man, and to like, that he would do something like that to you without even thinking about your feelings.

Ploa asserts that while she was always an exemplary student, this event motivated her to work even harder in school.

Interestingly, despite their refugee status, the women in my study share many attitudes with the voluntary immigrants described by Ogbu (1987, 1991). Ogbu argues that voluntary immigrants are motivated by a dual frame of reference, whereby they compare their life in the United States with life in their native country and conclude that things are better in their new country. It is important to point out that, as refugees, the women in my study do not match Ogbu's definition of voluntary immigrants. However, like Ogbu's voluntary immigrants, the women in my study hold folk theories of achievement that link education to socioeconomic mobility. Like voluntary immigrants, the Hmong women have a dual frame of reference, which also, in this case, is directly related to their understanding of gender and gender dynamics. Specifically, these Hmong American women compare the position of women in the United States to what they believe to be the position of women in Laos, and conclude that there is greater gender equality in the United States.

CULTURAL CHANGE AND RESISTANCE TO CHANGE

The women's desire for economic security, personal independence, and gender equality motivates them to pursue college educations. Their actions and desires are changing not only their own lives; they are also beginning to alter Hmong culture. Today, women like Moua and Joua are viewed as role models both by younger Hmong women and by older members of the Hmong community, who turn to Moua and Joua for advice and assistance. Joua and Moua work between and within the Hmong and mainstream communities. The very fact that Moua and Joua are seen as role models and leaders suggests that cultural expectations among the

Hmong regarding the education of women are changing. According to the 1990 U.S. Census, over one-third of the Hmong who have bachelor's degrees and nearly one-half of those with master's degrees are women.

Another indicator of cultural change is the fact that many Hmong women who interrupted their studies in order to follow traditional marriage patterns are now returning to school in increasing numbers (Fass, 1991). Several of my informants follow this pattern. Like the women in my study who are postponing marriage in order to pursue higher education, the married women are enrolling in college because they believe that education will lead to economic security. Returning to school after following traditional marriage patterns, these informants struggle to balance their family responsibilities and expectations with their school work. Family support for their pursuit of higher education varies. While some women report that their families encourage their decision to pursue higher education, others report being criticized by parents and in-laws for straying from their traditional roles as wives and mothers.

The women in my study who are mothers face the difficulty of finding safe and affordable child care for their children while they are at school. Those from more supportive families are often able to enlist the help of family members, but women who live far from their families or have unsupportive families are forced to turn to paid child care (e.g., baby-sitters, day-care centers, nursery schools). Many Hmong women find that child-care costs, which are roughly the same for families from all social-class backgrounds, are beyond their economic reach. Ironically, all of the women report that one of the primary reasons they decided to return to school was to improve economic conditions for their families, but they often find it difficult to improve their situations because the cost of child care is prohibitive.

Mao, a twenty-four-year-old who recently graduated from a small college with a degree in nursing, is one of these returning women. During her senior year in high school Mao eloped with a Hmong man ten years her senior. Although her husband followed the Hmong cultural practice and "captured" her in the middle of the night, Mao is quick to assert that this was a marriage of choice, not a forced marriage.[2] After graduating from high school, Mao settled into a life as a wife and mother. Two years after she had the first of her three children, Mao decided that she wanted to go to college in order to get a better job:

> Right after I finished high school, I didn't want to go on, you know? I just wanted to work and just, you know, earn money. But then I guess you can't earn money just, you know, not a lot of money anyway, just straight from high school anyway. So that's why I decided that, you know, I need to go back to school and get a degree . . . get more education.

Her greatest challenge as a student has been finding child care. Mao considers herself fortunate in that her husband, who does not have a college education, is very supportive of her pursuit of education. Although he does help with the children, he is often busy with his job for Head Start. Fortunately, during most of her college career, Mao has been able to arrange child care with other young Hmong mothers who live in her low-income housing complex. Two of the women with whom she shares child care most frequently are also pursuing their college degrees.

Bla, a twenty-two-year-old in her second year in college, is another returning student. Bla married her boyfriend during her junior year in high school in order to escape community rumors that she was "bad." After getting married, Bla transferred to a high school in the city where her new husband was attending college. Although she got pregnant during her senior year, Bla managed to graduate with her class. Two years after graduating from high school, Bla and her husband decided that they would have better economic opportunities if she returned to school to earn a college degree. Their dream is to move out of the low-income apartment in which they currently live and buy their own home. They believe that if they both earn college degrees and get good jobs, they will be able to achieve that dream.

Bla initially attempted to go to school full time, but has had to drop down to one or two courses per term because of difficulties finding safe and affordable child care for her two-year-old daughter. Pregnant with her second child, Bla is worried because she knows that affordable infant care is very difficult to find. Like Mao, Bla has shared child care with other young mothers in her housing complex, but her schedule often conflicts with the other mothers' schedules. Bla's mother has been particularly supportive of her return to school and has tried to provide child-care assistance, but she lives almost two hours away. Bla experimented with leaving her daughter at her mother's house during the week, but she has not done this recently because she finds the separation from her daughter too painful. When I asked Bla whether her in-laws ever help with child care, she shook her head and said that her husband's family does not believe that women should go to college.

Bla has also attempted to find paid child care for her daughter, but has found that to be too expensive. The university where Bla and her husband are students has a program that provides student-parents with up to $750 per semester to help cover the expense of child care. The amount given is based on financial need. During the 1995–1996 school year, Bla and her husband received $375 per semester, an amount too small to cover the cost of day-care centers in her area. Ironically, Bla works part time at a day-care center to help with the family finances, but she and her husband can't afford the cost of that center. Bla's difficulty finding child care has led her to conclude that she should have no more than two children. This decision to have a small family is a move away from the Hmong cultural norm of large families (Donnelly, 1994).

Although the number of Hmong American women who pursue higher education has grown, the women in my study continue to face many of the cultural barriers to education described by previous researchers (Donnelly, 1994; Rumbaut & Ima, 1988; Walker-Moffat, 1995). These women assert that they are concerned that the majority of Hmong girls and women still marry early and do not pursue four-year college degrees. At the Hmong Youth Conference in Washington, DC, the issue of early marriage came up in several student-led workshops. The women attending these workshops, in particular, expressed concern that Hmong girls are still marrying "too young," and that going to college is still the exception. These college women argued that early marriage among their peers will negatively affect the married women's economic and emotional lives.

In interviews and informal conversations with college women at the Hmong Youth Conference, I was told that while some girls are forced into early marriage by their families, many girls choose to marry early in order to escape parental control. The women in my study report that many of their friends see marriage as the only way to circumvent their parents' strict ideas about dating. In families that don't allow unchaperoned dating, for example, some Hmong girls find that marriage is the only culturally acceptable way to spend time alone with a boyfriend. One woman attending the Hmong Youth Conference said that she got married when she was in high school because she could not figure out another way to spend time with her boyfriend, that she had been "young and in love" and had "traditional parents who didn't understand." Lia talks about a friend who married early to escape her parents' authority:

> They got married because her parents wouldn't let them go out with each other and . . . [because] she always felt that she was doing things at home. She didn't have any freedom and she thought they just should get married.

According to Lia, this friend had imagined that marriage would give her freedom and independence, but has found out that marriage is not easy. Lia, who says her friend warns her not to make the same mistake, uses her friend's experiences to bolster her confidence in her decision to postpone marriage and to make her college education a priority in her life.

Another factor that leads to early marriage among Hmong girls and women is the fear that if they postpone marriage until after they graduate from college, Hmong men will consider them to be too old and undesirable. These fears are based on their understanding that Hmong men prefer young wives, a preference that has been documented by several scholars (Donnelly, 1994; Goldstein, 1985). In fact, Donnelly (1994) found that Hmong parents push their sons to marry young girls. The women in my study stated that their relatives often warn them that they will not find husbands unless they marry while they are still young.

Several women asserted that Hmong men's preference for young wives is connected to their preference for quiet, passive, and submissive wives whom they can control. The women have found that even college-educated Hmong men prefer to marry teenage Hmong girls. Several of my informants said they believe that most Hmong men view college-educated women as being too assertive and that they purposely choose young wives they can "boss around." Some women in my study argue that most Hmong men are insecure about losing their authority. According to Moua, Hmong men "are scared because they think all college women want to wear the pants in the family."

Hmong men's preference for younger wives concerns even women who are satisfied with their decision to postpone marriage. Lia, for example, is concerned that she might not be able to find a Hmong husband who will be interested in her and who will respect her:

> The thing, too, is that guys my age don't marry women — Hmong women my age. They marry younger women, and I don't really have that much. . . . I get worried every now and then. Am I gonna find a Hmong husband when I'm twenty-five? Guys who are twenty-five aren't gonna want to marry me. They'll want to marry someone younger.

Lia would ideally like to marry a Hmong husband, but like other college-educated Hmong women, she says that it is more important for her to find a husband who will respect her as an equal partner than to marry someone Hmong. She plans to look for a Hmong man to marry, but is open to marrying a non-Hmong. Sao, a twenty-five-year-old graduate student who is engaged to marry a Chinese immigrant from Taiwan, explained that she realized two years ago that she would not be able to find a Hmong man who would respect her. Like other women in my study, Sao believes that Hmong men prefer young women because they want passive wives. Sao maintains that once she accepted the fact that most Hmong men are sexist, she was open to marrying a non-Hmong. She says that marrying out of her ethnic group is a way to escape what she perceives as Hmong patriarchy. Similar research on out-marriage among Japanese American and Chinese American women suggests that some women out-marry in order to escape Asian patriarchy (Fong & Yung, 1995/1996). It is important to point out, however, that although Sao plans to out-marry, she insists that she will continue to assert a distinct ethnic identity as a Hmong person.

BLAMING THE VICTIM:
ANTI-IMMIGRANT RHETORIC AND WELFARE REFORM

In addition to the cultural obstacles these women face, it is crucial to point out that their ability to achieve their educational dreams is also influenced by larger social, economic, and political factors. In the 1990s, anti-immigrant sentiment and welfare bashing have created a hostile climate for Asian American and Latino immigrants and refugees (Suarez-Orozco, 1996), who are perceived to be a drain on the economy. They are simultaneously accused of taking jobs away from "real Americans" and living off the government (e.g., public assistance), which puts them in a no-win situation. Within this anti-immigrant rhetoric, the Hmong have been targeted and stereotyped as "lazy welfare recipients." In this section I focus on how the current social, political, and economic situation in the United States affects Hmong women's self-perceptions and their ability to reach their educational goals.

RESPONDING TO RACISM

My informants all spoke about the negative impact of racial and ethnic stereotypes on them and other members of the Hmong community. The women complained that the media characterized all Hmong as "lazy," "stupid," "backwards," and "foreign."[3] They were particularly upset by the stereotype that "all Hmong are on welfare." Many of these women have been targets of racist taunts. Mao, for example, recalls that as a teenager she was confronted by an elderly White woman one day on her way home from school:

> This lady say, "Why the Hmong . . . like why they on welfare?" So then she said, "Oh those Hmong just have a lot of kids, just stay home, you know, they have a lot of . . . just keeps having children, and just stay home, receiving aid, receiving all those benefits, just stay home, just keep on having kids. Why don't they — don't they just move back to their country?"

Such racist attacks ring in the ears of these women and remind them that some Americans don't want them to be here.

Some of my informants suggested that the Hmong should respond to these stereotypes by working hard to educate Americans about the history and accomplishments of Hmong Americans, a view shared by prominent Hmong American organizations. The Hmong American Partnership in Minnesota, for example, published a report that sought to "challenge the misconceptions of the Hmong and provide the public with a greater understanding of our complex situation" (Yang & Murphy, 1993, p. 1). Similarly, male and female students at the Hmong Youth Conference in Washington, DC, suggested that Hmong people need to do more "to educate Americans about the Hmong [situation]."

Some of my informants, however, assert more directly that the stereotypes of the Hmong are racist, ignorant, and unwarranted. Sao, for example, is particularly angry about what she sees as the dominant society's ignorance about welfare and the Hmong community. Although she believes in the value of educating Americans about the Hmong, she maintains that they need not be apologetic for being in this country or for receiving public assistance. Sao defends the Hmong people's right to receive public assistance, since they were U.S. allies during the Vietnam War:

> I think in this case the Hmong have every right to use the welfare system. . . . We fought along with the Americans. You know? We were on their side and we fought the communists for so long. . . . Thirty percent of us died. . . . When they came here they have no money, nothing. Only the clothes on their back, and so of course you have to start somewhere and so it is only right the government, since they make the promise, it is only right that they help these people start something.[4]

Sao is angry at politicians who claim that welfare perpetuates dependence. She is quick to point out that many Hmong people, like her own family, have successfully used public assistance to help them get started:

> Government needs to talk to people who benefit from welfare. The policy-makers, they don't understand the impact of the rules and regulations that they make. I wish that the policymaker will walk in shoes of a poor person for one day. . . . The system works! I mean, look at — look at me! Look at my family. We aren't on welfare [anymore] — all my brothers and sisters all work and it only took us less than seven years. . . . We started off on welfare and now we are off welfare.

Furthermore, Sao asserts, far from being a drain on society, the Hmong are becoming business and property owners who contribute to the economic growth of American communities.

Some of these women seem to have internalized the racism of the dominant society, questioning their own self-worth and worrying about what non-Hmong Americans think about them. In school, the self-doubt leads them to withdraw and remain silent in class. Blia, for example, explains that she is afraid to speak out in her college classes because she fears that all the non-Asians are judging her:

> College is really intimidating. I think I really feel, um, the fact that I'm a minority here. And I think that I'm inferior, I don't know as much. I don't have the

cultural background. I don't have the economic upbringing to perhaps know something.

Such insecurity and the internalization of racism appear to be more common among the younger women in my study who came to the United States as very young children. These women have few memories of life before coming to the United States, and many seem confused about the details of the Hmong involvement in the war in Vietnam. At the Hmong Youth Conference, for example, young men and women expressed confusion over the role of Hmong soldiers in the war. In their efforts to get "the facts about the war," the organizers of the Hmong Youth Conference invited Hmong elders and former members of the CIA to speak on a panel.

I would argue that the younger women's confusion regarding the Hmong involvement in the war and their uncertainty about the circumstances surrounding their arrival in the United States make it difficult for them to resist racist stereotypes. It is important to point out, however, that their naiveté about the Hmong experience is not simply a reflection of their age, but also a reflection of their education. When I asked my informants whether they had been taught in school about the role Hmong soldiers played during the war, most looked at me blankly. One stated that she remembered reading a bit about the Vietnam War in a textbook, but did not get any information about the Hmong. As is true of other minority groups, the absence of a culturally relevant pedagogy that teaches about the Hmong American experience and about the Hmong involvement in the war alienates Hmong students from their history (Ladson-Billings, 1995). I am not simply referring to a curriculum that includes information about minority culture and history. While it is certainly important to teach students about their history and culture, I would argue that it is also important to help them develop the critical skills necessary to challenge racism and other forms of inequality. In describing culturally relevant pedagogy, Ladson-Billings states: "Not only must teachers encourage academic success and cultural competence, they must help students to recognize, understand, and critique current social inequalities" (1995, p. 476). A culturally relevant practice that encourages critical thinking would help empower these Hmong students to resist racism.

IMPACT OF WELFARE REFORM

Policymakers, politicians, journalists, social workers, and members of the Hmong community have expressed concern over high levels of poverty and large numbers dependent upon public assistance among Hmong Americans (Fass, 1991; Rumbaut & Ima, 1988; Yang & Murphy, 1993). According to the 1990 Census, 61.8 percent of Hmong families in the United States lived below the poverty level in 1989, and 9,946 out of the 14,815 Hmong households in the United States (67.1%) received some form of public assistance. Despite room for concern, a closer look at the statistics provides some reason for optimism. For example, according to the 1990 Census, although two-thirds of all Hmong households in Minnesota receive some form of public assistance, more than a third of these households are made up of people who came to the United States after 1987 (Yang & Murphy, 1993). This may suggest that newcomers use public assistance to help them get established and move off of assistance once they are able to secure work, a view supported by my study, as most of my informants were raised in families in which public assistance was used as a transitional form of support. In general, these families depended on welfare until they were able to establish themselves financially, although those women raised by single mothers relied on public assistance long term.

Because of the relatively high numbers of Hmong Americans dependent on some form of public assistance, the current welfare reforms across the country will no doubt have an impact on the Hmong American community. The focus in the new welfare reform is to move people into the work force as quickly as possible. Many states will require recipients to work in order to receive support and will also limit the period for which support can be received (Haveman, 1996). The reforms are based on the assumptions that welfare discourages self-sufficiency and encourages dependence.

The state of Wisconsin, for example, which has one of the country's largest Hmong populations, has proposed a radical welfare reform plan (Wisconsin Works, or W-2). W-2 proposes that all assistance be time-limited and tied to work or other W-2 approved activities, not including training or education (Corbett, 1996). This work requirement will likely have a significant effect on Hmong families in Wisconsin who currently receive public assistance. Hmong adults with limited English-language skills may face serious barriers to employment. Language barriers are, in fact, a reality for a quarter of all welfare recipients (Haveman, 1996). The fact that W-2 payments do not include adjustments for the number of children in a family are potentially problematic for Hmong families, which are on the average larger than other American families (Rumbaut & Weeks, 1986).

For Hmong American women who are mothers and on public assistance, the full-time, year-round work requirement will create child-care concerns. Research shows that women with child-care problems are less likely to achieve self-sufficiency (Folk, 1996). Furthermore, researchers have found that for low-income mothers, child-care subsidies are crucial to becoming and remaining employed. Under W-2, families at or below 165 percent of poverty level who also meet all W-2 requirements are eligible for child-care subsidies for children under thirteen years of age. While these subsidies will help pay for child care, it is still unclear whether the supply of child care will be sufficient. Finally, it is crucial to point out that since child-care subsidies will only be provided for children under age thirteen, older children will run the risk of having no adult supervision after school hours and/or during the summer months.

Sao is particularly critical of the new welfare regulations that require work. In the following passage, she discusses the possible impact of welfare reform on Hmong who are single mothers and on their children:

> Now because of welfare reform or whatever they call it, I can see a lot of trouble already. A lot of the Hmong women that are here in America — a lot of them are single parent. You force women to go to work and the kids are left at home — Who are going to take care of their kids? . . . And then when they have no adult supervision they stay after school and they get involved with gangs.

Sao points out that single motherhood is a reality for many Hmong American women, a situation created not only by the death of a spouse or divorce, but also by the collision of the Hmong cultural practice of polygamy with U.S. laws. In Laos, the practice of polygamy meant that some Hmong men had more than one wife, as did the fathers of several of my informants. Because of the laws and cultural sanctions against polygamy in the United States, many women who are second or third wives of Hmong men raise their children as single mothers. Sao explained that her father had three wives in Laos, but after the war he officially separated from her mother. Thus, Sao's mother came to this country as the single mother of eleven dependent children. With eleven children, few marketable skills, and limited English-language ability, Sao's mother found it necessary to rely on public assistance. Sao maintains that this allowed her mother to be at home to provide the necessary guidance for her and her siblings, which she credits for the fact that she and all her siblings have been able to successfully finish some form of postsecondary education and find their way off public assistance and into jobs. Without adult supervision, Sao believes that both Hmong girls and boys will be drawn to gang involvement and all its attendant problems.

I would argue that the advent of W-2 could have a particularly harsh impact on Hmong daughters. With mothers having to "choose" work in order to receive public assistance, and with the prohibitive cost of child care, daughters in Hmong families are likely to be relegated to their traditional roles as the caretakers of younger siblings. Having to juggle such responsibilities with their school work may inhibit school persistence and achievement among these girls, making it more difficult for them to go to college.

Finally, the emphasis on work under W-2 and other welfare reform programs means that women will not be able to pursue higher education on a full-time basis while receiving public assistance. In my study, two women reported receiving some form of public assistance while attending college. Like the others in my study, these women see a college education as a way to get off welfare. Furthermore, the fact that child-care subsidies under W-2 are tied to work will mean that mothers will not be able to receive child-care subsidies to attend school, thereby inhibiting and most likely preventing any efforts on their part to educate themselves and become financially self-sufficient. And, given the Hmong cultural tradition of early marriage and motherhood, women who adhere most closely to the cultural norms will be most negatively affected by programs such as W-2, in that they will find it increasingly difficult to return to school once they have become mothers.

CONCLUSIONS

These women's stories demonstrate the complexity and texture of the lives of Hmong American women, even as journalists and scholars reduce their situation to one of pure cultural difference or symbolic exoticism. The culture in which Hmong American college women live is not simply a static entity, but rather a dynamic, shifting "work-in-progress" in which Hmong American college women act as agents of change through the expression of their hopes, dreams, and achievements, and through their adjustment to external political, economic, and social factors. Not only do the experiences of these women affect their own and future generations, they also have an impact on the older generations. However, despite evidence of cultural transformation that encourages school persistence, Hmong women still face cultural barriers to the pursuit of higher education demonstrating that cultural transformation is not a smooth process, but is fraught with tension and struggle.

In addition to ongoing cultural struggles, Hmong women face economic and racial barriers in their pursuit of higher education. With the prospect of welfare reform, such as Wisconsin's W-2, economic barriers to their pursuit of higher education could become even greater. I would argue that, although it is too early to say with any certainty, W-2 may be especially threatening to the educational aspirations of low-income Hmong American women who have followed the traditional Hmong practice of early marriage and motherhood.

The experiences of Hmong American college women illustrate the connection between cultural/private and structural/public concerns. In the face of structural limitations, any cultural change is limited in its potential to provide members of a minority group with the ability to fully pursue their dreams and transform the conditions of their lives.

NOTES

1. Newspapers and newsletters included the following: *Asian American Press*, St. Paul, MN: Asian Business & Community Publishing. *Asian Week: The Voice of Asian America*, San Francisco: Pan Asian Venture Capital Corporation. *The Hmong Free Press*, Minneapolis, MN: Sai Publishing. *Hmong Women Pursuing Education: A Newsletter Compiled by the Hmong Women Students at UW-Stout*, Menomonie, WI: Academic Skills Center, University of Wisconsin-Stout. *Wisconsin Hmong Life: A Monthly Publication of News and Events Concerning Hmong People*, Madison, WI: Hmong Refugee Committee, Bayview Center.
2. In an elopement, the man kidnaps or captures the woman, and after three days and three nights the couple returns to the home of the woman's parents and marriage is negotiated. Mao points out that she decided to run away with her future husband. For more on Hmong marriage customs, see Donnelly (1994), Meredith and Rowe (1986), and Vang (1981).
3. For more on the stereotyping of Southeast Asians, see DuBois (1993).
4. According to many Hmong refugees, the CIA promised that the United States would help and protect the Hmong in return for their help in the war. For a brief discussion of the role of the Hmong in the war in Laos, see Chan (1994).

REFERENCES

Abu-Lughod, L. (1991). Writing against culture. In R. G. Fox (Ed.), *Recapturing anthropology: Working in the present* (pp. 137–162). Santa Fe, NM: School of American Research Press.

Aguilar, J. (1981). Insider research: An ethnography of a debate. In D. A. Messerschmidt (Ed.), *Anthropologists at home in North America: Methods and issues in the study of one's own society* (pp. 15–26). Cambridge, Eng.: Cambridge University Press.

Balibar, E. (1991). Preface. In E. Balibar & I. Wallerstein (Eds.), *Race, nation, class* (pp. 1–13). New York: Verso.

Chan, S. (1994). *Hmong means free: Life in Laos and America*. Philadelphia: Temple University Press.

Corbett, T. (1996). Understanding Wisconsin Works (W-2). *Focus, 18*(1), 53–54.

Donnelly, N. (1994). *Changing lives of refugee Hmong women.* Seattle: University of Washington Press.

Dubois, T. (1993). Constructions construed: The representation of Southeast Asian refugees in academic, popular, and adolescent discourse. *Amerasia, 19*(3), 1–25.

Dunnigan, T. (1986). Processes of identity maintenance in Hmong society. In G. Hendricks, B. Downing, & A. Deinard (Eds.), *The Hmong in transition* (pp. 41–53). New York: Center for Migration Studies.

Erickson, F. (1997). Culture in society and in educational practices. In J. Banks & C. Banks (Eds.), *Multicultural education: Issues and perspectives* (3rd ed., pp. 32–60). Boston: Allyn & Bacon.

Fass, S. (1991). *The Hmong in Wisconsin: On the road to self-sufficiency.* Milwaukee: Wisconsin Policy Research Institute.

Fine, M. (1991). *Framing dropouts: Notes on the politics of an urban high school.* Albany: State University of New York Press.

Fine, M. (1994). Dis-stance and other stances: Negotiations of power inside feminist research. In A. Gitlin (Ed.), *Power and method: Political activism and educational research* (pp. 13–35). New York: Routledge.

Fish, A. (1991). *The Hmong of St. Paul, Minnesota: The effects of culture, gender, and family networks on adolescents' plans for the future.* Unpublished master's thesis, University of Minnesota.

Folk, K. (1996). The W-2 child care plan. *Focus, 18*(1), 66–68.

Fong, C., & Yung, J. (1995/1996). In search of the right spouse: Interracial marriage among Chinese and Japanese Americans. *Amerasia, 21*(3), 77–98.

Foster, M. (1994). The power to know one thing is never the power to know all things: Methodological notes on two studies of Black American teachers. In A. Gitlin (Ed.), *Power and method: Political activism and educational research* (pp. 129–146). New York: Routledge.

Goldstein, B. (1985). *Schooling for cultural transitions: Hmong girls and boys in American high schools.* Unpublished doctoral dissertation, University of Wisconsin-Madison.

Goldstein, B. (1986). Resolving sexual assault: Hmong and the American legal system. In G. Hendricks, B. Downing, & A. Deinard (Eds.), *The Hmong in transition* (pp. 135–143). New York: Center for Migration Studies.

Harrison, F. (1995). The persistent power of "race" in the cultural and political economy of racism. *Annual Review of Anthropology, 24,* 47–74.

Haveman, R. (1996). From welfare to work: Problems and pitfalls. *Focus, 18*(1), 21–24.

Hendricks, G. (1986). Introduction. In G. Hendricks, B. Downing, & A. Deinard (Eds.), *The Hmong in transition* (pp. 3–5). New York: Center for Migration Studies.

Hirayama, K., & Hirayama, H. (1988). Stress, social supports, and adaptational patterns in Hmong refugee families. *Amerasia, 14*(1), 93–108.

Koltyk, J. (1993). Telling narratives through home videos: Hmong refugees and self documentation of life in the old and new country. *Journal of American Folklore, 106,* 435–449.

Kondo, D. (1990). *Crafting selves: Power, gender, and discourses of identity in a Japanese workplace.* Chicago: University of Chicago Press.

Ladson-Billings, G. (1995). Toward a theory of culturally relevant pedagogy. *American Educational Research Journal, 32,* 465–491.

Lee, S. J. (1996). *Unraveling the "model-minority" stereotype: Listening to Asian American youth.* New York: Teachers College Press.

Lutz, C., & Collins, J. (1993). *Reading National Geographic.* Chicago: University of Chicago Press.

Meredith, W., & Rowe, G. (1986). Changes in Hmong refugee marital attitudes in America. In G. Hendricks, B. Downing, & A. Deinard (Eds.), *The Hmong in transition* (pp. 121–131). New York: Center for Migration Studies.

Oakley, A. (1981). Interviewing women: A contradiction in terms. In H. Roberts (Ed.), *Doing feminist research* (pp. 30–61). London: Routledge & Kegan Paul.

Ogbu, J. U. (1987). Variability in minority school performance: A problem in search of an explanation. *Anthropology and Education Quarterly, 18,* 312–334.

Ogbu, J. U. (1991) Immigrant and involuntary minorities in comparative perspective. In M. Gibson & J. U. Ogbu (Eds.), *Minority status and schooling: A comparative study of immigrant and involuntary minorities* (pp. 3–33). New York: Garland Press.

Peterson, S. (1988). Translating experience and the reading of a story cloth. *Journal of American Folklore, 101,* 6–22.

Razack, S. (1995). The perils of talking about culture: Schooling research on South and East Asian students. *Race, Gender, and Class, 2*(3), 67–82.

Reinharz, S. (1992). *Feminist methods in social research.* New York: Oxford University Press.

Rumbaut, R., & Ima, K. (1988). *The adaptation of Southeast Asian refugee youth: A comparative study.* Washington, DC: Office of Refugee Resettlement.

Rumbaut, R., & Weeks, J. (1986). Fertility and adaptation: Indochinese refugees in the United States. *International Migration Review, 20,* 428–465.

Said, E. (1978). *Orientalism.* New York: Random House.

Scott, G. (1988). To catch or not to catch a thief: A case of bride theft among the Lao Hmong refugees of southern California. *Ethnic Groups, 7,* 137–151.

Sherman, S. (1988). The Hmong: Laotian refugees in the "Land of the Giants." *National Geographic, 174,* 586–610.

Suarez-Orozco, M. (1996). California dreaming: Proposition 187 and cultural psychology of racial and ethnic exclusion. *Anthropology and Education Quarterly, 27,* 151–167.

Tapp, N. (1988). The reformation of culture: Hmong refugees from Laos. *Journal of Refugee Studies, 1*(1), 20–37.

Vang, K. (1981). Hmong marriage customs: A current assessment. In B. Downing & D. Olney (Eds.), *The Hmong in the West: Observations and reports* (pp. 29–45). Minneapolis: University of Minnesota, Southeast Asian Refugee Studies Project and Center for Urban and Regional Affairs.

Walker-Moffat, W. (1995). The other side of the Asian American success story. San Francisco: Jossey Bass.

Wolf, E. (1982). *Europe and the people without history.* Berkeley: University of California Press.

Yang, P., & Murphy, N. (1993). *Hmong in the 90's: Stepping towards the future.* St. Paul, MN: Hmong American Partnership.

Fact and Fiction:
Stories of Puerto Ricans
in U.S. Schools

SONIA NIETO

Puerto Rican youths have been attending U.S. schools for nearly a century. As a result of the takeover of Puerto Rico after the Spanish-American War, in the early 1900s Puerto Ricans began arriving in New York and other northeastern cities in increasing numbers. Sociologist Clara Rodríguez has suggested that all Puerto Ricans, regardless of actual birthplace, have been "born in the U.S.A." because all are subject to federal laws and to an imposed U.S. citizenship that was neither sought nor particularly desired (1991). One result of this citizenship, however, has been that Puerto Ricans have been free of the travel restrictions and similar limitations faced by other immigrants to the United States.[1] At first Puerto Ricans came in small numbers, but after the 1917 Jones Act was passed, which made Puerto Ricans U.S. citizens, the numbers grew steadily (Sánchez Korrol, 1983/1994). By the 1940s, a massive out-migration from the island was in progress, and at present, approximately two-fifths of all Puerto Ricans, or 2.75 million people, reside in the United States, a dramatic example of a modern-day diaspora (Institute for Puerto Rican Policy, 1992).

The Puerto Rican community is constantly changing as families seeking a better economic future regularly arrive in the United States, and return often to the island. This circulatory migration, called *vaivén* ("coming and going"), has helped to redefine immigration from the life-transforming experience that it was for most European immigrants at the turn of the century to "a way of life" for a great many Puerto Ricans in the latter part of the century (National Puerto Rican Task Force, 1982). The nature of the migration has also profoundly influenced such issues as language use, identity, and cultural fusion and retention.

Schools and classrooms have been among the sites most seriously impacted by the Puerto Rican presence in the United States, especially during the past two decades, during which Latino children have become the fastest growing ethnic group in public schools. A small number of Puerto Rican students have fared very well academically, and some have expressed gratitude for opportunities offered in U.S. schools that might have never been available to poor, working-class children in Puerto Rico (see, for example, the comments of many of the writers interviewed in Hernández, 1997). The majority, however, have had difficult and unsatisfactory

Harvard Educational Review Vol. 68 No. 2 Summer 1998, 133–163

experiences, including low levels of academic achievement, severe ethnic isolation, and one of the highest dropout rates of all groups of students in the United States (National Center for Educational Statistics [NCES], 1995). The troubled history of the education of Puerto Ricans in U.S. schools is almost a century old, and although it has been chronicled for at least seventy years, it is, in the words of Catherine Walsh, "a disconcerting history of which most U.S. educators are totally unaware" (1991, p. 2). Thus, in spite of Puerto Ricans' growing visibility, much of their history in U.S. schools has yet to be heard.

More careful thought is now being given to that "disconcerting history," especially to the human face of the experiences of Puerto Rican students in U.S. schools, and such consideration is evident in the research literature, especially in more recent ethnographic research studies. It is also evident in a growing body of fiction as, over the past two decades, Puerto Ricans and their experiences in U.S. schools have become more visible as either a primary or an incidental topic in children's, young adult, and adult literature. As an educational researcher, I have concentrated much of my professional and personal attention and energy on the education of Puerto Rican youths, and I have learned a great deal about the promises and pitfalls of education in the United States. As a student of literature, I have also been fascinated by the growing number of fictional stories of Puerto Rican youngsters in U.S. schools, represented by such writers as Piri Thomas, Nicholasa Mohr, Judith Ortiz Cofer, Martín Espada, and others.

Yet fiction is not generally regarded as a legitimate source of data in the educational research community because it is thought to be overly subjective, emotional, and idiosyncratic. Precisely because of the emotional charge of fiction, however, it can be a rich source of knowledge about people's lives and experiences. As Anne Haas Dyson and Celia Genishi have asserted, "Stories are an important tool for proclaiming ourselves as cultural beings" (1994, p. 4). Santa Arias (1996) has suggested that Latino writers serve an important function in that they redefine "the border" as a place of multiple realities and of rebellion. The literature they write, she says, can be understood as a bridge between cultures: "They not only write in order to present a testimonial of survival, but to intervene at various levels in a definition of these borderlands, of what it is like to live in between geographical, linguistic, and cultural worlds" (p. 238).

Fiction can be used in schools to make the lives and experiences of Puerto Ricans more visible than they have been. Stories can also serve as liberating pedagogy in the classroom because they challenge the one-dimensional and largely negative image of Puerto Ricans pervasive in U.S. society. These negative depictions can motivate Puerto Rican writers to present another facet of their community through their writing. One such writer, Jack Agüeros, notes that he feels an obligation "to present our people as we know them, from the inside, from the heart, with all the details (Hernández, 1997, p. 24). Such work can provide evidence of the debilitating experiences that some children have had, in addition to suggesting alternative and more positive possibilities for their future. Puerto Rican authors have written about schooling in the United States in numerous ways, from reports of confrontations with uncaring teachers and unthinking bureaucracies, to stories about teachers who have made a positive difference in the lives of children, to explorations of issues such as colonization, race, ethnicity, social class, and identity — all issues that are central to the lives of Puerto Rican youngsters. Jay

Blanchard and Ursula Casanova (1996) suggest that fiction can be a convincing source of information for teachers, as well as a catalyst for thinking about teaching and learning, as demonstrated in their recent text of short stories geared to preservice and practicing teachers. In their book, Blanchard and Casanova use stories to help illustrate significant themes in teaching, such as the role of families, the need to develop meaningful relationships with students, and the world of imagination.

In summary, the growing body of fiction about Puerto Ricans in U.S. schools is a fertile avenue for exploring and analyzing issues that have heretofore been largely invisible in educational research. By using the title "Fact and Fiction" in this article, I do not mean to suggest that educational research always represents facts, or "the truth," and that fiction is make-believe. Quite the contrary: because the fiction I have used in my analysis includes the voices and experiences of students themselves (or authors' recollections of their experiences as students), stories can frequently teach lessons about life and reality more dramatically and candidly than educational research. A merging of these two arenas of literature — fact and fiction — can be both engaging and illuminating. Before considering the common themes in the literature, I first provide an overview of the education of Puerto Ricans in U.S. schools.

PUERTO RICAN STUDENTS IN U.S. SCHOOLS

Puerto Ricans have achieved the questionable distinction of being one of the most undereducated ethnic groups in the United States. The story of this miseducation is infused with controversy concerning Puerto Rico's political status, conflicts over the role of culture and language in U.S. schools and society, harsh experiences with discrimination based on race, ethnicity, language, and social class, and the Puerto Rican community's determination to define and defend itself.

Almost from the time Puerto Rican students started attending schools in the United States, they have experienced problems such as high dropout rates, virtual absence from top ability groups, massive levels of retention, and low academic achievement (Association of Assistant Superintendents, 1948; ASPIRA, 1968; Margolis, 1968; Morrison, 1958; NCES, 1995; Walsh, 1991). The high dropout rate, for instance, is an issue that was discussed as early as 1958 in *The Puerto Rican Study*, a massive three-year investigation into the educational problems of Puerto Rican youngsters in New York City schools, who by then numbered almost 54,000. In the intervening forty years, when the U.S. Puerto Rican school-age population grew to nearly a million (Institute for Puerto Rican Policy, 1996), dropout rates as high as 70 to 90 percent have been consistently reported in cities throughout the Northeast (ASPIRA, 1993; Cafferty & Rivera-Martínez, 1981; Frau-Ramos & Nieto, 1993; U.S. Commission on Civil Rights, 1976).

As we shall see below, the standard explanations for the failure of Puerto Rican youths in U.S. schools have been rooted in the students themselves: that is, their culture (or lack of it), poverty, limited English proficiency, and poor parenting, among other issues, have been blamed for students' poor achievement (Nieto, 1995). On the other hand, schools' low expectations of these students, the poor preparation of their teachers, the victimization and racism they have faced, and the extremely limited resources of the schools themselves have rarely been mentioned as contributing to the lack of success of Puerto Rican students. Some of these problems are graphically documented in the poem "Public School 190, Brooklyn 1963" by Martín Espada:

> The inkwells had no ink.
> The flag had 48 stars, four years
> after Alaska and Hawaii.
> There were vandalized blackboards
> and chairs with three legs,
> taped windows, retarded boys penned
> in the basement.
> Some of us stared in Spanish.
> We windmilled punches
> or hid in the closet to steal from coats
> as the teacher drowsed, head bobbing.
> We had the Dick and Jane books,
> but someone filled in their faces
> with a brown crayon.
>
> When Kennedy was shot,
> they hurried us onto buses,
> not saying why,
> saying only that
> something bad had happened.
> But we knew
> something bad had happened,
> knew that before
> November 22, 1963. (1996, p. 25)

Another significant problem that has confounded the study of Puerto Ricans in U.S. schools is that historically much of the data have not been disaggregated according to ethnicity. Thus, Puerto Ricans are often lost in educational statistics labeled "Hispanic" or "Latino," as are Mexican Americans, Cubans, and Central and South Americans. There are valid reasons for using the overarching terms of Latino/a and Hispanic at times, including the fact that Latinos increasingly share physical space. This is the case, for example, with Puerto Ricans and Dominicans in the Northeast and Mexican Americans and Central Americans in California. Collectively, these groups have also tended to experience similar problems in education, housing, health care, and employment. However, the overarching terms do not recognize or take into consideration historic, regional, linguistic, racial, social class, and other important differences. Although many of the educational issues faced by Puerto Ricans are similar to those of Latinos in general, others are not. The tendency in research literature to lump all Latino groups together has resulted in muddling what might be sharp differences that could help explain how such issues as poverty, language dominance, political orientation, and school success or failure are manifested in different Latino ethnic groups.

As a subgroup within the Latino population, for instance, Puerto Ricans fare among the worst of all Latino groups in educational outcomes (Carrasquillo, 1991; Latino Commission, 1992; Meier & Stewart, 1991; Nieto, 1995), yet data to substantiate this situation are hard to find. For example, a national report by the National Council of La Raza found that more than one-third of all Latino children lived below the poverty line, compared with just one-eighth of White children (National Council of La Raza [NCLR], 1993). The even more distressing situation of Puerto Rican children is lost in these statistics, however, because the data were not disaggregated. Other research that centered specifically on Puerto Rican children found that they are at the *greatest* risk of being poor among other Latino ethnic groups, with a dramatic 58 percent living in poverty (ASPIRA, 1993; NCLR, 1993). Differences such as these may remain invisible unless the data are disaggregated. In this article, I use disaggregated data whenever possible, but I also use statistics on Latinos in general because they are more readily available.

RECURRING THEMES IN RESEARCH AND FICTION

Based on my reading of the literature in both educational research and fiction, I suggest that four interrelated and contrasting themes have emerged from the long history of stories told about Puerto Ricans in U.S. schools. They are: colonialism/resistance; cultural deficit/cultural acceptance; assimilation/identity; and marginalization/belonging. I explore here how each theme is illustrated in both research and fictional literature. To do this, I highlight significant literature in the educational arena, including historical analyses, commission findings and reports, and ethnographic studies. I also review and analyze works of fiction — short stories, novels, and poetry — that focus on the education of Puerto Rican students in U.S. schools. For every example of victimization or devaluation of Puerto Ricans there are also examples of resistance or affirmation, and these examples can serve as important lessons for teachers and schools committed to helping Puerto Rican students succeed in school.

Ultimately, these four themes lead to the broader discussion concerning care as a significant motif missing from the research literature on the education of Puerto Rican children. I further argue that it is only through care that we can ensure that Puerto Rican students receive the affirmation they so urgently need in U.S. schools.

Colonialism/Resistance

The role that colonialism has played in the education of Puerto Ricans needs to be understood precisely because Puerto Rico and the United States are connected through colonial ties. Although officially called a "territory" by the United States, Puerto Rico has virtually no control over its own destiny. For the past five hundred years, it has been little more than a colony, first of Spain and later of the United States. The fact that Puerto Rico and the United States were joined as a result of conquest (Rodríguez, 1991) is overlooked by historians, educators, and researchers, or minimized in much of the research literature. As a result, Puerto Ricans are generally perceived as simply one of the latest "newcomers" in the traditional European-style model of the immigration experience (Rodríguez, 1991). In fact, early writers such as the sociologist/priest Joseph Fitzpatrick focused on overpopulation as the overriding reason for the migration of Puerto Ricans to the United States (Fitzpatrick, 1971/1987a). Conveniently sidestepped is the contribution of U.S. imperialism to creating the structural changes that adversely affected the

Puerto Rican economy and that eventually led to the massive migration. These included the wholesale purchase of Puerto Rican farmlands by absentee U.S. landlords to grow and harvest sugar, in the process displacing an enormous number of local farmers. Many of these migrated to the United States (Melendez, 1991; Sanchez Korrol, 1983/1997). Later research, including Fitzpatrick's later work (1987b), challenged this initial analysis as overly simplistic (Bonilla & Campos, 1981; History Task Force, 1979; Meléndez, 1991; Rodríguez, 1991; Sánchez Korrol, 1983/1994).

Recent critical research has focused more carefully on the impact that Puerto Rico's colonial status has had on education, both on the Island and in the United States (*Centro,* 1997; Nieto, 1995, in press; Walsh, 1991). When people are stripped of their language and culture, they are also largely stripped of their identity as a people. However, dispossessing people of language and culture does not need to take place with the gun; it is frequently done more effectively through educational policies and practices, the effects of which can be even more brutal than those of the gun. The violence that takes place within schools and classrooms is more symbolic than real. According to Pierre Bourdieu (1977), symbolic violence refers to the maintenance of power relations of the dominant society through the manipulation of symbols.

Given Puerto Rico's longstanding colonial relationship with the United States, it is not surprising that the schools in Puerto Rico have been and continue to be sites of symbolic violence. In a groundbreaking study of the Americanization of schools in Puerto Rico, Aida Negrón de Montilla documented how the United States began to change educational policies and practices almost as soon as it took possession of the island in 1898. Some of these changes were blatant, such as language policies that attempted to wipe out the Spanish language. Within the first several decades, however, it became apparent that total obliteration of the language was impossible, both because the policy was not working and because many Puerto Ricans perceived it as a crude example of cultural imperialism. By the late 1940s, the United States had settled for enforced ESL instruction in all island schools. Other colonizing policies in the schools included the wholesale adoption of U.S. textbooks, curriculum, methods, and materials in island schools; the imposition of the Pledge of Allegiance and other patriotic rituals; and the preparation and expectations of teachers as agents of English and U.S. culture (Negrón de Montilla, 1971).

The symbolic violence represented in these policies is translated into stories that are usually told in sardonic but amusing ways. For instance, the stories of Abelardo Díaz Alfaro are hilarious examples of colonialism gone awry. In "Santa Cló va a La Cuchilla" (1962), Santa Claus, with all the trappings of his Yankee identity, including a sweltering red suit, shows up in La Cuchilla, a rural community with no understanding of this cultural icon. The story is a humorous example of how colonies are saturated with culturally meaningless symbols, while culturally meaningful ones — in this case Los Reyes Magos, or the Three Wise Men — are displaced or disparaged.

In another story, "Peyo Mercé Enseña Inglés" ("Peyo Mercé Teaches English"), Díaz Alfaro (1978) relates the panic experienced by a rural teacher who speaks only Spanish when he receives the mandate from the central office to teach his students English: Peyo Mercé is horrified when he realizes that he has to teach "inglés en inglés!" ("English in English!") (p. 98). The mandate, a historically accurate event, makes for a comical story told with great humanity and insight. Like all good teachers, Peyo Mercé tries to find something in the U.S.-imposed textbook to which his students can relate, and he comes upon a picture of a rooster. Using the picture, he instructs the children to say "cockle-doodle-doo," the sound that roosters make in English. As the story concludes, one of the young students can no longer accept the lie that he and his classmates are learning: he rejects both the English of the rooster and, presumably, the cultural imposition that it represents by stating emphatically that perhaps this is *another* kind of rooster, but that the roosters in *his* house clearly say "¡cocoroco!" — the sound made by roosters in Spanish.

Other examples of the link between politics and education in the early colonization of Puerto Rico by the United States were the establishment of para-educational organizations and activities — for example, the Boy Scouts, the Girl Scouts, and the Future Homemakers of America — and the substitution of Puerto Rican holidays with U.S. holidays, such as Washington's Birthday and Thanksgiving (Negrón de Montilla, 1971). Ironically, even the U.S. celebration of independence became an official holiday in the colony. In fact, the colonial presence is felt most strongly through the manipulation of the tastes, values, and dispositions of the Puerto Rican people. In a scene from *When I Was Puerto Rican*, Esmeralda Santiago (1993) recounts how the mothers of the children in Miss Jiménez's class were asked to attend a meeting with experts from the United States who would teach them "all about proper nutrition and hygiene, so that we would grow up as tall and strong as Dick, Jane, and Sally, the *Americanitos* in our primers" (p. 64). At the meeting, the experts brought charts with unrecognizable food staples:

> There were carrots and broccoli, iceberg lettuce, apples, pears, and peaches. . . . There was no rice on the chart, no beans, no salted codfish. There were big white eggs, not at all like the small round ones our hens gave us. There was a tall glass of milk, but no coffee. . . . There were bananas but no plantains, potatoes but no *batatas* [sweet potatoes], cereal flakes but no oatmeal, bacon but no sausages. (p. 66)

At the end of the meeting, the mothers received peanut butter, cornflakes, fruit cocktail, peaches in heavy syrup, beets, tuna fish, grape jelly, and pickles, none of which formed part of the Puerto Rican diet, and the mother of the protagonist, Negi, concluded, "I don't understand why they didn't just give us a sack of rice and a bag of beans. It would keep this family fed for a month" (p. 68). Such extracurricular educational policies imposed U.S. mainstream cultural values, tastes, and attitudes on Puerto Rican children and their families.

Along with their luggage and other prized possessions, Puerto Rican families also bring with them to the United States this legacy of colonialism. Officially U.S. citizens, Puerto Ricans are not national immigrants, and therefore it is their language, culture, and ethnicity, rather than their nationality, that separate them from their U.S. peers (Cafferty & Rivera-Martínez, 1981). Because the colonial relationship has made Puerto Rican migration a constant experience, in the process it has created "the students in between," those who spend time on both Island and mainland (Quality Education for Minorities Project, 1990). One consequence of colonialism is that issues of identity, belonging, and loyalty are at the very core of the psychological dilemmas faced by Puerto Rican youngsters, and even adults, who know only too well what it means to be a "cultural schizophrenic." In fact, the image of an air bus connecting Puerto Rico to New York has made its way into popular Puerto Rican fiction through Luis Rafael Sánchez's story, "The Flying Bus," in which Sánchez describes one of the passengers as "a well-poised woman . . . [who] informs us that she flies over *the pond* every month and that she has forgotten on which bank of it she really lives" (1987, p. 19; emphasis in original). Joy De Jesús has described the resulting identity crisis in this way:

> What makes growing up Puerto Rican unique is trying to define yourself within the unsettling condition of being neither here nor there: "Am I black or white?" "Is my primary language Spanish or English?" "Am I Puerto Rican or American?" For the Puerto Rican child, the answers to these questions tend to be somewhere in between, and never simple. (1997, p. xviii)

Sandra María Estevez poetically expresses the same sentiment of being "in-between," in "Here":

> I am two parts / a person
> boricua/spic
> past and present
> alive and oppressed
> given a cultural beauty
> . . . and robbed of a cultural identity (1991, p. 186)

Stories about divided identities and loyalties, even among children, are common in the work of Puerto Rican writers. Abraham Rodríguez's "The Boy without a Flag" is a prime example of this idea. After listening to his father denounce U.S. imperialism in Puerto Rico and throughout the world, the eleven-year-old protagonist decides that he will no longer salute the U.S. flag. When his teacher asks him to explain this decision, he announces, using the very same words he had heard his father use, "Because I'm Puerto Rican. I ain't no American. And I'm not no Yankee flag-waver" (1992, p. 18). The principal, who tries to convince him that this posture may in the long run jeopardize his future, asks: "You don't want to end up losing a good job opportunity in government or in the armed forces because as a child you indulged your imagination and refused to salute the flag?" (p. 26). The young boy is crestfallen when he realizes that his father is not only embarrassed by his behavior but has, in fact, sided with the principal, a position he has no doubt taken to protect his son. Martín Espada tells a similar story through the poem "The Year I Was Diagnosed with a Sacrilegious Heart":

> At twelve, I quit reciting
> the Pledge of Allegiance,
> could not salute the flag
> in 1969, and I,
> undecorated for grades or sports,
> was never again anonymous in school. (1993, pp. 72–74)

José Angel Figueroa echoes this theme in "Boricua," a poem that speaks of cultural and political conflict. Referring to education, he writes

> s c h o o l s
> always wanted
> to cave in your
> PuertoRican Accent
> & because you
> wanted to make it
> you had to pledge
> allegiance lefthanded
> because you
> had lost your soul
> during some english exam. (1991, p. 222)

These flag stories allegorically describe resistance to colonialism even among young children.

Colonial status cannot explain all of the educational problems experienced by Puerto Rican students in U.S. schools. Although it is true that the educational instability that results from moving back and forth can lead to low academic achievement, poor language skills, and high dropout rates, there are many Puerto Rican youngsters who do not move back and forth between Puerto Rico and the United States and therefore do not experience this kind of educational disruption. By and large, however, they also experience educational failure. Some theorists have even speculated that colonial status per se may have an impact on students' actual academic achievement (Gibson & Ogbu, 1991; Ogbu, 1987). John Ogbu's (1987) theory concerning *voluntary* and *involuntary* minorities is helpful in understanding this phenomenon. According to Ogbu, it is important to look not simply at a group's cultural background, but also at its political situation in the host society and the perceptions it has of opportunities available in that society. Thus, the major problem in the academic performance of U.S. Puerto Ricans is not that they possess a different language, culture, or cognitive or communication style than students in the cultural mainstream. Rather, the nature of their history, subjugation, and exploitation, together with their own responses to their treatment, are at the heart of their poor academic achievement (Ogbu, 1987).

Because the problem of the poor academic achievement of Puerto Rican youngsters cannot be blamed simply on the legacy of colonialism, I now turn to an exploration of a related concept, the pressure to assimilate, and its effect on the education of Puerto Rican students.

Assimilation/Identity

In the United States, public schools have always had a pivotal role in assimilating immigrant and other nonmainstream students because they have historically stripped them of their native cultural identity in order to impose the majority culture on them. The creation of the common school during the nineteenth century was based in part on the perceived need to assimilate immigrant and other students of widely diverse backgrounds (Katz, 1975). Hence, although the "melting pot" has been heralded as the chief metaphor for pluralism in the United States, a rigid Anglo-conformity has been in place for much of U.S. history. According to Joel Spring (1997), schools in the United States have assimilated students with practices that include flag ceremonies and other patriotic celebrations, the replacement in school curricula of local heroes with national ones, a focus on the history and traditions of the dominant White culture, and the prohibition of native language use in the school. The educational establishment repeated this process, at least in part, in schools in Puerto Rico, and it has been part of the educational landscape since the U.S. takeover of the island in 1898.

These socializing and assimilating agents, then, are no strangers to Puerto Rican students when they enter U.S. schools. Assimilation for Puerto Rican children continues in U.S.-based schools, usually in the urban centers of the Northeast. The image of decaying urban schools, graphically portrayed by a number of Puerto Rican writers, serves as a metaphor for the assimilation of newcomers. Historically, most newcomers to the United States have been poor, uneducated, and relegated to the urban ghettos from which earlier immigrants had fled. Schools in these urban ghettos often were old, worn, and dilapidated. Judith Ortiz Cofer, for instance, describes her first encounter with a school in Paterson, New Jersey, as follows:

> The school building was not a welcoming sight for someone used to the bright colors and airiness of tropical architecture. The building looked functional. It could have been a prison, an asylum, or just what it was: an urban school for the children of immigrants, built to withstand waves of change, generation by generation. (1990, p. 61)

In a powerful novel about a young girl's abuse-filled childhood, Alba Ambert compares the physical presence of her school in New York City with the apparent indifference of the staff who work there:

> Public School 9 was a red-brick structure built at the turn of the century. It loomed on 138th Street across from the Puerto Rico Theater like a huge armory vigilantly surveilling students, teachers, and staff who scuttled in and out of its wide staircase. . . . Teachers and principal lingered at the shore, their backs turned to the island of isolation in which the children lived. From the periphery, they looked away and refused to learn the language of the dispossessed. (1995, p. 113)

For El Cortes (1998), assimilation is portrayed through the rancid smells that are a result of the humiliation faced by children who throw up when they are prohibited from speaking Spanish, forced to eat strange foods, or ridiculed by their teachers for their customs and values:

> School smells is a mess of bad smells and altogether they make one great big bad stink. Vegetable soup with smelly onions in it and rotten orange peel smells get mixed up with the King Pine old mop bleach smell and all of that gets mixed up with . . . throw up. School smells.

Assimilation takes place in numerous ways, and examples of this process, as well as its detrimental effects, abound in fact and in fiction. For instance, the extensive

1976 report by the U.S. Commission on Civil Rights concerning Puerto Ricans in the United States found that young people identified the schools' unresponsiveness to their cultural backgrounds as a primary reason for dropping out of school. Underpinning the pressure to assimilate newcomers is the ideology of "colorblindness"; that is, the view that failing to see differences epitomizes fairness and equality. *The Losers,* one of the early comprehensive reports on the education of Puerto Rican students in the United States, was commissioned by ASPIRA, an educational and leadership advocacy organization focusing on Puerto Rican youths. The report, among the first to challenge the prevalent melting pot ideology, persuasively challenged the ideology of colorblindness by focusing on the Puerto Rican children's teachers — mostly White, middle-class women with little or no personal or professional experiences with the Puerto Rican community:

> Denying her prejudices, the teacher also denies genuine differences among her students. . . . There is, of course, something to be said for the egalitarian belief that all people are basically similar; but teachers who deny authentic cultural differences among their pupils are practicing a subtle form of tyranny. . . . That is how the majority culture imposes its standards upon a minority, a cruel sort of assimilation forced onto children in the name of equality. (Margolis, 1968, p. 7)

In some cases, the situation has changed very little in the intervening three decades. A recent ethnographic study by Ellen Bigler (1997) in a classroom with a sizable proportion of Puerto Rican students in a small upstate New York town documented that almost all the teachers, most of whom were White, were uncomfortable acknowledging cultural, racial, and ethnic differences among their students; they insisted that they wanted to treat all their students "the same."

Schools also promote assimilation by mythologizing what Bigler calls "ethnic success stories" (1997, p. 9). The model for these Horatio Alger–type success stories is the struggling European immigrant who makes good by learning English and adapting to the cultural mainstream. The teachers and other residents of the town who perpetuated these stories were unaware of how Puerto Rican migrants differed from earlier European immigrants, due to their experiences with colonization, racism, and a different economic situation. One middle-school teacher remarked: "Why are these kids doing this? Why are they not speaking English when they can? Why aren't they trying to fit into the mainstream? . . . They're no different than earlier waves. They worked, they learned the language, and that was your key to success" (p. 9).

One of the earliest and most exhaustively documented ethnographies concerning Puerto Rican children was carried out in 1965 in an East Harlem school (Bucchioni, 1982). Published years later, the study chronicled one case after another in which pressures toward assimilation took place in classrooms every day. In this particular study, the teacher recounted "the ethnic success story" when the children began to question why they lived in tiny, cramped apartments and shared a bathroom with other families, rather than in the kinds of spacious houses in middle-class neighborhoods that they were learning about in school. Juan, one of the children, mused aloud that only very rich people could live in those houses, to which his teacher Miss Dwight responded, "Not exactly rich, Juan. But they do work hard, and every day" (p. 210). When Juan answered that his father *also* worked hard, even on Sundays, Miss Dwight replied:

> It is difficult, sometimes, to earn enough money to do everything we want. It's important for you to remember that your work in school will some day help you to get a better job, earn more money, and live in a good home. . . . But let us remember that while we work toward something better, we must accept what we have now and try to appreciate the good things we have. (p. 210)

In the young-adult novel *Nilda*, Nicholasa Mohr articulates a cruder version of this myth through her character Miss Langhorn, who precedes the daily Pledge of Allegiance with "more or less the same speech": "Brave people they were, our forefathers, going into the unknown where man had never ventured. They were not going to permit the Indians to stop them. This nation was developed from a wild primitive forest into a civilized nation" (1986, p. 52).

The pressure to assimilate is also evident when schools identify the Spanish language as a problem. The first large-scale study of Puerto Rican children in the New York City schools, *The Puerto Rican Study* (Morrison, 1958), attempted to define and propose positive solutions to the problem of academic failure. It also identified the continuation of spoken Spanish in the home as "the chief deterrent" to Puerto Ricans' lack of academic progress. Several years later, the ASPIRA study roundly criticized this position and found the same message of "Spanish as a problem" still evident in many schools:

> In their eagerness to erase Spanish from the child's mind and substitute English, the schools are placing Puerto Rican children in an extremely ambiguous role. They are saying, "Forget where you came from, remember only where you are and where you are going." That is hardly the kind of message that inspires happy adjustments. (Margolis, 1968, p. 9)

Not only has the Spanish language been prohibited in the schools, but Puerto Rican students' accents and dialects have been disparaged as well. In Nicholasa Mohr's *Nilda*, she describes in comic detail how Miss Reilly, the Spanish teacher in the all-female school attended by Nilda, speaks with a thick American accent while insisting that Castilian Spanish is the "real Spanish." She continues, ". . . and I am determined, girls, that that is what we shall learn and speak in my class; nothing but the best!" (1986, p. 214). Castilian Spanish raises issues of power and privilege because the general public, as well as many non-Latino Spanish teachers, consider it to be the variety of Spanish of the highest prestige. Nilda's experience has been shared by many Puerto Ricans and other Latinos, who end up either failing Spanish or dropping it.

Over the years, both fiction and research have chronicled the practice of Anglicizing students' names. In *The Losers*, Margolis documents a typical example: "José González, a kindergartner, has given up trying to tell his teacher his name is not Joe. It makes her angry" (1968, p. 3). Thirty years later, Ellen Bigler found a remarkably similar situation in her ethnography of an upstate New York school. There, a teacher Anglicized Javier to Xavier, saying that "it would be better in the long run for him to have a more American-sounding name" (1997, p. 13). The same scenario forms the basis for the story in Alma Flor Ada's novel for young children, *My Name Is María Isabel* (1993). María Isabel Salazar López, a new third-grader, is given the name "Mary" by her teacher to distinguish her from the other two Marías in the classroom. María Isabel has a hard time remembering her new name and she is repeatedly scolded by her teacher for not responding when called on. María Isabel loves her name because it includes the names of both her grandmothers. When the teacher assigns her students a composition entitled "My Greatest Wish," Maria Isabel tells the teacher in her essay why her name is so important to her and why her greatest wish is to be called by her real name. In this case, there is a happy ending: the teacher, basically a sensitive and caring person, calls her María Isabel the very next day. Unfortunately, in real life, it is not always this way.

Puerto Rican resistance to assimilation has been visible in the educational literature, as well as in fiction. Educational literature has rationalized assimilation on many grounds: the very creation of the common school was based on the need to homogenize millions of European immigrants into U.S. mainstream culture (Appleton, 1983; Katz, 1975). The schools' reaction to the cultural and linguistic differences of Puerto Ricans and other students of color have been even more negative, and for many years they resulted, for example, in prohibitions on using Spanish in the schools (Crawford, 1992). Recent research on cultural and linguistic identity has challenged the long-standing conventional wisdom that in order to get ahead one must sacrifice one's identity. In the case of Spanish, for instance, Ana Celia Zentella's study (1997) of language practices among Puerto Rican children growing up in a low-income community in New York City found that the most academically successful students in the study were also the most fluent bilinguals. They also happened to be in bilingual rather than monolingual classes. The reluctance to drop Spanish has been found in reports as long ago as the ASPIRA study, *The Losers* (Margolis, 1968). A more recent study cited by Kenneth Meier and Joseph Stewart (1991) found that Puerto Rican parents, more than any other Latino parents, wanted their children to retain their Spanish while they also wanted their children to become fluent in English. Resisting the push for assimilation, Puerto Rican students and their communities have always attempted to claim and maintain their identities, even within the school setting. In the Puerto Rican community, there has been an insistence that one can be *both* Puerto Rican *and* a good student, *both* English- *and* Spanish-speaking; in a word, that one can be bilingual and bicultural.

Linguistic and cultural maintenance have implications for academic success. For instance, a study by Jean Phinney (1993) of high school and college students of diverse racial and ethnic minority backgrounds found a significant correlation between ethnic identity and positive self-esteem. This link has important implications for student achievement. For example, in case studies of Puerto Rican and Vietnamese adolescents in a Boston bilingual program, Virginia Vogel Zanger (1987) found that the students' sense of stigmatization had a negative impact on their academic development. Another convincing counter-argument to the perceived need to assimilate is found in research on Cambodian refugee children by the Metropolitan Indochinese Children and Adolescent Service. In this study, researchers found that the more the children assimilated into U.S. mainstream culture, the worse was their emotional adjustment (*New Voices*, 1988). Another study of Southeast Asian students found that higher grade point averages correlated with *maintaining*, rather than wiping out, traditional values, ethnic pride, and close social and cultural ties with members of the same ethnic group (Rumbaut & Ima, 1987).

In research with academically successful students of diverse backgrounds, I also found that there was a marked desire on the part of most to maintain their cultural and linguistic identification (Nieto, 1996). Further, in another study of high-achieving, college-bound Latino students in a comprehensive Boston high school, Zanger found similarly that these students voiced a tremendous resistance to assimilation. Referring to the pressure to assimilate that she felt from her teachers, one young woman stated, "They want to *monoculture* [you]" (1993, p. 172). These Latino students also demonstrated great pride in their cultural background and articulated a desire to be accepted for who they were. In the words of one student, "You don't need to change your culture to be American" (p. 175).

Cultural Deficit/Cultural Acceptance

In the search for explanations for the dismal educational failure of Puerto Rican students, a number of theories concerning cultural acceptance and "cultural deficit" have been used over the years. Numerous commissions, panels, and councils, as well as many individual researchers, who have studied the plight of Puerto Rican students in U.S. schools have used labels ranging from "problem" to "culturally deprived" to the more recent "at risk" to characterize these students (Nieto, 1995). Such labels are at the very core of the deficit theories that began to define Puerto Rican students almost from the time they first entered U.S. schools. For example, a 1935 report by the New York City Chamber of Commerce described Puerto Rican students in general as "slow learners" (Sánchez Korrol, 1994). The previously cited *Puerto Rican Study* (Morrison, 1958) likewise indicated that teachers and schools largely viewed Puerto Rican students' home language and culture as shortcomings and barriers to their education. Another early report stated that "some observers are of the opinion that the Puerto Rican, as well as members of the other Spanish-speaking groups, is less inclined to seek out educational advantages and follow them up by regular attendance than individuals of some of the other cultural groups" (Chenault, 1938/1970, p. 145). In another example, a teacher made the following comment about her Puerto Rican students: "The only way to teach them is to repeat things twenty-five times unless for some reason it means something to them" (Sexton, 1965, p. 58). Much of the early research literature similarly characterized Puerto Rican students as impulsive, undisciplined, and troublesome, all traits thought to be inherited from their families and which made them incapable of profiting from their education (Nieto, 1995).

That idea of cultural deficit has translated into lower teacher expectations for many Puerto Rican students. For instance, Virginia Vogel Zanger's (1993) research among high-achieving Latino students found that their perceptions of teachers' failure to push them was experienced emotionally as abandonment. Similar findings have been expressed over and over in the research literature (Darder & Upshur, 1993; Hidalgo, 1992; Margolis, 1968; National Commission, 1984). Fiction literature repeats this theme. *A Perfect Silence* (Ambert, 1995), for example, describes low expectations in depressing detail:

Teachers never expected the children, who were mostly Puerto Rican and Black, with a smattering of Irish and Italians too poor to have fled the ghetto, to occupy the ivy-scented halls of distant universities or mark history with distinguished feats. Teachers felt grateful beyond their expectations when girls turned twelve without "getting themselves pregnant," and boys managed to elude reform school. (p. 113)

Clearly, teachers, schools, and society in general have assumed that the problem of Puerto Rican students' failure lies with the students themselves, be it in their culture, family, genes, or lack of English skills. Although such problems as poverty, racism, poor language skills, neglect, abuse, and crime cannot be dismissed as contributing to the academic failure that some Puerto Rican youngsters face, deficit explanations have rarely considered how schools and society have been complicitous in causing these failures. Instead, deficit explanations have often considered students and their families solely responsible for failure. These theories have influenced the framing of the problems, as well as proposed solutions to them.

The paradigm of cultural deficiency was nowhere more clearly and destructively articulated than in *La Vida,* an extensive anthropological investigation of one hundred Puerto Rican families living in poverty in New York City and San Juan, Puerto Rico (Lewis, 1965). *La Vida* personified "the culture of poverty" and its negative ramifications for future generations through an in-depth study of the Ríos family, whom author Oscar Lewis described as "closer to the expression of an unbridled id than any other people I have studied" (p. xxvi). A particularly insidious description of his subjects reads:

> The people in this book, like most of the other Puerto Rican slum dwellers I have studied, show a great zest for life, especially for sex, and a need for excitement, new experiences and adventures. . . . They value acting out more than thinking out, self-expression more than self-constraint, pleasure more than productivity, spending more than saving, personal loyalty more than impersonal justice. (Lewis, 1965, p. xxvi)

Characterizations such as these left a mark on how U.S. society in general, and schools and teachers in particular, were to view the Puerto Rican community for decades.

The schools' perceptions of Puerto Rican students have often echoed those of Lewis. For example, Eugene Bucchioni's ethnography of a school in Spanish Harlem documented the conversation of two teachers in the hall: " 'The Puerto Ricans seem to learn absolutely nothing, either here or at home.' 'Yes,' said Miss Dwight, 'all they seem to care about is sleeping, eating, playing, and having parties'" (1982, p. 202). In Alba Ambert's novel *A Perfect Silence,* the narrator describes teachers' attitudes about their Puerto Rican students that speaks volumes about their teachers' lack of cultural knowledge:

> They expressed shock that little girls would have their ear lobes pierced, a savage tribal custom that, they thought, had to be some sort of child abuse. They criticized when children were absent from school to care for younger siblings if a mother had to run errands, or if they had to translate for a sick relative in the

hospital. They accused children of cheating when they copied from each other's homework. (Ambert, 1995, p. 113)

The assumption that what needs changing are the students is still prevalent in many schools and is revealed in much of the research on Puerto Rican education. In their study of four public schools with large percentages of Latino children, Antonia Darder and Carol Upshur (1993) found that most teachers in the schools mentioned the problem of poor achievement as residing in the children's lack of conceptual understanding in English, lack of motivation, and lack of retention, while only occasionally mentioning the inadequate curriculum, the negative views of staff towards bilingual education, or their lack of cross-cultural understanding. Puerto Rican children in the four schools had quite different ideas about improving their schooling. When asked what they would like school to be like, they mentioned, among other things, the need to feel safe, to have newer and more interesting books and computers, and to have humorous and friendly teachers who would not yell at them (Darder & Upshur, 1993).

In *The Losers,* Margolis documents the following scene demonstrating how teachers assume Puerto Rican students' culture to be a barrier to their academic achievement: "An honor student asked her counselor for a chance to look at college catalogues. 'Is that Italian or Spanish?' asked the counselor, looking at the name on the girl's card. 'Spanish? Now this is just my opinion, but I think you'd be happier as a secretary'" (1968, p. 3). Another scene, striking in its similarity, was recounted several years later during the public hearings held by the U.S. Commission for Civil Rights in preparation for their report on Puerto Ricans in the United States. There, a high school student from Pennsylvania told the commission of her repeated attempts to gain admission to an academic course. Her counselor, she said, warned her that "I should not aim too high because I would probably be disappointed at the end result" (1976, p. 108).

For many years, another common practice in schools was to place students back at least a grade when they arrived from Puerto Rico, a practice based on the dubious assumption that this would help them learn English and catch up academically. The effect of retaining students was found to be "particularly acute" by the U.S. Commission on Civil Rights, and it was described by one witness from Massachusetts as a leading cause for the high dropout rate:

They came from Puerto Rico, they're in the 10th, 11th, or senior year of high school. . . . They came to Boston and they placed them in the 6th and 7th grades. You're wondering why they dropped out. . . . Here's a kid trying to learn and he automatically gets an inferiority complex and quits. (1976, p. 101)

This experience is echoed in the novel *When I Was Puerto Rican,* when the author tells the story of Negi, unceremoniously put back a grade despite her excellent academic record simply because she does not speak English. Negi, however, fights back, convincing the principal that she is eighth-grade material: "I have A's in school Puerto Rico. I lern good. I no seven gray girl" (Santiago, 1993, p. 226). Fortunately, he changes his mind and places her in an eighth-grade class (albeit 8-23, the class for the lowest achieving students and those labeled as learning disabled). By the following year, Negi is placed in one of the top ninth-grade classes, and from there she goes on to a top-rated public high school and then to Harvard.

Needless to say, this story is pure fiction for all but a tiny minority of Puerto Rican students, most of whom have neither the wherewithal nor the resources to make the demands that Negi was able to make.

Although U.S. public schools have been the setting of most stories of Puerto Ricans, a small number have focused on Catholic and independent schools (Rivera, 1982; Vega, 1996). The cultural rejection faced by Puerto Ricans in these settings has been of a different kind than that faced in public schools. In *Family Installments,* Edward Rivera (1982) tells the story of Santos Malánguez and his family, who move to New York City from Puerto Rico and enroll Santos in second grade at Saint Misericordia Academy (affectionately dubbed Saint Miseria's) for Boys and Girls in East Harlem. Catholic school differed from public schools in many ways — notably in the strict rules, the heavy doses of homework, the high expectations of all students, and the corporal punishment — but Puerto Ricans were still generally assumed to be of inferior genetic stock. These seemingly contradictory attitudes were well described in Rivera's story: "There was something both cold-hearted and generous about our nuns that gave at least some of us reason to be grateful our parents had signed us up at Saint Miseria's" (p. 74). Specifically, there is the humorous scene in which Sister Felicia, without consulting with Santos's parents, decides that he and a number of other children are charity cases. Since they are preparing for their First Communion, she marches off with them to *La Marqueta,* the Puerto Rican market in Spanish Harlem, to buy their outfits for the big day. Rivera describes the patronizing attitude of the nuns: "First they hit you and make certain embarrassing hints about your family habits and your man-eating ancestors, and then they treat you to a free purchase of clothes" (p. 78).

Deficit explanations for students' academic failure were accepted fairly consistently and uncritically until the late 1960s and 1970s, when Puerto Rican educators and researchers themselves were more visible in the research studies, commissions, and panels studying the education of Puerto Rican youths (Nieto, 1995). In short, the research literature until quite recently tended to highlight what Puerto Rican youngsters *did not have, did not know,* and *could not do,* and, as a result, neglected also to consider what students *already had, knew,* and *could do.*

The development of cultural awareness represents a step away from the view that students' native languages and cultures hinder their learning. For instance, in research that was part of the report of the Latino Commission of the New York City Board of Education, Clara Rodríguez (1991) found substantial differences between two high schools with high dropout rates and two with low dropout rates. At the schools with low dropout rates, she found that cultural sensitivity was either present or neutral, that is, there was a feeling among the students that their culture would not work against them, and that they would be treated fairly in spite of their culture. Rodríguez notes that "in the absence of cultural sensitivity, an acceptable surrogate seemed to be neutrality toward cultural differences combined with good teaching" (1991, pp. 45–46).

Teachers and schools step closer to cultural acceptance when they acknowledge the Spanish language and the Puerto Rican culture as important resources and talents. For instance, Lourdes Díaz Soto, in research with parents of both low- and high-achieving Puerto Rican children, discovered that the parents of the high-achieving children preferred a native language environment at home to a far greater extent than did the families of lower-achieving children (1993). Similarly, the Massachusetts Advocacy Center found that bilingual programs can actually act as a "buffer" to prevent some students from dropping out of high school (Massachusetts Advocacy Center, 1990). In the short story "School Smells," El Cortes lovingly recalls Miss Powell, her favorite teacher, who used the students' language and culture in positive ways:

> In second grade when we spoke Spanish, we didn't get yelled at — SPEAK ENGLISH. NO SPANISH. YOU'RE IN AMERICA NOW — like it was a sin. . . . Miss Powell had us teach her and the kids who didn't know Spanish some words and we wrote invitations to the mothers to visit. They came and told stories about how it was when they were kids in Puerto Rico and we told it in English for the kids who didn't know Spanish. (1998)

In recent research among Puerto Rican families, Carmen Mercado and Luis Moll (1997) demonstrate an even closer step to cultural acceptance. Using a "funds of knowledge" perspective based on the assumption that all families have cultural resources that can be used in the service of their children's learning, the researchers asked their graduate students, all bilingual teachers in New York City, to investigate the knowledge and practices that their students' families possessed. As a result of the research, the teachers, some of whom felt that they already knew their students quite well, were surprised at the wealth of sociocultural knowledge and practices in the families, resources of which even the families themselves are not always aware. These included entrepreneurial skills, knowledge of health and medicine, and musical talent.

Jo-Anne Wilson Keenan, Jerri Willett, and Judith Solsken, a classroom teacher and two university faculty members who engaged in collaborative research in the teacher's second-grade classroom for two years, described a similar finding. Their research (1993) focused on schools' need to change in order to accommodate and serve the children in them, in contrast to the conventional wisdom that students and their families need to do all the changing. Through a series of inspiring anecdotes, the authors documented how the families of the students changed the culture of the classroom. There was, for instance, the story of Blanca Pérez's father, a cartoonist and martial artist, who visited the classroom. The authors concluded: "Jimmy Pérez does not typically spend his days in an elementary school classroom. Yet this gentle and immensely talented man is capable of teaching many things" (p. 59). In addition, the authors explained how Jo-Anne, the teacher, attempted to learn Spanish, and how her attempts were appreciated by the parents: "As I risk speaking in another language, others feel free to take the same risk. As our struggle to appreciate each other's languages becomes public, language differences are no longer a barrier but common ground for generating conversations about language and cultural differences and similarities" (p. 63). When teachers and schools accept and, even better, when they affirm the language and culture of their Puerto Rican students, they also send students the message that their identity is not a barrier to their education. In the numerous examples above, we have seen that when teachers perceive only deficits in their students' backgrounds, the students' learning is not promoted. Conversely, when teachers see their students' individual and cultural talents, students are encouraged to continue their education.

Marginalization/Belonging

Marginalization has been a common theme in much of the research and fiction literature concerning Puerto Ricans in U.S. schools for many years, and it is no more poignantly expressed than in this segment of the poem "Broken English Dream" by Pedro Pietri:

> To the united states we came
> To learn how to misspell our name
> To lose the definition of pride
> To have misfortune on our side . . .
> To be trained to turn on television sets
> To dream about jobs you will never get
> To fill out welfare applications
> To graduate from school without an education . . . (1977, p. 22)

Puerto Rican youths have often felt that they simply did not belong in U.S. schools, and this feeling of alienation was well described by Piri Thomas in his 1967 novel, *Down These Mean Streets:* "School stunk. I hated school and all its teachers. I hated the crispy look of the teachers and the draggy-long hours they took out of my life from nine to three" (p. 64). In fact, for Thomas, sneaking out of school was like "escaping from some kind of prison" (p. 64). Research literature reflects these ideas. For example, ASPIRA conducted a survey in several schools to determine the adjustment of newly arrived students and found a good deal of alienation among Puerto Rican students:

> The conclusion of the survey, in short, was that despite the genuine good-will and effort of hundreds of teachers, many Puerto Rican children were being left out, were not participating in classroom activities, were not learning. Quietly and unobtrusively, they were "sitting out" months and years of their allotted school time. (Margolis, 1968, p. 125)

Almost two decades later, the National Commission on Secondary Education for Hispanics reached a similar conclusion:

> The fundamental finding of the National Commission on Secondary Education for Hispanics is that a shocking proportion of this generation of Hispanic young people is being wasted. Wasted because their education needs are neither understood nor met, their high aspirations unrecognized, their promising potential stunted. (1984, n.p.)

Marginalization often begins when Spanish-speaking students enter schools and find that their only means of communication is neither understood nor accepted. In the 1965 study, Eugene Bucchioni describes the role of the Spanish language for Puerto Rican students: "Its use symbolizes the cultural understanding and unity of Puerto Rican pupils, especially when confronted by an outsider who . . . represents the imposed authority and control of a superordinate group" (1982, p. 234). Using the Spanish language among themselves represents one of the few instances in which Puerto Rican students can create a sense of belonging. Marisol, one of the students I interviewed for a previous study, talked of her need to speak her native language in school even though she was fluent in English. She described a problem she had with a former teacher who had prohibited her from speaking Spanish in class: "I thought it was like an insult to us, you know? Just telling us not to talk Spanish, 'cause [we] were Puerto Ricans and, you know, we're free to talk whatever we want. . . . I could never stay quiet and talk only English, 'cause, you know, words slip in Spanish" (Nieto, 1996, p. 157).

For Puerto Rican students, speaking Spanish generally represents nothing more than solidarity and belonging, but it is often interpreted as a lack of respect.

In *Silent Dancing*, Judith Ortiz Cofer recounts her experience with a teacher who struck her on the head when she thought she was being disrespected. Actually, Judith did not understand English. This was to be a painful but quickly learned lesson: "I instinctively understood then that language is the only weapon a child has against the absolute power of adults," she concluded (1990, p. 62).

Alba Ambert also powerfully describes the alienating experience of school when her protagonist Blanca is placed in a class for the mentally retarded because she cannot speak English:

> During that year in a class for the mentally retarded, Blanca drew pumpkins in October, colored pine trees in December, and cut out white bunnies in April. She also picked up some English. When Blanca was able to communicate in English, school authorities no longer considered her retarded and placed her in a classroom for children without the deficiency of not knowing the English language. (Ambert, 1995, p. 79)

Marginalization, however, is not simply related to the lack of English-language skills. Many students have expressed feeling marginalized because their culture, their social class, their traditions, and the values of their families are different from the culture found in mainstream schools. Virginia Vogel Zanger's (1993) study of high-achieving, college-bound Latino students in a Boston high school exemplifies this marginalization. Even the words that the students in her study employed to describe their perceived status within the school were striking examples of alienation: these included terms such as "not joined in" and "out to the edge," and prepositions such as "below," "under," "low," and "down." Further, Johanna Vega, in recounting her experiences of going from the South Bronx to becoming a scholarship student at Groton, a posh independent school in Massachusetts, writes of the terrible "psychic wounding" that she underwent for four years (1996).

When my colleague Manuel Frau-Ramos and I questioned young people in an exploratory study of dropouts in Holyoke, Massachusetts, we heard one student explain, "I was an outsider." When we asked Pedro, one of the students who was still in school, if the alienation he felt was due to his level of English proficiency, he said, "No, it is not the English . . . that's not the problem. . . . I don't know how to explain it, I don't know" (Frau-Ramos & Nieto, 1993, p. 160). Another student, José, explained that he "felt alone" at school, adding, *"Tu sabes, no son los míos"* ["You know, they are not my people"]. When we asked Pedro if he had any recommendations for teachers and schools to help solve the dropout problem among Puerto Rican students, he said, *"Hacer algo para que los boricuas no se sientan aparte"* ["Do something so that the Puerto Rican students would not feel separate"] (p. 161). That feeling of separateness is another word for marginalization.

Contrasting that feeling of separateness documented by Manuel Frau-Ramos and me is an immensely successful program for Latino students studied by Jeannette Abi-Nader (1993), which suggests that a sense of belonging can counter the cultural isolation that Puerto Rican students feel. One of the keys to the program's success was the teacher who directed the program by incorporating motivational strategies that built on the students' culture and their need for family-like affection and caring. In other words, the teacher created a world in the classroom in which the students felt they "belonged." The students in turn described him as "a father, brother, and friend to us."

CONCLUSION: CARE AS THE MISSING INGREDIENT IN THE EDUCATION OF PUERTO RICANS

I began this article by stating that the general public knows very little of the history of Puerto Ricans in U.S. schools, and this is indeed true, although a great deal has been written on the subject. For instance, the ASPIRA report on the education of Puerto Ricans, written thirty years ago (Margolis, 1968), pointed out that an impressive bibliography of 450 articles and studies focusing on the issue of Puerto Rican children in U.S. schools had already been compiled by 1968. More research might point to better solutions, but it may also only point to more solutions that are rejected, ignored, or overlooked. The major problem, however, seems to be not the lack of data, but rather the lack of will and resources to remedy the educational problems that Puerto Rican students face.

This is the point at which the use of fiction with fact can make a difference in the education of Puerto Rican students. The examples of fiction used in this article, almost all written by Puerto Ricans, represent the lived experiences of Puerto Rican students themselves. They are not clinical or sterile descriptions of faceless students in nameless schools; instead, these works of fiction serve to make the educational research come alive and make it harder to ignore or reject the facts described in educational research literature. Using fact and fiction together can be a powerful way of making the problems that Puerto Rican students face more visible to those who can make schools caring and affirming places, that is, the teachers, administrators, and policymakers.

The message that emerges from this study of fact and fiction is one that underlies all the others: *the care or rejection experienced by Puerto Rican students in U.S. schools can have a significant impact on their academic success or failure.* Research by Victor Battistich, Daniel Solomon, Dong-il Kim, Meredith Watson, and Eric Schaps (1995) indicates important connections among caring communities, the identification that students make with learning, and their academic achievement. These researchers examined relationships between students' sense of school community, poverty level, and their attitudes, motives, beliefs, and behavior in twenty-four elementary schools. Because Puerto Rican students live in greater poverty than those from most other groups, one of the major conclusions of the study has especially important implications for them: "Although the deleterious effects of poverty are well known, the most encouraging aspect of the present findings is the suggestive evidence that some of its negative effects can be mitigated if the school is successful in creating a caring community for its members" (1995, p. 649).

According to the National Commission on Secondary Education for Hispanics (NCSEH), "Hispanic students almost unanimously identified 'someone caring' as the most important factor in academic success" (1984, p. 13). Students attribute academic success to this quality of "caring" in their schools. As one young woman in the NCSEH report explained, "I got pregnant and I thought I'd never be anybody but I came here and the teachers and the kids gave me love and I know I'll make it" (p. 29). In an ethnographic study of Puerto Rican adolescents who had dropped out of school and were now attending an alternative school (Saravia-Shore & Martinez, 1992), the researchers documented numerous similar examples of conflicting values of home, peers, and schools. Students were happy with the alternative schools because they felt that teachers there cared about them, whereas criticisms of their previous schools included teachers' lack of respect, care, and concern: "They would say things like, 'Do you want to be like the other Puerto Rican women who never got an education? Do you want to be like the rest of your family and never go to school?'" (p. 242).

Research and fiction often associate caring with Puerto Rican or other Latino teachers (Hornberger, 1990; Latino Commission, 1992; Mercado & Moll, 1997; Montero-Sieburth & Pérez, 1987; National Commission on Secondary Education for Hispanics, 1984). It is important, however, to mention that, in both fact and fiction, caring is not exclusive to Latino teachers. Non-Latino teachers, who represent the vast majority of teachers of Puerto Rican youngsters, also show care and concern for their Puerto Rican students (Abi-Nader, 1993; Ada, 1993; Ambert, 1995; Cofer, 1990; Mercado & Moll, 1997; Mohr, 1979; Santiago, 1993; Vega, 1996). Many commissions and reports have called for hiring more Latino teachers (Latino Commission, 1992; Meier & Stewart, 1991; Morrison, 1958; National Commission on Secondary Education for Hispanics, 1984; U.S. Commission on Civil Rights, 1976), a recommendation that makes eminent good sense. However, the literature is clear that while being Puerto Rican can be an advantage to teaching Puerto Rican youths, non-Puerto Rican teachers can also be extremely effective with them.

Latino youngsters explicitly mention "love" as the factor that can make or break their experiences in school. Voices recorded in the research literature from the 1950s until today suggest that the importance of caring and the price of rejection have always been significant, but no one chose to listen to them. This was true in research as early as *The Puerto Rican Study* (Morrison, 1958), when children and their parents were interviewed: "There were instances where, from the child's viewpoint, the present teacher, compared with previous teachers in Puerto Rico, seemed uninteresting, lacking in affection or in kindness" (p. 133).

Almost thirty years later, research on the strategies used by a bilingual teacher to relate to her Latino students also identified *cariño,* or endearment — especially as evident in hugging and other displays of affection — as a key element in the success of Latino youngsters. She identified herself as a "teacher, friend, mother, social worker, translator, counselor, advocate, prosecutor, group therapist, hygienist, and monitor" (Montero-Sieburth & Pérez, 1987, p. 183). A few years later, Nancy Hornberger's (1990) study of successful learning contexts draws a similar conclusion: in the Puerto Rican classroom that she studied, she found that the teacher openly displayed tenderness and affection, as well as a "motherly concern" for her students, expressions typical of the Puerto Rican community. Nitza Hidalgo explains the importance of this kind of interpersonal support: "Because of the propensity to place value on interpersonal relationships within the culture, the relationship between the teacher and Puerto Rican student becomes vital to the educational achievement of the student. Students have to feel liked by the teacher; they gain strength from their relationship to their teachers (1992, p. 36). A young woman in Zanger's research described the experiences of Latino students and the cost of rejection: "They just feel left out, they feel like if no one loves them, no one cares, so why should they care?" (1993, p. 176). Still more recently, one of the Latina teachers in the research by Carmen Mercado and Luis Moll described how she viewed her profession: "It is not an 8:40 to 3:30 P.M. job but an extension of my life, as if it were part of my family" (1997, p. 31).

Fiction echoes the importance of caring that many have overlooked or ignored in the research literature. Alba Ambert's *A Perfect Silence* beautifully expresses this sentiment when she describes a number of exceptions to Blanca's generally uncaring and unfeeling teachers. Mrs. Wasserman, the teacher who first recognized the abuse Blanca had experienced, kept a collection of children's books in the classroom that Blanca transformed into "dreams of possible worlds" (1995, p. 114). Her second-grade teacher, Mrs. Kalfus, once kissed Blanca's swollen cheek when she had a toothache: "Years later, Blanca, who forgot much of her disrupted childhood, remembered that kiss" (p. 115).

Similarly, Mr. Barone, the guidance counselor in *When I Was Puerto Rican* (Santiago, 1993), sees promise in Negi and pushes her to go to an academic high school. The ensuing scene, in which Negi tries out for Performing Arts High School by reciting a monologue she memorized in a thick Puerto Rican accent using English that she does not understand, is a hilarious and touching example of care and concern in the fiction about Puerto Rican students in U.S. schools. By going out of his way to help Negi apply to a school with rigorous standards, Mr. Barone exemplifies how teachers and other educators can make caring and concern a vital part of the school community.

But what exactly does it mean to create such a caring community? The literature and research that we have seen describe "caring" as providing affection and support for students, building strong interpersonal relationships with them and their families, learning about and from them, respecting and affirming their language and culture and building on it, and having high expectations of them. Caring implies that schools' policies and practices also need to change because simply changing the nature of their relationships with teachers and schools will not by itself change the opportunities the children are given. Hence, changing both personal relationships among teachers and Puerto Rican students and the institutional conditions in their schools is essential if these students are to become successful learners.

These changes are, however, not enough. Care is demonstrated as well through the provision of adequate resources to ensure that learning can take place. The poignant plea of a student who addressed the National Commission on Secondary Education for Hispanics (1984) is even more explicit: "We work hard and we try and our teachers care, but we are not treated fairly. Our school is poor. If this commission cares, please make something happen" (n.p.). The commission's final word, that Latinos "are our children, a generation too precious to waste" (p. 45), is worth repeating if we are serious and truly care about creating the possibility of success for more Puerto Rican students.

NOTE

1. Puerto Ricans are not "immigrants" in the traditional sense of the word, since they arrive in the United States as citizens. They are also not strictly "migrants," since they have not simply moved from one geographic part of a culturally connected society to another. Some scholars refer to Puerto Ricans living in the United States as *[im]migrants,* highlighting the hybrid nature of their status. See, for example, Marquez (1995).

REFERENCES

Abi-Nader, J. (1993). Meeting the needs of multicultural classrooms: Family values and the motivation of minority students. In M. J. O'Hair & S. J. Odell (Eds.), *Diversity and teaching: Teacher education yearbook 1* (pp. 212–236). Ft. Worth, TX: Harcourt Brace Jovanovich.

Ada, A. F. (1993). *My name is María Isabel.* New York: Atheneum.

Ambert, A. (1995). *A perfect silence.* Houston, TX: Arte Público Press.

Appleton, N. (1983). *Cultural pluralism in education: Theoretical foundations.* New York: Longman.

Arias, S. (1996). Inside the worlds of Latino traveling cultures: Martín Espada's poetry of rebellion. *Bilingual Review/Revista Bilingüe, 21,* 231–240.

ASPIRA of New York. (1968). *Hemos trabajado bien: Proceedings of the ASPIRA National Conference of Puerto Ricans, Mexican-Americans, and Educators.* New York: Author.

ASPIRA Institute for Policy Research. (1993). *Facing the facts: The state of Hispanic education, 1993.* Washington, DC: ASPIRA.

Association of Assistant Superintendents (1948). *A program of education for Puerto Ricans in New York City.* Brooklyn: New York City Board of Education.

Battistich, V., Solomon, D., Kim, D., Watson, M., & Schaps, E. (1995). Schools as communities, poverty levels of student populations, and students' attitudes, motives, and performance: A multilevel analysis. *American Educational Research Journal, 32,* 627–658.

Bigler, E. (1997). Dangerous discourses: Language politics and classroom practices in Upstate New York. *Centro, 9*(9), 8–25.

Blanchard, J. S., & Casanova, U. (1996). *Modern fiction about schoolteaching: An anthology.* Needham Heights, MA: Allyn & Bacon.

Bonilla, F., & Campos, R. (1981). A wealth of poor: Puerto Ricans in the new economic order. *Daedalus, 110,* 133–176.

Bourdieu, P. (1977). *Outline of theory and practice.* Cambridge, Eng.: Cambridge University Press.

Bucchioni, E. (1982). The daily round of life in the school. In F. Cordasco & E. Bucchioni (Eds.), *The Puerto Rican community and its children on the mainland* (3rd rev. ed., pp. 201–238). Metuchen, NJ: Scarecrow Press.

Cafferty, P. S. J., & Rivera-Martínez, C. (1981). *The politics of language: The dilemma of bilingual education for Puerto Ricans.* Boulder, CO: Westview Press.

Carrasquillo, A. L. (1991). *Hispanic children and youth in the United States: A resource guide.* New York: Garland.

Centro. (1997). Special issue on the education of Puerto Ricans, *9*(9).

Chenault, L. R. (1970). *The Puerto Rican migrant in New York City.* New York: Columbia University Press. (Original work published 1938)

Cofer, J. O. (1990). *Silent dancing: A partial remembrance of a Puerto Rican childhood.* Houston, TX: Arte Público Press.

Cortes, E. (1998). School smells. Unpublished manuscript.

Crawford, J. (1992). *Hold your tongue: Bilingualism and the politics of "English only."* Reading, MA: Addison-Wesley.

Darder, A., & Upshur, C. (1993). What do Latino children need to succeed in school? A study of four Boston public schools. In R. Rivera and S. Nieto (Eds.), *The education of Latino students in Massachusetts: Research and policy implications* (pp. 127–146). Boston: Gastón Institute for Latino Public Policy and Development.

De Jesús, J. L. (Ed.) (1997). *Growing up Puerto Rican.* New York: William Morrow.

Díaz Alfaro, A. (1962). Santa Cló va a La Cuchilla. In W. E. Colford (Ed. and Trans.), *Classic tales from Spanish America* (pp. 206–210). New York: Barrons Educational Series.

Díaz Alfaro, A. (1978). Peyo Mercé enseña inglés. In K. Wagenheim (Ed.), *Cuentos: An anthology of short stories from Puerto Rico* (pp. 98–107). New York : Schocken Books.

Díaz Soto, L. (1993). Native language for school success. *Bilingual Research Journal, 17* (1/2), 83–97.

Dyson, A. H., & Genishi, C. (1994). Introduction. In A. H. Dyson & C. Genishi (Eds.), *The need for story: Cultural diversity in classroom and community* (pp. 1–7). Urbana, IL: National Council of Teachers of English.

Espada, M. (1993). The year I was diagnosed with a sacrilegious heart. In M. Espada (Ed.), *City of coughing and dead radiators* (pp. 72–74). New York: W. W. Norton.

Espada, M. (1996). Public School 190, Brooklyn, 1963. In M. Espada, Ed.), *Imagine the angels of bread* (p. 25). New York: W. W. Norton.

Estevez, S. M. (1991). Here. In F. Turner (Ed.), *Puerto Rican writers at home in the U.S.A.: An anthology* (pp. 186–187). Seattle, WA: Open Hand.

Figueroa, J. A. (1991). Boricua. In F. Turner (Ed.), *Puerto Rican writers at home in the U.S.A.: An anthology* (pp. 221–224). Seattle, WA: Open Hand.

Fitzpatrick, J. P. (1987a). *Puerto Rican Americans: The meaning of migration to the mainland.* Englewood Cliffs, NJ: Prentice-Hall. (Original work published 1971)

Fitzpatrick, J. P. (1987b). *One church, many cultures: Challenge of diversity.* Kansas City, MO: Sheed & Ward.

Frau-Ramos, M., & Nieto, S. (1993). 'I was an outsider': Dropping out among Puerto Rican youths in Holyoke, Massachusetts. In R. Rivera and S. Nieto (Eds.), *The education of Latino students in Massachusetts: Research and policy implications* (pp. 147–169). Boston: Gastón Institute for Latino Public Policy and Development.

Gibson, M. A., & Ogbu, J. U. (Eds.). (1991). *Minority status and schooling: A comparative study of immigrant and involuntary minorities.* New York: Garland.

Hernández, C. D. (1997). *Puerto Rican voices in English: Interviews with writers.* Westport, CT: Praeger.

Hidalgo, N. M. (1992). *"i saw puerto rico once": A review of the literature on Puerto Rican families and school achievement in the United States* (Report No. 12). Boston: Center on Families, Communities, Schools and Children's Learning.

History Task Force, Centro de Estudios Puertorriqueños. (1979). *Labor migration under capitalism: The Puerto Rican experience.* New York: Monthly Review Press.

Hornberger, N. (1990). Creating successful learning contexts for biliteracy. *Teachers College Record, 92,* 212–229.

Institute for Puerto Rican Policy. (1992). The distribution of Puerto Ricans and other selected Latinos in the U.S.: 1990. *Datanote on the Puerto Rican community, 11.* New York: Author.

Institute for Puerto Rican Policy. (1996). The status of Puerto Rican children in the U.S. *IPR Datanote, 18.*

Katz, M. B. (1975). *Class, bureaucracy, and the schools: The illusion of educational change in America.* New York: Praeger.

Keenan, J. W., Willett, J., & Solsken, J. (1993). Constructing an urban village: School/home collaboration in a multicultural classroom. *Language Arts, 70,* 56–66.

Latino Commission on Educational Reform. (1992). *Toward a vision for the education of Latino students: Community voices, student voice* (Interim report of the Latino Commission on Educational Reform). Brooklyn: New York City Board of Education.

Lewis, O. (1965). *La vida: A Puerto Rican family in the culture of poverty, San Juan and New York.* New York: Vintage.

Margolis, R. J. (1968). *The losers: A report on Puerto Ricans and the public schools.* New York: ASPIRA.

Marquez, R. (1995). Sojourners, settlers, castaways, and creators: A recollection of Puerto Rico past and Puerto Ricans present. *Massachusetts Review, 36*(1), 94–118.

Massachusetts Advocacy Center. (1990). *Locked in/locked out: Tracking and placement practices in Boston public schools.* Boston: Author.

Meier, K. J., & Stewart, J., Jr. (1991). *The politics of Hispanic education: Un paso pa'lante y dos pa'tras.* Albany: State University of New York Press.

Meléndez, E. (1991). *Los que se van, los que regresan: Puerto Rican migration to and from the United States, 1982–1988. New York: Commonwealth of Puerto Rico, Department of Puerto Rican Community Affairs.*

Mercado, C. I., & Moll, L. (1997). The study of funds of knowledge: Collaborative research in Latino homes. *Centro, 9*(9), 26–42.

Mohr, N. (1979). *Felita.* New York: Dial Press.

Mohr, N. (1986). *Nilda* (2nd ed). Houston, TX: Arte Público Press.

Montero-Sieburth, M., & Pérez, M. (1987). *Echar pa'lante,* moving onward: The dilemmas and strategies of a bilingual teacher. *Anthropology and Education Quarterly, 18,* 180–189.

Morrison, J. C. (1958). *The Puerto Rican study, 1953–1957.* Brooklyn: New York City Board of Education.

National Center for Educational Statistics. (1995). *The educational progress of Hispanic students.* Washington, DC: United States Department of Education, Office of Educational Research and Improvement.

National Commission on Secondary Education for Hispanics. (1984). *"Make something happen": Hispanics and urban school reform.* Washington, DC: Hispanic Policy Development Project.

National Council of La Raza. (1993). *Moving from the margins: Puerto Rican young men and family poverty.* Washington, DC: Author.

National Puerto Rican Task Force. (1982). *Toward a language policy for Puerto Ricans in the U.S.: An agenda for a community in movement.* New York: City University of New York Research Foundation.

Negrón de Montilla, A. (1971). *Americanization in Puerto Rico and the public school system, 1900–1930.* Río Piedras, PR: Editorial Edil.

New voices: Immigrant students in U.S. public schools. (1988). Boston: National Coalition of Advocates for Students.

Nieto, S. (1995). A history of the education of Puerto Rican students in U.S. mainland schools: "Losers," "outsiders," or "leaders"? In J. A. Banks & C. A. M. Banks (Eds.), *Handbook of research on multicultural education* (pp. 388–411). New York: Macmillan.

Nieto, S. (1996). *Affirming diversity: The sociopolitical context of multicultural education* (2nd ed.). White Plains, NY: Longman.

Nieto, S. (Ed.). (in press). *Puerto Rican students in U.S. schools.* Mahwah, NJ: Lawrence Erlbaum Associates.

Ogbu, J. U. (1987). Variability in minority school performance: A problem in search of an explanation. *Anthropology and Education Quarterly, 18,* 312–334.

Phinney, J. S. (1993). A three-stage model of ethnic identity development in adolescence. In M. E. Bernal & G. P. Knight (Eds.), *Ethnic identity: Formation and transmission among Hispanics and other minorities* (pp. 61–79). Albany: State University of New York Press.

Pietri, P. (1977). Broken English dream. In P. Pietri (Ed.), *Obituario puertorriqueño* (pp. 18–43). San Juan, PR: Instituto de Cultura Puertorriqueña.

Quality Education for Minorities Project. (1990). *Education that works: An action plan for the education of minorities.* Cambridge, MA: Author.

Rivera, E. (1982). *Family installments: Memories of growing up Hispanic.* New York: William Morrow.

Rodríguez, A., Jr. (1992). *The boy without a flag: Tales of the South Bronx.* Minneapolis, MN: Milkweed Editions.

Rodríguez, C. (1991). *Puerto Ricans: Born in the U.S.A.* Boulder, CO: Westview Press.

Rumbaut, R. G., & Ima, K. (1987). *The adaptation of Southeast Asian refugee youth: A comparative study* (Final Report.) San Diego, CA.: Office of Refugee Resettlement.

Sánchez, L. R. (1987). The flying bus. In A. Rodríguez de Laguna (Ed.), *Images and identities: The Puerto Rican in two world contexts* (pp. 17–25). New Brunswick, NJ: Transaction Books.

Sánchez Korrol, V. E. (1994). *From colonia to community: The history of Puerto Ricans in New York City.* Berkeley: University of California Press. (Original work published 1983)

Santiago, E. (1993). *When I was Puerto Rican.* Reading, MA: Addison-Wesley.

Saravia-Shore, M., & Martinez, H. (1992). An ethnographic study of home/school role conflicts of second generation Puerto Rican adolescents. In M. Saravia-Shore & S. F. Arvizu (Eds.), *Cross-cultural literacy: Ethnographies of communication in multiethnic classrooms* (pp. 227–251). New York: Garland.

Sexton, P. C. (1965). *Spanish Harlem.* New York: Harper & Row.

Spring, J. (1997). *Deculturalization and the struggle for equality: A brief history of the education of dominated cultures in the United States.* New York: McGraw-Hill.

Thomas, P. (1997). *Down these mean streets.* New York: Vintage Books.

U.S. Commission on Civil Rights. (1976). *Puerto Ricans in the continental United States: An uncertain future.* Washington, DC: Author.

Vega, J. (1996). From the South Bronx to Groton. In L. M. Carlson (Ed.), *Barrio streets, carnival dreams: Three generations of Latino artistry* (pp. 83–99). New York: Henry Holt.

Walsh, C. E. (1991). *Pedagogy and the struggle for voice: Issues of language, power, and schooling for Puerto Ricans.* New York: Bergin & Garvey.

Zanger, V. V. (1987). *The social context of second language learning; An examination of barriers to integration in five case studies.* Unpublished doctoral dissertation, Boston University.

Zanger, V. V. (1993). Academic costs of social marginalization: An analysis of the perceptions of Latino students at a Boston high school. In R. Rivera and S. Nieto (Eds.), *The education of Latino students in Massachusetts: Research and policy implications* (pp. 170–190). Boston: Gastón Institute for Latino Public Policy and Development.

Zentella, A. C. (1997). *Growing up bilingual: Puerto Rican children in New York.* Oxford, Eng.: Basil Blackwell.

Youth Speak Out

These brief pieces have appeared previously in *New Youth Connections* and *Foster Care Youth United*, two magazines published by the New York-based organization Youth Communication, and in *Peaceworks*, a publication of the American Friends Service Committee, which is located in Cambridge, Massachusetts. By including these young people's perspectives, we hope to provide a more complete account of the challenges facing youth as they grow up in a violence-filled world.

A Dream Guy, a Nightmare Experience

ANONYMOUS

I'm lying on the floor, in a dark room, unable to move. Then I see him, standing over me, laughing. I try to move, but I'm paralyzed. He gets closer and closer and right when he's about to kiss me, I wake up, screaming. After that I'm too upset to go back to sleep, so I sit up and cry all night.

My nightmares aren't as vivid as before, but they're there. Just when I think it's finally over, the memories come back to haunt me. I keep thinking that maybe I could have done something to prevent it. Maybe if I hadn't been such a sucker for a happy ending. Maybe if I had thought ahead. Maybe . . . Maybe . . .

I Was 13

We didn't go to the same schools but he lived in the neighborhood, and was always hanging around. I used to see him in the morning, before school. He was about 16, kind of tall, with short, dark hair, and the most beautiful grey eyes I've ever seen. He'd say "hi" when he saw me and even though I didn't really know him, I started to like him. Occasionally, I'd stop and talk to him — nothing too personal. We talked about the movies we'd seen, music and stuff like that. I began to look forward to our little talks, and was disappointed when I didn't see him around the school. I was 13 at the time.

One day, after school, he was waiting for me. I was with my friend Charlene. We were talking outside the school and I pretended that I didn't see him. He kept trying to get my attention, but I pretended not to notice. I don't know why — maybe I didn't want Charlene to know I had a crush on him.

He Carried My Books

When I said goodbye to my friend, I walked slowly to the end of my block. "Hello," he called out to me. I turned, slowly, and smiled at him. "Hi, Eric," I said shyly. "Where are you going?" he asked. I told him I was going to the train station. He asked if he could walk me there, and, being the lovesick puppy that I was, I said, "Sure."

He carried my books and we talked all the way to the train station. When we arrived, he asked if he could have my phone number. I was so excited that I gave it to him without any hesitation.

He called that night. We talked for at least two hours. He told me that he lived with his aunt and his brother. He said he'd been wanting to talk to me for a while, that he liked me and wanted to get together sometime. That phone call made me the happiest person in the world. After I got off the phone with him, I called some of my friends and told them. Being liked by a guy made me feel important.

A Small Kiss

The next time I saw him, he walked me to the train station again, and we talked some more. Then he kissed me goodbye. It was just a small kiss, but it made me feel wonderful. I was convinced he was a great guy.

He called me again that night. We talked for a while, and just as I hoped, he "popped the question."

"Yes! I'll go out with you!" I half screamed. For the rest of the night, I was practically floating in mid-air, I was so happy. "Somebody loves me," I thought.

We were "boyfriend and girlfriend" for a grand total of five days. He called me and we saw each other throughout the week. Then after school on Friday, he was waiting for me in our usual meeting place, on the corner by the schoolyard. He said he wanted to take me someplace special that afternoon. I was thrilled. I thought maybe we would go to the movies or something. "But first," he said, "we have to stop by my house for a minute."

It was a pretty big apartment, but it looked like it hadn't been cleaned in years. He brought me into the kitchen and got a glass of water. Then we went into the living room and sat on a sofa with the stuffing coming out of it. He told me to leave my books on the floor. Then he turned on the television and shut off all the lights and said, "We'll go in a minute. I'm tired. I want to rest for a second. Sit down with me." So, I did.

This Doesn't Feel Right

We sat in the darkness and watched TV for a while. I asked him where his aunt and his brother were. He stared at me with those eyes and replied, "out" plain and simple. He was acting kind of weird, but I didn't want to say anything, because I thought he might get mad or something. He took my hand and started to kiss me. At first it was kind of nice. But then he started getting too aggressive, putting his hands in places they didn't belong.

I remember thinking to myself, "This doesn't feel right. What's he doing?" I started getting scared and told him to stop. But he didn't. I tried pushing him away, but I was too small. He was a lot bigger than me. He forced himself on top of me and pulled my pants down. No matter how much I struggled, he wouldn't let up. He held me down by the shoulders and raped me. I was crying and screaming, "No! Stop! Please stop!" But he wouldn't. Exhausted from crying and trying to get him off me, I stared into the blackness, tears sliding off of my cheeks.

It all happened very fast. As soon as I could, I fixed my pants, tried to wipe the tears away, and got the hell out of there. I walked the eight blocks to the train station and waited for the train in a daze. I kept telling myself that it didn't really happen, that it couldn't really happen — not to me.

The Trip Home

On the train this guy pressed up against me and tried to talk to me. I just turned around and walked through to the other car. Then I caught this girl looking at me, like she knew. I gave her a really ugly stare and she looked away, embarrassed.

When I finally made it home, the first thing I did was jump in the shower. I washed my entire body, but I just couldn't seem to feel clean. I dried myself off and put on some clean clothes. Then I looked at the clothes I was wearing at the time it happened. I noticed blood on my pants and shirt. I had a small cut on my chest and my legs were scraped up — I guess from struggling. I took the clothes, balled them up and put them in a plastic bag. I carried them to the incinerator and threw them out. Then I went into my room, lay down on my bed and cried. Thank God my mother wasn't home.

I didn't want to think about it, but I couldn't help it. I'll never forget the look he gave me afterwards. It was like he was proud of what he had done. Then something else popped into my mind: What if I get pregnant? I closed my eyes and tried to block the thought. (Thankfully, I wasn't, but I was really scared for a while.)

Playing Sick Seemed the Only Escape

I saw him once more afterwards when I went to the store with Charlene one day after school. I was getting some juice and, while I was walking up to the counter to pay for it, he and two of his friends came into the store. My heart raced and I dropped the bottle. It smashed on the floor, but I didn't hear it. Charlene grabbed me and pulled me out of there. She knew something was wrong, but she kept her mouth shut. I didn't leave my house for a few weeks after that. I was afraid I might see him again. I was staying home more and more. Playing sick seemed to be the only escape.

One day, my best friend was over at my house, and I decided to tell her. I just couldn't keep this horrible secret inside of me any longer. "Kate, I need to tell you something," I said. I took a deep breath and sat down. "Kate," I tried to go slowly, but the words raced out of my mouth. "I was going out with this guy and I thought he was really nice but he wasn't. Kate, you're my best friend and I want you to help me. I was raped."

Kate just stared at me, in shock. Then the expression on her face changed to one of disbelief. "Well," she said, "How do you know if he really raped you?" I couldn't believe it. My best friend, doubting me, almost accusing me of lying. Things between us were never the same from then on. I can't say that I hate her, because I don't. I just don't talk to her — about anything.

Telling Someone — Getting Help

Eventually, I told some friends and a few adults. I am happy to say that all of them really helped me. They always listened when I needed to talk, anytime. Even if it was 3:30 in the morning, and I had trouble sleeping, I could call them up and they'd help me get through it. Now I really regret not speaking to anyone sooner.

It happened almost three years ago, but I still think about it as though it were yesterday. I have to stop asking myself if it was my fault, if I "asked for it." It wasn't my fault, I didn't ask for it. I had no control over the situation. The only thing I did wrong was wait so long to get help.

Rape is a horrible thing, I know that now. You have to be aware. You have to be careful. It can happen to anyone. And yes, you can be raped by someone you know. One minute you're watching TV, riding along in a car, getting help with homework. The next minute you're fighting to get away, gasping for breath, staring off into the blackness. If it does happen to you, remember, it's not your fault. Tell someone fast. Get help. It'll really make a difference later on.

Harvard Educational Review   Vol. 65 No. 2 Summer 1995, 258–261

When Things Get Hectic

JUAN AZIZE

Last summer I was headed to the bodega around my block to get a hero when I saw my boy Deps step to some kid I'd never seen before. Being the nosy friend that I am, I went over to see what the problem was. "Yo Deps, what's going on man?" I said.

"This b—ch ass n—ga got an eye problem." Deps answered.

"Whatever man," said the kid. I noticed he got scared when I came over, knowing there were two of us now and this wasn't his neighborhood.

But fighting over a bad look wasn't exactly the move. "Yo, forget about that sh—t man," I said. "He don't want no beef."

"So why he trying to scope if he don't want none?" said Deps.

"I wasn't scoping at you man," answered the kid.

"Yo man, squash this bullsh—t already so I could get my sandwich," I told Deps. "My stomach is growling."

"Aaiight man, just don't be trying to act like you represent around here." Deps told the kid. They both gave each other the hand along with dirty looks and slow moves.

After the fake pound, I went inside the store to get my salami and cheese and Deps tagged along. About 15 minutes later there we were chilling in front of my house. It was really hot and we were trying to throw girls in front of the hydrant and munching down that delicious hero when, all of a sudden, a blue Corolla with tinted windows rolled up in front of us.

Drive-By Time

I knew right away this was the kid Deps was riffing to. I remember the hero losing its delicious taste. The girls were still teasing us, trying to get us to chase them, when Deps tapped my leg cause he knew what time it was. Before I could yell "duck," I saw the back window roll down enough for a gun to fit through. I grabbed Deps like a reflex and we both hit the floor at the same time two bullets hit the side of my house.

The car was long gone before me and Deps had a chance to feel burnt. All of a sudden the girls didn't want to play anymore and it wasn't that sunny. I never knew things could get to that point so fast. A dirty look setting bullets off didn't make any sense. What if they had caught us from behind? What if they had shot one of the girls? What if my mother had been standing there?

It really made me think deep. I wanted to kill those guys, I was so steamed. I was confused. I was flipping. I rode around with my friends looking for that blue Corolla for that whole week. Deps got a gun that same day hoping they were going to come back, which didn't happen.

Blasted over Something Stupid

This kind of thing goes on all the time: "Yo, you heard who got shot?" "I ran into some beef today." "Yo man, bring a shank just in case." I am sick and tired of hearing it. Violence surrounds us everywhere: school, work, even in front of your crib. That's the number one reason for deaths among teens in New York City. Kids nowadays are ready to kill each other over the dumbest things.

I know a lot of kids who are scared one day they are just going to get blasted for something stupid like that. There are so many other kids out there with guns, knives, and short tempers.

I live in Corona, Queens and when the weekends come I feel like I am in a battle zone. Before trooping it out to a jam I always have to make sure I am rolling with my little crew in case things get hectic. Most of the jams I've been to end up with a shootout or a rumble.

And this stuff doesn't just go down where I live. In school all the gossip in the hallway is about things happening in the streets. I know lots of people also carry weapons to school but the beef is outside most of the time.

There was this time, last year in my old school, when my boy Duzer was supposed to shoot a fair one with another kid in school, so my little crew got together to keep it a fair fight.

Shanked over a Girl

When eighth period came we all hit the handball courts. While Duzer hopped around to get ready, I saw kids pulling shanks and hammers out of their Jansports. I knew this wasn't going to be no fair fight, fake gangstas put that out of style trying to find the easy way out.

It started to get hectic: people were getting shanked up and hammered down. I was playing it safe and taking them sucker punches every chance I had. It was an

---

GLOSSARY

Beef — a problem or dispute.

Shank — a boxcutter or any sharp object other than a knife. Also the act of cutting someone.

Crib — house, apartment . . . the place where you live.

Bodega — corner grocery store.

Scope — look or stare at somebody.

Squash — the process of solving a problem without violence.

Represent — the act of standing up for something, a neighborhood, a certain place, for yourself, etc.

Pound — the hand change of two people when greeting.

Fair one — a fair fight, one on one.

Catch their back — back somebody up, being there for them.

Blasted — get shot up bad.

Trooping out to a jam — to go to a party.

Rolling deep — hanging out with a lot of people.

Finesse — the style or way people carry themselves.

Riff — to argue or dispute over something.

Get hectic — get wild, violent, or out-of-hand.

5-0s — the cops, police.

Hype — the excitement or the high feeling inside during a wild event.

Front — back down or hide from the truth, pretend to be something you're not.

Strapped — armed with a gun.

Glock — a powerful type of gun.

Nine — a 9-mm handgun.

Jansport — a brand-name of backpacks.

---

even rumble, not counting the fact that they had more weapons. (I admit I was scared to death about them hammers.)

When the 5-0's rolled up we were gone with the wind. A couple of kids couldn't run so they stayed on the floor covering their sore spots. My boy Eliester had a thin slice on his neck and had to get 11 stitches. The rest of us had shanked jackets and arms, nothing serious (thank God).

We ran to the hospital about 10 blocks away. About a half hour later, after the hype went down, I stopped Duzer in the waiting room and asked him what the beef was all about. I almost started to laugh when I heard the answer: "He was trying to tell me who I wasn't allowed to talk to," answered Duzer. "Yo, I was up on that b—ch way before that n—ga even dreamed about it."

A girl! I didn't understand. One of our boys gets sliced in the neck with 11 stitches and three other kids were left on the floor bleeding like cold. This sh–t was pathetic, killing each other over a girl who's probably ready to move on to the next man. Eight tracks make better sense than that.

Your Boys Are Your Boys

I am not gonna front though. If my boys get into more senseless beef, I am still going to catch their backs and I won't stop to ask them what the problem is. Adrenalin flows faster than questions, and my boys have always been there for me when I needed them without asking questions and trying to talk it out.

I guess it must be written in that invisible book that knows everything, the one where ladies go first and actions speak louder than words. The funny thing is, I follow that book. If my boys have beef again I'll be there asking mute questions that come out too late. It's like a reflex. It shouldn't be, but it is. Your boys are your boys. I do stop to think about it, but only after it's too late, after the damage is already done.

Harvard Educational Review   Vol. 65 No. 2 Summer 1995, 262–264

This article was taken from *Things Get Hectic: Teens Write About the Violence that Surrounds Them* by Youth Communication, copyright 1998 by Youth Communication/New York Center, Inc. Reprinted by permission of the publisher, Simon & Schuster, Inc., New York. All rights reserved. For more information, write to Youth Communication, 224 W. 29th St. 2nd Fl., New York, NY 10001.

Keep It Real!

JUAN AZIZE

What do I think causes all of the violence? Finding the answer to that is the hardest part. When you start to break things down, you realize it goes way beyond respect. Maybe it's the stress we are all under or that we are trying to prove something.

Alcohol and drugs is another big part of it. They kill so many brain cells you start to forget you live in New York City.

I look at it this way: If I am going to have beef I am going to have beef worth having. Not over a girl, a bad skeem, a stupid remark, or any other petty things. I am going to make sure before I go all out that it's for a good cause. What is a good cause for me? Somebody trying to kill me, rob me, or anybody that touches my mother. A little violence won't hurt in those cases.

Besides that, you got to keep it real. The last thing in your mind should be a Glock or a black jack, that's all unnecessary violence. Nobody has to go that far unless it is life-threatening. There are many kids out there who only get down when they are strapped or rolling deep. Remember, the real people won't need that when they blow your finesse. And you aren't always going to have your gun or your crew to hide behind. Slow down or it's going to happen when you are not looking.

You should only try to get respect if disrespected, without letting things get out of hand. I'm not saying it's easy, trust me. Nowadays there is no respect, everyone wants to be bigger than the next guy. But real people keep it real. They are the ones that go all with their hands and not with their guns, knowing it will give them both a chance to come back. Like that rap song goes: "Leave your nines at home and bring your skills to the battle."

We should all try to calm down. Violence won't solve anything in the long run. We have to grow up and realize there are other ways to solve a problem — talking it out and mediating and sometimes even ignoring it. We've got to try to remember a lot of kids are getting killed over little problems that could have been easily solved.

In the past three years, I've lost three of my boys to senseless violence. Every time it happens, the rest of us get together and make a mural on the wall. For me, the hardest part is figuring out what colors and design to use. How are we supposed to concentrate without the whole crew? Even the invisible book doesn't have an answer to that one. It doesn't have a special chapter on consequences.

We all have one life to live, let's keep it real. 'Cause I am tired of trying to figure out colors and designs for my friends' memorials. Wouldn't you be?

This goes out to SEN and to all those who have fallen to violence. Rest In Peace. Nobody is ever promised tomorrow. Increase the peace.

Harvard Educational Review   Vol. 65 No. 2 Summer 1995, 265

This article was taken from *Things Get Hectic: Teens Write About the Violence that Surrounds Them* by Youth Communication, copyright 1998 by Youth Communication/New York Center, Inc. Reprinted by permission of the publisher, Simon & Schuster, Inc., New York. All rights reserved. For more information, write to Youth Communication, 224 W. 29th St. 2nd Fl., New York, NY 10001.

L.A. RIOTS: *Some Serious Déjà Vu*

PART I.   MOHAMAD BAZZI

One image of the Los Angeles riots I will never forget is a picture I saw in the newspaper of a stripped, burned-out car sitting in the haze in the middle of a desolate avenue. As soon as I saw it, I felt numb. I heard the gunshots, sensed the terror. For a moment I was back on the streets of my native Beirut.

The scene reminded me of Al-Shayah, the inner-city Lebanese neighborhood where I grew up. My block was on a busy street, by Beirut standards. It was also a favorite target of trigger-happy Christian militia snipers. When gunfire erupted — sometimes killing innocent bystanders — everyone would run for cover, leaving the whole street deserted, dead.

I lived a few hundred feet from the "green line," an invisible but lethal marker which divided the Christian East and Muslim West sectors of Beirut for more than 15 years.

Back in 1943, when the Lebanese people achieved independence from France, the departing French set up a plan to insure that Muslims and Christians got equal representation in the new government. But in practice, their plan proved unfair, divisive, and contributed to the outbreak of civil war.

Christians, who made up a slight majority at the time, got most of the money and power. A few Muslims managed to prosper and join the ranks of the middle and upper classes, but many more were shut out by the green lines.

In 1975, after decades of unemployment, crumbling schools, rampant poverty and a general atmosphere of frustration and hopelessness, the poor finally took to the streets. They've been there ever since.

See any similarities? I do.

In a way, Los Angeles has its own green line. It is a border that separates South-Central and other neighborhoods like it from mainstream America, and it's patrolled by L.A.P.D. snipers.

The people of South-Central Los Angeles and the people of West Beirut have a great deal in common. Both are minorities, both are alienated. The Muslims of West Beirut, like L.A.'s Blacks and Latinos, have long been excluded from the national political and economic life. In both places the inequities were built into the system from the beginning.

Many of those who have been doing the fighting in Lebanon for so long are just like me — young men between the ages of 16 and 25, reared in neighborhoods like Al-Shayah. We have wrestled with the same problems that led our American counterparts to set L.A. ablaze: lack of job opportunities, inadequate schools, and a system that doesn't work for us.

In Beirut, as in L.A., young men have resorted to crime and violence. Gangs thrive in both worlds. In L.A. they have names like "Crips" and "Bloods." In Lebanon they take forms like the Hezbollah — the Shiite Muslim "Party of God." For nearly 20 years, young men have formed the backbone of most of these groups. To this day, the neighborhood militia still offers Lebanese youth their most lucrative job opportunities.

The city of Beirut lies in ruins. Those buildings that haven't been completely bombed out are scarred by bullet holes. Most families have lost loved ones in the fighting.

Is Los Angeles destined to become an American Beirut? Is New York? Atlanta?

Not if the powers that be heed Los Angeles Mayor Tom Bradley's call for "economic empowerment" for young minority men. Not if they work to bring inner-city schools back to life and fully address the other roots of urban poverty and injustice.

Otherwise, I and others who came to this country after experiencing the terrors of Beirut are in for some serious déjà vu.

PART II.   ROHAN A. DEWAR

Now do you get it? Did it finally sink in? Does this stop all your dreamy talk about how "Everything is gonna be alright" and "Don't worry, be happy"? Good. Now it's time to face reality. If nothing else, this whole Rodney King issue — the court case and the riots — should have opened your eyes.

Now tell me that racism in America's judicial system died out after the civil rights movement and I'll laugh right in your face. News flash! It's always been here. Racism is a fact of life, or rather, a way of life here in the good ol' U.S. of A.

But don't worry.

This whole Rodney King issue will be forgotten. Just like Arthur McDuffie. Just like Philip Pannell.

I bet you don't even know who Arthur McDuffie is. I didn't until a few weeks ago. He was a Black man who, after an eight minute high speed chase, was beaten savagely by police officers in Miami, Florida in December of 1979. (Sound familiar?)

Four officers were put on trial, but the trial was moved from Miami, which had a substantial Black population, to Tampa, which was predominantly White. There were no Black jurors. The officers were all found not guilty of all charges, despite the evidence. After the officers were acquitted rioting broke out — residents of Miami went looting, vandalizing, and murdering.

Does all this ring a bell? It should. It's almost exactly what happened with the Rodney King case. So, as you see, the King case is really nothing new. It's just that the media coverage and our memories don't last long on issues like police brutality against minorities and our failed criminal justice system.

Same Old Story

It's the same cycle over and over again. First, something like the Rodney King case comes up, then we start feeling angry, and occasionally we'll even go on a march. Then the issue dies down, we put it in the back of our minds. And later we just forget about it. Then, when another cop brutalizes a minority, we get all surprised and start trying on tennis shoes for the next march.

Can you still remember Philip Pannell? He was that 16-year-old kid who was shot in the back by Police Officer Gary Spath in Teaneck, New Jersey on April 10, 1990. Here's where our justice system failed us that time: first the case was tried in Bergen County, New Jersey, which was only 4% Black.

Second, every single member of the jury in the Teaneck case was White.

Third, and probably most unfair of all, members of the jury in the Teaneck case had ties to the police department. One of the jurors was the son of a retired police officer and another had two brothers-in-law who were cops! And these people are supposed to be impartial?

Get the picture? Police brutality against minorities has been going on for a long time and I can guarantee you it will continue until we stop forgetting about it and all the other injustices in our criminal justice system.

The judicial system has always been unfair to minorities. The problems didn't clear up after the McDuffie case or the Teaneck case. So why did people stop protesting?

Why did it take the Rodney King video to get people up off their butts? You want to bring about change? Then get on out there and challenge the injustices we're all facing. And don't stop until you can breathe easy in front of the cops, the judge, and the jury.

Harvard Educational Review   Vol. 65 No. 2 Summer 1995, 266–268

"Educate Us"

LIVEDA C. CLEMENTS

From the back of my closet I retrieved my black dress and shoes. This attire was one I rarely liked to wear. While I was driving to the church, various scenes jogged through my mind, reminding me of my friend. Yet, at that very instant, images of what I might see today collided with each and every scene. My train of thought was immediately broken when I saw the mass of people crowding the church doorway. We had gathered to give our respects to another young, black male who had become an innocent victim of circumstance and in so doing had become an inspiration of many of my future goals.

When I was inside the church, a feeling of amazement overwhelmed me. Each pew, chair, and standing area was occupied by a soul filled with sorrow. I would have thought it was a Sunday service if I had not heard the shrilling cries of loss.

As I walked closer to the casket my legs became like rubber bands, tears descending from my eyes like water dripping from a leaking faucet. Then, there rested before me my friend. I had only known him for a brief period, yet long enough to realize that he and I shared many similar goals and expectations.

He had a great dream of becoming a criminal justice lawyer. He had chosen this career because the belligerent attitudes that have been generated by today's black youth worried him tremendously. He wanted to be a contributor to the rehabilitation of those who commit immoral acts. He wanted to assist in restoring the remains of the inner city. He had many goals which he intended to accomplish. Many of his immediate concerns centered around preparing for a successful future. He anticipated finishing high school with complimentary grades and subsequently attending a university.

He expressed himself by transforming endless thought into elaborate pictures. Many of his pictures were abstract drawings, which told a story that only he could understand. Other pictures exemplified the suffering of black people. He was a perfect example of who I am today, not only because our dreams, goals, and choices of expression joined hand in hand, but also because we faced an everyday obstacle — living in the inner city of Boston. Boston is an environment that shares only a small portion of its success with Black America, and it is a locality where drugs and lawless acts become synonymous with life for many.

Unfortunately all of his great dreams of success, of goals and opportunities, were shattered by one bullet. Now I am here to pursue both his dreams and my goals.

Education, acquiring general knowledge and developing the power of reasoning and judgement, is the solution to the problem of violence. If the student population were better educated their perception of life, motivation, and sense of destination would be generated toward success, as opposed to the existing conditions of: gaining respect by committing unlawful acts, selling drugs in order to make easy money, and maintaining a nonchalant attitude in an effort to survive. Further steps need to be taken in order to thoroughly supply schools with proper materials, effectively keep drugs and weapons out of the schools, productively decrease the student drop-out rate, and continuously offer students with the potential to progress and succeed in better opportunities. Education is and will ultimately be the solution to the existing problem.

Harvard Educational Review   Vol. 65 No. 2 Summer 1995, 269–270

Women Are Under a Rap Attack

YELENA DYNNIKOV

Free expression is great as long as someone's got something to say. Censorship is wrong if it prevents people from voicing their opinions on political and social issues. Discussions of topics like sexual preference, animal rights, and whether or not abortion should be legal are examples of what should not be censored. When you stand up for what you believe in and tell people about it, you're making an important statement. It is your right under the First Amendment of the Constitution to do so. In cases like these, censorship is not acceptable and cannot be tolerated.

But I have to admit there are times when I think censorship just might be a good idea. Like when I hear music that is insulting and degrading to women. Free expression receives a slap in the face when so-called "artists" use their First Amendment rights to demean women and send the message that we're all "stupid tramps."

Rappers or Cave Men?

A good example is "A B–tch Iz a B–tch" by NWA. This rap is just an endless stream of curses and threats of violence against women. And Awesome Dre is anything but awesome in his rap, "Sex Fiend." He seems to think that having sex with any girl he sees is his right: "Don't have to have permission 'cause I'm Awesome Dre." He believes women were created for the sole purpose of satisfying a man. I think he needs to change his name. How about Stone Age Dre, the caveman rapper?

When I hear songs like these, my jaw hardens and I shake with anger. I remember my first reaction to hearing Ice-T rap, "You know you want to do it too . . . you say you don't but I know you do." Fear rose up inside me. Are there really men out there who feel this way? "We both want it. Don't make it tough girl," Ice-T continued.

I pressed the "stop" button on my Walkman to reassure myself that it could be stopped. That I could shut him up. But as silence filled the air, I questioned my action. What did I shut up — Ice-T or my Walkman? When guys on the street start following you and hassling you because they think you're good for only one thing, how do you shut them up? There's no stop button to use on them.

Degrading Stereotypes

So many rap songs follow the same pattern — they create negative stereotypes of women and then use those stereotypes to legitimize treating women like dirt. It's an endless cycle. Women are first degraded and lowered: "Are you that funky, dirty, money-hungry, scandalous stuck-up, hairpiece wearing b–itch? Yup, you probably are!" ["A B–tch Iz a B–tch" by NWA] The girl's personality and credibility is lowered to that of a carrot stick.

These rappers never want to get to know the women they pursue. In fact, they proudly admit that they're only after one thing. "Kickin' conversation, ain't talkin' down nothing. When all that's really on your mind is what? Let's get butt naked and f—k." ["GIRLS, L.G.B.N.A.F." by Ice-T] And if a woman doesn't leap at the chance, she is immediately branded a b–tch. "When you say 'hi,' she don't say 'hi.' Are you the kind that think you're so damn fly? B–tch, eat sh–t and die!" ["A B–tch Iz a B–tch" by NWA]

We're Not Sex Toys

These raps suggest that women are plastic dummies with no brains, no ambitions, no personalities, and no feelings. They are portrayed by the "artists" as purely shallow sex toys. A girl's only function is to please the guy and after that she's discarded.

By now, you may be thinking, "What is she so worked up about? It's only music." It's because I think music is the only form of communication that really reaches a person. It steals the breath. It speaks to the heart. It moves the soul. It speaks even when no words are added and when accompanied by words, music can move boulders. It can also crash boulders if misused.

I hear lots of teens say that just because you hear something in a song does not mean that you'll go out and do it. Although that may be true, one cannot deny that music can affect and influence a person subconsciously.

Let's say a guy is out with a girl and wants to have sex with her but she says "No," but another part of him is hearing Ice-T sing, "You say you don't want it but I know you do." A whole crew of rappers has hammered into his head the idea that you don't have to take what the girl says seriously, that having sex with who you want, when you want, is a guy's right. And anyway, deep down she really wants it, no matter what she says. The line between fantasy and reality may get confused. Some guys might start to think that saying "No" is just another way of saying "Convince me." But it's not. A guy who doesn't listen when a woman says "no" is a rapist.

Let's Boycott

I think some of these songs put women in real danger (in addition to being ignorant and offensive). I wish they could be censored but I doubt that will happen. But there are things that can be done. Look at what happened with Ice-T's song "Cop Killer." Whether or not you agree with the people who were offended by that song, you have to admit that they were effective — they got it taken off the album. If enough people complained against songs that are threatening to women, maybe we could get some of those taken off the air.

Refusing to buy and support those tapes is a way of fighting the stereotype of women they are putting out. If you hear an offensive song on the radio that hurts you personally, act on it. Call up the radio stations that play it and tell them that they have lost a listener because of that particular song. Write to the record company that produced it and tell them why you refuse to buy their records. A campaign like this can work if we make it work!

Harvard Educational Review   Vol. 65 No. 2 Summer 1995, 271–273

What Are They Trying to Prove?

MELISSA LEE GRUENLER

Last year three young men lured Julio Rivera into a deserted schoolyard in Queens. Two of them beat him repeatedly with a hammer and a wrench, and the third finished him off by stabbing him in the back. Then they left him there to die.

The youths who murdered Rivera had two things in common: they were all between the ages of 15 and 25 and they all hated him because he was gay.

A lot of young guys feel threatened by gays and lesbians. They call them names, make jokes about them, and, according to Naomi Lichtenstein of the Gay and Lesbian Anti-Violence project, are responsible for a "vast majority" of attacks like the one against Rivera.

Why would anyone hurt or kill someone just because that person is different? The most basic reason is fear, fear of the unknown. "People think we are a whole different species," said Angel Star, 20, a gay student at Harvey Milk HS in Manhattan. "Because you don't understand someone, you become afraid of him or her."

In the case of young men, the fear is even greater because, deep down, they are not 100% sure of who they are. When they can't accept the possibility that they might be gay themselves, says Lichtenstein, "they go out looking for targets, saying subconsciously, 'That one's the f—got, not me' . . . they literally want to get rid of the other person as a way of getting rid of the feelings in themselves. Of course it won't work; violence solves nothing."

Real Men Don't Have to Prove It

Another reason is the pressure to be a "real man." A lot of young guys believe a man has to have sex with women and fight a lot. Most of these hate crimes start when a guy wants to prove to himself and his buddies that he's a man. So he'll say, "Let's go beat up a junkie or a f—g."

Lichtenstein says older men tend to be more secure. "They don't need to prove anything," she explained. "And they've learned other ways of solving their own problems without hurting someone else."

But it's not just teens who are anti-gay, it's our whole society: parents, teachers, religion, the media — even the law. In movies and on TV young people see images of homosexuals as criminals and child molesters, according to Andy Humm of the Hetrick Martin Institute for Gay and Lesbian Youth. It's practically forbidden to air programs that show two homosexual people together.

The Roman Catholic Church teaches that it's wrong to be gay or lesbian and the military throws people out if they're even suspected of it. In some states (not New York) there are still laws forbidding homosexuals to make love. Until 1973 the nation's psychiatrists considered being gay a mental illness.

1 in 10

There is such a lack of understanding about homosexuals that even their parents often turn against them. Parents tell their kids: " 'I'd rather have a junkie than a gay son,'" says Angel, "[or] 'I'd rather you be a slut than for you to like [other] girls.' . . . They'd rather have their child destroy their life and be miserable, than be gay."

It's no wonder a lot of teens grow up prejudiced against gays. Whether they learned those values at home, in church, in school, or from TV, homosexuality threatens a lot of people's "views on how the world should be," says Lichtenstein. Their belief in the traditional family is so narrow that anything else is wrong. So they go out and beat somebody up.

Experts agree the best way to change that is through education. Most people are not taught that one out of ten people in the United States is gay. "Society takes for granted [that] everyone is straight or that everyone should be," said Angel.

People need to understand that it's normal to be gay, lesbian, or bisexual. "[It] doesn't make someone less of a man or woman," explained Lichtenstein. "A man or woman is not defined by who they love."

Like Racism

There was a time when Blacks were separated to the point where they had to use their own water fountains. Yet they drank the same water White people did. The only thing different about them was the color of their skin. Blacks went through a lot to prove they are equal. Well, gays are fighting for the same thing.

We all know that disliking someone because of color is being prejudiced and it's wrong. When teens think they're better than someone because he or she is gay, when they avoid the person or make rude comments, then they're being bigots just like the Ku Klux Klan. We are all human beings. Before you start to look for a reason to hate, look for a reason to love.

Harvard Educational Review   Vol. 65 No. 2 Summer 1995, 274–275

From Fighta to Writa:
How a Friend Changed My Life

KENYETTA IVY

I came into the system in '92. It was in the summer. I remember the night I went to Light St., my first group home.

I arrived at 1:30 in the morning. When I entered the house I was scared, 'cause I always heard that people died in group homes. When I got inside, the girls were all sitting in the lounge. There were 25 girls in the house.

I stayed there for only a month, because I started hanging with the wrong crowd. I was smoking weed, drinking, and fighting. I was considered the baddest girl in the house. They had to get me out of there, so they moved me to another group home.

This one was called Coney Island Diagnostic. It had four girls living there. But I was kicked out 'cause I broke a girl's jaw. Me and the girl were screaming in the hall after the staff went to bed. The next day the girl told the staff it was my fault. I got in trouble for that, so I hit her. When I left for school the staff said don't come back, so I didn't.

America's Most Wanted

I went to my grandmother's house and stayed there for two weeks. I was getting badder and badder. My friend's mother said I would be on "America's Most Wanted" at age 16. I told her, "Ha, I fooled you, I'm in a group home." I thought everything was a joke.

When I left my grandmother's house, I went to my old group home, Sheltering Arms. My male friends would pay me to get them girls they could have sex with. They called me a female pimp. I was asking myself, "How can I do this to another girl?" But I didn't care.

In October, 1992, I went to court to get placed into another group home. It was a few days after my 17th birthday. They placed me in a 30-day transitional center in Brooklyn.

This was a group home I fell in love with. I loved it so much 'cause all we did was smoke weed and have fun. I had a crew in there called B.M.P. (Blunt Master Possie). We broke every rule in the book.

I eventually had to leave because my 30 days were up.

This time they moved me to a lockdown in Queens. It was a co-ed group home, boys and girls. I went there with the intention of leaving. I was going to leave "By Any Means Necessary," so that's just what I did.

Me and the few friends I made in the three weeks I was there beat up this girl. The girl thought she was all that. My friends grabbed the girl outside the house. We beat her so bad she pressed charges.

When we got to the police station, they said I was going to jail. I was scared but I really didn't care. I stayed at the station for a few hours, then was let go. I went back to the group home. The next day I got moved again.

Eight Group Homes

Moving from place to place was fun at first. By February of '93 I had been in eight group homes, picked up a tag name, and had over 20 fights. (My tag name was Bonnie, as in "Bonnie and Clyde," the bank robbers.)

My last group home was back in the Bronx again. When I got there, I was wondering how long I would stay — a month, a week, a day, or at the rate I was going, an hour.

Staff seemed nice at first. Most of the time I stayed to myself, because the girls didn't come home until night time.

The coolest girl in the house was Kathy. I thought she was cool from the first time I met her because she was so quiet. But when I would start fights with the girls in the house, if they said something wrong to me, Kathy would jump right in.

The staff in the house said that Kathy acted like my mother or something. She would always get me out of trouble. I still fought, but I was starting to slow down. See, every time I got into a fight, Kathy would take me for a walk.

Kathy was the only one who ever (I mean ever since I was born) encouraged me to make something out of myself. She told me fighting was not the move. I looked at her as a mother figure, because she treated me like she really cared and I knew she did.

I always thought that the people I hung out with cared, but I was wrong. Kathy said that if they cared for you, they wouldn't tell you to do bad things, such as smoking and stuff, but the right things. I knew she was right, because when I followed her advice I always had a positive outcome.

Could It Be She Was Changing Me?

Kathy and I were hanging out more and more. After a while, I started calling her my best friend. The staff became jealous, because at one point Kathy had been close to them. She used to tell them her problems, but now she was confiding in me.

Staff started calling me "sneaky" and told the other residents not to trust me. Kathy said, "Bonnie, you're not sneaky, they just don't understand you."

In the system, residents understand other residents 'cause they have almost the same problems. Staff thinks and looks at it another way. So they put us down mentally, emotionally, sometimes physically. Kathy said that I just needed someone to care for me.

She would always tell me it was positive over negative, and that if you respect a person, you will get the same respect back. I became a positive person. I was given a single room. When I first arrived I was on restriction every day, and now I was never on restriction.

It came to the point that when I saw a fight, I would try to break it up. I never knew a person could change someone that much, but Kathy changed me. She gave me a heart I could not get anywhere else. I think that if I hadn't met Kathy, I would still be listening to those people who call themselves my "friends."

Me and Kathy made big plans to go to college and then into the health field. I stayed in my room and wrote poems while she practiced dancing.

We were chosen to see Mayor Dinkins for a special discussion on youth. (Back in the days, the only person I thought I would be chosen to see was the judge.)

A Friendship Lost

Every night before I went to bed, I would thank God for a friend like her. Now I think that maybe that wasn't enough.

One day me and Kathy got into a fight because I called her a b–tch. I was only playing, but she took it the wrong way. We got into a verbal fight. I got mad and said a lot of things that hurt her.

She always told me you can't break up a true friendship, but I now realize that you can after I felt the pain of losing a friend.

I miss Kathy and still love her dearly. After a while I gave up on getting our friendship back, 'cause I kept trying and it wasn't working.

Now I'm still on the right track and still thinking of the advice she gave me. I thank God for the good times as well as the bad. Although we are no longer friends, I just don't know where I would be without her.

I know if God wants it, we will be friends again, and I hope that day is soon.

Harvard Educational Review   Vol. 65, No. 2 Summer 1995, 276–278

Un Colegio Brega con la Muerte

MICHAEL QUINTYNE

Traducción: Personal de NYC

La gente que no conoce el colegio Thomas Jefferson cree que es un infierno. Se imaginan que los estudiantes son unos delincuentes que venden drogas y traen armas. Pero según Eric Alexander, 17, que está en su último año en "Jeff," la escuela es más bien como una familia.

"La mayor parte de los estudiantes se respeta," dijo Eric. "Y la mayor parte de los maestros los tratan como si fueran sus propios hijos."

El 26 de febrero, Eric estaba en el pasillo del segundo piso rumbo a su clase cuando sintió los balazos que dejaron a dos estudiantes muertos. Eric corrió a la oficina del decano. Como muchos de sus compañeros, quedó aterrorizado y confundido.

Según la profesora de historia, Sharon King, en el momento en que sonaron los balazos, la directora, Carol Beck, salió de su oficina y empezó a llevar los estudiantes al auditorio. "Corrió el riesgo de que le pegaran un tiro," dijo King.

"La Sra. Beck se mantuvo valiente en todo momento," acertó Melissa Baltazar, 14. "Es la clase de persona que siempre mira hacia adelante — nunca para atrás . . . No creo que esta escuela pudiera sobrevivir sin ella."

Después del asesinato, Melissa dijo que suspendieron las clases. "Sólo había aulas a donde ir y los maestros te dejaban expresar los sentimientos para que no reprimieras nada."

Solidaridad ante la Tragedia

Los profesores también estaban frustrados y asustados. Sin embargo, Melissa dijo que no lo mostraron. Tenían que mantenerse firmes para apoyar a los estudiantes.

Eric dijo que muchos de los estudiantes en su primer año querían trasladarse a otro colegio de una vez. "Los demás muchachos tratamos de convencerles que no se fueran porque necesitamos su apoyo."

Mientras todos hablaron bien del colegio, la mayoría concedió que las calles que lo rodean están llenas de narcotraficantes y pistoleros, y que eso influye en los estudiantes.

"La escuela está bien. No le pasa nada a la escuela," dijo Kerry Collins, 18, una miembra del equipo de campo y pista. "Sólo que queda en un barrio malo."

King estubo de acuerdo. "Se puede conseguir un revólver en cada esquina de East New York," dijo. "¿Ves una biblioteca en cada esquina?"

Algunos jóvenes traen los problemas al colegio consigo. "Los muchachos vienen de varios proyectos [de vivienda] creyendo que el suyo es mejor que otros," explicó Melissa. "Eso es lo que trae la violencia . . . No es la escuela sino los muchachos que entran."

Kerry dijo que muchas veces la presión de los compañeros contribuye a los problemas. Dijo que a veces un muchacho está dispuesto a dejar pasar una mala situación sin que se ponga violenta. "Pero su amigo va a tratar de calentar las cosas . . . decirle m—cón o lo que sea para que haga algo [estúpido]."

La Situación Queda Clara

Sin embargo, parece que los estudiantes en Jefferson han aprendido mucho de la tragedia.

"Ian [uno de los muchachos que murió] fue popular con mucha gente," dijo Melissa. "Cuando ven morir a uno de sus amigos saben que fácilmente pudo haber sido uno de ellos mismos . . . Ahora, los estudiantes entienden que los revólveres no son juguetes . . . Cambian sus actitudes de una manera positiva."

"Muchos [estudiantes] quedan traumatizados," explicó King. "Creo que todo este lío se les está poniendo más claro ahora . . . No creo que quisieran que algo así jamás sucediera otra vez. Es una manera bien dura de aprender pero lo captaron."

Los estudiantes dicen que los detectores de metal deben de haber sido instalado antes. Después del primer acontecimiento en que un estudiante fue asesinado en el pasillo el pasado noviembre, la junta de educación contrató un equipo de seguridad para visitar la escuela una vez por semana con detectores de metal. Desde el segundo asesinato en febrero, han estado allí todos los días. "Ahora están haciendo todo lo que pueden," dijo Kerry.

Todas las personas que entrevisté estaban de acuerdo en que los detectores de metal y más guardias eran importantes "pero no deben tratarnos como si estuviéramos en la cárcel," dijo Eric.

La Seguridad Es una Curita

King dijo que le molesta ver a los estudiantes registrados, tratados como criminales, y esperando media hora para pasar la inspección por la mañana. "La seguridad equivale a poner una curita al problema," insistió. "Tenemos que empezar a desarrollar el carácter del estudiante." A ella le gustaría ver más programas especiales, alguna clase de "entrenamiento para la madurez" en el currículum, y más profesores negros, hombres que puedan servir de modelos de conducta.

Los estudiantes están de acuerdo con que se requeriría más que guardias y detectores para hacer las escuelas verdaderamente sanas. "Había un montón de policías patrullando el segundo piso donde mataron a los dos muchachos," dijo Melissa. "No importa cuántos policías haya, todo depende de la actitud de los estudiantes. Son ellos los que van a acabar con la violencia que sucede en la escuela."

Harvard Educational Review   Vol. 65 No. 2 Summer 1995, 279–280

"Start with Love and Attention"

TYRONE SUTTON

As a young man growing up in the Roxbury area of Boston, I have lost a handful of close childhood friends to senseless violence. I've seen the stillness on my partner's face as he lay motionless in a wooden box. I've seen the tears on so many faces, enough to last a lifetime. I've heard the sorrow-filled screams of families, young and old, ring in my ear until I could no longer acknowledge them. I've seen the sacred title of mother and father be slipped out of the grasp of grieving parents. I myself have felt my heart stop in the face of death, and wondered would I be next?

All of this grief and anxiety before the age of eighteen has for me built a strong character. I knew that at the tender age of fifteen my fellow peers and I had no business at a funeral trying, unsuccessfully, to come to terms with the death of one of our own. Although this is just one facet of life in Roxbury, it is a very serious issue which needs to be addressed.

As a youngster, I was raised to believe that there is a love and respect shared by everyone throughout the ghetto, but it seems we've replaced those feelings with anger and envy. Where did we go wrong? Or should I say, where did the adults responsible for these children go wrong? I think it is obvious that how you behave and interact with others begins at home. We pick up character traits from our surroundings, and if we're around those who have no respect, love, or morals for themselves, we too develop those tragic flaws.

Therefore, you see, in order to stop the violence in Boston we have to start with the love and attention a child needs from his or her immediate family. The children of Boston need role models other than basketball stars or rappers. They need local teachers, relatives and mentors to help them reach for reality-based goals. When a child can't make his or her dream come to life, they feel hopeless, betrayed and frustrated, and they vent their frustrations through violence and drugs. If Boston had a system of community leaders who would take the youth of their neighborhood under their wing to initiate change, I believe the difference would be evident. All any person needs is love, attention and understanding. It's when these necessities are denied to them, that they feel they have no alternative but physical hostility. It's time for us to stop selling ourselves short on a beautiful community that could be, and start working towards a better environment for all.

Harvard Educational Review   Vol. 65 No. 2 Summer 1995, 281

Section Two

community and popular education

The Algebra Project:
Organizing in the Spirit of Ella

ROBERT PARRIS MOSES
MIEKO KAMII
SUSAN McALLISTER SWAP
JEFF HOWARD

The United States is beginning to address, in a fundamental way, the teaching of mathematics in its middle schools. The National Science Foundation (1989), for instance, has issued a request for proposals to develop materials for middle school mathematics instruction that sets out the technical elements of the problem in great detail. At the heart of math-science education issues, however, is a basic political question: If the current technological revolution demands new standards of mathematics and science literacy, will all citizens be given equal access to the new skills, or will some be left behind, denied participation in the unfolding economic and political era? Those who are concerned about the life chances for historically oppressed people in the United States must not allow math-science education to be addressed as if it were purely a matter of technical instruction.

The Algebra Project, a math-science program in Cambridge, Massachusetts, has organized local communities to help make algebra available to all seventh- and eighth-grade students, regardless of their prior level of skill development or academic achievement. The project's philosophy is that access to algebra will enable students to participate in advanced high school math and science courses, which in turn are a gateway for college entrance. The project offers a new curriculum and a five-step curricular process for sixth graders that provides the following: a smooth transition from the concepts of arithmetic to those of algebra, increasing the likelihood of mastery of seventh- and eighth-grade algebra; a home, community, and school culture involving teachers, parents, community volunteers, and school administrators in activities that support students' academic achievement; and a model of intellectual development that is based on motivation rather than ability.

The belief that ability is the essential ingredient driving intellectual development and is necessary for mastering advanced school mathematics is the basis for the differentiation in mathematics curricula at the eighth-grade level as well as the widespread practice of offering eighth-grade algebra only to students who are "mathematically inclined" or "gifted." The developers of the Algebra Project have

Harvard Educational Review Vol. 59 No. 4 November 1989, 423–443

called upon the traditions of the civil rights movement to assist communities in organizing a challenge to the ability model and its institutional expressions.

TRADITIONS OF THE CIVIL RIGHTS MOVEMENT IN MISSISSIPPI

Through the Public Broadcasting System's (PBS) *Eyes on the Prize* series, the American public has been given an opportunity to revisit the civil rights movement's community mobilization tradition. Masses of people were mobilized to participate in large scale events such as the Birmingham campaign, the March on Washington, and the Selma-to-Montgomery March, which were aimed at achieving equal access for Southern Blacks to public facilities and institutions. The tradition is epitomized by Dr. Martin Luther King, Jr., who lifted the movement by inspiring immense crowds in vast public spaces.

Within the civil rights movement was an older, yet less well known, community organizing tradition. This tradition laid the foundation for Mississippi Freedom Summer (1964), which revolutionized race relations in Mississippi, and for the Voting Rights Act of 1965, which altered politics throughout the South during the last quarter of this century. Its leader was Ella Baker, a community organizer and *fundi* whose wisdom and counsel guided the Black veterans of the first wave of student sit-ins through the founding and establishment of the Student Nonviolent Coordinating Committee (SNCC).[1] She inspired in SNCC field secretaries a spiritual belief in human dignity, a faith in the capacity of Blacks to produce leaders from the ranks of their people, and a perseverance when confronting overwhelming obstacles. Baker symbolizes the tradition in the civil rights movement of quiet places and the organizers who liked to work in them.[2] Just as her spirit, consciousness, and teaching infused the Mississippi Movement, they permeated the Algebra Project from its inception.

Three aspects of the Mississippi organizing tradition underlie the Algebra Project: the centrality of families to the work of organizing; the empowerment of grassroots people and their recruitment for leadership; and the principle of "casting down your bucket where you are," or organizing in the context in which one lives and works, and working the issues found in that context.[3]

Families and Organizing

Of central importance to the Mississippi Movement was the capacity of Black families to adopt, nurture, love, and protect civil rights organizers as if they were family members. This practice, known in the literature as "informal absorption," allowed SNCC and CORE (Congress of Racial Equality) field secretaries and organizers to move from place to place in Mississippi with scarcely a dollar in their pockets, knowing full well that a family welcome awaited them at the end of their journeys. The absorption of civil rights organizers into Black families was spiritual gold for the Mississippi Movement, and it empowered movement organizers with the one credential that they could never earn: being one of the community's children. This credential contradicted the label of "outside agitator" used in Mississippi by the White power structure to negate the impact of the movement. By the same token, movement organizers empowered their adoptive families by reinforcing and enlarging the connections between them and the larger movement family, with its extensive networks across the land.

Grassroots People and Grassroots Leadership

The Mississippi Movement's message of empowerment for grassroots people was delivered to the entire country on national television at the 1964 Democratic National Convention by the Black sharecroppers, domestic workers, and farmers who formed the rank and file of the Mississippi Freedom Democratic Party (MFDP). Thereafter, the message of empowerment was carried by Black and White community organizers into many areas of community activity, including education, health, welfare, religion, and politics. However, neither the MFDP nor other grassroots organizations took root and flourished into a strong national movement for empowering Black people. The echoes heard — from the Democratic party to the federal government and from the religious sector to public school systems — were the same: institutionalizing empowerment in the hands of Black "folk" is too risky a notion to attract lasting political support.

The issue of community empowerment in the public schools, first raised by Black community organizers in Harlem in 1965, also found expression in White, liberal America. For example, in 1969 the Open Program of the Martin Luther King, Jr., School was established as a magnet program in the Cambridge public schools, in part because of the clamoring of Cambridge parents for more open education programs for their children, and in part because of the response to desegregation of the Cambridge schools.[4]

"Cast down your bucket where you are"

To master the art of organizing that strives to empower grassroots people, one needs to learn to "cast down your bucket where you are." In 1976, Bob and Janet Moses, both former organizers for SNCC in Mississippi, cast down their bucket in Cambridge and looked to the Open Program of the King School as a place to educate their children.[5] What would later become the Algebra Project began in 1982 when their eldest daughter, Maisha, entered the Open Program's eighth grade.

THE ALGEBRA PROJECT

Before 1982, Moses, whose background included teaching secondary school mathematics in New York City and in Tanzania, had been teaching math to his children at home. Maisha, now a junior at Harvard University, recalls these lessons, conducted weekly during the school year and daily during the summer and vacations:

> Doing math at home was always a lot harder than math at school. It was somewhat like a chore. In our family, extra reading with my mom when we were much younger and math with my dad was part of our responsibility in the family, like taking out the garbage or doing the laundry.

Moses faced a familiar challenge: the resistance of adolescent children to performing what they regarded as a "household chore." Maisha explains:

> As we were getting older, it was a lot harder to get us to do math at home. We battled a lot more and complained. "Why do we have to do this? No one else has

to do this." Dad would say, "It's important. I want you to do it. You need to do it." But we wouldn't be satisfied. I didn't really want to do it. Dad would have to sit there and force answers out of me. Finally he decided that the only way to get me to do algebra was to go into school.

In the fall of 1982, Mary Lou Mehrling, Maisha's eighth-grade teacher, invited Moses into her seventh/eighth-grade classroom to work with Maisha and three other eighth graders on algebra. That spring, Maisha and two others took the Cambridge citywide algebra test that was offered to students who wished to bypass Algebra I and go directly into honors algebra or honors geometry in the ninth grade. All three passed, becoming the first students in the history of the King School to be eligible to pursue the honors math and science curriculum at Cambridge's only high school, Cambridge Rindge and Latin.[6]

With one eye on his eldest son, who was about to enter the Open Program's seventh grade, Moses decided to continue working the next year (1983–1984) with Mehrling and another seventh/eighth-grade teacher. The number of eighth graders studying algebra with Moses increased to nine. Partway through the year, the teachers selected seven seventh graders they thought were likely to begin algebra the following year, creating the first group of "high-ability" seventh graders for Moses to direct. That spring, all nine of Moses's eighth graders took the citywide algebra test, and six passed.

In the following year the program expanded again, but it was no longer quite the same. As early as 1983–1984, it was evident that in spite of the commitment to meeting the educational needs of all its pupils, mathematics instruction in the Open Program was unwittingly skewed along racial lines.[7] Children in the two seventh/eighth-grade classrooms were clustered into separate ability groups: above-grade-level tracks primarily composed of middle-class Whites; below-grade-level tracks made up almost exclusively of Blacks and other children of color; and grade-level tracks that were racially mixed. The Open Program's system of ability groups effectively shunted most students of color onto the no-algebra track, imbuing too many youngsters with the self-fulfilling notion that little was expected of them.

Additionally, Moses and Mehrling became aware that some high-achieving Black males felt uncomfortable joining the algebra group, for it meant being separated from their friends who were on other math tracks. On the whole, young people feel the need to be as similar to their peers as possible. Separating academically talented adolescents from their peers for the sake of participation in the academic "fast track" potentially aggravates the anxiety that accompanies adolescents' identity development.[8] Moreover, enduring attitudes toward math are shaped by math instruction at the seventh- and eighth-grade levels. Traditionally, very few new math principles are introduced in these two grades, when attention focuses instead on review (Usiskin, 1987). Moses and Mehrling hypothesized that using the seventh and eighth grades to lay a groundwork of competence in algebra might enhance students' general self-confidence and provide them with the mathematical background necessary for advanced high school courses.

The Mississippi Movement's organizing tradition utilized everyday issues of ordinary people and framed them for the maximum benefit of the community. In Mississippi the issue was the right to vote; technically: "What are the legal, judicial, political, and constitutional obstacles to the right to vote? How can we initiate court cases, introduce legislation, and mobilize political support to remove these obstacles?" SNCC and CORE workers pursued this goal by establishing beach-heads, through Black families, in the most resistant counties throughout the state. But the Mississippi organizers did something of even greater importance, and that was to conceive of the issue of voting in its broadest political sense. Midway through voter registration efforts, they began to ask themselves and the Black community: "What is the vote for? Why do we want it in the first place? What must we do right now to ensure that when we have the vote, it will work for us to benefit our communities?" After the organizers and key community groups had worked and reworked these and other questions, they shifted the organizing strategy from increasing voter registration to laying the basis for a community-based political party, which eventually became the Mississippi Freedom Democratic Party. Creating a new political party became the Mississippi Movement's focus, because of its greater potential for involving community people in a substantive long-term effort. Participants would come to own the political questions and their responses to them.[9]

In the Open Program the everyday issue was teaching algebra in the seventh and eighth grades. Moses, the parent-as-organizer in the program, instinctively used the lesson he had learned in Mississippi, transforming the everyday issue into a broader political question for the Open Program community to consider: What is algebra for? Why do we want children to study it? What do we need to include in the mathematics education of every middle school student, to provide each and every one of them with access to the college preparatory mathematics curriculum in high school? Why is it important to gain such access?

By linking the content of math education to the future prospects of inner-city children, Moses transformed what had previously been a purely curricular issue into a broader political question. Drawing on his experience as an organizer, educator, and parent, Moses transformed the dialogue among parents, teachers, and school administrators in the Open Program into one that centered on questions that would get at the heart of educational practice: How can a culture be created in the Open Program in which every child is expected to be as good as possible in his or her mathematical development? What should the content of middle school mathematics be? What curricular processes make that content available to all students?

A cornerstone of the evolving Algebra Project thus became the expectation that every child in the Open Program could achieve math literacy, an ethos powerful enough to suffuse both the peer and adult culture. The components of this effort included changing the content and methods of teaching math, involving parents in activities that would enable them to better support their children's learning, teaching students to set goals and motivating them to achieve, and reaching out to Black college graduates in the Boston area who would serve as tutors and role models of academic success.

Teachers as Learners

From the beginning, Mehrling and Moses modeled the notion that there is no shame in confessing ignorance — if it is the first step in learning. Mehrling, an ex-music teacher, took courses in mathematics, beginning with algebra, and eventually achieved state certification in math. But she did something more profound: she turned her inexperience with math content into a component of learning by adopting a position of mutual inquiry with her students and by presenting herself to them as a learner. As she states, she "developed methods of responding to students' questions that helped both the students and me to think through the problems." When she had questions, she would ask Moses for help, on the spot:

> Presenting myself as a learner, in front of my students, helped me to understand what they were experiencing, and helped them to feel comfortable asking for help. Students no longer felt threatened if they did not understand a problem or a concept, for they saw that we all were learners and we all learn in different ways.

Because Mehrling presented herself openly and honestly as a student of the subject she was teaching, she was able to help build her students' confidence. She overtly transmitted the message, "if I [your teacher] can risk embarrassment to learn this subject, surely you can, too." But she also conveyed to them a powerful latent message:

> I am confident that people who don't know this subject can learn it; to learn it they have, at all times, to be ready not to pretend to understand what they do not truly understand; to learn it they must be comfortable asking for help and willing to risk embarrassment.

Mehrling's message recapitulated a memorable message that Fannie Lou Hamer and others conveyed at the height of the MFDP challenge to the Democratic National Convention of 1964 — confidence that people who did not know the business of politics could learn it by asking direct questions and risking embarrassment. Each confronted their inexperience with honesty and integrity, turning potential liabilities into strengths.

Involving Parents

From its inception, the Open Program had evolved a set of policies and practices that encouraged parents' active involvement in staff hiring, curriculum development, observation and evaluation of teachers, and governance and administration of the school. Parental involvement in the Algebra Project grew naturally in this context.

Parents who served on the program's seventh/eighth-grade committee in 1984–1985 concluded that decisions about studying algebra in the seventh and eighth grades could not be left up to individual sixth graders. These children were too young to fully understand the long-range implications of their decisions for college entrance. Nor should such decisions rest solely with the teachers, curriculum coordinators, or school or district-wide administrators, each of whom had their own ideas about who should study algebra and in which grade. Rather, parents needed to be involved in making educational choices for their children at both individual and policymaking levels. They also had to be better informed about details of the middle school math curriculum so that they would be able to make informed decisions and protect the best interests of their children.

During the spring of 1985, a parent from the Open Program's seventh/eighth-grade committee collaborated with Moses to distribute a letter to the parents of all the sixth graders, asking whether they thought that every seventh grader should study algebra, and whether they thought their own child should study algebra in the seventh grade. In reply, a few parents said they thought that some seventh graders probably weren't ready, but no parent thought his or her own child should be denied access to algebra in the seventh grade. Exposing the contradictions between parental assessments of their children's capabilities and curricular assumptions at the community level provided a means for building consensus around educational outcomes for all children.

This was the catalyst for inviting all Open Program children entering the seventh grade in the fall of 1985 to study algebra three times a week. With the exception of a few eighth graders who in their teacher's judgment were not ready, the invitation to study algebra was extended to the entire eighth grade as well. The consensus statement from parents launched a change in school policy and culture. Currently, every Open Program student is expected to study algebra in the seventh and eighth grades.

As the project evolved, parental participation increased as parents volunteered in classrooms and participated in workshops on student self-esteem and achievement. Parents from throughout the King School were invited to attend "Honors Bound" parent groups, which prepared students of color to accept the challenge of taking honors courses in high school and created a home-school culture that would nurture and support serious intellectual effort. A Saturday morning algebra course for parents was offered, teaching algebra in the same way that it was being taught to their children.

Parents who took algebra during the Saturday classes committed themselves to making the project "theirs" in a fundamental sense. A grateful parent captured the multiple dimensions of this experience in a 1987 letter to the Cambridge School Committee:

> This program exemplifies to me all that I hope most for in the education of my daughter and other young people in our community: a positive orientation to learning; a rich understanding of advanced mathematics; recognition of the relationship between what is learned in the classroom and what goes on in life; and a sense of personal empowerment.
>
> As a sixth grader in her first year in the program, my daughter began to overcome her fear of math and distorted perceptions of what she is capable of doing and why it is important. I believe this was due to several factors, including the climate of learning in the classroom (in part, a sense that students, teachers and aides alike were learning *together*); the demystification of the subject by relating it to life experiences; and by the fact that her mother, along with other parents and community members, was simultaneously overcoming latent math panic by taking the course on Saturdays.
>
> This experience not only helped me understand the program (and learn math); it also greatly enhanced my comprehension of the life of the school and neighborhood community and of problems that as a citizen I can help to resolve.

Parents were barraged with letters and opportunities to talk, to ask questions, and to join in planning, all as an acknowledgment of the centrality of parents in the construction of a home-school culture of high achievement.

Creating a New Teaching and Learning Environment for Math

As an adjunct to opening up algebra to all seventh and eighth graders in 1985, ability grouping was replaced with individual and small-group instruction. Students were taught skills for learning hard material "on their own." In conferences with teachers, students were asked to set their own short-term objectives (for example, deciding how many lesson sets they wished to complete each week), and longer-range goals (for example, deciding to prepare for the citywide test). Parents were informed about the goals and were asked to sign their child's goal statement each semester. The pace and scope of students' mathematical studies therefore came under student control. Mehrling tells a story that reflects the individual and group motivation that such goal-setting can foster:

> Andrea spoke up at one of our first meetings and said, "I'm going to do four lessons a week because I want to finish such-and-such by the end of seventh grade, so I can finish the book by the end of the eighth grade, so I can be in honors geometry in the ninth grade." This was a twelve-year-old. The others looked at her — this hadn't come from a teacher — and said, "Are you crazy?" She said, "That's what I'm going to do." Bob [Moses] was there, and he started to frame for them why what Andrea had just done was a very mature and farsighted act, and how maybe they weren't ready to do that yet. But it gave Andrea a lot of support and affirmation for having said that in the group. And it changed what the others were going to say next. Everything from then on was in terms of Andrea: "Well, I'm not going to do quite what Andrea is, but . . ."

Students also learned to work harder than they had before. They were encouraged to develop habits of concentration, patience, and perseverance in approaching their daily math work. Students decided which of several resources to consult — the textbook, the instructor, or a peer — when they had a question or ran into difficulties in solving a problem. Teachers met with small groups for brief lessons on specific concepts and regularly held small-group review sessions. Reflecting on this decision, Mehrling recently explained:

> Adolescent learners can sometimes interrelate with materials, and it's not nearly as threatening as interacting with an adult. If they can go to an adult to ask a question about the materials when they're ready to go to an adult, it's wholly different from being in a group, being pinpointed and put on the spot, and feeling vulnerable about the pieces they don't have in place yet. Once they start to interact with materials, they get not only very possessive of them, but very reluctant to go back to any kind of teacher-directed lessons. They're empowered, in a curious way, around materials — something I would never have even thought about. The Open Program generally is a very teacher-intensive kind of program. We motivate, we bring in materials from everywhere, and our teaching is interpersonal. We discovered at the seventh- and eighth-grade level that that was one of the problems with students who felt vulnerable: it put them on the spot.

As part of the new curricular, pedagogical, and social environment for studying math, the seventh- and eighth-grade teachers assumed the role of "coach" as opposed to "lecturer" in their relationship with students.

The project produced its first full graduating class in the spring of 1986. When they entered high school the following autumn, 39 percent of the graduates were placed in Honors Geometry or Honors Algebra. Not a single student in that cohort ended up at Cambridge Rindge and Latin School in lower-level math courses, such as Algebra I.

Curricular Expansion

By 1986, attention turned to the preparation of students for seventh-grade algebra. With all students in the seventh and eighth grades taking algebra, lower grade teachers began to question the adequacy of their own math curricula as preparation for algebra. To address this question systematically, the entire staff of the Open Program participated in a year-long institute centered on the question of math literacy.

After the institute, teachers at all levels (K–8) implemented new curricula in mathematics appropriate for the age and grade levels they taught. Some teachers found it unsettling to devise their own curricular practices around the needs of children and their own teaching styles. The results of the Algebra Project suggest that flexibility leads to better pedagogy. For example, when fifth/sixth-grade teachers tried a materials-centered approach with sixth graders that had worked very well at the seventh/eighth-grade level, they found that younger children, accustomed to more teacher-centered instruction, needed more teacher-child and small-group interaction in the sixth-grade transition curriculum. The teachers modified their classroom technique, but retained the principle of encouraging greater self-reliance in finding answers to problems. Improved adaptation of curriculum was itself beneficial. But equally important, this process gave teachers the same sense of empowerment experienced by students. Teachers who participated in the innovation and trained themselves in how to present the curriculum were more likely to understand, appreciate, and foster the skill of self-education that was central to the Algebra Project. One teacher explained:

> Bob was affirming what we were doing while he was helping us change. He didn't come in and say, "We're throwing this out, it's junk." He came in and said, "You guys are great. Wanna try something different?" When we asked, "How will it work?" he turned it around and asked, "Well, how do you think it should work? What do you want to have happen?" He didn't really give us a way, which admittedly was frustrating, but it also gave us ownership around it. Bob didn't have all of the answers. At first I was really annoyed that he was making me go through this process. I kept saying, "Bob has an agenda. Why doesn't he tell us? We're wasting so much time!" But he knew that it had to come from us. He knew he couldn't impose, because he didn't know what would work. He wasn't a classroom teacher. He just had the vision. If he could help us catch the vision, we would make it work.

A second outcome was that Moses agreed to develop a curriculum for the sixth grade that would provide a conceptual transition from arithmetic to algebra. The main features of what has come to be called the Algebra Project, and the philosophy that guided its construction, are discussed below.

What to Teach and How to Teach It

The opening of algebra to everyone in 1985–1986 gave Moses the opportunity to work closely with several students who had great difficulty with the initial chapters of the algebra textbook. In particular, one Black male student took many months to complete the first few lessons. Moses wondered precisely where the student's conceptual knot lay. Was it possible to lead the student from arithmetic to algebra by mapping a conceptual trail, beginning with concepts that were obvious and proceeding by equally obvious steps?

After working with a number of students who were having difficulty, Moses came to the conclusion that the heart of the problem lay in their concept of number. In arithmetic, the distinctive feature of a number is magnitude or quantity. In algebra, a number has two distinctive features: one is quantitative; the other is qualitative and must be explicitly taught. Students of arithmetic have in their minds one question that they associate with counting numbers: "How many?" Students of algebra need to have two: "How many?" and another questions, such as "Which way?" as points of reference for the intuitive concept of opposites. Children understand the question, "Which way?" from their early years, but it is not a question that they associate with numbers. The number concept used in arithmetic must be generalized in algebra, and failure to make this generalization blocks students' understanding. Once students have generalized their concept of number, they must also generalize their knowledge of basic operations such as subtraction.

Moses gradually arrived at a five-step teaching and learning process that takes students from physical events to a symbolic representation of those events, thereby accelerating sixth graders' grasp of key concepts needed in the study of algebra.[10] The five steps are:

1. Physical event
2. Picture of model of this event
3. Intuitive (idiomatic) language description of this event
4. A description of this event in "regimented" English
5. Symbolic representation of the event

The purpose of the five steps is to avert student frustration in "the game of signs," or the misapprehension that mathematics is the manipulation of a collection of mysterious symbols and signs. Chad, a young Black seventh grader, recently looked up from reading a page in the first chapter of a traditional algebra text and said to his mother, "It's all just words." For too many youngsters, mathematics is a game of signs they cannot play. They must be helped to understand what those signs *really* mean and to construct for themselves a basis of evidence for mathematics. When middle school students use the five-step process to construct symbolic representations of physical events (representations that they themselves make up), they forge, through direct experience, their own platform of mathematical truths. Their personally constructed symbolic representations enter into a system of mathematical truths that has content and meaning.

At the Open Program, students initiate this process with a trip on the Red Line of Boston's subway system (the physical event). This experience provides the context in which a number of obvious questions may be asked: At what station do we start? Where are we going? How many stops will it take to get there? In what direction do we go? These questions have obvious answers, forming the basis for the mathematics of trips. When they return, students are asked to write about their trip, draw a mural or construct a three-dimensional model, make graphs for trips that they create, and collect statistical data about them. The purpose is to fuse in their minds the two questions "How many?" and "Which way?" and to anchor these questions to physical events.

Students then use this process to explore the concept of equivalence in the broad cultural context of everyday events, such as cooking, coaching, teaching, painting, and repairing. They explore any concept in which object A is substituted for object B to achieve a certain goal. They conclude the discussion of equivalence in subway travel with open-ended constructions of equivalent trips, leading to an introduction of displacements as "trips that have the same number of stops and go in the same direction."

Once displacements are introduced, they investigate the concept of "comparing" as a prelude to generalizing their concept of subtraction. Most algebra texts introduce subtraction as a transformed addition problem. Students are asked to think of subtraction $(3 - (-2) = +5)$ as "adding the opposite" or "finding the missing addend" $(3 - ? = 5)$, which provides one group of signs as a reference for another. But students look for concrete experiences, pictures, or at least a concept, to link directly to algebraic subtraction. The problem is compounded because students have overlearned "take-away" as the concept underlying subtraction. In algebra, "take-away" no longer has a straightforward application to subtraction. Within a couple of months of beginning algebra, students confront subtraction statements that have no discernible content, have only indirect meaning in relation to an associated addition problem, and are not at all obvious.

To give additional content, meaning, and clarity to subtraction in beginning algebra, students begin with the physical event of comparing the heights of two students, Coastocoast, who is six feet tall, and Watchme, who is four feet tall. The class works with a picture of this event, generating questions that can be used to compare heights:

1. Which one is taller?
2. What is the difference in their heights?
3. How much shorter is Watchme than Coastocoast?
4. Who is shorter?
5. How much taller is Coastocoast than Watchme?

In arithmetic there are two subtraction concepts, the concept of "take-away" and the concept of "the difference between." The latter provides the appropriate entry into subtraction in algebra, as illustrated in the above set of questions. Students will readily identify an answer to the second question by subtracting to find the difference in the heights. This prepares them to accept subtraction as the best approach to answering comparative questions — questions that belong to algebra and not arithmetic.

The answers to these questions are carefully processed in three stages: intuitive language, regimented English, and symbolic representations. "How much taller is Coastocoast than Watchme?" is explored in the following way:

- *Intuitive language:* "Coastocoast is two feet taller than Watchme."
- *Regimented English:* "The height of Coastocoast compared to the height of Watchme is two feet taller."
- *Symbolic representations:*

    (5a)   H(C) compared to H(W) is $2'$ ↑
    (5b)   H(C) − H(W) = $2'$ ↑
    (5c) $6'$ ↑ − $4'$ ↑ = $2'$ ↑
            (that is, $6'$ is $2'$ taller than $4'$)

"How much shorter is Watchme than Coastocoast?" proceeds along a similar track.

- *Intuitive language:* "Watchme is two feet shorter than Coastocoast."
- *Regimented English:* "The height of Watchme compared to the height of Coastocoast is two feet shorter."
- *Symbolic representations:*

    (3a)   H(W) compared to H(C) is $2'$ ↓
    (3b)   H(W) − H(C) = $2'$ ↓
    (3c) $4'$ ↑ − $6'$ ↑ = $2'$ ↓
            (that is, a height of $4'$ is $2'$ shorter than a height of $6'$)

This way of comparing physical quantities is easily reinforced with work stations at which students compare weights, lengths, temperatures, and speeds. They may return to their experience on the subway to compare positions of stations on the Red Line, using the following model:

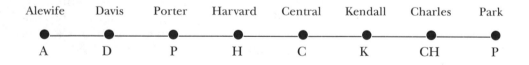

Alewife	Davis	Porter	Harvard	Central	Kendall	Charles	Park
A	D	P	H	C	K	CH	P

When asked, "What is the position of Harvard compared to Kendall?" students work through the following steps:

- *Intuitive language:* "Harvard is two stops outbound from Kendall."
- *Regimented English:* "The position of Harvard compared to the position of Kendall is two stops outbound."
- *Symbolic representations:*

    (a)   P(H) compared to P(K) is 2
    (b)   P(H) − P(K) = 2

In a similar way the question, "What is the position of Kendall relative to Harvard?" yields

$$P(K) - P(H) = 2$$

As soon as integers are introduced as a system of coordinates, students are ready to generate their own subtraction problems. The notion of an arbitrary point of reference having been introduced earlier, systems of coordinates are assigned to the stations, with the zero point alternately assigned to various stations. Each assignment generates a different subtraction problem for the question, "What is the position of Harvard relative to Kendall?"

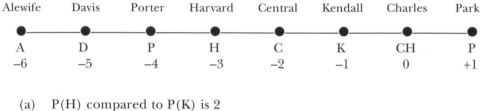

Alewife	Davis	Porter	Harvard	Central	Kendall	Charles	Park
A	D	P	H	C	K	CH	P
–6	–5	–4	–3	–2	–1	0	+1

(a)   P(H) compared to P(K) is 2
(b)   P(H) – P(K) = 2
(c)   –3 – (–1) = –2

By similar reasoning, the question, "What is the position of Kendall relative to Harvard?" yields

$$P(K) - P(H) = 2$$
$$-1 - (-3) = +2$$

The opposite comparisons [P(H) compared to P(K), and P(K) compared to P(H)] lead to opposite expressions [(–3) – (–1), and (–1) – (–3)] as well as opposite integers [(–2) and (+2)], in a way that gives direct, intuitive meaning to subtraction of integers and provides students and teachers alike with control over the generation of simple subtraction problems and equations. The curriculum and curricular process used in the sixth grade have made algebra accessible for all middle school students. The project has demonstrated that all seventh- and eighth-grade students in the King School's Open Program can study algebra, and that the entire school community expects them to do so.

Community Participation in Creating a Culture of Achievement

For youngsters who have felt excluded from the culture of academic achievement in school, the expectation that they, too, can learn is crucial. During the 1987–1988 school year, the project's response to children who did not think they were likely to succeed in math was to institute a series of measures designed to create a culture of mathematical and scientific literacy, not only in the Open Program, but in other programs within the King School as well. The Seymour Institute for Advanced Christian Studies, a service organization conceived by Black Harvard graduates to support community-based development in urban areas, provided Black role models to go into classes to tutor students and to run before-school algebra study halls four mornings a week. The study halls were open to seventh and eighth graders from all of the King School's four programs. The tutors, who came from

Harvard, MIT, Wentworth Institute, and Boston University, established relationships with individual children and became role models of academically successful young adults for seventh and eighth graders to emulate. A Harvard Law School student and tutor wrote:

> I have been impressed by the fact that these seventh and eighth graders are able to read and understand their math textbooks, already have some understanding of algebraic concepts, and are willing to come out at 7:30 A.M. in order to work on their mathematical skills. . . . The students in the Algebra Project are able to help themselves, and each other, by using their books. Helping each other has another important role in the Project. I believe that it is their friendships that keep them coming to early morning study halls; relationships that support educational achievement are being established outside the classroom.

As the Algebra Project developed, the message that each child could learn was more systematically articulated by the Efficacy Institute.[11] Emphasizing confidence and effective effort as key ingredients in the process of intellectual development, the Efficacy model provides educators, parents, and students with an explicit alternative to the ability model of learning. Efficacy assumes that children, who are well enough endowed to master the fundamentals of language at an early age, are fully capable of learning mathematics. In order to learn, children are required to marshal effective effort. They must learn to work with commitment, focused attention, and reliable strategies. When learning is perceived as a function of effective effort, one seeks factors inhibiting children when they are having difficulties learning or understanding a concept, rather than looking for "disabilities" that prevent learning.

Many children of color learn from an early age that there are doubts concerning their capacity to develop intellectually. Messages communicated from school (low-ability placements in the primary grades), from peers (pervasive anti-intellectualism within the peer group), and the media (expectations of inferiority) all serve to impress upon them that they may not be up to the task of advanced studies. The lack of confidence engendered by the internalization of these messages shapes the meaning of any failure ("I guess this proves I'm not smart") and undermines the capacity to work ("Why bang my head against the wall if I'm unable to learn the stuff anyway?").

To redress these circumstances, Efficacy works to plant an alternative idea in the child's mind: "If I work hard enough, I can get smart."

Confidence	$\rightarrow$	Effective Effort	$\rightarrow$	Development
(Think you can)		*(Work hard)*		*(Get smart)*

Emphasis is placed on the process of development and some measure of control is returned to the child.

Teachers are the carriers of Efficacy ideas, and it is to them that responsibility falls for building confidence and shaping strong effort in children. Teachers attend an intensive, five-day seminar to learn the Efficacy model of development and study its implications for their own teaching. They are then provided with a formal curriculum to use with their students over the course of an academic year.

The curriculum gives teachers and students a shared language and a conceptual framework for reworking questions, such as why a particular child has been unable to "do math" in the past. The teacher is able to impress upon the child that learning is a function of effort, not of innate ability. The curriculum helps the students to raise their consciousness so they can affirm for themselves their own need for self-development. Such affirmation on their part is a critical prerequisite to confronting obstacles to their own development and acquiring attitudes and habits that will ensure success in many endeavors, including the algebra program.

In 1988, a sixth-grade teacher in the Open Program began teaching the Efficacy curriculum to all the sixth graders twice a week. She explains:

> We all consider ourselves to be good teachers, and yet we know that we are failing some students. Bob talked to us about a way that could help us to help those children achieve. We realized what that will mean not only to those students but to all of the children in our classrooms, and from there, what that will mean to the community at large.

The Project Continues

The Algebra Project continues at the Open Program. The Efficacy and algebra curricula are taught to sixth graders, and algebra is studied by all seventh and eighth graders. The project is now challenging other schools to make the political decision to alter their own math curricula. For example, discussions are proceeding with administrators and teachers in Boston, where three schools have volunteered to experiment with both the Efficacy and Algebra Project curricula and receive training in their implementation. Moses has also begun to train selected middle school teachers in Atlanta. Currently, the project is exploring relationships with school systems in other cities.

CONCLUSION

Community Organizing and Educational Innovation

The community organizing approach to educational innovation differs from traditional educational interventions in several important ways. The principle of "casting down your bucket where you are" stands in marked contrast to research programs originating in universities, where scholars design interventions they hypothesize will result in outcomes that they articulate in advance and that are replicable. Researchers in universities and consulting firms must have well-designed, highly articulated interventions in order to convince funding agencies that their projects have promise. Depending upon the focus of the investigation, the researcher generally targets selected neighborhoods, schools, or organizations for participation based on their demographic or similarly quantifiable characteristics. Additionally, researchers have intellectual roots in their own disciplines and view problems through lenses that are consonant with their disciplines, rather than through the eyes of a community.

In contrast to the university-based researcher, the organizer working in the tradition of Ella gradually becomes recognized by community members as having a commitment to their overall well-being. The organizer immerses himself or herself in the life of the community, learning its strengths, resources, concerns, and ways of conducting business. The organizer does not have a comprehensive, detailed plan for remedying a perceived problem but takes an "evolutionary" view of his or her own role in the construction of the solution. He or she understands that the community's everyday concerns can be transformed into broader political questions of general import. The form they will take is not always known in advance.

Once political questions are identified, the organizer's agenda must remain simultaneously focused and fluid — sharply focused on the long-range goal, but fluid with respect to how the goal will be attained. The organizer seeks out views of community participants who have strong interests in the issue and informally educates community members who are uninvolved but whose interests are at stake. It is the organizer's task to help community members air their opinions, question one another, and then build consensus, a process that usually takes a good deal of time to complete.

Improving the mathematics curriculum and curricular process in a middle school has gradually become the focus of the Algebra Project. At the outset, Moses did not know that the project would become a vehicle for raising questions about ability grouping, effective teaching for children of color, or the community's roles in educational decisionmaking. He did not imagine that it would trigger an interest in teaching algebra to inner-city middle school students beyond his daughter's classroom.

As we have seen, the program's innovations relied on the involvement of the entire community: teachers, parents, school administrators, students, tutors, and consultants from the Greater Boston community. In her review of programs that have been helpful in breaking the cycle of disadvantage, Lisbeth Schorr (1988) highlights the importance of comprehensive, flexible, and intensive approaches to reform:[12]

> Many interventions have turned out to be ineffective not because seriously disadvantaged families are beyond help, but because we have tried to attack complex, deeply rooted tangles of troubles with isolated fragments of help, with help rendered grudgingly in one-shot forays, with help designed less to meet the needs of beneficiaries than to conform to professional or bureaucratic convenience, with help that may be useful to middle-class families but is often irrelevant to families struggling to survive. (pp. 263–264)

The work of discovering new solutions, building a broad base of support, and overcoming barriers takes time. Moses's effort to work with teachers, parents, and administrators to transform the middle school mathematics curriculum and curricular process in the Open Program began seven years ago. We note that it took fifteen years for James Comer's efforts at comprehensive reform in two New Haven schools to yield striking improvements in test scores (Comer, 1980, 1988).[13] Durable reforms are possible, but there are no shortcuts in bottom-up implementation.

In the Open Program, faculty volunteered to participate, committing themselves to working together to discover better ways to teach math and struggling to reach consensus. Parents were deeply involved as learners, supporters, contributors, and decisionmakers. Students voluntarily set goals for themselves and came to 7:30 A.M. study halls four mornings a week. School administrators supported teachers as they tried out new strategies, worked to secure funding, and acted as spokespersons for the project. The strengths of various contributors were recognized, and they were empowered to adapt, create, and evaluate their progress in attaining a shared vision.

Others have learned that it is through struggling with a problem and shaping the solutions that commitment to change really occurs. Schorr (1988) reports:

> Dr. Comer wanted to make sure I understood that the essence of his intervention is a process, not a package of materials, instructional methods, or techniques. "It is the creation of a sense of community and direction for parents, school staff, and students alike." (p. 234)

Comer is pointing to the fact that significant innovations must transform the culture, and transformation requires a broad base of voluntary support. It is crucial that participants have time to understand an idea, explore their commitment, and adapt the innovation to their needs.

Henry Levin (1988) also emphasizes the importance of process.[14] He states:

> Underlying the organizational approach are two major assumptions: First, the strategy must "empower" all of the major participants rather than decrying their weaknesses. (p. 5)

Many will find it useful to follow the precept "cast down your bucket where you are," as Jaime Escalante did in Los Angeles when he began offering calculus to disadvantaged youth. The starting point for reform is less important than whether the issue is powerful and inspiring enough to generate enthusiasm, reveal broader political questions, compel devoted leadership, and serve as a vehicle for community commitment.

Funding to Support Innovation

The Algebra Project would not have developed as it did had it not been for the MacArthur "no strings attached" Fellowship that allowed Moses to work in the Open Program for five years without having to account for the way he spent his time. Subsequent funding has been difficult. For eighteen months, Wheelock College in Boston supported Moses as he looked for resources to provide release time for teachers, cover materials and reproduction costs, and secure consultation from the broader academic community. Moses is still spending an enormous amount of time trying to secure long-term funding to support the continuation and dissemination of the Algebra Project.

Finding support can be a depleting struggle for many innovative efforts. National funding sources are hesitant to fund projects with grassroots leadership, a community focus, a long time frame, and a philosophy that casts educational issues in political as well as technical terms. Declining state and local budgets also threaten commitment to comprehensive, long-term reforms. But only when major political questions are addressed (for instance, that *all* children can benefit from and should have access to algebra in their middle school years) can we discover the most appropriate ways to organize knowledge, develop curriculum, and encourage home, school, and community participation.

Transforming School Culture

Teachers and parents in the Open Program came to believe that ability grouping in mathematics seriously impaired the capacity of middle school females and students of color to learn as well as they might. Questioning the policy was the first step toward comprehensive change. Others concur that differentiating students harms those who are disadvantaged or placed in lower tracks.[15] After articulating a vision of high expectations in algebra for all students, participants worked to transform the culture of the school, so that policies, teaching strategies, and the Efficacy curriculum could together help students.

The project speaks to the importance of family as a link to school success. Henderson (1987) concludes her review of research concerning parental involvement in student achievement by categorically stating that "the evidence is beyond dispute: parent involvement improves student achievement" (p. 1). This finding holds for middle- as well as low-income families, at different grade levels, and within a broad spectrum of interventions. As the U.S. population becomes more diverse, it is absolutely fundamental that schools join with families to define and support school success. Continuity between home and school must be forged for all children, and we must draw on the strengths and resources that families can provide.

Curriculum and Curricular Process

Among the strengths of the faculty and volunteers in the Open Program was their curiosity about why some children were not succeeding in mathematics and their willingness to explore the possibility that their own teaching strategies might be a factor. Moses and the teachers became classroom researchers — analyzing student errors, locating conceptual knots, and experimenting with materials and teaching processes that might improve students' mathematical development. A sixth-grade transition curriculum that allows students to relate everyday experiences to mathematical concepts represented symbolically should be disseminated widely.

In 1964, national attention was focused on the disenfranchised citizens of the South. In 1989, another kind of disenfranchisement exists, as many poor, indigenous, and immigrant children of color are denied access to programs and teaching that support their success in school. The success of the Algebra Project stands as a challenge to public school teachers, administrators, scholars, and, most important, those individuals who have traditionally advocated for the democratization of the society and schools: Will you wage a campaign for mathematical literacy, which acknowledges that every middle school student can and should learn algebra while simultaneously empowering the child's community and family? Will you organize in the spirit of Ella?

NOTES

1. *Fundi* is a Swahili term for a person who has an expertise valued by society, and who passes on his or her art to the young by example and instruction. Ella Baker was a fundi to the SNCC workers learning the art of community organizing.
2. One such quiet place was Amite County, in a remote corner of southwest Mississippi, where E. W. Steptoe's family welcomed Bob Moses, SNCC's first field secretary, into

the community in the summer of 1961. Mr. Steptoe was president of Amite County's NAACP chapter in the late 1950s when the county sheriff raided a chapter meeting and confiscated the group's books, thus exposing the members to economic reprisals and physical danger. By the time the first wave of SNCC organizers spread out across the rural South, activities at places like the Steptoe farmhouse had ground to a halt.

3. "Cast down your bucket where you are" was used by Booker T. Washington in an address at the Atlanta Exposition, September 18, 1895.

4. The King School is a large, modern facility built on the site of a school that had served Cambridge's Black community for many years. By the late 1970s, the King School housed four programs for grades K–8: a regular program composed of personnel from the former school; a magnet Open Program; and smaller bilingual and special needs programs.

5. Because some but not all authors of this article are also the subjects of discussion, we have chosen to use third-person references throughout to avoid confusion.

6. The fourth student opted to go to a private high school, and did not take the test.

7. See Delpit (1986) for a discussion of the differences between the instructional needs of mainstream and minority children.

8. See Fordham (1988) for a discussion of the tensions high-achieving Black students feel when they strive for academic success.

9. It was only in Mississippi, where the entire state was structured along a community organizing tradition, that the issue of the right to vote was perceived as a broad political question.

10. This model is a synthesis of ideas derived from three sources. The first was the Open Program itself. Moses observed teaching practices in the Open Program and attended workshops with teachers in which Virginia Chalmers and others explained the teaching and learning ideas that they had developed for primary grades. The second was Quine's (1981) notion of "mathematization in situ." "A progressive sharpening and regimenting of ordinary idioms: this is what led to arithmetic, symbolic logic, and set theory, and this is mathematization" (p. 150). Quine insisted that "set theory, arithmetic, and symbolic logic are all of them products of the straightforward mathematization of ordinary interpreted discourse" (p. 151). The third source was Dubinsky (1987), who shared his insight that in the future, mathematics education would center on a "fixed curricular process" rather than a "fixed curriculum."

11. The Efficacy model of intellectual development is based on motivation. The role of motivation in self-development was studied by Jeffrey Howard, Director of the Efficacy Institute, who, in collaboration with educators, developed the model summarized here.

12. As a participant of the Harvard University Working Group on Early Life and Adolescence, Lisbeth Schorr believed that with the knowledge currently available, society could prevent the damaging outcomes for adolescents associated with disadvantage, such as teenage pregnancy, juvenile crime, school failure, and unemployment. She visited an array of health and education programs that were successful in interrupting the cycle of disadvantage and discovered that what the programs had in common was a comprehensive, flexible, and intensive approach to reform.

13. In 1968, James Comer, a psychiatrist at the Yale Child Study Center, began a program of reform in the two New Haven schools that had the lowest achievement scores and the worst attendance and behavior records in the system. Today, although the community is still impoverished, these demonstration schools now boast top achievement scores in the New Haven system (ranking third and fourth), no serious behavior problems, and superior attendance records. The critical components of the reform, now disseminated to fourteen other sites, include a school planning and management

team (composed of the principal, parents, and teachers), a mental health team that provides coordinated services to children in conflict, and extensive parent involvement.

14. Henry Levin is the director of the very successful Accelerated Schools Project in the San Francisco Bay Area, whose mission is "bringing children into the educational mainstream so that they can fully benefit from future schooling and their adult opportunities" (1988, p. 3).

15. Levin (1988) argued that the major reason for the failure of many disadvantaged children is low teacher expectation, which in turn leads to pull-out programs based on tedious drill-and-practice curricula. Peterson (1989) conducted a study in Utah, concluding that ability grouping is harmful to remedial students, and that participation in accelerated programs is a more effective route to higher achievement.

REFERENCES

Comer, J. (1988). *Maggie's American dream*. New York: New American Library.

Comer, J. (1980). *School power*. New York: Free Press.

Delpit, L. (1986). Skills and other dilemmas of a progressive Black educator. *Harvard Educational Review, 56*, 379–385.

Dubinsky, E. (1987). *How Piaget's and related work should influence K–12 curriculum design*. Unpublished manuscript.

Fordham, S. (1988). Racelessness as a factor in Black students' school success: Pragmatic strategy or Pyrrhic victory? *Harvard Educational Review, 58*, 54–84.

Henderson, A. (1987). *The evidence continues to grow: Parent involvement improves student achievement*. Columbia, MD: National Committee for Citizens in Education.

Levin, H. (1988). Don't remediate: Accelerate. In *Proceedings of the Stanford University Centennial Conference, Accelerating the Education of At-Risk Students*. Stanford, CA: Stanford University, Center for Educational Research.

National Science Foundation. (1989). *Materials for middle school mathematics instruction*. Catalog of Federal Domestic Assistance No. 47.067, Materials Development, Research, and Informal Science Education.

Peterson, J. (1989). Remediation is no remedy. *Educational Leadership, 46*(6), 24–25.

Quine, W. V. (1981). *Theories and things*. Cambridge, MA: Harvard University Press.

Saxon, J. H., Jr. (1982). *Algebra I: An incremental development*. Norman, OK: Saxon.

Schorr, L. (1988). *Within our reach: Breaking the cycle of disadvantage*. New York: Anchor Press/Doubleday.

Usiskin, Z. (1987). Why elementary algebra can, should, and must be an eighth-grade course for average students. *Mathematics Teacher, 80*, 428–437.

The authors wish to thank the following people for their contributions to this article: Theresa Perry, Daniel Cheever, Barney Brawer, Ceasar McDowell, and, finally, the teachers and administrators of the Open Program of the Martin Luther King, Jr., School.

The Reading Campaign Experience within Palestinian Society: Innovative Strategies for Learning and Building Community

MUNIR JAMIL FASHEH

Many societies, especially those within what is usually referred to as the Third World, are increasingly facing conditions that are dismantling the social, economic, cultural, educational, spiritual, and psychological fabrics that have been crucial to their survival for centuries. These conditions are due both to factors that are external to a society — such as the influence of multinational corporations or coups imposed by outside governments — and to factors that are internal to a society — such as members' perceptions or internal conflicts among groups. In addition to such dismantlement, most Third World societies live with problems stemming from dependency. The role of cultural hegemony in producing this dependency of the Third World on the Western World is tremendous (Freire, 1970).[1]

Palestinian society, which faces many of these internal and external conditions, has had to deal with still another factor: Israeli occupation. Since 1967, Israel has confiscated much of the land in the West Bank and over one-third of the Gaza Strip (Aronson, 1994).[2] In addition to land, the occupation authorities control the region's water and raw materials. Economic markets, formal education, and official media and information sources are also under Israeli control. Israeli-ordered closures of all Palestinian schools and universities, which in some cases lasted more than four consecutive years, including the period between 1987 and 1992, are one significant example of Israeli control and disruption of Palestinian life.

The effect of Israeli occupation on Palestinian education has been particularly drastic. A study conducted by the Tamer Institute for Community Education between 1990 and 1991 (Tamer Institute, 1991), which assessed fourth- and sixth-grade students' achievement in math and Arabic, indicated that the deterioration of Palestinian education has reached emergency proportions.[3] A more recent study (National Center for Educational Research and Development, Jordan, 1993) conducted by the Tamer Institute and UNICEF, which was part of a twenty-country comparative study involving eighth graders' achievement in science and mathematics, shows that West Bank students ranked last in academic achievement among all students studied. These studies were conducted after schools had been

Harvard Educational Review Vol. 65 No. 1 Spring 1995, 66–92

closed by the Israelis for two years; during those two years, all students were promoted to the next grades, as if they had attended school.

Even when Palestinian schools are open, the methods of teaching used and the facilities available are deficient and obsolete, and have deteriorated since the Israeli occupation. By 1976, for example, there was no longer a single librarian or lab technician in government (public) schools in the West Bank (which had been run by Jordan before 1967 and by Israeli military authorities since 1967). Since 1978, all training courses and workshops for government school teachers have ceased to exist.[4] During the occupation, lists of Israeli banned books have continued to expand. Today's curriculum and textbooks continue to be alien and dry and to ignore the voices and experiences of the learners and teachers, and the context in which they live (see, for example, Fasheh, 1990, and Mahshi and Bush, 1989).

The amount of time and energy required to deal with the underlying problems of cultural dependency and societal dismantlement undermines Palestinians' ability to deal with other challenges, including the increasing needs and demands of educating children and youth. Dependency is visible in the way that Palestinian cultural products are being supplanted by imported children's characters, such as Walt Disney characters or the Ninja Turtles, and by foreign television programs, magazines, and formal education. These objects and images substitute for real learning and authentic forms of education, and play an enormous role in daily Palestinian life.

Dismantlement and dependency tend to cultivate a society's acceptance of superficial or symbolic improvements. In my thirty years of experience in various Palestinian educational settings, I have often seen superficial and symbolic improvement that disguises real deterioration underneath: Palestinian students acquire diplomas but no learning abilities; they learn textbook theories but not the ability to construct their own explanations of experiences and phenomena.[5] Schools encourage ready-made solutions and discourage experimentation and innovative ideas. Palestinians build universities that lack good libraries and that impede students' development of the abilities to express, organize, and produce knowledge; and they build structures and organizations that lack community bonding and community spirit. Enacting visible, but often merely symbolic, improvement without deeper and longer lasting change deceives people and blinds them from seeing the opportunities that are being lost, as well as what could and should be done instead. Palestinians need to create alternatives in their minds and in their practice to deal with current challenges and the increasing demands on formal education.

I am convinced that, although many of the problems Palestinians face are caused by outside factors, the solution can only come from within. Blaming outside forces alone will not take us very far, just as merely blaming germs for our sickness will not cure us: we must instead make our bodies immune. Thus, strengthening our bodies, our collective, and our spirit — that is, building the internal strength of individuals, of institutions, and of the community — should be the strategic and pivotal theme of our thinking and our actions.

The challenge to Palestinians is to develop the means and strategies that foster our survival and continued growth as individuals, as institutions, and as a community. Such strategies must be innovative, effective, relatively simple and inexpensive, easily replicable, and able to be implemented with available resources. Like all other societies, the Palestinians' primary resource, which cannot ever be taken away, is the human resource. Our people are our hope for survival and development. Developing this treasure should be the main concern and focus of our thought and action. The foundation for developing this resource — the human treasure — lies in community building. And the foundation of community building lies in community education.

The recent reading campaign of the Tamer Institute is an instructive and inspiring example of community education that embodies many aspects mentioned above. Palestinians' most important need, from the Institute's perspective, is to acquire the means to learn, communicate, and produce culturally, maintaining the vitality of Palestinian society through the creation of books, stories, plays, literature, theories, and perspectives. Before I describe the campaign, however, I would like to explain briefly what I mean by community, community building, and community education.

ON COMMUNITY, COMMUNITY BUILDING, AND COMMUNITY EDUCATION

When I talk about community building, I do not mean that currently there is no Palestinian community and that we have to build one. We do have a community; the challenge we face is, rather, how to ensure its continuity and growth — not only as individuals or as ethnic or separate groups, but as a community.

One can best understand community and community building through experiencing them and reflecting on these experiences. Like most Palestinians, my personal experience of community started at home. When I was growing up, I was deprived of many material things, including having a house, which was taken from my family by the Israelis in 1948 when I was seven years old. As a result, I was also deprived of a bed of my own for several years (we were two families living in one room). I was often deprived of enough food and sometimes even of water, which had to be rationed. I was deprived of toys and other things that children usually have at that age. But I never felt deprived of the warm, sincere, and loving feelings of the "small community" of my family at home. This was the basis of my developing a sense of community and of my ability later to facilitate building community spirit in other settings: among teachers with whom I worked as the head supervisor of math instruction in the West Bank in the 1970s; among people of various ages with whom I worked when I created the voluntary community work movement in the West Bank in the early 1970s (Fasheh, 1988); among students when I was Dean of Students at Birzeit University in the 1980s; and among my colleagues in the various places in which I have worked.

All these experiences of community were deep and far-reaching, but no doubt the peak of community feeling at a national level was the one I experienced during the first two years of the *intifada* in 1988–1989. The intifada, which means "shaking off the dirt" in Arabic, came about through a collective reaction within the Palestinian community in the West Bank and Gaza Strip to the total absurdity of the Israeli occupation. It arose not out of a plan, but because the situation became so unbearable that people, as a community, just decided to take action to end the occupation, or die.[6]

What was common to my experiences in these communities was that they were powerful and unforgettable, with a sense of meaning and purpose. There was no attempt to wipe out differences; instead, in relation to certain issues such as common goals and actions, individual differences within these communities were transcended. In other instances, differences were a source of argument, struggle, and growth. Also common to my various experiences of community was my sense of safety: I was accepted by members of the community and was able to express my ideas and feelings. Mistakes were not considered personal traits but a natural part of growth — and I was learning and growing. I felt that communication was possible and sincere. I felt that the value of mutual support was part of the group's thinking and behavior. And, last but not least, my experiences of community included a decisionmaking process that I find superior to the often-acclaimed democratic process (which in practice often boils down to casting votes). In fact, we resorted to the democratic process only in instances where communication at a more human and profound level was not possible. In other words, we voted when we were at a low point in our ability to communicate with and relate to one another.

Community Building

Community building takes place at both "visible" and "invisible" levels. Such activities as building physical institutions and social organizations and bringing in technology are manifestations of community building at the visible level. Building at this level, however, is short-lived if it is not accompanied by building at the invisible level — that is, at the human level and at the institutional development level. Through my twenty-three years of involvement in community education, I have come to think of community building at the invisible level as taking place through five sublevels:

1. developing the ability to express personal experiences and observed phenomena
2. developing the ability to redefine terms and concepts, to explain experiences and phenomena, and to see "wholes" (i.e., to construct one's own knowledge)
3. developing the ability to generate, acquire, and manage information
4. building social formations (such as small groups or teams) and forms of communication that are effective in solving problems and addressing needs
5. building at the spiritual and value-development level as part of building a common vision

Since these sublevels are obviously connected to language (expression), thought, social organization, and values, the centrality of culture and cultural production in community building is both obvious and crucial.

Building through institutional development encompasses all five sublevels. Institutional development refers to developing an environment within an institution that is conducive to learning, commitment, and taking initiative. Institutional development also includes the development of participants' internal ability to deal with interpersonal problems, with feelings of self-defensiveness, with values of winning and control, and so on. Developing an institution's environment and individuals' capacities are what I mean by community building at the invisible level.

An integral part of community building at the invisible level is what I call "cultural products," which may take the form of articles, books, drawings, songs, or plays; ideas, methodologies, or theories; reading clubs or discussion groups; the development of libraries; or the development of illustrators and youth leaders. Such products can serve as a source of economic return and can also inspire feelings of self-worth, both at the individual and national levels.

The relevance and quality of any society's cultural products characterize the value of that society and insure its viability and continuity. A culture that hopes to survive on what it produced in the past is like a person who hopes to survive on what he or she ate in the past: such reliance is not possible. To survive and develop, a community or group must constantly produce culturally.

Fortunately, most of the basic ingredients that we Palestinians need to build and develop our community exist: a common language, common history and culture, common land, common needs and realities, and a common destiny. At the same time, we also have ingredients that complement our commonalities, such as diversity and exposure to other cultures. However, a crucial ingredient that is missing from Palestinian society (and perhaps many others as well) — one that is absolutely essential to community building — is learning, or, better stated, acquiring the means to learn, communicate, build, and produce. Neglecting this element in the face of current challenges will have disastrous consequences for the Palestinian community in the future.

Acquiring the means to learn is a much more basic need than acquiring ready-made knowledge and technical know-how. The first belongs to the invisible level, the second to the visible level. In other words, acquiring the means to learn is more important and more fundamental than acquiring the right to an education. For example, if people have the *right* to express themselves, that does not necessarily mean that they have the *ability* to do so. But, people with the *ability* to express themselves will find a way to communicate their ideas. The "means to learn" refers to the abilities that I mentioned earlier in relation to community building at the five sublevels. Expressing personal experiences, debating them with others in small groups, and, as a result, building together new understandings and explanations, having access to information, and building new bonds and vision among people that transcend self-interests are, I believe, the main means to help people learn. Usually, however, these means are neglected because they are less visible than those skills traditionally taught in schools and require more time, patience, effort, and creativity, as well as a different perception and a different set of skills.

Recent developments indicate that many Palestinians are again falling into the trap of making improvements at the visible, superficial level while ignoring crucial needs at a deeper and more fundamental level. This situation had occurred in the late 1970s, when money poured in from various Arab governments and international aid agencies and university facilities were constructed, leading people to believe that physical structures were all that were needed to build a university. In my opinion, the creation of the United Nations Relief and Works Agency (UNRWA) in 1952 to "help" Palestinians has contributed, among other things, to Palestinians' expectations that they will receive provisions without having to make any effort themselves. Programs of relief under certain circumstances are needed, but attempts must be made to ensure that these programs do not create a dependency relationship on the donors and do not rob recipients of their self-worth and their ability to meet their own needs.

Currently in education, remedial and compensatory work for students and condensed training courses leading to a degree for teachers are the main strategies to improve education in the West Bank. These improvements, while helpful, are not enough to address the needs of Palestinian children and youth. Students' lack of opportunity to acquire the habit of reading, the skill of personal writing, and the value of good books, for example, still needs to be addressed. These are part of what I referred to earlier as access to information and the value of information — that is, *the means to learn.*

It is difficult to tell how developments in the current Middle East peace talks will affect Palestinian youth and children, but my guess is that such developments will increase their feelings of frustration and helplessness. I worry that these developments will open the doors for youth to become increasingly enveloped by materialistic values, despite a continued lack of means, and to pursue the values of individual gain and profit at the expense of the common good, community needs, and asserting and creating alternatives.

Innovative solutions are needed. The Tamer Institute reading campaign is one attempt to deal with current issues, not only in terms of stopping the deterioration of formal education, but also in terms of contributing to what I have referred to as community building.

COMMUNITY EDUCATION

The foundation for community building lies in community education, which cannot take place without community action. Often, a problem or an event focuses people's collective energies on solving a problem or changing a situation. The most significant characteristic of community education is linking expression to thought and action with the aim of building a viable community.

Let me use an example from the Tamer Institute's reading campaign to illustrate the connections among expression, thought, and action in community building. The voluntary youth groups within the reading campaign focus their energies on encouraging people to read, especially through visits to places like schools, homes for the elderly, and mosques. Part of their "job" is to record and articulate their experiences and ideas, debate their ideas and understandings, and decide about actions and carry them out. Thus, connectedness between language, thinking, and practice is an integral part of the group's function and work. This linkage takes place in small groups whose aim is to contribute to the building of a viable community.

Community education as we conceive and practice it at the Tamer Institute is based on the following convictions:

• Language is connected to thought and action, with the aim of building a viable community;
• Acquiring the means to learn is more important than acquiring ready-made, prepackaged knowledge;
• Going through processes, not acquiring products, is what develops human resources;

- Creativity and innovation are at least as important as material resources in building a viable community;
- The experience of every individual, without exception, is valuable. There is no person who does not (usually unconsciously) try to understand his or her own experiences and surrounding events. These attempts are the foundation of real diversity in any community and the basis of real learning. From these premises about the importance of honoring each person's experience stems my conviction that the biggest enemies of any community and of learning in general are a dichotomous, either-or orientation in thinking and a single-answer approach in teaching;
- No community development or community building can occur without the gradual emergence of a discourse and a social momentum around community issues and action;
- Youth and women are the two most important actors in community building, at least in our experience at the Tamer Institute. Although there are barriers for women due to their position in Palestinian society, in terms of community building (and the reading campaign in particular), I believe that women are better equipped to participate than men. Women's sense of community is ingrained in their experience and upbringing. Women, for example, usually do not think only of themselves when they want to do something, but also consider how their action affects their children, their family, and others. Furthermore, women have significant influence on the upbringing of children, and women's and youth's relative marginalization by dominant ideologies makes them more willing to accept change and to build differently. In my experience, expression, small groups, and cultural production do not form a threat to dominant groups, such as men. Thus, members of dominant groups have not interfered in the reading campaign so far.

The Tamer Institute's reading campaign is a program in community education at a national level that addresses many convictions and needs mentioned above. The remainder of this article describes how the campaign embodies these aspects of community building.

THE READING CAMPAIGN WITHIN PALESTINIAN SOCIETY

Circumstances that seem hopelessly bad could, in reality, be a signal or an opportunity for real hope and real change. Going through a crisis seems to me to be the most crucial factor in changing convictions and patterns of thinking and behaving, not only in Palestinian society, but in any society. For such change to happen, however, people must be ready to learn and be ready to build on their learning and on the resources of their community. Innovative ideas and an experimental spirit are usually harder to accept when existing conditions seem to be functional. People experiencing a crisis or living under seemingly hopeless conditions are usually more open and receptive to ways that would be considered radical, alien, or impractical under normal conditions.

Our experience with the reading campaign confirms this observation. The campaign was launched at a time when conditions in the West Bank and the Gaza Strip seemed desperately bad and constantly deteriorating. People's response, enthusiasm, and readiness to join in the campaign's activities by far exceeded our expectations.

Over the years, the habit of reading has not been actively encouraged within Palestinian society. Moreover, the tradition of evening meetings, where relatives and neighbors met and talked about daily events and personal experiences (and which were a main vehicle of learning when I was growing up), has completely given way to the domination of TV and video since the late 1970s. The situation within Palestinian society is similar to that in many other societies, where people have become passive, sitting in front of a distorting and paralyzing screen, swallowing sound and picture. Under these conditions, reading is the only hope to obtain relevant information that is usually suppressed or ignored in schools and official media. Reading remains the central means for students to acquire necessary skills, such as those related to language acquisition and expression, and thus increase their chances to obtain education and succeed in schooling if they so choose. Reading and the resulting personal growth will continue to form the foundation for self-learning and meaningful understanding.

February 13, 1992, marked the launch of the reading campaign, following more than eight months of discussion and preparation. Discussions involving teachers, educators, professionals, and grassroots practitioners (such as those working with women's committees and health groups) focused on the worsening condition of Palestinian education and on the feasibility of using a reading campaign to address unmet needs. The general feeling at the beginning was that although the ideas behind the campaign were important and timely, the campaign itself would be difficult to implement. Many participants were doubtful and asked how we were going to encourage and convince people to read. We started thinking of ways that would take us away from the traditional "preaching" methods and closer to what would be appealing, especially to children. We had to think of ways to fight the negative attitudes toward reading developed in schools, where reading, in general, is seen as a duty or a chore. We knew we had to make the campaign "fun" so that it would not just admonish people — "You must read: it is for your own good" — but would actively involve them in their own learning. We decided to focus on the theme of "traveling through reading," for which we designed a "passport to reading."

The other "fun" aspect of the campaign is its main character, Nakhleh ash-Shiber, a stage character who goes on tours, performing and engaging children in all kinds of activities at schools and other centers. Nakhleh appears on the campaign logo saying, "I READ," thus modeling the behavior rather than using the preaching form: "You should read."

The reading campaign is an all-encompassing activity that goes beyond teaching the technical skill of reading to integrate, in a dynamic and complementary way, a variety of projects that make the campaign special. In addition to the passport and the Nakhleh character, the reading campaign includes several activities: producing materials and books; encouraging children and youth to express themselves through writing, acting, and — more recently — the use of puppets; starting or developing libraries; and encouraging and establishing volunteer groups (among both adults and youth) to help in various campaign activities.

On the day the campaign was launched, activities took place in some schools, public libraries, and other social institutions and community centers in areas of the West Bank and the Gaza Strip.[7] The distribution of passports began on that day. We encouraged interested groups and individuals to participate in the campaign in a manner most adaptable to their means and interests. In one area, for example, a group of people organized a book fair open to all; in another area, Nakhleh ash-Shiber gave a performance; and in others, adult volunteers assisted by taking participants to the local library or to buy a book at a local bookstore. Our emphasis was on getting local groups to initiate whatever they could, or found appropriate, or wished to do in their own localities. We communicated the importance of local initiatives through personal contact with schools, libraries, and interested individuals, as well as via two special pages in the local newspaper supervised by the Tamer Institute.

The "Passport to Reading"

For a people who for decades have been consistently denied an identity and a sense of belonging, who have been forced to live with increasing restrictions on movement and travel, and who have been facing an increasing fragmentation of their society, the passport to reading has been a very appealing idea. It meets the psychological and educational needs of both children and adults. Within the first year, a total of almost 80,000 passports were acquired by people from different regions and of various age groups, though mainly by children between the ages of seven and thirteen. That the campaign has been successful under Palestine's extreme conditions does not mean, however, that the idea would not appeal to children living under different, more normal, conditions.

Altogether, seven different-colored passports exist. The first passport has twelve "visas," with each visa representing the reading of one book. After children finish a book, they receive a "visa stamp" in their passport from an appropriate "authority" like a librarian, a teacher, a person working in a community organization, or a parent. The visa stamps these volunteer authorities use are usually those that belong to their respective institutions or organizations, and sometimes the stamp is just as simple as a parent's or teacher's signature. Before stamping the passport, however, the authority asks the child questions about the book. The purpose of such questions is not to test children but, rather, to expand their horizons. A typical question might be: "If you were to finish the story you have just read, how would you finish it?" Some authorities choose other requirements for stamping passports, such as asking the child to summarize the book in one or two written pages.

Each successive passport requires three more visas than the preceding one for completion, so that after children finish all seven, they will have read 147 books. At that point, the passport holder will become eligible to be a member of a Nakhleh ash-Shiber reading club, which we are encouraging schools, public libraries, and various community organizations to establish. These reading clubs are not only concerned with reading, but also with writing and with "discovery" (nature) trips within the nearby environment. By the summer of 1994, several such reading clubs had formed throughout the West Bank, involving mainly children under age twelve. Sometimes, several clubs meet together in order to exchange ideas and experiences or to plan activities.

One important aspect of the campaign is the fact that each passport costs about 42 U.S. cents. Two-thirds of the proceeds stay in the school or location where the passports are sold, to be used for buying books or improving the local library. In this way, any financial support gained from passports is distributed widely in the community and in relation to the effort exerted by that community. This practice allows the children to feel that they are supporting their school or local library, because they are told how their contributions will be used.

The passports have been educational in raising children's awareness of the conditions under which they live. One question young children often asked, especially at the beginning of the campaign and especially in the Gaza Strip, was whether they could use the passports to travel: the severe restrictions on travel imposed by Israel on the Palestinians makes traveling — even to Jerusalem — an unattainable dream for most Palestinian children. Sometimes we discuss with children how, under conditions of political oppression, "passports to reading" can provide a cultural sense of belonging and a means for youth to travel through the books they read.

"Nakhleh ash-Shiber": The Children's Character

I believe that two basic needs of almost all children are the need to express themselves freely and the need for role models, both real and cultural. One of the main themes of the Tamer Institute is encouraging expression in various forms. We feel that theatrical expression should become an integral part of education, both in and out of schools. Children find in the most basic form of theater — that of playing a role or a character — an outlet for their ideas, feelings, fears, hopes, and expectations. For example, children often impersonate the adults around them, create their own plays, and choose the street or yard as their setting; they don't need to dress up or rehearse, nor do they require a stage or an audience. Even when children write, the most common form, in our experience, is dialogue with some narrative in between.

Nakhleh ash-Shiber, the central character of the campaign, is a Palestinian comic stage character created by two Palestinian actors in 1986. Because Nakhleh usually performed in school settings, the closing of Palestinian schools by Israel in December 1987 made it impossible for his performances to continue, and he stopped performing in early 1988. In 1989, a group of Palestinian educators, artists, and writers became interested in developing this theater persona into a special Palestinian character, mainly for children, who would be able to say simply and spontaneously what parents, teachers, and politicians usually mystify. Using his own words, Nakhleh is a "nonperson" in that he represents every person through his voicing of communal concerns. He is in contradiction first and foremost with himself. His name — the first contradiction in his life — literally means in Arabic "palm tree span of the palm," a combination of a palm tree (a tall object) and "the palm of the hand" (a short object). He makes children laugh and clap and sing under conditions that otherwise reflect suffering, death, sadness, anger, and lack of hope. He challenges normality per se and does it naturally and spontaneously through the questions he asks. He raises issues that no one else dares raise, such as questions related to political matters or to conventional ways of raising children. He is a deeply moral person, with an intense love for life and children, and he is so human that he provokes us to see our hypocrisies.

During the first two years of the campaign, Nakhleh performed more than 250 times in various places around the country. Performances took place in schools,

The campaign poster, depicting Nakhleh ash-Shiber and a tent home transformed by books and reading into a happier place where children can learn and play.

community centers, centers for children with special needs, and religious institutions. Performances in refugee camps were done in cooperation with UNRWA. The children's reaction, especially in the Gaza Strip, was overwhelming: they would often welcome the character with cheers and singing as he approached the place of performance. Although we usually allow a maximum of eighty children at any single performance, in some places it is hard to control the situation, and the number reaches three to four hundred. The actor portraying Nakhleh is a master on the drums. When he uses them in his performances, children start clapping and singing, and sometimes even dancing. Nakhleh also invites children to tell stories or jokes and recite poetry. Children seem to find all these ways of expressing themselves invigorating; they sometimes get so excited and loud that the performance must be interrupted.

In addition to promoting Nakhleh on stage, the Tamer Institute is trying to promote the character in other media, such as cartoon strips, educational materials, and videotapes. Soon after launching the reading campaign, a special weekly page for youth carrying Nakhleh ash-Shiber's name was created in the most widely read Palestinian daily, *al-Quds*. This page facilitates interaction among youth and also serves as a forum for their ideas, feelings, experiences, fancies, and expressions.

More recently, the Tamer Institute rented a small place in Jerusalem where Nakhleh started working with children, as well as with preschool and elementary teachers, in puppet-making and the use of puppets as tools for education and self-expression. These techniques can be used in various settings, including schools, summer camps, and youth centers.

Creative Writing Activities

The special weekly page in *al-Quds* newspaper, which first came out on April 2, 1992, welcomes contributions from youth, such as fiction, stories, dreams, and poems, and discussions of issues ranging from early marriage to their worries, fears, and hopes for the future. In April 1994, the Tamer Institute published a book that contains about seventy of these youths' contributions to the newspaper page. Over the past couple of years, we have also contacted a number of youth who have shown potential as writers to form a core group of young writers to help in supervising and developing the page, and who we hope will be editors of a magazine for and by youth in the future.

In addition to the newspaper page, writing workshops are being conducted in various settings. Four such workshops are worth mentioning: the first involves Palestinian women writers; the second involves female university students; the third is for girls between nine and sixteen years of age in summer camps; and the fourth aims at producing a handbook on the "writing process" to be used by teachers of Arabic in elementary classes.[8]

Writing as a vehicle for personal and communal expression is an important aspect not only of education, but of life itself. This is especially true in the context of the *intifada* and the particular Palestinian experience, where the neglect of self-expression, especially in the form of writing, is so serious. As long as the Palestinians and other marginalized people do not find the means by which to inscribe themselves and their presence in the records of history, they will remain an easy target for marginalization and distortion. Children and youth, who represent a sizable segment of the Palestinian population, have been going through disturbing

During Nakhleh's performances, children are invited to laugh, clap, and sing, or to relate stories, jokes, and poems.

and powerful experiences, which at times cause high levels of anger and frustration, yet they are without any outlet for their emotions.

Expressing one's own experiences and getting involved in community programs such as the reading campaign are healthy and constructive ways of dealing with the problem of oppression. They provide a means for youth to gain a voice and feelings of self-worth and to make sense of what otherwise seems to be a brutal and senseless world around them. In the context of the current Middle East peace talks, this crucial segment of the population must not be neglected; the future of the region will depend, significantly, on how youth perceive themselves and the world around them.

Development of Volunteer Groups

Eleven regional reading campaign volunteer committees have been instrumental in spreading the word about the campaign, in distributing passports and other materials, and in advising the Tamer Institute.[9] Volunteers are both adults and youth. Despite harsh restrictions on travel imposed by Israeli authorities, attempts to establish volunteer groups continue and, in fact, gain more importance and urgency.[10]

Although the role of adults is crucial in coordinating campaign activities in their respective regions, and sometimes in supervising youth activities, special effort has been made to involve students, mainly those between ages thirteen and sixteen and university students, in reading campaign activities. By the summer of 1994, youth groups were active in five regions. A sixth group, based in Gaza, could not continue its meetings and activities due to the conditions in that area. These

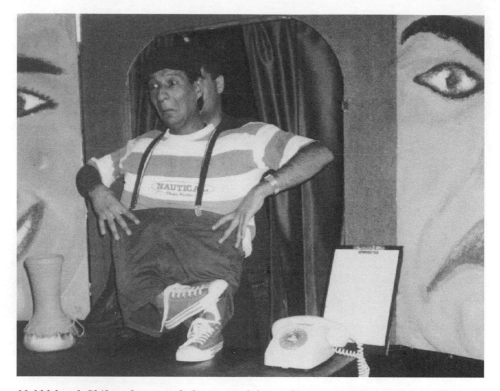

Nakhleh ash-Shiber, the central character of the reading campaign, challenges "normality" through the questions he asks.

youth groups, referred to as "Palm Groups," are formed at the initiative of people in each region.

The Institute's function is primarily to publish and distribute whatever we receive from the various groups about their activities, ideas, and experiences; to help establish bylaws and other organizational matters concerning the functioning of the groups; and to issue membership cards for volunteers. The Institute also conducts training workshops for youth and organizes activities that will bring youth from various regions together.

What stands out clearly and powerfully in our experience with youth volunteer groups is that through such small groups, rather than through grand, "national" designs and plans, individual and community development can be combined. Individuals develop themselves by learning how to discuss issues and reach decisions within meetings, choose a leader for their group, keep records, and follow up on group decisions. It is through small groups that work within a larger network and with a common purpose and vision that individuals and communities are transformed. In the case of the reading campaign, transformation (in terms of their abilities to express, organize, act, and acquire access to information) takes place through youths' helping conduct activities, including Nakhleh's performances; distributing materials; and propagating the importance of reading, writing, and community action. I have found that the foundation for building a viable community lies in this combination of personal growth and community development.

For example, the Jerusalem group has been coordinating their work with an elderly group. They visit elderly people in their private homes or in homes for the elderly and read to them. They also encourage older people who have good reading skills and an engaging reading style to visit schools and read stories to the children. For Mother's Day in March 1993, the group adapted a story on motherhood, which was written by an elderly woman, for the stage. Travel restrictions, however, made the preparation and performance impossible; thus the performance had to be postponed.

The volunteers' enthusiasm naturally differs from one person to another and from one location to another. One impression that was confirmed through our experience, however, is that youth are, in general, "practical idealists." They are eager to translate their hopes and ideals into reality. Under appropriate conditions, youth are natural "doers," volunteers, and creators. Having meaning in their lives and feeling a sense of belonging seem to drive them to act. The types of actions youth take, however, depend to a large extent on the prevalent values and surrounding conditions. As a young volunteer commented: "Since I joined the reading campaign as a volunteer, I feel like I have gained a new and big family." Another volunteer said: "Since I joined the group, I have discovered new things in me which I did not know before. I discovered that I can present my ideas clearly in meetings." A third said: "When I started coming to the meetings, at first I enjoyed them. But when we started visiting some schools and libraries and got negative responses, I wanted to leave. But then I looked at the notebook where we recorded what we have done, I was amazed at how much was done and I decided to stay."

The father of one volunteer was not happy with all the time his daughter was putting into the campaign and the fact that the meetings included both boys and girls, and so he decided to attend a meeting. After the meeting, members of the staff had a constructive discussion with this father — a discussion that convinced us of the need to produce a pamphlet for parents explaining the function of the volunteer program within the campaign.

The development of volunteer groups around the country is an integral part of the reading campaign, and we view youth as the backbone of the volunteer corps. We are convinced that without them, the campaign will not grow or last. These volunteer groups are crucial in building a social base for meeting other basic needs (such as the skills related to societal organization, including debating issues, holding each other accountable, and taking collective actions) in the community, both now and in the future. Through the Institute's various youth projects, we hope to contribute to the development of a genuine and constructive Palestinian youth culture.

Production of Materials and Books

Some materials for the campaign were produced centrally by Tamer Institute in order to ensure that the quality and the message were consistent in all parts of the country. Almost all campaign materials carry the campaign logo with Nakhleh declaring, "I READ," the campaign slogan. We also encourage regional groups and institutions to produce additional materials as they deem necessary. Campaign materials prepared by Tamer Institute include:

- a general brochure explaining (in Nakhleh's questioning style) the campaign
- a poster portraying reading as being fun
- passports to reading
- a story about reading and about books for children who are beginning to read
- posters for the "Special Reading Weeks," commemorating the first and second anniversaries of the campaign

One problem we faced from the outset was the lack of good books written in Arabic, especially for children. In general, libraries — where they exist — are poorly stocked and contain books that are old and falling apart. It was obvious that in this case we needed to work at the "visible level" in the short term, importing books from Arab countries, and at the "invisible level" in the long-term, producing local books and magazines. One group whose work we found complemented our own in this area is the Arab Resource Collective located in Lebanon and Cyprus. Part of their work is to translate and adapt reading materials, especially those geared to children and mainly related to health, such as David Werner's books and the Child-to-Child series that are produced at the Institute of Education, University of London.[11] In fact, Tamer Institute helped in translating and adapting some of the pamphlets in the Child-to-Child series, which includes eight story books for children ages six to nine. These books were popular with the young children in the campaign.

Writing, publishing, and importing and exporting books are activities that should accompany any successful reading campaign. Our experience since launching the campaign was so encouraging that we began to consider establishing a publishing house. We wanted to concentrate on publishing materials that are of excellent quality, both in form and in content, and that reflect people's personal experiences or creative activities. The first phase of establishing such a house began in January 1993. By the summer of 1994, three new books had been published, and three others were in their final stages.[12]

Other Activities and Materials Related to the Reading Campaign

Individuals, organizations, and businesses in the community have initiated the development of other types of activities and materials, and their initiative has been a welcome surprise. Examples of these other materials include audiovisual aids, toys, and games. One project that arose unexpectedly from the community was a set of poems, on the theme of reading and books, composed by a Palestinian lawyer from the town of Jenin on the West Bank. We published some of the poems in the special section of *al-Quds*. Sabreen, a Palestinian musical group, liked the poems and composed music for some of them. Booklets of the poems will be published by the Tamer Institute and will be distributed along with a cassette of the songs. An ice cream maker in the West Bank asked for permission to use the logo of the reading campaign on his ice cream cones, which he began doing in the summer of 1992. Other companies, especially on the first anniversary of the campaign, produced materials such as hats, rulers, pens, and key holders carrying the logo of the reading campaign. Altogether, about 10,000 items were produced and distributed during the special reading week in February 1993.

Starting and Developing Libraries

Local libraries and school libraries, in the relatively few places they exist, are poor, not only in books but also in the activities they offer. Most schools either lack libraries or have inactive ones. The school libraries that do exist are disorganized. Usually a teacher in the school is responsible for keeping records of the books checked out or in; usually the books fill only a cupboard in the teacher's room. Moreover, all libraries, including university libraries, regularly receive lists of banned books from Israeli authorities. These lists include thousands of books, mostly about Palestine and Islam, but also by such writers as Franz Kafka and Pablo Neruda.

The library subproject of the reading campaign has two objectives: to support local initiatives to create libraries and to develop and enrich existing libraries. Our efforts to fulfill these objectives have assumed different forms. We have established reading clubs and sought ways to add books to existing libraries (for example, local libraries keep two-thirds of the proceeds from passports in order to buy new books). We have tried to attract more readers to libraries through activities such as story-telling, writing workshops, or Nakhleh ash-Shiber's performances. More recently, we have provided a specialist on library science who can help in training and in organizing existing libraries.[13]

Thus far, success in starting new libraries or developing existing ones has depended to a large extent on the presence of enthusiastic and concerned teachers and parents. In several places, establishing a new library or activating an existing one was done in conjunction with establishing volunteer groups in the village. The pattern that seems to be successful in establishing such libraries and volunteer groups has been for a teacher or group of teachers to invite interested adults and students to a meeting with people from the Tamer Institute, and there to engage with them in a discussion concerning the reading campaign.

The following story of one teacher's efforts to develop a library is an inspiring example of many of the aspects of community building discussed in this article. An elementary school teacher from a poor, remote village called us at the Tamer Institute and expressed her enthusiasm about the campaign. She wanted to know how she could obtain books, or money to buy books, in order to start a small library in her school. I told her that every place has to initiate ways to carry this responsibility themselves. Her reply was, "Oh! That's a nice idea." I didn't know whether she was just being cordial and was really frustrated by my answer, or whether she really believed in what I said. About a month later, however, she called and, sounding happy, said, "Let me tell you what happened. I asked each student in the two classes I teach to try and save two to three New Israeli Shekels (about $1) and buy a book. Now we have seventy-seven books, and the children themselves are taking care of the borrowing process." She added, "Even my relationship with my students has improved."

This story is a small but powerful example of what I have tried to describe as community building. In this instance, the sense of community in the school has been enhanced through the class's response to creating a library. At least in the context of this small activity, the teacher has been able to move from being a knowledge-giver to a knowledge-facilitator. The activity allowed both teacher and students to gain a new sense of responsibility and respect for themselves and for one another. They were able to build their sense of self-confidence and self-worth because they were encouraged to do things by themselves using what they already had. Although their action of collectively organizing and running a library was small and local, it was also part of a larger national campaign that involved many others in the community. Finally, the activity added a way for the teacher and her students to increase their access to information and opened up the possibility of discussing and expressing their reactions to what they read and discuss. In many ways, then, this activity exemplifies community building at the invisible level through the social, spiritual, organizational, and psychological dimensions and, most importantly, through helping people acquire the means to learn. It is a concrete example of how the teacher and her students empowered themselves through their participation in the campaign.

Accomplishments of the First Year

The two newspaper weekly pages ("Educational Affairs" and "Nakhleh ash-Shiber") supervised by the Tamer Institute were the main means through which the Institute and teachers, students, librarians, and parents communicated about the reading campaign. These means were augmented by Institute members' visits to the various locations, by their direct communication with volunteer groups, and by people visiting the Institute. Questionnaires were also used to solicit information from people concerning the campaign and to evaluate its effectiveness. One such questionnaire was distributed in January 1993, almost a year after launching the campaign.[14] One method we used to obtain feedback was to visit the various locations and discuss the questions with coordinators while they completed the questionnaire, a procedure that built on Palestinians' cultural preference for oral communication. This process also produced more depth and details for us than we would have obtained from written responses alone.

The information gained from the questionnaires was beneficial to the local coordinators, as well as to us, in terms of clarifying aspects of the campaign and exploring new ways of encouraging activities and communicating with people in the future. Most of the adults who were active in the campaign were teachers and librarians, and the campaign was most widely accepted among children between six and sixteen years of age. At the local level, most activities were centered around reading stories, holding contests, displaying book exhibits, discussing how to use libraries, and scheduling performances by Nakhleh. Increases in the number of library users occurred in several places, especially in elementary schools for girls.

There was widespread agreement among respondents that the passport was a good idea for motivating children to read, as well as for addressing other needs of children. In fact, the only objection to both the passport and the Nakhleh character came from some educators in education departments within Palestinian universities! Their objections centered around their claim that the character is not serious enough, that he does not have a clear message, and that the passport starts with his name rather than with the name of a political person. The reason for their objections could lie in the fact that such activities undermine the concept and the practice of control that usually accompany dominant perceptions of education (see, for example, Freire, 1985, and Argyris, 1982).

A common complaint from people in various locations was the fact that the Tamer Institute was almost always late in providing passports to those who requested them and that this affected children's enthusiasm.[15] Some other complaints, however, such as those related to expectations that the Tamer Institute would give money or donate books, reflect a dangerous tendency I have noticed over the past few decades in which many Palestinians (perhaps like many others in the Third World) expect things to be both immediately available and free.

Both the campaign brochure and the sticker were popular, but we were criticized often for not using the Palestinian headdress for Nakhleh ash-Shiber. Our response was, first, that we wanted to be true to the character as it was created on stage by the two Palestinian actors and, second, that Palestinians have for so long stressed symbolism over reality that it is time for somebody, like Nakhleh, to reverse priorities and put what is real first. In our opinion, what is real here are the Palestinian people, the land, and daily aspects of life. One symbol, which was used in the poster to represent the Palestinian experience, was a drawing of a book in the form of a tent. A tent is a powerful image, because many Palestinians have been violently expelled from their homes in the years since 1948. This time, however, the "tent" is inhabited by happy and active children, rather than by people expelled from their homes.

One can also measure the success of the campaign by people's enthusiasm for their local community actions and initiatives. Some of these have been mentioned above; other examples include contributions from individuals and businesses. For example, one successful businessman, who saw his nine-year-old daughter read for the first time, contributed the amount needed to produce passports for all the students in his daughter's school. We felt that the enthusiastic response to the campaign was also evident in an initiative by the French Cultural Centers in Gaza and in Jerusalem, which asked permission to produce a similar "passport to reading" in both Arabic and French to use in their centers. In addition, the Swedish International Development Authority (SIDA) invited us to participate and make a presentation about the reading campaign at the International Book and Library Fair in Gottenburg in October 1994.

The campaign also attracted the attention and financial support of international bodies, as well as Palestinian groups in the United States, such as the Jerusalem Fund and United Palestinian Appeal.[16] Arabs in some Arab countries, especially Jordan, Lebanon, and Yemen, also were enthusiastic and inspired by our efforts. In Jordan, for example, the association of librarians decided to adopt the passport idea, as did groups such as the United Nations and international aid organizations working in Palestinian refugee camps in South Lebanon. Yemeni groups working with children extended an open invitation for people at the Tamer Institute to visit Yemen and talk to various groups about the campaign.

Another sign of enthusiasm for the campaign is reflected in the fact that other groups in the West Bank are starting campaigns in their own areas of work or interest. For example, the Early Childhood Resource Center in Jerusalem started a campaign addressing the rights and needs of young children. A second group, the Association of Arab Hotels and Travel Agencies in Jerusalem, working in cooperation with a Palestinian nonprofit organization, the Economic Development Group, started a campaign to encourage internal tourism, especially among school students. In addition, in 1994, a group of concerned Palestinians, in cooperation with the United Nations Development Program (UNDP) in Jerusalem, launched a campaign concerning the conservation of water, its importance and value, and the dissemination of pertinent information. All these groups have approached the Tamer Institute in order to coordinate their work and activities with the reading campaign so that we might help spread word of their projects.

Our emphasis during the second, and now the third, year has been on developing and activating libraries, on developing our work with youth in volunteer groups, and on writing and publishing relevant materials. To these ends, a retreat for all youth volunteers and a panel conducted by youth on their experiences with community work, teamwork, and leadership are scheduled for early 1995. In addition, the specialist librarian previously mentioned will first activate public libraries, and then gradually add school libraries.

The Special Weeks Commemorating the First and Second Anniversaries of the Reading Campaign

A "special week" (February 11–18, 1993) was designated in order to organize activities commemorating and expanding campaign activities. An ad hoc committee consisting of individuals from various regions who are active in the campaign was formed to initiate and coordinate national activities during that week, and local committees, meanwhile, organized local activities. One national activity was the "I Contributed a Book" subcampaign. In each town, public libraries, schools, mosques, churches, or cultural centers served as collection sites for books donated by individuals, which were then distributed to schools or centers that needed them. As a receipt for every book donated, a donor received a sticker with the words "I Contributed a Book." Another national activity was a special play by Nakhleh ash-Shiber, which was prepared to be performed especially in places that did not have the chance to have him during the previous year. In addition, public libraries in almost all towns collectively donated one hundred yearly memberships to children who had checked out the most books during the previous year. Further, several bookstores declared a discount of 15 to 20 percent on all their books during the special week.

Sadly, commemoration of the reading campaign's second anniversary was canceled due to the massacre in a Hebron mosque committed by a Jewish settler on February 28, 1994.[17]

CONCLUSION

I began this article by saying that Palestinian society, like many societies in the Third World, is facing a serious state of dismantlement. As a result of the peace accords, we are currently witnessing some changes and improvements at what I have been referring to as the visible level, such as our ability to raise the Palestinian flag. However, control of water, land, and movement of people remains completely in the hands of the Israeli military. Similarly, although administration of education is under Palestinian authority, all the previous military orders and rules concerning education remain intact, to be changed only through Israeli consent.

Matters at the deeper, invisible level are most likely going to deteriorate even further. In my opinion, the accords currently being implemented, if not challenged and debated, will most likely lead to the transformation of Palestinian society from a people who have a history, a dream, and a sense of community into isolated and separate groups living on fragmented pieces of land. These groups will have no sense of community, spiritual bonding, or history, no access to natural resources, and no access to Jerusalem.[18] The self-rule as we see it implemented is not much different from the self-rule that was given to Blacks living in areas like Treskei and Seskei under the apartheid government in South Africa. In our case, the Israeli government continues to make decisions concerning resources, movement, foreign affairs, and access to important information, such as the distribution of the population and the amount of water under the West Bank and Gaza. In short, current trends seem, at best, to be transforming Palestinians from a cohesive cultural community to a group of individuals fighting over consumer goods. In my experience, disaster is usually on the way when things seem to be improving at visible or symbolic levels while deteriorating at deeper, less visible levels.

This is not a call for despair but, rather, a call for action. Hope is probably the strongest human emotion. But hope does not come through wishing alone. It comes through imagining alternatives to what exists and through action. Demanding more and better schools, for example, is not realistic under the conditions that currently exist in many societies, including Palestinian society. And even if demanding more and better schools were realistic, it is not enough. In fact, such a demand may blind us from seeing crucial but neglected needs, from imagining alternatives, from being more honestly responsible, and from thinking creatively about what we can do.

In this article, I have described one innovative project, the reading campaign within Palestinian society, which depends to a large extent on local resources. Yet, this project can also have far-reaching impact in terms of addressing crucial needs and changing perceptions, convictions, and patterns of thinking and behaving. The campaign can also influence Palestinian society by developing personal and social habits and values crucial to both individual and community development. The most important of these values encouraged in the campaign, in my opinion, is placing primary responsibility for learning on children and their families. The family can be effective when parents or older siblings read to young children, or encourage each other to read or write together. In addition, by being active in the reading campaign, youths can learn to be more involved in family and community affairs and development. Moreover, current conditions in most societies that expose children and youth to so many dangers — such as the prevalence of cars and weapons, drugs and food additives, and daily consumption of junk information (mainly through television) — clearly bring to mind that there is no substitute for the family in addressing children's learning and growth needs.

One of the innovative aspects of the reading campaign is that it mobilizes and increases the "yield" of available resources. Most of what we have used in order to generate the momentum within the campaign was already present. Pulling together material, human, and institutional resources in ways that are acceptable and nonthreatening to people has been a key factor in generating this momentum. The campaign is also an innovative project in that it employs simple and pivotal, but powerful and effective, ideas. The implementation is not an arbitrary process, but a purposeful one. It follows practical steps that are in contrast to more familiar attempts to increase reading through compulsory activities, which so often are ineffective, or with the big centralized plans and grand designs that are usually imposed from above and outside. Such plans and designs are like storms, and storms usually disrupt life. Our campaign is more like a tender, refreshing breeze, invigorating people and bringing them hope. Finally, the campaign provides many avenues for people to learn and is based on the premise that change is an opportunity for each person to learn and develop.

The reading campaign also demonstrates what I refer to as "acquiring the means to learn" and incorporates the five sublevels of community building I described at the beginning of this article. The campaign increases people's ability to express themselves (for example, through the youth page and during Nakhleh's performances); that is, to build at the level of creative cultural expressions (sublevel 1). It increases people's ability to redefine the meanings of words in their own minds, in light of their own experience, and in order to develop a new understanding of what goes on around them (sublevel 2). For example, through their involvement in the volunteer youth groups (Palm groups) and in the Nakhleh ash-Shiber reading clubs, children and youth develop authentic meanings for words such as leadership, community work, teamwork, and democratic practice. This article itself is an example of building at sublevel 2, as it develops new understanding and knowledge of what a campaign could be and what community building is. Further, the campaign helps produce new information — for example, through publications and information about children via their passport applications — and increases people's access to information by developing and revitalizing existing libraries (sublevel 3). It increases people's ability to communicate through, for example, the youth page, to build networks, and to develop youth through, for example, voluntary youth groups (sublevel 4). The campaign is a forum that gathers people together and helps them communicate with one another, and, at the same time, it brings out the diversity that exists in almost every community (sublevels 4 and 5). The campaign adds to people's sense of belonging, togetherness, and common good that is crucial to community building. It helps people create new values, attitudes, and priorities in the Palestinian community (sublevel 5).

Moreover, the campaign is breaking many of the boundaries built around us as Palestinians: geographical, psychological, legal, political, social, and cultural. It is a free and liberating action initiated under conditions that for many years have lacked both freedom and liberty. It is an idea that uses a constructive rather than an analytical approach to development and to solving problems. The campaign functions by changing not only the supply of reading materials, but also the demand for them. It is a meaningful and useful activity in a community that currently lacks any such activities for children and youth at the national level. And, no doubt, teachers' participation in the reading campaign — and not in the typical training workshops — is a more effective approach to teacher development. Last but not least, the reading campaign can contribute in a pragmatic way to economic activity and self-sufficiency through publications, performances, and other cultural products. Such cultural products can also reduce cultural dependency on dominant ideologies and commercial cultural commodities.

Reading is not an alien idea to the Arab culture, one of whose main principles is "Read in the name of your God," the first commandment in the *Qur'an.* Reading forms a natural and attainable way of uniting Arabs culturally and intellectually, which is a prerequisite for political, social, and economic unity.

NOTES

1. I choose to use the term "Third World," despite its being inaccurate and having negative connotations, at least in part because it is a more commonly recognized option than more appropriate terms, such as "Human World," "Marginalized World," or Samir Amin's (1974) "the Periphery." My choice reflects my beliefs that the "Third World" is not necessarily "developing" and, furthermore, that nations in this region are not necessarily striving to emulate "Western World" development.

2. Prior to 1948, the state of Palestine, which included what is now referred to as Israel, the West Bank, and the Gaza Strip, existed along with Jordan on the east side of the Jordan River. In 1948, Israel was created, while the West Bank eventually came under the control of Jordan and the Gaza Strip under Egyptian administration.

    After the creation of Israel, Palestinians were dispersed: some lived in what became Israel, some in the West Bank, some in the Gaza Strip, and others throughout Arab countries, mainly Jordan, Syria, and Lebanon. After the Israeli occupation of the West Bank and the Gaza Strip in 1967, Palestinians living under Israeli control inhabited four different regions with four different identities: Israel, the West Bank, the Gaza Strip, and East Jerusalem. Palestinian society has been fragmented even more since the recent signing of the peace accords by the addition of two new, small regions (one-half of Gaza and Jericho) to the "map."

3. The Tamer Institute, which I cofounded with Beth Kuttab in 1989, is a pioneering education initiative that came about as a natural and necessary response to the realities and needs of the Palestinian community in the West Bank and the Gaza Strip. The Institute is helping to develop a new orientation in Palestinian education through its projects, which include a reading campaign — the focus of this article — teacher development, educational materials, and seminars.

4. Between 1973 and 1978, during my tenure as head supervisor of math instruction in all West Bank schools, I was in charge of all training courses, in all subjects.

5. In these thirty years, I have been a math and science teacher at the elementary, secondary, and college levels; dean of students at Birzeit University; and head supervisor of math instruction for all West Bank schools. I have directed teacher-training programs; established several community and children's programs; published a magazine on teaching math and several books on education, math, and religion; headed the nonprofit Economic Development Group; and cofounded and directed the Tamer Institute.

6. The intifada, however, was unable to reach its full potential due to harsh and what I consider to be unwarranted Israeli measures, such as imprisonments, deportations, demolitions, killings, and an August 1988 law that criminalized activities such as communal farming and teaching children. In March 1988, four months after the intifada started and as a result of school closures, various forms of popular education had begun to flourish, one of which was teaching children in their neighborhoods. The August law succeeded in stifling such attempts when they were just blooming. The Tamer Institute's reading campaign is another attempt that depends mainly on individual effort and addresses part of the need created by school closures.

7. I say some schools because government (or public) schools in the West Bank and the Gaza Strip, as well as Arab public schools in Israel, were forbidden by Israeli authorities to take part in campaign activities.

8. We focused in our early workshops on women mainly because they showed more interest and because Palestinian women and girls (like women and girls in many other places) have fewer opportunities to voice their opinions.

9. These areas consist of Jerusalem, Ramallah, Nablus, Hebron, Gaza, Khan Yonis, Rafah, Jenin, Akka, Bethlehem, and Nazareth.

10. The harshest such measure has been the closing of Jerusalem to Palestinians living in the West Bank and the Gaza Strip. This closing means breaking the West Bank geographically into two parts, because no one can travel through Jerusalem. This has affected our staff's ability to reach our office, as well as to reach half of the West Bank, the Gaza Strip, Jerusalem, and the Galilean region, where a large concentration of Palestinians live. Consequently, we were forced to move our office in December 1993 from Jerusalem to Ramallah on the West Bank.

11. These and other publications are available from Arab Resource Collective Ltd., Resources for Community Health and Development, P.O. Box 7380 Nicosia, Cyprus, or P.O. Box 5916-13, Beirut, Lebanon.

12. The three published books, all in Arabic, are *Nakhleh Loves Books,* a book for children; *The Bird of Writing, The Wings of the Pen,* a collection of seventy contributions by youth who wrote for the special newspaper page; and *Proceedings of the Seminar "Towards Rebuilding Palestinian Society,"* which was conducted by the Tamer Institute. The three publications in progress are: *The Rush of Words,* a handbook for Arabic teachers on the writing process; *Who Makes History,* a handbook on oral history for history teachers; and *Integrating Art into the Teaching of Math,* for children in the first three grades.

13. It is unfortunate that at a time when Palestinians most need development in certain areas, including library services, six posts were abolished by the UNRWA Headquarters. Besides the library services specialist, the other posts that were abolished were for art, home economics, physical education, special education, and vocational training. These terminations affect UNRWA schools, which serve about one-quarter of the students in the West Bank and Gaza Strip.

14. The regions that were included in the evaluation were Jerusalem, Nablus, Jenin, Jericho, Akka, Ramallah-Bireh, Nazareth, and the Gaza Strip. The questionnaire consisted of questions in five main categories: demographic information; activities in the particular locations; campaign materials (i.e., the brochure, the sticker, the passport, the poster); financial matters (such as how many passports they sold, how proceeds were spent, etc.); and the relationship with the Tamer Institute (such as coordination of meetings, follow-up, whether the Institute did its part and what it promised, whether information in the two newspaper pages was clear).

15. One reason for the delay was that we did not anticipate the extent of involvement and enthusiasm that children manifested. Another reason was that the Institute lacked an efficient internal organization to collect our share of the money from passport sales so that we could order new ones.

16. These international bodies include the European Union, the Canadian government, an Italian cultural organization, Christian Aid, the British World University Service, the Mennonite Central Committee, and the Swedish government.

17. The second anniversary special week had been scheduled for March 17–24, 1994, at the request of teachers and administrators who felt that March would be a better month of the school calendar than February for the celebration. Thus, the massacre interrupted the commemoration.

18. To clarify the importance of Jerusalem to Palestine, imagine England with the English having no access to London except through permits given to less than 5 percent of the population! But, as compensation, English communities around London would be allowed to raise the British flag and to have British police.

REFERENCES

Amin, S. (1974). *Accumulation on a world scale: A critique of the theory of underdevelopment.* New York: Monthly Review Press.

Argyris, C. (1982). *Reasoning, learning, and action.* San Francisco: Jossey-Bass.

Aronson, J. (1994, September). Settlements remain a key factor in current stage of negotiation. *Report on Israeli settlements in the occupied territories* (vol. 4, no. 5). Washington, DC: Foundation for Middle East Peace.

Fasheh, M. (1988). *Education as praxis for liberation: Birzeit University and the Community Work Program.* Unpublished doctoral dissertation, Harvard Graduate School of Education, Cambridge, MA.

Fasheh, M. (1990). Community education: To reclaim and transform what has been made invisible. *Harvard Educational Review, 60,* 19–35.

Freire, P. (1970). *Pedagogy of the oppressed.* New York: Herder & Herder.

Freire, P. (1985). *The politics of education.* South Hadley, MA: Bergin & Garvey.

Mahshi, K., & Bush, K. (1989). The Palestinian uprising and education for the future. *Harvard Educational Review, 59,* 470–483.

National Center for Educational Research and Development, Jordan. (1993, March). *Student achievement in Jordan and the West Bank: A comparative perspective* (Publication series no. 17).

Tamer Institute. (1991). *Assessment of achievement in Arabic and math of fourth and sixth grade students in the Central region of the West Bank.* Jerusalem: Author.

Literally thousands of people contributed to the success of the reading campaign and, thus, directly or indirectly, to this article; it is not possible to mention all of them here.

However, I would like to mention a few: Claude Isacov, Fadia Salfiti (coordinator of the campaign), Serene Huleileh (coordinator of publications and production), Yaqoub Abu Arafeh and Mohammad Ammous (both of whom perform Nakhleh ash-Shiber), Jamil al-Qiq (the main illustrator of campaign materials), Nihaia Abu Nahla (the main volunteer coordinator of the campaign in the Gaza Strip), Tayseer Masrieh (from Turbo Design, Inc., in Ramallah, the company that designed most of the materials), Nadia Ghattas, Issa Saba (from the YMCA in Gaza), Rana Barakat, Jamal Haddad, Nida Abed Rashid, Ali Touqan (from the Nablus public library), Mary Fasheh (the specialist librarian), Nasr ed-Din Anabtawi (the lawyer who composed the poems), Sabreen (the musical group that composed the music), Hussein Ghaith, Fateh Azzam, Nayef Jaber, Suhair Sleiman, and the young volunteers. For further information on the reading campaign, contact Tamer Institute, P.O. Box 25223, Shufat, Jerusalem.

Bilingual Education for
Puerto Ricans in New York City:
From Hope to Compromise

SANDRA DEL VALLE

In 1975, the U.S. Commission on Civil Rights quoted a leading Puerto Rican educator on the issue of education and language:

> Our definition of cultural pluralism must include the concept that our language and culture will be given equal status to that of the majority population. It is not enough simply to say that we should be given the opportunity to share in the positive benefits of modern American life. Instead, we must insist that this sharing will not be accomplished at the sacrifice of all those traits which make us what we are as Puerto Ricans. (U.S. Commission on Civil Rights, 1975, p. 103)

In looking for "equal status" on the mainland for the Spanish language and Puerto Rican culture, this educator reflected a popular attitude among Puerto Ricans that gave rise to their support for bilingual education. Bilingual education is a method of teaching a language to speakers of another language using the students' native language to some extent. The extent to which native language is used depends on the nature and goals of the program. For example, developmental bilingual education (DBE) is contrasted with transitional bilingual education programs (TBE). In this article, TBE is considered an assimilationist program in which the educational system usually takes a top-down approach that leaves the affected community with no real decisionmaking power. Teachers are trained to teach the "standard variety" of the minority language. The student body is usually exclusively language minority and the program usually lasts three years. While it may begin with the use of the native language, this language is phased out in a short time in favor of the majority (target) language. The oppositional model to this assimilationist model is the pluralistic model, or DBE, in which the native language is developed along with the target language (Dicker, 1996).

Mainland Puerto Ricans see bilingual education not only as a method to educate language-minority students, but also as a means to realize the promise of equal citizenship in the educational arena. Their vision of bilingual education was one in which the native language — that is, Spanish — was a valuable building

Harvard Educational Review   Vol. 68 No. 2 Summer 1998, 193–217

block with which they could learn English without sacrificing academic achievement or their native language.

By 1995, the character of Puerto Rican demands for bilingual education had changed dramatically. In *Bushwick Parents Organization v. Mills,* the Bushwick Parents Organization (BPO), a Puerto Rican–dominated parents' organization, supported a lawsuit against Richard P. Mills, New York State's Education Commissioner, which stated that:

> [A] forbidding system of bilingual education has been permitted to emerge in New York City which fails to provide [limited English proficient] children with adequate instruction in English, the critical skill they need to participate fully in the educational and economic opportunities American society offers. (*Bushwick Parents Organization v. Mills,* 1995)

Support for bilingual education and the maintenance of native languages as a goal for Puerto Ricans was no longer to be taken for granted. In the twenty years between these two statements — that is, the U.S. Commission on Civil Rights and the BPO lawsuit — bilingual education has suffered on the local and national level from a variety of factors, including compromised decisionmaking by professionals, lack of information about the goals and methods of bilingual education among language-minority communities, a gap between professional policymakers and the grassroots communities they served, a suspicion by the majority culture of bilingual education's goals, and the perception that it is a failed practice that only serves the entrenched self-interest of professional Latinos (Moran, 1986).

In this article, I discuss the struggle for bilingual education as a fight for civil rights in which lawyers and litigation have played a large role. I specifically examine the role of Puerto Ricans in New York City in these struggles. An important issue to be examined is the fatal gap between two visions of bilingual education — the vision of the grassroots Puerto Rican community that saw bilingual education as educational enrichment, and the remedial model that was ultimately adopted and advanced by lawyers and other professionals in the courts. I also examine the effects of that gap today and its contributions to the development of *BPO v. Mills.* Finally, I discuss the current antibilingual climate, the growth in immigration from Central and South America and Asia to cities like New York, the school reform movement, and the implications these hold for the future of bilingual education.

FEDERAL DECISIONMAKING AND ITS IMPLICATIONS FOR BILINGUAL EDUCATION

Federal decisionmaking in language and education has operated on the legislative and judicial levels. The first and earliest interventions were legislative and sought to fund special English-language instructional programs for language-minority students. The second set of interventions, never fully defined, attempted to define the contours and prohibitions of language-based discrimination. Both tracks, however, shared and have been defined by a vision of bilingual education as a "deficit" and have assumed, if not a "blame the victim" mentality, at least a "change the victim" mentality. The first track found its expression in Title VII of the Elementary and Secondary Education Act (1968), also known as the Bilingual Education Act. The judicial track can be seen in the U.S. Supreme Court case, *Lau v. Nichols* (1974). The development and implications for bilingual education of both tracks are discussed below.

The Legislative Track: The Bilingual Education Act

The national audience first became aware of the educational underachievement of language-minority students in the late 1960s, with the issuance of the National Education Association (NEA) report entitled, "The Invisible Minority, *Pero No Vencibles*," which focused on the educational plight of Mexican American children. The NEA report focused on Arizona's educational neglect of its Mexican American students in Tucson and became the impetus for a later Tucson conference that involved influential congressmen. José Cardenas, a southwestern educator, spoke about the terrible quality of education for Tucson's Mexican American students, saying that "almost anything is better" than what they were receiving (Crawford, 1991, p. 41). The increasing political clout of Mexican American students and the emergence of radical groups, such as the Crusade for Justice, that grew out of the community's frustrations in dealing with an unresponsive government made education a priority issue (Baez, 1995). The Tucson conference proposed developmental bilingual education programs extending from preschool into the high school years as at least one remedy for the "miseducation" of Mexican American children.

The growing Puerto Rican community in New York also received attention. Although Puerto Ricans had been officially recognized as U.S. citizens since 1917, those who migrated to the states were subjected to the same type of racial, ethnic, socioeconomic, and linguistic discrimination as were Mexican Americans in the Southwest. When they entered the U.S. schools with only limited English ability and a poor rural education, they encountered schools unprepared for their needs, teachers untrained to educate "foreign" pupils, outdated textbooks with no bearing on their lives or histories, and a school system generally prepared only to conform students to a White, middle-class model of success (Castellanos, 1985). Meanwhile, the Puerto Rican community was already experimenting with bilingual education. The Puerto Rican Study conducted in 1958 by the Board of Education of the City of New York recommended the use of the native language, and even native-language retention, as a way to address the high Puerto Rican dropout rate (Board of Education of the City of New York, 1958). By the mid-1960s, groups like ASPIRA,[1] United Bronx Parents, and the Puerto Rican Educators Association were promoting bilingualism and multiculturalism as goals for the system's bilingual education programs (Baez, 1995).

Responding to the increased attention given to Latino education issues, Congress passed the 1968 Bilingual Education Act. The legislation was lauded by education advocates and Latino supporters for placing the educational needs of language-minority children at the forefront of national education policymaking. However, it defined the problem in terms of English-language proficiency rather than the educational under-attainment of all language-minority children. Not surprisingly, the legislation defined simply teaching children English as the solution. The Bilingual Education Act defined bilingual education as a remedial effort to make students dominant in English only, thereby a de facto squelching of possibilities for the development of bilingualism. In other words, "remedial" was defined as compensatory in terms of not knowing English, as opposed to viewing proficiency in a native language as an asset to which English could be added. The compromised nature of what was won through this legislation was not lost on Puerto Rican bilingual education advocates:

> I wish to stress that I realize the importance of learning English by Puerto Ricans and other minority groups living in the United States. But I do not feel that our educational abilities are so limited and our educational vision so short-sighted that we must teach one language at the expense of another, that we must sacrifice the academic potential of thousands of youngsters in order to promote the learning of English, that we must jettison and reject ways of life that are our own. (S. Polanco-Abreu, quoted in Crawford, 1991, p. 38)

The act also issued no guidelines in the development of programs; instead, it relied on local districts, which often had little expertise or incentive, to address the "special" needs of language-minority students. Congress also prioritized poor families as program recipients and, by injecting an unnecessary poverty criteria, stamped the "compensatory" label firmly on bilingual education. The act also appeared to condone the racial segregation of language-minority children. Without guidance and with only limited funding, districts and parents accepted the segregation of these students as programatically necessary (children needed to be grouped together by language in order to be served) and fiscally required (the inclusion of Anglos, who were difficult to attract anyway would water down the funds available to language-minority students) (Castellanos, 1985). Housed in poor, already-segregated Latino schools, bilingual programs were new, underfunded, and already seen as remedial efforts rather than as magnets to draw students not zoned for these schools (Castellanos, 1985; Crawford, 1992). These early decisions, which reflect an ambivalence toward bilingual education and federal educational interventions, reverberate even today in the heated debate over bilingual education.

The Judicial Track: Lau v. Nichols

Bilingual education *seemed* to receive another boost in 1974 when the U.S. Supreme Court held in *Lau v. Nichols* that schools must address the English-language "deficiencies" of English Language Learners (ELLs),[2] who, according to the decision, could not simply be allowed to sit in the classroom and neither comprehend nor participate. The Court ruled that such a state of affairs was the denial of equal educational opportunity.

Lau began as a reaction by Chinese parents to a San Francisco education desegregation case that they feared would jeopardize their bilingual programs. Approximately half of the Chinese schoolchildren who needed language support services were receiving them, prompting parents to go to court to demand bilingual education programs in their neighborhood schools. Controversy over exactly what the Chinese parents were demanding marked the lower court proceedings. The parents' lawyers asked for "bilingual compensatory education in English" (Baez,

1995, p. 129). The court interpreted this as demanding special non-English courses, and circuit judges responded by stating that

> the State's use of English as the language of instruction in its schools is intimately and properly related to the educational and socializing purposes for which schools were established. This is an English-speaking nation. (*Lau*, 1974)

A dissenting judge resisted this interpretation that translated the parents' demands as a plea for their children to learn only English. Even sympathetic judges were confused, however, finding that "the children do not seek to have their classes taught in both English and Chinese. All they ask is that they receive instruction in the English language" (*Lau*, 1974, p. 801).

When the Supreme Court reviewed the case, the lawyers decided not to request that the Court mandate any particular educational methodology. Although the Court essentially precluded rampant "sink or swim" methods of education, it did not explicitly endorse bilingual education either. In fact, it endorsed no particular methodology, but left that choice up to school administrators. The Federal Office of Civil Rights read *Lau* as requiring transitional bilingual education programs and developed "Lau Guidelines" that were to be used by school districts when developing programs for language-minority schoolchildren. Although hailed for acknowledging the legitimate educational needs of these children, *Lau* did not find a constitutional violation of the children's rights. For instance, the Court could have found that it was a violation of the Fourteenth Amendment's Equal Protection Clause not to provide special language programs for these children. Such a ruling would have put *Lau on the same footing as Brown v. Board of Education* and would have raised the moral stakes for providing language-minority students a proper education, not to mention raising the national visibility of these students. A decision based on the Constitution might have been used to strengthen programs and substantially increase spending for language-minority students. Most significantly, such a decision could have led to the use of a results-based approach to the education of these students, in which program effectiveness would be measured by the academic success of students. Instead, it decided the case on the basis of Title VI of the Civil Rights Laws, which precluded recipients of federal funds from discriminating on the basis of national origin. Further, equal educational opportunity was defined by the Court as a mechanism for ensuring access to English-language instruction only; the Chinese community's aspirations for a truly bilingual, bicultural education got no real hearing and were not reflected in the Court's decision. Despite its limitations, *Lau* became the template used for fashioning bilingual education litigation and its consequent remedies.

New York City

Latino education litigation began in New York City and elsewhere as a grassroots movement to address the inequities in schooling for Puerto Rican students regardless of their language dominance. The Puerto Rican agenda for education reform was comprehensive and holistic — it demanded respect for the language and culture and home life of Puerto Rican children. It further demanded that Puerto Rican children's home language be used as an asset in building toward bilingualism rather than as a deficit. It went beyond these cultural issues to seek greater numbers of Latino teachers, better links between schools and families and communities, and far greater community control of schools than the large, bureaucratic, Anglo-dominated school system offered (National Puerto Rican Taskforce on Educational Policy, 1982; Pedraza, 1997).

In the early 1970s, the energetic and politically active Puerto Rican community in New York had enjoyed a series of educational victories because of grassroots activism. For example, in 1973, in the middle of a school redistricting fight, community pressure kept East Harlem, a Puerto Rican stronghold, in a single school district rather than allowing its divisions to divide the neighborhood into two districts (Pedraza, 1997). The East Harlem Puerto Rican community was not new to educational struggles; from the 1920s to the 1960s, it had been involved in progressive educational reform that brought about the East Harlem Block School, an innovative school founded by Black and Puerto Rican parents.

ASPIRA of New York v. Board of Education

ASPIRA of New York was founded in 1961 as a nonprofit educational and leadership development agency dedicated to serving the Puerto Rican community in New York City (*ASPIRA v. Board of Education,* 1973). Clearly, the existing educational system was failing Puerto Rican students in 1970; 51 percent of non-Hispanic Whites over the age of twenty-five had graduated from high school, as opposed to 20 percent of Puerto Ricans; only 1 percent of Puerto Ricans were college graduates (Wagenheim, 1975). In 1947, an estimated 25,000 Puerto Rican students were in the New York City school system (Falk & Wang, 1990); by 1972, that number had risen to 245,000, with an additional 38,000 students from non-Puerto Rican Spanish-speaking nationalities. About 40 percent of the Puerto Rican children spoke Spanish only, requiring an unprepared school system to quickly develop approaches and curricula to properly educate them (Falk & Wang, 1990). In 1966, with Puerto Ricans constituting 21 percent of New York City's public school enrollment, ASPIRA issued *The Losers* (Margolis, 1968), a report documenting the system's failure to educate its Puerto Rican students. In creating its agenda for education reform, ASPIRA decided to press for bilingual education as a method, not only as a means of addressing the miseducation of Puerto Rican children, but also as an organizing tool and a means of "preserving community identity" (Falk & Wang, 1990, p. 6).

The Puerto Rican grassroots community wanted to see a revitalized educational experience for their children that respected their cultural and linguistic backgrounds and that developed students' Spanish literacy, while at the same time giving those students who needed it the opportunity to learn English. Most importantly, the problem was not defined as one resting within Spanish-dominant children. It instead framed the problem as a school system that did not respond to the needs of all Puerto Rican children, regardless of their dominant language. Although bilingual education was deemed a worthy goal in itself, it was seen as part and parcel of what the educator Jim Cummins (1986) would later call a "framework for intervention" for language-minority students. By itself, bilingual education could not address the underachievement of language-minority children in the United States. Cummins argued that a theory of intervention addressing the power relations between majority and minority cultures was needed. Since school culture simply reflected the imbalance of power between majorities and minorities in society generally, it required a mediating construct to help minority children succeed in school despite their subjugated status. The extent to which minority students' language and culture were valued and incorporated in the school was one factor in empowering minority students. In 1973, Latino educators defined cultural pluralism as their rationale for bilingual education. By "cultural pluralism" they meant a respect for cultures other than the majority, other-than-English language acquisition, development of a positive self-image, and equality of educational opportunity (Cardenas, 1995).

To achieve this goal, individual Puerto Rican parents and ASPIRA decided to go to court to press for reforms in the school system. ASPIRA was represented in court by the newly formed Puerto Rican Legal Defense and Education Fund (PRLDEF), an organization formed in response to the outcry over the education of Puerto Rican children and the demand for litigation. The resulting case was one of the earliest to establish a legal federal mandate for bilingual education as a method of ensuring an equal educational opportunity for students who were not proficient in English. It was also notable because the case involved the largest school system in the nation at that time, as well as the largest plaintiff group, with over 80,000 children potentially affected (Santiago-Santiago, 1986). The case was settled with a court-monitored consent decree setting up a transitional bilingual education program that became a model for school districts facing similar litigation throughout the nation.[3]

The available research, the spirit of educational innovation, and the Puerto Rican community's activism could have turned the case into not just landmark but legendary litigation for bilingual education. Instead, the litigation, following the parameters of *Lau,* closely defined the class-action group only as those Spanish-surnamed children who needed English-language remediation. Afraid that *Lau* would not succeed in the Supreme Court, lawyers stopped short of asking for a developmental model of bilingual education and instead urged and secured a transitional model. One commentator noted that, given the high level of energy in the Latino community in New York City at the time, the "professional class managing the litigation" should not have "held back" by allowing the recently decided *Lau* case to dominate the bilingual litigation strategy (Baez, 1995, p. 179). As a result, these grassroots organizations would not see their vision for a truly transformative education secured. Instead, in the consent decree and subsequent rulings, Judge Marvin E. Frankel described plaintiffs' monolingual non-English-speaking children as "disturbed, deprived, culturally ghettoized" since they were not academically successful (*ASPIRA v. Board of Education,* 1975, p. 1164).

The dissonance between community wishes and litigation objectives in ASPIRA was marked. While ASPIRA's leaders and the lawyers agreed on following a modest strategy to secure transitional services, other community members wanted bilingual programs that would maintain and further develop the Spanish language and culture in addition to academic support programs that would help all Puerto Rican/Latino students (Baez, 1995). Although ASPIRA's leaders, the lawyers, and university professionals worked together on the case, neither frontline teachers nor average parents whose children would be affected by the outcome even knew of the litigation or of the resulting consent decree (Santiago-Santiago, 1986).

After the decree, community activists and bilingual education advocates stressed the continuing need for struggle in this area, particularly since the consent decree had only partially fulfilled their demands:

> Many [ASPIRA and other advocates, as well] fully realized that the decree would not ensure equal educational opportunity for all 253,452 Puerto Rican children in the City's schools. At best, the decree had the potential of assisting those most in need — Puerto Rican and Hispanic LEP children. This meant that equal educational opportunity for approximately 60 percent of the population, which had varying degrees of proficiency in English and were not eligible for the [consent decree] program, remained virtually unaddressed. (Santiago-Santiago, 1986, p. 161)

Many felt that the decree represented an assimilationist model of education that did not address the essential concerns of the Puerto Rican community — that is, the need, as expressed by Cummins, to have schools respect the Spanish language and the social, familial, and civic culture of Puerto Rican students. The decree did not attempt to realize these broader goals, and there remains a sense that the professionals handling the litigation compromised a visionary idea of education for a quicker legal victory (Falk & Wang, 1990).

Ten years after the litigation, ASPIRA convinced the Educational Priorities Panel (EPP), a fiscal educational watchdog in New York City, that the consent decree's promise was still not being fulfilled. As a result of their collaborative efforts, EPP issued an influential report, *Ten Years of Neglect: The Failure to Serve Language Minority Children in the New York City Public Schools* (Willner, 1986), which documented the decree's inadequacies, reporting that 40 percent of the ELLs entitled to bilingual services were not receiving them. Their report became the fountainhead from which more negotiations with the Board of Education sprang.

Indeed, despite its attempt to promote Puerto Rican empowerment, *ASPIRA v. Board of Education* is one of the least community empowering of the bilingual education litigation cases of the 1970s (Baez, 1995). It did little to change power relations in the school system, did not address the unequal learning opportunities of Latino/Puerto Rican children as a whole, did not change schools into centers for community learning and empowerment, and did not address the low expectations often held for Latino/Puerto Rican students. The litigation, however, did force the New York City public school system to acknowledge at least some of the needs of Puerto Rican children, increased the influence of ASPIRA on educational policymaking, and continues to force the Board of Education to offer bilingual education programs. Further, the requirement that the school system hire teachers proficient in English and Spanish created a cadre of teachers within the system to help monitor the consent decree and develop more holistic linguistic programs. Unfortunately, the emphasis on bilingual education has continued to obscure the need for greater systemic reform. Twenty years after the ASPIRA consent decree, with Latino children comprising 35 percent of the school system and growing, Latinos are still concentrated in the worst performing schools in the city and are subjected to poor, underfunded, remedial bilingual programs (Latino Commission on Educational Reform, 1992).

EFFECTS OF THE LITIGATION MODEL
ON BILINGUAL EDUCATION NATIONALLY

The flawed legal strategy pursued in bilingual education litigation was exemplified but not confined to New York City.[4] Given the narrow parameters of litigation within which complex community needs must be fitted into the technical strictures of a complaint, Latino education litigation nationally devolved within a short time into litigation *only* over the needs of non-English-dominant students, or ELLs, at the expense of the majority of English-speaking, second- and third-generation Latino children, who were also being neglected by the educational establishment. The litigation model pursued in New York City and nationally had three interrelated and unfortunate results that are still being felt today. Discussed in greater detail below, these results have helped increase the vulnerability of bilingual education programs. From allowing bilingual education to be treated as a panacea for school systems' failing to educate language-minority students to then limiting the scope and goals of the programs, these factors have had a corrosive effect on public support for bilingual education.

1. *An artificial and unworkable limitation on the kind of educational litigation that could be fashioned for language-minority children.* By developing cases that relied exclusively on the educational needs of ELLs, lawyers ended up without a legal strategy that addressed the legitimate and compelling educational needs of all other Latino and language-minority children — that is, children who come from a language-minority background but are proficient in English. TBE ended up being used as a panacea to cure the ills of an educational system that consistently failed to address the needs of language-minority children. Rather than seeing *Lau* as a small and hopeful sign that the needs of language-minority children could be addressed in courts, lawyers took *Lau* as the last word on equal educational opportunities for these schoolchildren and failed to continue to push for a Constitutional guarantee for bilingual education.

The status of Puerto Ricans as migratory citizens caught between two cultures was likewise never explored as a possible legal hook. For at least a decade, Puerto Ricans had argued that their status as citizens of both Puerto Rican and Anglo cultures and languages required that mainland schools incorporate their linguistic needs in their instructional methods. Unfortunately, these possibilities were never fully explored by lawyers leading bilingual education litigation, and there are still no viable legal strategies today that place the language-minority children's educational needs generally before courts or policymakers.

2. *Dysfunction between community wishes and litigation obligations.* While the Latino community in New York City and elsewhere called for the transformation of schools into nurturing environments in which their children could succeed, the litigation focused exclusively on ELLs. Prior to 1974, Latino education litigation nationally was notable for its grassroots foundation (Baez, 1995). Nationalist Latino groups from the Northeast and Southwest, and parents' groups such as the United Bronx Parents, headed by Puerto Rican Evelina Antonetti and *El Comité de Padres* in Boston, were instrumental in raising parents' consciousness of the need

for concerted community action, as well as in educating them about democratic education principles (Baez, 1995). The litigation that occurred until the mid-1970s transformed the greater Latino community precisely because it sprang from that community, changed parents through the litigation process, and created a new educational experience for all — that is, for parents and students, English proficient or not.

After *Lau*, however, the community's vision of educational reform was lost in the push by leaders and lawyers for "quick fix" remedies that ignored the complex issues raised by parents. Some commentators have argued that the role of lawyers, judges, and national policymakers undermines the necessary community choice over and control of bilingual education policy (Baker & de Kanter, 1986). Naturally, it can also be argued that lawyers, judges, and national policymakers are the only people small minority communities can turn to if their larger political subdivision — that is, their school district or local government — does not value their language heritage (Teitelbaum & Hiller, 1977). Either way, the impact of federal litigation on a community's voice and empowerment can be substantial.

3. *Institutionalization of transitional bilingual education (TBE).* Finally, lawyers and national policymakers did succeed in raising the awareness of the needs of ELLs to a previously unheard of level (Baker & de Kanter, 1986). Unfortunately, lawyers also ended up institutionalizing TBE and shaping a deficit-based, remedial type of bilingual education that begins with the premise that the most important educational objective for a language-minority student is to learn English, and then measures program success by how quickly students are transitioned into English (Puerto Rican Legal Defense and Education Fund, 1972). Yet, that shape neither fulfills the promise of bilingual education nor consequently serves the vibrant and multifaceted communities that still await the transformative educational litigation they originally sought.

From 1974 to 1981, the presumed legal mandate for bilingual education was lost. In 1983, the Supreme Court withdrew from *Lau*'s interpretation of Title VI, which only required that the challenged action or policy have a negative effect on the protected group. The Court decided that Title VI required that a plaintiff show that the recipient of federal funds *intended* to discriminate (*Guardians Association v. Civil Service Commission of New York*, 1983). In 1974, the Equal Educational Opportunities Act (EEOA) was passed, a statute generally intended to address busing for desegregative purposes. The statute, however, contained a provision that mandated equal educational opportunities for ELLs.[5] With the waning influence of *Lau*, the EEOA became the prime vehicle for bilingual education litigation. The EEOA allowed plaintiffs to proceed with an "effects test" of discrimination; that is, they would not have to prove intentional discrimination. However, the EEOA's provisions have been read as giving local educational agencies (LEAs) wide latitude in their decisionmaking without providing penalties for abuse of discretion.[6]

Further, Reagan and Bush federal court appointees began retreating from a federalist approach to civil rights and relying more on LEAs' discretion. Despite the landmark that *Lau* represented, the case served as a viable precedent for a bilingual education mandate for only seven years, from 1974 to 1981. In 1981, in *Castañeda v. Pickard*, the Fifth Circuit Court of Appeals, which has jurisdiction over six states, including Texas and Florida, read civil rights laws as requiring only that districts somehow meet the language needs of ELLs, but not necessarily through bilingual education.[7] As the means of doing so in *Castañeda*, the Fifth Circuit Court of Appeals outlined a three-pronged test to determine whether a local educational agency was meeting its requirements towards ELLs under the EEOA: 1) the LEA must use a methodology for teaching English that is supported by some experts in the field or that is considered a legitimate experimental strategy; 2) the LEA must dedicate sufficient resources to the program to make it work; and 3) after a reasonable trial period, the program must indeed succeed in teaching the students English. *Castañeda* signaled a federal retreat from bilingual education and a continuing reluctance on the part of courts to mandate educational policymaking for local districts.

Although *Castañeda* is not a Supreme Court decision and technically does not overrule *Lau*, it has been cited or referred to by courts throughout the nation as reflecting the legal standards for serving ELLs.[8] Given *Lau*'s weakness and the lack of political support for bilingual education, *Castañeda* has generally been taken as the best bilingual education advocates can hope for in the foreseeable future. Ultimately, this means that litigation cannot force school districts with no specific bilingual education consent decrees or state laws to develop these programs in cities such as New York. Consent decrees that pre-date *Castañeda* are increasingly open to attack as inflexible mandates at a time when the federal government is looking to expand school districts' autonomy. With the federal retreat from bilingual education and its growing unpopularity, consent decrees like ASPIRA, once seen as minimal starting points for greater educational reform, become the ceiling for litigatively enforceable rights.

CURRENT CLIMATE

Today, many effective and operational bilingual education programs are being lost because language has long been seen as a proxy for ethnicity, and the maintenance of minority languages as a threat to a national identity (Fishman, 1989). In 1981, Joseph Califano, then Secretary of Health, Education, and Welfare, remarked that bilingual programs had become "captives of the professional Hispanic and other ethnic groups, with their understandably emotional but often exaggerated political rhetoric of biculturalism" (Califano, 1981, p. 313). Indeed, in 1985, U.S. Secretary of Education William Bennett said that the "original purposes" of the Bilingual Education Act of 1968 had been "perverted and politicized," and that a "sense of cultural pride cannot come at the price of proficiency in English, our common language" (Moran, 1993, p. 274). Educator Sonia Nieto notes that

> bilingual education is a political issue because both the proponents and opponents of bilingual education have long recognized its potential for empowering these traditionally powerless groups. Because it represents the class and ethnic group interest of traditionally subordinate groups and comes out on the side of education as an emancipatory proposition, it is no mystery that bilingual education has been characterized by great controversy. (Nieto, 1996, p. 194)

Sociolinguist Joshua Fishman, linking bilingual education with ethno-linguistic diversity, has found that

> from the very beginning of speculative social theory, ethnicity has been primarily associated with its debits, rather than with its assets. The view [that] ethnolinguistic diversity is itself nothing but a byproduct of poverty and backwardness is a recurring theme in both modern liberal and conservative thought. Why are such destructive myths so hard to combat? Myths are vested interests and vested interests produce their own intellectual blinders, even when they are entertained and adopted by folks who are modern, progressive and even intellectual. Power is a scarce commodity and power-sharing is never engaged in voluntarily. Ethnolinguistic aggregates are suspected of power aspirations and ethnolinguistic pluralism is considered a bad risk, insofar as potentially fostering such aspirations rather than overcoming them. (Fishman, 1989, pp. 561–563)

The attacks on bilingual education today are based not only on ethnicity principles, but on the popular issue of "standards" as well. Since the program is seen as benefiting only minorities, it is assumed that it coddles students and lowers their threshold of success rather than ensuring educational excellence in two languages.[9] This new tactic has had a divisive effect on Latinos, who are left insisting that they want the very best for their children — that is, to learn English as a way into the middle class. Bilingual education detractors have used these protestations as "proof" that Latinos don't support bilingual education (Center for Equal Opportunity [CEO], 1996b). Using Latinos as opponents of bilingual education is very valuable to these detractors, as it helps insulate critics from charges of discrimination. Indeed, they can charge that bilingual education or a failing segregated system is itself discriminating against Latinos, the single largest ethnic group receiving bilingual education services, nationally and in New York City (Garvin, 1998; Meyers, 1998). This is not surprising, since the limitations of bilingual education that have made it vulnerable to attack were embedded in its defining moments more than twenty years ago.

Bushwick Parents Organization v. Mills

Many of these issues were reflected in a lawsuit that arose in New York City when the Bushwick Parents Organization (BPO) filed a lawsuit attempting to dismantle bilingual education in the city (*BPO v. Mills*, 1995). Latino parents — including mostly Puerto Ricans who were backed by a large church-run parents' organization that, in turn, was helped in its lawsuit by conservative think tanks and a large private law firm — filed the suit. BPO complained that their members' children were being misplaced in bilingual classes, were learning neither English nor Spanish adequately in those classes, and were unable to remove themselves from the program without having their loyalty to their "ethnicity" questioned.

Sadly, the Bushwick school district in Brooklyn, New York, with a poverty rate of over 90 percent, is like many other districts in which Puerto Rican and Latino students predominate (Board of Education of the City of New York, 1997a). According to state standards, its boundaries contain four "failing" schools. In half the middle schools, less than a quarter of the students read at grade level; in no middle school were half the children reading at grade level (Public Education Association, 1994). Despite these glaring inadequacies throughout a failing school system, the lawsuit focused only on the failures of the bilingual education programs.

One year prior to the filing of this lawsuit, former schools chancellor Ramón Cortines issued results of a longitudinal study that severely undermined the credibility of bilingual education in New York City because of its finding that ELLs in ESL-only classrooms learned English faster and academically outperformed their counterparts receiving bilingual education (Board of Education, 1994). The methodologically flawed study received enormous media attention, as the *New York Times* featured the findings on a front page usually reserved for national and international news. The study has since been repeatedly cited as the last word on the state of bilingual education in New York (Berman, 1998; CEO, 1996a; Garvin, 1998).

The repercussions of the report reverberated through the BPO lawsuit. The report was used to argue that any state practices that allowed children to remain in bilingual education for longer than three years was tantamount to educational malpractice and was attached to the complaint as support for the plaintiff's contentions. The BPO sued the State Commissioner of Education, saying that enforcement of a fortieth percentile cutoff score on English-language assessments before a child was no longer considered an ELL, and therefore no longer eligible for English-language support services, was "arbitrary and capricious," as it allowed students to remain too long in bilingual education classes. The lawsuit, however, was legally meritless. The commissioner's reliance on individual student performance on the assessments was appropriate, and the use of a fortieth percentile was a codified educational decision that no court, lacking pedagogical expertise, would second guess. The court ruled that how the assessments were being used were appropriate.

Although quickly dismissed, the lawsuit grabbed national headlines, as moderate and liberal press rushed to cover a story where Puerto Rican parents criticized bilingual education (Amselle, 1996; "Parents worried," 1996; Steinberg, 1995). The press, however, did not cover the strong support that existed for bilingual education in the Bushwick community among Puerto Ricans, and even among the Puerto Rican leadership of the BPO (M. Diaz, personal communication, 1995). The lawsuit had a corrosive effect on the Bushwick community, with support for bilingual education becoming the driving issue in school board elections and people within BPO resigning over the lawsuit. The activist Latino parents whom BPO attracted could have used the opportunity of community mobilization to shift its emphasis to achieve a more systemic reform in District 32, which would have addressed the educational failures of the district as a whole rather than focusing only on bilingual education programs. Instead, national conservative groups, such as the Center for Equal Opportunity (CEO, 1996a),[10] used the lawsuit to further their own agendas in opposition to bilingual education by attempting to intervene in the lawsuit.

The growing lethargy among the Puerto Rican and Latino community in New York about bilingual education helped create the climate for filing the lawsuit. The battle for bilingual education was considered won with the signing of the ASPIRA consent decree. In fact, new, younger heads of Puerto Rican organizations, as well as newly immigrating parents and new teachers, had no notion of the history and, most importantly, did not even know of the decree's existence, let

alone its significance. After the decree was signed it continued to be monitored —
and still is — by lawyers at the Puerto Rican Legal Defense and Education Fund:
community monitoring, such as was done by ASPIRA to gather data for the building of the ASPIRA lawsuit, would not become a feature of the decree. By the time
the Bushwick parents' unhappiness with their district was translated into a bilingual education lawsuit, there were no other parents or alternatives on the grassroots level to BPO's divisive guidance. Never truly allowed to take its form from
the aspirations of parents, bilingual education in New York City was now being attacked by Puerto Rican parents.

Bilingual education at the college level was made the scapegoat in a battle over
graduation requirements at Hostos Community College in the South Bronx in
spring 1997. There, a contest of wills between the former chancellor of the City
University of New York and newly appointed, conservative Board of Trustee members erupted into a controversy over whether the college, with a mission to educate poor, immigrant students and use bilingual education, was undermining
graduation standards. Although the issues surrounding the graduation standards,
especially the writing assessments, were complex, the media concentrated only on
the issue of whether the use of bilingual education was necessary, appropriate, or
standards-eroding (Chan, 1997; "Shortchanging students," 1997; "Failure at
Hostos," 1997; "No substitute," 1997).

The same concern over erosion of standards was used in the debate over new
high school graduation standards proposed by New York State Commissioner of
Education Richard P. Mills. Under Commissioner Mills's proposal, all graduating
seniors would have been required to take and pass more rigorous exams in a variety of subject areas before being allowed to graduate. Previously, seniors could
have chosen to take less rigorous exams and graduate with a lesser "local" diploma
rather than the more prestigious "Regents" diploma. The tests for the local diploma, however, were available in a variety of languages. The debate over whether
to even offer the new exams in languages other than English was a hot one. Over
and over, there was a concern that translation of tests would somehow lower standards rather than ensuring that all children were actually meeting the high standards expected of all seniors. After being repeatedly tabled by Board of Regents
member Saul Cohen, the chair of the Committee on Elementary and Secondary
Education who opposed the translations, the translations were finally approved
only for those students entering the New York State school system after ninth
grade and only after the commissioner issued a statement stressing the need for
intensive English-language instruction. How the plan to effect this statement will
interact or collide with the ASPIRA consent decree in New York City remains to be
seen. However, one could argue that it was again this aged decree that was used to
stop the commissioner from issuing a statement that would have promised total
English-language immersion for all ELLs in exchange for the translation of the
tests and in direct violation of the decree.

Despite this modest victory, bilingual education throughout New York State is
in jeopardy. Although the state currently has a strong bilingual education law, the
Board of Regents recently indicated that it wanted to "massage" the law to allow
for "intensive English-language instruction." This terminology has not yet been
defined by the Board of Regents or Commissioner Mills, but unhappiness with the
current levels of English-language instruction in bilingual education programs is

palpable.[11] If the state moves away from bilingual education, as many other states already have done, it will be looking for major compromises from ASPIRA on its consent decree, the only legal impediment to the statewide elimination of bilingual education. In the ensuing political and legal struggle, ASPIRA and its lawyers at PRLDEF cannot be perceived as only representing a handful of elites or the interests of bilingual teachers. The support for bilingual education and the consent decree must return to the grassroots level, to students in the programs and their parents.

The transitional nature of bilingual education programs also makes it difficult to develop a movement. By its nature, those most affected by the elimination of bilingual programs are the most recent immigrants — those who have been in the school system for less than three years. A population generally economically vulnerable and dealing with the social and cultural dislocations involved in immigrating, they usually have little time and energy for involvement in educational struggles that are not directly personal, especially when the need for English-language support services is seen as a temporary measure to be exhausted within one to three years. The reputation of bilingual education as a remedial program for poor children who cannot meet the same expectations as Anglo students hardly makes it a sympathetic cause. Already, bilingual programs are seen as stigmatizing and the first step to a lower academic track. In summarizing immigrant students' educational experiences in New York City, Francisco Rivera-Batiz noted that

> the participation of students in . . . programs [for limited English proficient students] frequently places them in a separate track in schools, a track which often has lower expectations of their students, and lower outcomes. The progress of the students is not monitored adequately, and many wind up graduating from high school without ever attending the regular school program. Furthermore, LEP students do not have the same access to the services available to students in mainstream programs. (Rivera-Batiz, 1996, p. 29)

Regardless of the accuracy of this assessment, the public perceives "LEP programs," especially bilingual education programs, as palatably negative.

RECOMMENDATIONS AND FUTURE POSSIBILITIES

Bilingual education is being attacked not only by conservatives who fear its capacity to empower minorities, but by liberals as well, who see poorly devised and implemented programs as a hindrance to the academic success and assimilation of language-minority, especially Latino, students. Turning the tide for bilingual education will be difficult; given the political nature of bilingual education, simply strengthening programs, as at least one commentator has suggested, will not be sufficient (Krashen, 1996). Instead, a reinvigorated, multitiered advocacy strategy must be pursued that should weave together the following elements:

Develop committed bilingual education teachers. Bilingual education was funded and mandated before there were sufficient numbers of teachers to make it a reality. Poorly implemented programs, implemented either by hostile, uninterested teachers and districts or by well-meaning but untrained staff has had a negative impact on the ability of many to wholeheartedly support bilingual education. Community monitoring of bilingual education's implementation and the professional development of teachers can help ensure that we have defensible programs. Community-based organizations that operate youth programs should be sharing the history, politics, and empowering nature of bilingual education with their students. Even if the students do not want to become bilingual education teachers, they can become a resource to the greater community on the ideas and ideals of bilingual education.

Respond to the changing Latino demographics in New York City. Recent immigrants have been arriving at New York City's schools in record numbers over the past several years. In 1989, New York City's public schools had 36,000 recent immigrant enrollees; by 1995 that number had increased to 134,875 (Rivera-Batiz, 1996).[12] The percentage of immigrant children enrolled in the city's schools rose from 20 percent in 1989 to over 30 percent in 1995; the number identified as "recent" immigrants (three years or less in the state's schools) rose from 3.8 percent in 1989 to 12.8 percent in 1995 (Rivera-Batiz, 1996). The range of languages now represented in bilingual education and ESL classes in the state is over 172, with Spanish, Haitian Creole, Chinese, Russian, and Korean as the largest language groups (Kadamus, 1997).

Generally, immigrants, especially Latino immigrants, experience the same poor education as Puerto Ricans. They attend overcrowded, highly segregated schools within Anglo-dominated school systems. There is a threat that low-literacy ELLs who need intensive instruction in their own languages before they can learn English will instead be referred to special education classes, as was done with Puerto Rican children decades ago. After much pressure, the Board of Education released a study in 1997 documenting that Latino children are the most underrepresented ethnic group in gifted and talented programs (Board of Education, 1997b). The vast majority of the districts do not even have a way to measure giftedness in ELLs, and thereby automatically exclude them from New York City's best programs. In short, the civil rights issues that confronted Puerto Ricans in the 1950s and 1960s are still being felt today by the newer Latino subgroups.

Puerto Ricans can play a role in shaping the terrain of a possible new movement by sharing their history of struggle and educational activism to pushing for holistic school reform. Rather than continuing to push for remedial bilingual education as an end in itself or simply monitoring the consent decree, the emphasis needs to be on bilingual education as a component of remaking schools. Providing bilingual education alone will not address immigrant children's needs, which may range from having access to schools that prepare them for the Regents exams to ensuring that their classrooms are small enough to handle the diversity in languages and literacy levels that they present.

Contextualize bilingual education within a struggle for educational reform. Some advances have already been made in placing bilingual education as an enrichment model in a variety of smaller, dual-language, developmental schools throughout the city. Backed by a large grant from the Annenberg Foundation, these schools have a greater autonomy and can develop creative curriculum and hire teachers who are dedicated to serving a particular school population.

Since 1994, six new small schools for predominantly Latino schoolchildren with an emphasis on bilingualism have been or are in the process of being created in

New York City. The first of these schools, the Leadership Secondary School, was opened in 1994 on the basis of recommendations by the Latino Commission on Educational Reform, a commission of thirty-five parents, students, teachers, administrators, researchers, and concerned citizens chaired by Manhattan Board of Education member Luís O. Reyes.

After the commission created five more schools with an emphasis on the education of ELLs and Latinos, a Latino education network, funded by the Annenberg grant, was created to provide a forum in which the schools can share their technical and pedagogical knowledge with each other. Most importantly, the schools' leaders are trying to develop a curriculum to achieve biliteracy on a high school level that could be used city-wide. These leaders, overwhelmingly Puerto Rican, are unabashedly using bilingual education and the goal of biliteracy as a central piece in the creation of their schools. The schools also are striving to create "a sharing, supportive, nurturing learning environment in our schools that is student-centered and encourages a holistic approach to education; educational excellence to cope with and succeed according to and beyond traditional 'standards'; bilingual literacy; proactive participation in the movement for civil and human rights; empowering and creating new leaders" (Latino Network Members, 1997, p. 1).

These schools, however, serve only a portion of the thousands of Latino children in New York City's public schools. Further, as unzoned schools of choice, only the most educated and politically savvy parents will be able to negotiate their children's way into them. The schools and their creators, however, can be a rich resource for remaking the image of bilingual education from the "forbidding" system the Bushwick parents felt they had to fight their way out of into a magnet for all children.

Develop support for bilingual education among various ethnic and linguistic minority groups. Since its inception, the general public has viewed bilingual education as a special education component for Latino children. This perspective is not coincidental, since the Bilingual Education Act was intended to redress the educational under-achievement of Latino children. Advocates expanded the potential beneficiaries to include other language groups when they realized that the act would have greater support if it included other groups; they also felt morally obligated to include other groups suffering the same educational neglect (Crawford, 1992, p. 41).

Other linguistic groups besides Latinos support bilingual education and benefit from these programs. New York City hosts transitional and developmental bilingual programs in a rainbow of languages, reflecting a concern for native-language retention among other language groups. If the base of support for bilingual programs is to widen, which seems critical, then Latinos and other language groups must highlight and nurture cross-cultural support for these programs. Latinos have to be willing to share leadership in this area with other groups, and other language groups have to make advocacy for bilingual education a visible priority for their organizations.

Puerto Ricans can be instrumental in this area, since they have been at the forefront of the bilingual education struggle. Puerto Ricans have established organizations for which bilingual education is a top agenda item. Unfortunately, many of these organizations have either been overwhelmed by their own needs or lulled into a false sense of security by the provision of federal and state laws on bilingual education. These organizations need to reinvigorate their bilingual education strategies by reaching down to the grassroots level, as well as across to other language groups. To date, that outreach has either not been done or done halfheartedly. Collaboration — sharing of strategies, joint events, sessions on cross-cultural understanding — needs to be developed by grassroots organizations on the local level. Latino bilingual education teachers can be especially helpful as they reach out to their colleagues in ESL or other bilingual programs to share information on building successful programs. Recognizing the political nature of bilingual education, they can strategize with each other, their parents, and their students on building cross-cultural support for bilingual education in their own communities.

Build coalitions with mainstream, nonethnic education groups such as the National Education Association (NEA), the Educational Priorities Panel (EPP), and the recently created Campaign for Fiscal Equity in New York City. Wade Henderson of the Leadership Conference on Civil Rights has declared that "coalition politics is the politics of the future."[13] These national groups usually have access to larger audiences and are not perceived as having a particular ethnic special interest to promote. Both the EPP and the NEA were significantly involved in raising the profile of the education of language-minority children, both nationally and locally. No single civil rights issue calls for such coalition-building as bilingual education. Hampered by the public's perception of it as remedial, segregatory, failing, and promoting the special interests of professional Latinos, the investment and support of mainstream education agencies is critical to reshaping public perception.

Develop leadership among parents and students who benefit from bilingual programs. Bilingual education opponents have successfully painted a portrait of bilingual education advocates as self-interested elites who think they "know better" than immigrant parents about educating their children, often to the detriment of the child and against the parents' best instincts. If the advocacy for bilingual education continues to rest on the shoulders of professionals alone, it will not succeed (Callaghan, 1997; CEO, 1996b; Garvin, 1998).

Involve lawyers to the extent necessary to prevent the dismantling of community-supported bilingual programs currently in existence. Lawyers can help communities in building organizations and coalitions to advance the goals of bilingual education, as well as in devising legal strategies that might address a community's educational issues. However, the legal role cannot and should not dominate the strategic thinking of a community seeking empowerment. The past struggles in New York City and elsewhere have taught us that lawyering should take place within a context of community support, mobilization, and leadership, or it may cause as much damage as good.

CONCLUSION

National policymakers, federal courts, and advocacy organizations have raised the nation's consciousness on issues affecting language-minority students. The fact that the merits of bilingual education are even heatedly debated owes much to their efforts to keep the pedagogy viable in even the most politically conservative times. However, these forces, perhaps because of their very nature — institutional-ized, mainstream, national in scope — have also contributed to the compromised nature of bilingual education, making it especially vulnerable to attack.

The current sociopolitical and legal climate requires that national policy-makers, federal courts, and advocacy organizations continue to play a role in de-fending bilingual education programs. However, that role must be constructed differently than it has been; it must take its cues from parents, students, and local grassroots organizations. These entities must make more extensive efforts to edu-cate the communities they wish to represent, and they must be willing to be as radi-cal and hopeful, as daring and as resourceful as the Puerto Ricans who fought for bilingual education twenty-five years ago and the new immigrants who will con-tinue to fight for it in the future.

NOTES

1. ASPIRA is Spanish for "aspire" and is intended to convey the hopes of young Puerto Ricans, as well as to serve as a symbol of their struggle to attain those hopes and dreams. ASPIRA, which was established in 1961 in New York City, organizes Puerto Rican high school and college youth into clubs, where they learn leadership and problem-solving skills while engaged in community action projects. Youth also use ASPIRA resources to develop and implement a plan for completing their education.
2. "English Language Learner" (ELL) denotes someone who does not speak, read, and/or write in English at the academic level of their peers. Most school districts and the federal government use the more pejorative "limited English proficient" (LEP) to designate the same population. The "ELL" designation, however, stresses that the student already has native-language strengths and should not be defined solely in re-lation to their need to learn English.
3. A consent decree is an agreement between two parties to a litigation that is moni-tored by a court. A violation of a term in the consent decree enables the original party to seek relief in the court. A consent decree can be modified by the agreement of all parties or by the court after a hearing.
4. For instance, in *Serna v. Portales* (1974), elementary-grade Spanish-surnamed chil-dren in Texas were to receive between forty-five and sixty minutes of bilingual in-struction per day. High school students were to be given access to "ethnic studies" only. In *Otero v. Mesa County Valley School District* (1975), the court completely rejected bilingual education programs as a remedy for the academic failure of Chicano schoolchildren in Colorado, finding instead that socioeconomic factors, not school districts, were to blame.
5. The Equal Educational Opportunities Act (1968) states: "No state shall deny equal educational opportunity to an individual on account of his or her race, color, sex or national origin by the failure of an educational agency to take appropriate action to overcome language barriers that impede equal participation by its students in its in-structional programs."
6. The Elementary and Secondary Education Act states, "the term 'local educational agency' means a public board of education or other public authority legally consti-tuted within a State for either administrative control or direction of or to perform a service function for, public elementary or secondary schools in a city, county, town-ship, school district, or other political subdivision of a State, or such combination of school districts or counties as are recognized in a State as an administrative agency for its public elementary or secondary schools."

7. A federal Circuit Court of Appeals is the highest federal court in a region just below the U.S. Supreme Court. It interprets and defines the law for the states within its jurisdiction. However, because of common law principles of comity, other federal circuits presiding over other states will give great weight to how a sister circuit has interpreted the law and may adopt that interpretation.

8. See, for example, *Teresa P. v. Berkeley* (1989). In 1985, *Castañeda's* standards were also adopted by the OCR as the measure for compliance with Title VI when proceeding with a disparate impact theory (Williams, 1991).

9. For instance, in a *New York Post* editorial, one commentator noted that the bilingual education mission of Hostos Community College in the South Bronx really meant that "[y]ou can't expect poor immigrants to do college-level work." The Hostos attitude recalls the enslaving mentality of the 1960s welfare movement (Berman, 1998).

10. Founded by Linda Chavez, formerly of U.S. English, the Center for Equal Opportunity is a right-wing think tank opposing bilingual education, affirmative action, and other minority benefit programs.

11. These remarks are based on the author's attendance at the January 14, 1998, meeting of the Board of Regents Subcommittee on Elementary and Secondary Education.

12. These are conservative estimates based on the number of children eligible for Emergency Immigrant Education assistance.

13. Remarks made at the NAACP Legal Defense and Educational Fund's Civil Rights Conference at Airlie, Virginia, in October 1997.

REFERENCES

Amselle, J. (1996, September 30). Ingles si! *National Review, 18,* 52.

ASPIRA of New York, Inc. v. Board of Education, 58 F.R.D. 62 (S.D.N.Y. 1973).

ASPIRA of New York, Inc. v. Board of Education, 394 F. Supp. 1161 (S.D.N.Y. 1975).

Baez, L. A. (1995). *From transformative school goals to assimilationist and remedial bilingual education: A critical review of key precedent-setting Hispanic bilingual litigation decided by federal courts between 1974 and 1983.* Unpublished manuscript.

Baker, K., & de Kanter, A. (1986). Assessing the legal profession's contribution to the education of bilingual students. La Raza Law Journal, 1, 295–329.

Berman, R. (1998, January 9). Hostos' war on English and success. *New York Post,* p. 27.

Board of Education of the City of New York. (1958). *The Puerto Rican Study, 1953–1957.* New York: Author.

Board of Education of the City of New York. (1994). *Educational progress of students in bilingual and ESL programs: A longitudinal study, 1990–1994.* Brooklyn, NY: Author.

Board of Education of the City of New York. (1997a). *Facts and figures.* New York: Author.

Board of Education of the City of New York. (1997b). *Programs serving gifted and talented students in New York City public schools, 1995–1996* (Division of Assessment and Accountability). New York: Author.

Bushwick Parents Organization v. Mills, 5181 Civ. 95 (Sup. Ct. New York.) Verified Petition (1995).

Califano, J. A., Jr. (1981). *Governing America: An insider's report from the White House and the cabinet.* New York: Simon & Schuster.

Callaghan, A. (1997, August 15). Desperate to learn English. *New York Times,* p. 31.

Cardenas, J. A. (1995). *Multicultural education: A generation of advocacy.* Needham, MA: Simon & Schuster.

Castañeda v. Pickard, 648 F. 2d 989 (5th Cir. 1981).

Castellanos, D. (1985). *The best of two worlds: Bilingual-bicultural education in the U.S.* Trenton: New Jersey Department of Education.

Center for Equal Opportunity. (1996a). *The failure of bilingual education.* Washington, DC: Author.

Center for Equal Opportunity. (1996b). *The importance of learning English: A national survey of Hispanic parents.* Washington, DC: Author.

Chan, Y. (1997, May 21). CUNY flap as school lowers bar on English. *New York Daily News,* p. 6.

Crawford, J. (1991). *Bilingual education: History, politics, theory and practice* (3d ed.) Los Angeles: Bilingual Educational Services.

Crawford, J. (Ed.). (1992). *Language loyalties: A source book on the official English controversy.* Chicago: University of Chicago Press.

Cummins, J. (1986). Empowering minority students: A framework for intervention. *Harvard Educational Review, 56,* 18–36.

Dicker, S. J. (1996). *Languages in America: A pluralist view.* Clevedon, Eng.: Multilingual Matters.

Elementary and Secondary Education Act, Chap. 47, 20 U.S.C.A. § 2891.

Equal Educational Opportunities Act, 20 U.S.C.A. § 1703(f) (1968).

Failure at Hostos College. (1997, May 23). *New York Post,* p. 34.

Falk, R., & Wang, T. (1990). ASPIRA v. Board of Education: *La lucha para la lengua: The slow vindication of educational rights.* Unpublished manuscript.

Fishman, J. (1989). *Language and ethnicity in minority sociolinguistic perspective.* Clevedon, Eng.: Multilingual Matters.

Garvin, G. (1998, January). Loco, completamente loco: The many failures of bilingual education. *REASON Magazine Online.*

Guardians Association v. Civil Service Commission of New York, 463 U.S. 582 (1983).

Kadamus, J. (1997, April 14). *Building capacity: Addressing the needs of limited English proficient students.* Albany: New York State Education Department.

Krashen, S. D. (1996). *Under attack: The case against bilingual education.* Culver City, CA: Language Education Associates.

Latino Commission on Educational Reform. (1992). *Toward a vision for the education of Latino students: Community voices, student voices.* Brooklyn: Board of Education of the City of New York.

Latino Network Members. (1997, June) Memorandum to Beth Lief, Sara Schwabacher, and Michael Webb.

Lau v. Nichols, 414 U.S. 563 (1974).

Margolis, R. J. (1968). *The losers: A report on Puerto Ricans and the public schools.* New York: ASPIRA.

Meyers, M. (1998, February 17). The bilingual dead-end. *New York Post,* p. 25.

Moran, R. F. (1986). Foreword — the lesson of Keyes: How do you translate "The American dream"? *La Raza Law Journal, 26,* 255–319.

Moran, R. F. (1993). Of democracy, devaluation and bilingual education. *Creighton Law Review, 26,* 274.

National Puerto Rican Taskforce on Educational Policy. (1982). *Toward a language policy for Puerto Ricans in the U.S.: An agenda for a community in movement.* New York: Research Foundation of the City University of New York.

Nieto, S. (1996). *Affirming diversity: The socio-political context of multicultural education* (2nd ed.). White Plains, NY: Longman.

No substitute for English. (1997, May 23). *New York Daily News,* p. 42.

Otero v. Mesa County Valley School District, 408 F. Supp. 162 (D.C. Colo. 1975).

Parents worried bilingual ed hurts students. (1996, February 28). *Education Week,* p. 1.

Pedraza, P. (1996–1997). Puerto Ricans and the politics of school reform. *Journal of El Centro de Estudios Puertorriqueños, Winter,* 74–85.

Public Education Association. (1994). *A consumer's guide to middle schools in District 32, Brooklyn.* New York: Author.

Puerto Rican Legal Defense and Education Fund. (1972). Brief *Amicus Curiae* in support of petitioners in *Lau v. Nichols.*

Rivera-Batiz, F. (1996). *The education of immigrant children: The case of New York City* (Working Paper No. 2). New York: International Center for Migration, Ethnicity and Citizenship of the New School for Social Research.

Santiago-Santiago, I. (1986). *ASPIRA v. Board of Education* revisited. *American Journal of Education, 95,* 149–199.

Serna v. Portales, 499 F. 2d 1147 (10th Cir. 1974).

Shortchanging students at Hostos. (1997, May 23). *New York Times,* p. 30.

Steinberg, J. (1995, September 19). Lawsuit is filed accusing state of overuse of bilingual classes. *New York Times,* p. A1.

Teitelbaum, H., & Hiller, R. (1977). Bilingual education: The legal mandate. *Harvard Educational Review, 47,* 138–170.

Teresa P. v. Berkeley, U.S.D., 724 F. Supp. 698 (N.D. Cal. 1989).

U.S. Commission on Civil Rights. (1975). *Report on Puerto Ricans in the United States: An uncertain future.* Washington, DC: Author.

Wagenheim, K. (1975). *A survey of Puerto Ricans on the U.S. mainland in the 1970s.* New York: Praeger.

Williams, M. L. (1991). *Policy update on schools' obligations toward national origin minority students with limited English proficiency.* Washington, DC: U.S. Dept. Of Education, Office for Civil Rights.

Willner, R. (1986). *Ten years of neglect: The failure to serve language-minority students in the New York City public schools.* New York: Educational Priorities Panel.

Memorias de una Vida de Obra
(Memories of a Life of Work):
An Interview with Antonia Pantoja

Antonia Pantoja is one of the best known Puerto Rican women activists alive today. Born on September 13, 1921, into a politically active working-class family in Punta de Tierra, Puerto Rico, Pantoja witnessed her family's and her community's fight against oppression in Puerto Rico. From an early age, she was involved in political activities and the struggle for freedom among her people. Pantoja attended the University of Puerto Rico in the late 1930s, and left before graduating to become an elementary school teacher.

In 1944, at the age of twenty-three, Pantoja moved to the United States. Settling in New York City, she worked with children while attending Hunter College to complete her bachelor of arts degree. Pantoja spent most of her working life in New York City, where she organized several important community-based organizations that are still active today.

In 1962, she founded ASPIRA, the Spanish word for "aspire." This organization brings together Puerto Rican and other Latino high school and college students into clubs, where they learn leadership and problem-solving skills while working in community action projects. Other institutions Pantoja was instrumental in building include the Puerto Rican Association for Community Affairs (PRACA), the Puerto Rican Forum, Boricua College, the Puerto Rican Community Development Project, the Puerto Rican Research and Resource Center in Washington, DC, and PRODUCIR ("to produce")[1] in Puerto Rico.

Pantoja's activism is an example of a distinct style and philosophy of female leadership. In her various leadership roles, she has stressed collective decision-making; developing new leaders, especially among youth; and the good of the group over the personal gain of the individual.

In 1972, Pantoja moved to California, where she became a faculty member at San Diego State University and director of the school's social work program for undergraduate students. She was instrumental in establishing the university's Graduate School for Community Development, working with students to plan and design this school, which gives students the opportunity to work within and strengthen different communities.

---

[1] Inspired by the phrase of the nineteenth-century Puerto Rican physician, poet, and revolutionary Ramón Emeterio Betances, "*Producir es servir a la humanidad*" ("To produce is to serve humanity").

Harvard Educational Review   Vol. 68 No. 2 Summer 1998, 244–258

Pantoja moved back to Puerto Rico in 1984, where she has continued her spirited activism and community involvement. Pantoja became involved in PRO-DUCIR, a community-based organization that promotes economic self-sufficiency by developing a local economic infrastructure and creating economic links outside the community. To this day, Pantoja, now in her late seventies, remains active in projects and social movements related to the struggles of Puerto Rican people.

In 1996, President Clinton awarded Pantoja the Medal of Freedom for her community work. In 1997, the Mexican Fine Arts Museum in Chicago named Pantoja a woman who reflects the spirit of Sor Juana Inés de la Cruz, a seventeenth-century Mexican poet, intellectual, and philosopher. This distinction has been awarded to Isabel Allende in 1994, to Nobel Peace Prize winner Rigoberta Menchu Tum in 1995, and to Gwendolyn Brooks in 1996.

Interviewer Wilhelmina Perry is an African American educator who has known Antonia Pantoja for twenty years as a colleague, friend, and fellow worker. Pantoja and Perry have been members of the faculty of San Diego State University and worked together to create the Graduate School for Community Development, where both were administrators and faculty. They have also worked together in developing PRODUCIR, have coauthored several articles, and have joined in many projects of community research, community education and training, and community art activities. Perry and Pantoja share a political and philosophical commitment to the struggle to eliminate social, political, and economic injustice.

What early experiences in Puerto Rico influenced your ideas and thinking about social justice?

There are several specific incidents that I can vividly recall, and there are also patterns of relationships that I feel have affected me greatly. First, I should say that my grandfather was a cigar factory worker and a very strong union person. I personally witnessed the struggle of my family, friends, and neighbors in organizing to gain better working conditions and better wages. I was the only child in the family, and my relationship with my grandfather was very important to me, both in terms of his affection for me and in terms of his thinking. My grandfather's efforts at organizing resulted in severe physical violence against him and against his fellow workers. They won the strike, but the company then packed up their machinery and left Puerto Rico. Everyone lost their jobs. I can still remember the sense of outrage and powerlessness that we all felt. We literally had no rights. My life's work has always been influenced by the memory of this inequity.

I remember as a child leaving school to attend political rallies for the independence of the Island. I was curious about particular leaders and about the world of ideas. When my mother found out about my attendance at the rallies, she was both angry and afraid. I wondered why we could not express our rights and talk about our desires for the destiny of our country.

Growing up in Puerto Rico, other things also disturbed me. It was very clear to me that I was growing up as a poor Black child. I do not know how people cannot be conscious of themselves in their social setting, as many people are. I attended Central High School in the city of San Juan, and felt discriminated against because my clothing was that of a poor child. I was a frail female child who wanted an education in a society where male children were preferred. During my childhood in

Puerto Rico, before Operation Bootstrap,[2] the country was extremely economically depressed. But still you must remember that there has always been "the correct family name," "the debutantes' balls," and the "upper social class." As a child of ambitions and dreams, I required access to the resources that were out of my immediate reach. I aspired to a high school and university education during a time when no one or very few from Barrio Obrero, the neighborhood where I lived, had such dreams. Recently, I attended a reunion of Central High School, where I was being honored. All the graduates of my old home neighborhood were there. I felt particularly honored, and I know that they sincerely shared the stage with me. It was a victory, in a sense, for all of us. Of course, today they are also all professionals and leaders in their respective circles.

You must also remember what it means to be Black in Puerto Rico. During my early years, I was very much aware of my physical difference: my hair, my color, my size, and shape were not at all like the models that were projected as good or beautiful. Even today, people still believe that the Puerto Rican Barbie Doll represents us all. I am still involved in the fight against racism in Puerto Rico. In fact, in May 1998 I am participating with Marta Moreno Vega in a conference on racism in Puerto Rico.

I participated last year in the annual conference of the Civil Rights Commission in Puerto Rico. The topic of my presentation was "Does Racism Exist in Puerto Rico?" I used this opportunity to talk about the lack of symbols and images of the Black population in our country. I also talked about my visits to local prisons in Puerto Rico, where so many of the young male prisoners are Black Puerto Ricans. This situation is slowly changing, but within the Puerto Rican society we have little understanding of our own racism. We like to talk about our difference from the United States. With regard to my interests in the situation of racism in Puerto Rico and in correcting this injustice, I am providing some support to my young nephews and nieces, who are publishing a new magazine, *In the House.*

What experiences in your life have shaped your political ideas?

I grew up in Puerto Rico prior to the years of Luis Muñoz Marín. At that time of extreme poverty on the Island, workers were oppressed by large U.S. companies. In my community of Barrio Obrero, most working families were supported by income from the American Tobacco Company. Their lives were hard and full of injustice. Labor union organizing was an important tool for demanding rights. I remember nights when my grandfather, one of the major organizers, would hold strategy meetings in my house. I was very young, but I remember the arguing, the excitement, and the implied danger in it all. Workers were frequently beaten when strikes were organized. As a small child, I was learning of injustices, but I was also learning that you must fight back. Sometimes you fight even when your life is in danger.

---

[2] Operation Bootstrap was an economic development program started under the leadership of Governor Luis Muñoz Marín in the early 1950s. Muñoz Marín's policies, designed to bring industry into Puerto Rico in order to create jobs, brought about economic development that helped move the Island out of a state of abject poverty, but also deepened the Island's economic dependence on the United States.

During those years, there were also strong feelings of nationalism among many groups of workers, although they were frequently covert, because those were days in which you could be jailed for your expressions alone.

Later, when I came to the United States, I first lived with a group of artists in Greenwich Village in an old church. I imagine we were early "hippies." We talked a lot about the arts, but we also talked a lot about social conditions in the world. Many of my friends had parents who had come from Europe and had fled countries of oppression. Our house was a hub of activity for people with progressive political ideas.

For five years I lived in this setting. The group with whom I lived had friends from the Lincoln Brigade who had fought in the Spanish Civil War, members of the Baha'i faith, anarchists, socialists who were Trotskyites, socialists who were Leninists, philosophers, labor union leaders, poets, artists. This was the environment where I became a New Yorker and where I learned of the oppression and the colonization of other people. I came in contact with the histories of political movements — the Spanish Civil War, the Russian Revolution, the destruction of the Jews by the Nazis in Europe, the destruction and enslavement of Africans brought to the United States. I learned about all of these things, and in the process I learned to speak English fluently. This house in which I lived was a living school.

After years of this type of living, I reached out for some order in my life. I took a job working with children and also returned to school. I had only received a normal school certificate at the University of Puerto Rico. A normal school certificate was given upon completion of two years of college. With the certificate, you were eligible to teach in the lower grades of the elementary school. I worked in East Harlem while attending Hunter College to complete my bachelor of arts degree. I was an older student and I sought to make relationships with others. I learned that there were two or three Puerto Rican students on campus, and we began to meet. The group extended itself to other Puerto Rican students in other colleges of the city. We became a family, and because I was older and had more experience, I became the leader of the group. We used this group to politicize ourselves, as well as to find social supports. The group further extended to include factory workers and other young adults who were eager to meet, discuss ideas, and organize for action. We began to collect data on the situation of school dropouts, the situation of poverty as it affected our families, and the growing problem of gang activity among our youth. We not only studied, but we also organized action projects to address these situations. We were the only group of this kind working in our community. The majority of the Puerto Rican groups were hometown clubs that held dances to raise money to help each other when families had a need.

This original group named itself the Puerto Rican Association for Community Affairs (PRACA).[3] We became known as the "young Turks" because we questioned the leadership style existing in New York, which had been brought to us from the Island. We strongly believed that these leaders were not knowledgeable of the problems of the New York Puerto Ricans because they did not acknowledge the racist nature of the oppression that they were suffering. Racism was one of the issues that we had not recognized while living in Puerto Rico. There were three

---

[3] PRACA, a full-blown social service institution established in the 1950s, dedicates most of its resources to work with children in adoption, foster care, and in its bilingual nursery. It also offers services for leadership development and works on women's issues.

groups of Puerto Rican New Yorkers: those who emigrated during the 1920s and the 1930s, those who had emigrated during the 1960s, and a small group of young people who had been born in the city. This last group understood racism because they had established contact with the Black community and their struggle.

Many years later, while living and teaching at San Diego State, where I became the director of the social work program for undergraduate students, I learned how to teach social policy. My mentor was an African American, also from New York City. This relationship brought a fundamental change to my understanding of the nature of racism, oppression, and exclusion as weapons of sustaining the relationship between those who are privileged and those who are excluded. In more recent years, my teaching and writing have reflected a more clearly articulated political position.

Your early life experiences and your grandfather greatly influenced your life. Have there been other strong influences?

As a student, I was greatly influenced by literature and philosophy. You must remember that during my youth, education in Puerto Rico concentrated heavily on literature. Two writers of great importance in shaping my ideas were Miguel de Unamuno and José Ortega y Gassett. Unamuno inspired me because he emphasized the importance of living life fully and passionately with meaning. As a child, these ideas were romantic, but as I matured I came to a fuller understanding of the importance of living a life that would be one of accomplishments and benefits — not for oneself but for the lives of others. Very early in my life I came to understand that one has a responsibility to make the time and length of your life count for something worthwhile. As a child, I always felt that this was a noble cause — to live a life of meaning.

I grew up as a child very much influenced by remarks that my grandmother made about me. When people came to visit the house, my grandmother would always say, "Toni, show people your hands. This child has a special destiny!" How could I set aside such a prophesy? My grandfather would always tell me that I carried his name and that I should carry it proudly. When I began ASPIRA there was one exercise I did right away with the youth — in fact, I still do this exercise today. I ask them to repeat their names several times strongly and in a loud voice. When we started ASPIRA, the Puerto Rican youth were ashamed of their names. Their teachers were mispronouncing their Spanish names. In fact, they were saying the names in English or simply changing the names by shortening them or changing the letters. The children were too afraid to make the corrections. Not only was the name changed, but their self-image was also being changed.

In your life, how have experiences of discrimination and injustice influenced your vision and your commitment to institution building?

Very early in my work in the community, it became evident that we Puerto Ricans needed to build institutions that would provide for our needs in a manner that we could use them: by speaking to us in a language that we could understand and by considering that certain ways had no meaning to us because we were from another cultural context. This was the reason why those of us who began working together in the 1960s decided that instead of bringing Puerto Ricans to existing agencies, where they were not being adequately served, we needed to build our own institutions. One case in point was the placement of children in foster homes or with adoptive parents. I came in contact with the fate suffered by Puerto Rican children who were placed in non-Puerto Rican foster homes. Many of these children were confused and becoming self-haters. They were in boarding homes, institutional settings, or in foster homes where they were being lost as Puerto Ricans, or they were learning that they should forget their language, their parents' customs, and their origins. Over the objection of all the established foster care and adoption services in New York, we were able to establish our own institution, the Puerto Rican Association for Community Affairs, or PRACA.

What do you consider has been your most important contribution to the life of the Puerto Rican community in the United States?

Obviously, ASPIRA has had the greatest impact on my life, and on the lives of Puerto Rican youth in New York City and other cities where ASPIRA is established. I feel proud and rewarded that the basic model and philosophy of work remain fundamental to ASPIRA's operation after all these years. As I travel around the United States, it is clear that "Aspirantes" live and work around the country. Perhaps there are even Aspirantes in Europe and other parts of the world. I hear so many stories of the impact of ASPIRA on the lives of people! Two Aspirantes from the early years are people who have taken very seriously the commitment of leadership. Of course, these two are just a small example of the contributions of many others who are working, through their commitments, to change the life situations for others in our community. One is today the president of the Borough of the Bronx of New York City. He supports issues and agencies that serve our community. The other Aspirante is a vice-president at the Children's Television Workshop, where she makes available bilingual materials to Puerto Rican day-care and nursery programs. She is also active on the boards of ASPIRA of New York and PRODUCIR, Inc. Today Aspirantes' stories have just as much impact because our communities are beset with crime and tremendous obstacles that must be overcome.

I discover not only participants whose lives have been changed, but I also meet staff members whose lives have taken on greater meaning and value because they are engaged in work they consider to be important. Numerically, the graduates of ASPIRA range in the thousands. For New York alone, I believe the figure is 35,000.

If one examines the model and work of ASPIRA, ideas of culture and language are fundamental to its conceptualization and philosophy for action. Why were these important in building a foundation for your work?

Language is fundamental to a community's ability to communicate and to know and understand their environment, and to the ability to locate oneself and others in the social context. Language is the bloodstream where culture flows. Language and culture are the essence of one's identity. In New York, I found that the Puerto Rican youth had no sense of their parents' homeland and culture. They were losing their language and were ashamed of who they were, they had internalized the projections of self and group worthlessness that they were receiving from their teachers, the police, and the workers in agencies that were supposed to serve them. The message was clearly sent that to be Puerto Rican was to be worthless. Puerto Rican youth in New York needed to discover their language and culture in order to possess the strength of personality to believe in themselves. You must remember, in those years, for any people of color to think in this way was dangerous. It was considered extremely radical. ASPIRA had its critics and friends, but I was being pushed from both sides to forget about culture and language. Some people, especially the New York Board of Education, wanted these students to fit into the larger society and forget about being Puerto Rican.

ASPIRA, of course, is always identified as an educational institution, but I consider that all my work has always been about community development and providing resources for people to develop their personal and social strengths within the context of their cultural origins and the physical or national communities in which they live. In this sense, to my way of thinking, I have always been doing community development work, although it might have been characterized by others as education or social service work. The proof of this statement is in the thousands of Aspirantes who hold a strong sense of identity as their base of operation and at the same time have formed networks of personal and working relationships that extend across the United States. To my way of thinking, the economic aspect of my current work is new. New because I did not previously have an understanding of this dimension as it operates in our community or in the larger society. Now I fully understand the role of economic injustice and exclusion as it has destroyed our communities. For me, at this time, the most significant pursuit is restoring and creating economic justice for our communities. I see this goal not solely in terms of the individual pursuits, but as a pursuit for a collective community.

On the subject of ASPIRA, tell us how the symbol of the pitirre *and the name ASPIRA were chosen and why.*

We wanted a name and a symbol that our people would know and that would have meaning for us as a people. The name was selected as the command for the verb "to aspire." We wanted our youth to feel the sense of command and urgency in the name. As graduates, they would become Aspirantes, indicating that they had responded to the call. You know that ASPIRA has other symbols and ceremonies that are also significant to its mission. The pitirre was selected as a symbol because it is a bird in Puerto Rico, small but strong and clever. It could do battle with the mighty *guaraguao* (chicken hawk). We all felt that we were the small bird, David fighting the mighty Goliath.

Why did you come to the United States?

I had been a teacher in the hills of Puerto Rico, and I was the only working adult in my family. My income helped to support the others. We did not have public welfare in those days. I had not been paid for four months, and the pressures of my responsibility weighed heavily on me. We were being bombarded with information on new low-cost airplane fares, and many of my neighbors had left for the States. They would always return well dressed and with what seemed to us lots of money. The United States, with all its wealth and opportunities, became our dream for a future. Of course, we could not have known about the negative aspects of life there. No one talked about those things. I decided to leave for the United States. I was twenty-three years old. You could not get a permit to travel without a valid reason, since this was wartime. I applied to medical school at Columbia University, and I was accepted. I had no intention of going, but it was a way to get to the United States because medical students had a priority to travel. I became one of the "Marine Tigers," traveling the Atlantic Ocean during wartime. Later, I learned that those of us who emigrated during the 1960s were all called "Marine Tigers" because there was a freighter by that name that had brought some Puerto Ricans from the Island to the United States. The name was used by other Puerto Ricans who had lived in the United States for many years prior to our arrival, and was used in a derogatory manner to refer to us as unsophisticated and inexperienced. I traveled on the SS *Florida*, which docked in New Orleans, where I was introduced to racism. Three other young Puerto Ricans whom I met on the boat stayed with me while we waited to board the train to New York. We could not find a restaurant that would serve us. I still remember that, but at the time we did not recognize that we did not receive service because we were Black.

In reading some of your speeches, interviews, and articles, I notice that you have maintained a continuous personal struggle with the United States. What is at the root of this struggle?

My strong love/hate relationship with the United States is based on the imperialistic relations it has towards the Third World and non-White nations of the world. The United States invaded our Island one hundred years ago, and still remains on the Island as the conqueror who owns us.

The invasion of our country and its occupation up to the present day is one of the most glaring examples of the empire in possession of the land of a weaker nation. The United States also owned the Philippine Islands and Micronesia. At present, it still owns Guam and the Virgin Islands. In the United States, communities of people of color immigrating in search of a better way of life receive unequal resources, unequal representation before the law, and unequal access to the channels of justice. Non-White (and poor White) communities suffer as internal colonies.

The love part of my internal contradiction is based on the personal knowledge that in the United States there are and always have been movements of social justice that have succeeded in bringing changes before the law to redress the injustices. One must recognize and admire this aspect of the peoples of the United States.

You have received many honors and accomplished many things, yet you still seem to feel a great sense of identification with people who are "powerless." How do you explain this?

Yes, I think that you are correct. I still feel, somewhere inside myself, the vulnerability of my early days. This is not to say that I am not proud, completely self-assured, and a warrior. But in some respects, I hope that I never lose this vulnerable quality. It is the thing that keeps me discontent and fighting all the time. They call me an activist. Sometimes I feel offended by this label, because I think of myself as an educator, a writer, an institution-builder. Other times I consider this a great honor.

What is your position with regard to the situation of women in the Puerto Rican community?

I have always worked with a strong group of women around me in institution-building activities. Despite the minority status of women, I have always believed that our organizations, our communities, and our society would be well served by having the special attributes that women bring to their responsibilities. Of course, you cannot generalize about differences between males and females, but the input of women is frequently characteristically different. We tend not to seek power simply for personal gains. We are more concerned with using power to acquire resources to improve the life of our community. I have spoken on many occasions, very vocally, about the abuses of power by many of our male leadership in New York who have lost their professional careers or political positions because of their lack of community commitment and their pursuits of personal gains. I have always believed that leadership of institutions should change and give opportunities to an emerging leadership. Too frequently, one person or a small group in leadership never let go of the reins. When women are excluded, either from being officeholders or from networking relationships, it is wrong.

You have taught at many universities, so I know that you are aware that many educators consider education not to be political, but rather that education should remain "objective." How would you answer these people?

Education is always political in its methodology, its curriculum, and the arrangements it uses to administer its product. One need only read the history of the development of education in the schools of Puerto Rico. From this experience, as well as the experiences of other countries, including the United States, we know that education is used by the ruling classes or ruling power to promote certain ideas and to create a body of workers and professionals who respond to a vision of society that those in power hold. This is why we have fought so hard for community control of schools and for representation of our communities on local school boards as administrators and as trustees. You have a perfect example now in New York in the case of Eugenio María de Hostos Community College. The new administration has ordered that English proficiency be a requirement for graduation. This is a clear imposition of a political ideology. The same thing is happening in Puerto Rico. We could argue whether this is a good thing or a bad thing. The basic point is that the position represents the political ideology of those in power, and they are using their power to impose their will on all the people. There are other cases that we can cite. Something as simple as the wearing of school uniforms represents a set of values imposed by those in control of decisions about behavior. I would think that there are few academics who could continue to argue such a naive position following the civil unrest of the 1960s. Those who continue to argue that education is or should be "objective" ignore the history and sociology of education.

Since 1984 you have been involved in community economic development work. This focus is a shift from working in educational institutions. Why this shift?

In 1984, I returned to Puerto Rico after forty years in the United States. I had decided to retire in a village similar to the one where I had begun my early life as a teacher. My colleague and I bought a farm in the rain forest and decided that we would live a simple rural life. Neighbors found out that we had taught in California and that I had been a founder of ASPIRA. We were invited to a community meeting to present ourselves. At the meeting, the members of the civic and social association asked us to work directly with the community in bringing employment opportunities to our area. A resident committee was organized, and after a period of planning we began to develop goals, a work model, and a plan of action for the new organization, which we named PRODUCIR, "to produce." We have worked in PRODUCIR for the last twelve years. PRODUCIR was organized in 1986 with residents of a local village in Cubuy and Lomas of Canovanas. The corporation is owned and operated by local residents with the primary objective of improving the economic and social conditions of the residents.

This work was very important in realizing that to change a condition of poverty and dependency a community could begin a process of restoration of its basic functions. The most important function of a community is its economic function through production, distribution, and consumption. This is the way jobs are created and important resources are produced. If the economic function is not alive in a community, the community will die. We began the restoration of a local economy in our village by helping farmers learn new food-growing methods, and by constructing a small shopping center to open small businesses that would bring services that did not exist into the area. We also organized a community credit union. The growing of food products to sell in downtown supermarkets and the establishment of an array of small businesses to sell to community members started a good combination of economic activity. This would bring new money in, sell services and goods to improve the quality of life of the residents of the community, and leave savings in the credit union. The new economic activity employed people. As we have left PRODUCIR in the hands of the people of the community, it has secured funds to build a medical center, develop housing for low-income people, and start an educational project to help high school youth attend the university in pursuit of health careers so that they can eventually work in the medical center. The Board of Directors is negotiating to bring a factory that will employ 150 people, with the help of the Small Business Administration and the U.S. Department of Commerce.

In what activities are you now involved?

I am now working with the board and personnel of PRODUCIR, as an unpaid consultant. This action is a result of both my philosophy of work and my style of work. The project belongs to the residents of that community. When we began the work over twelve years ago, we made an agreement with the members of the planning committee that they must eventually take full responsibility for the work. In all the work that I have done in the United States, I have left the institution that I helped create because I believe that one should not hold on to an entity. There should be an opportunity for new leadership to develop and for new ideas to be born.

Currently, my health is good and I still feel energetic. I would like the opportunity to return to work with ASPIRA in terms of assisting them in the development of a community financial lending institution.

Your work has continued for over forty years. What motivates you to continue even after you have retired twice?

A firm belief in the possible achievement of a just society where we can all live with our differences — racial, cultural, age, sexual preference, and religion — without having to suffer punishment and where we can develop to our fullest potentials. If each one of us does one piece of the total work that must be done, this goal can be achieved. I am motivated by the desire to contribute towards building a more humane and just society. I am also motivated from another direction: I do not wish to live in a society where I see crime, poverty, sickness, and other social problems. I want to change these things. The motivation comes from the noble pursuit as well as the intolerance that I have for social injustice. To me, these are related factors, but they do not always operate in unison.

What things are happening that give you a sense that some positive activities are occurring in our society?

As I mentioned earlier, our communities now have large groups of professionals, elected officials, and public officials throughout the United States. We know that there are emerging communities of middle-class Puerto Ricans. We have the National Puerto Rican Coalition to thank for this information. We also have business people and individuals in the arts and sciences. Although our numbers are still relatively small when compared to other Spanish-speaking groups, the growth is reason to applaud.

In spite of the severe cutbacks in public funding to community organizations, Puerto Rican communities have continued to retain control and operation of their major institutions. Hopefully, we can still say this ten years from now. Although some of the same problems continue to exist, new problems have been added: AIDS, teenage crime and violence, and the number of children living in poverty continue to be unacceptable, as do school dropout rates and high levels of unemployment among our youth. We cannot afford to feel content or satisfied, although our community enjoys increased levels of individual accomplishments and successes. In fact, I was recently in Chicago where I participated in a reception for potential mentors for agencies serving Latino youth. I was greatly impressed by the number of young professionals who are coming forward to lend a hand to a younger person. This individual success now exists, but we cannot let the success of a few individuals cause us to forget that our future is at great risk if we do not continue to eliminate the problems. I recently received an invitation to serve on a national steering committee to address the condition of AIDS in the Latino community. I was horrified to learn of the projections for the devastating effect that this epidemic will have on our communities. In all my life, we have never faced such a devastating future. There is much work to be done.

One of the issues that I address constantly when asked the question that you asked has to do with the situation of leadership in our communities. We must require and support a leadership base made up of persons who are committed, honest, and responsible. They must be men and women, youth, seniors, homosexuals, and persons from various segments of the community who are committed to social justice and a more humane society. They must be responsible representatives of the people who are their constituents. None of us can afford to violate ethical rules or acquire power and resources to serve our own personal ends. I have never been a person who likes to emphasize how good things are. In fact, I have been accused of being overly critical. Since my life is guided by a vision of a humane and just society, I judge by what still needs to be done. This gives me and others much continuing work. I believe that one must be judged by the significance of one's contributions to others.

If you were to revisit or reconsider the work that you have done, how would you change any of your goals or activities?

Of course, you must remember that hindsight is always an easy way to consider that now you are correct. But I would say that when I started, if I had had a better political understanding of why people are poor, I would have developed a model of work that directly addressed economic injustice. I do not know how ASPIRA might have been different. Many of the Aspirantes moved on to universities and had enough of a start to expand their own understandings and activities. For me, I am now committed to working with various ASPIRA affiliates to teach and work out an institutional component that will assist them in creating financial entities that can collectively pool sums of our monies and use them for community economic development activities. We are especially thinking of lending and credit activities, saving and investment activities. In my way of thinking, this new work agenda that I have set for myself brings my life's work full circle.

What lessons would you like to share with future generations?

I think that one of the most difficult things for young people to understand is that life is a struggle. It never ends. And in this regard the struggle for justice and freedom must continue. The work must be linked from one generation to another, and we must see ourselves as links. Everyone has a part to play. No one can afford to sit on the sidelines. What affects one of us affects all of us. No one can really escape the experiences of injustice when the group is colonized. Our individual rights, as well as the rights of our communities in the United States and in our Island home, are at stake. When I came to Puerto Rico on my first return trip, I was very sick with asthma. I could not find work. I was generally discouraged and felt I should return to the States, although I had been told the environmental conditions were detrimental to my life. In Puerto Rico you could not find work unless you could prove to have done political work for the party in power. I decided to return to the States where the Puerto Rican Forum was the vehicle to get a grant from the Ford Foundation to develop a Puerto Rican Research Resources Center in Washington, DC. The research center then became the instrument to organize the Universidad Boricua with a grant from the Office of Education. (Department status had not yet been given. The office was under the Department of Health, Education, and Welfare.) During that time, a strong political activist visited my home. This was during the 1970s, and the struggle of communities of color to obtain their rights had evoked such a strong repressive reaction that I had arrived at the point that I believed that a more active struggle was necessary. At this point I thought I should leave my work and studies and join the direct struggle. This young political activist said to me, "You are not joining the direct struggle. Everyone has a part to play and your part is to teach." I learned very much that day. I learned that everyone in his or her own way must become an actor and play the part for which one is most suited.

Part Two

learning from struggles

learning from struggles

Part Two of this book is organized around two themes: national liberation and changing scholarship in academia. The first section discusses the experiences and politico-pedagogical positioning of groups who have struggled to organize in spite of the many layers of economic, gender-related, and colonial yokes that oppress them.

The second theme, changing scholarship in academia, is intended as a double entendre. On the one hand, this section reflects the stimulating and responsive scholarship that is emerging as a result of profound and dynamic intellectual, cultural, and methodological changes that are occurring in academia. On the other hand, such scholarship also speaks to the historically invisible and marginalized populations that are staking their claims within academia.

NATIONAL LIBERATION

Of course, the line between the two themes in this part is a fabricated one for the purposes of conceptual organization. The scholars who write of national liberation movements, and the education at the core of those movements, are also changing the scholarship in academia, as are many of the scholars in this book. For instance, in *Nationalist Ideologies, Neighborhood-Based Activism, and Educational Spaces in Puerto Rican Chicago*, Ana Y. Ramos-Zayas argues that schooling cannot be divorced from the political and socioeconomic forces governing neighborhood development. In doing so, Ramos-Zayas reenvisions both the study of schooling and the very definition of liberatory education. Ironically, Ramos-Zayas discovers that when schools encourage and facilitate the process whereby Puerto Rican students see beyond the rhetoric of democracy to the reality of colonialism, rather than losing hope for change, the students become agents for change at the local, national, and international level.

In addition to reenvisioning scholarship, the three chapters in the national liberation section are clearly focused on the educational experiences that emerge when groups mobilize their intellectual and cultural energies for national liberation. Ramos-Zayas, as mentioned above, writes of a Puerto Rican school in the United States based upon a nationalist (Puerto Rican) ideology. In the next chapter, *Women and Education in Eritrea: A Historical and Contemporary Analysis*, Asgedet Stefanos tackles as her central questions whether, and to what extent, Eritrean women have been achieving emancipation in postcolonial Eritrea. She then examines what role education has played in that process. Stefanos clearly articulates the challenge of liberation for all, and the central role of education in a period that followed great struggles for freedom from colonial rule.

Finally, in *The Palestinian Uprising and Education for the Future,* Khalil Mahshi and Kim Bush address the educational and liberatory potential of a popular uprising (the *intifadeh*) against colonial rule. Mahshi and Bush review the current educational system in the West Bank and Gaza, and analyze the intifadeh as a catalyst for educational change. The authors argue that "the intifadeh has erased traditional lines that divide educators and citizens, creating a laboratory for dramatic changes in all areas of education." In addition to discussing the nature of the challenges involved in such a change, Mahshi and Bush encourage debate among educators in Palestine and in the international educational community, thus contributing to the changing scholarship that is the central theme of the following section.

CHANGING SCHOLARSHIP IN ACADEMIA

It is worth repeating that the scholars featured in this section share at least one commonality with the scholars of the previous section: the ultimate source of their active engagement with the academy is the recognition of the struggles of the communities with which they are concerned. The notion of struggle, and the recognition of the communities that struggle mightily against oppressive systems of education, is the thread that weaves this tapestry of resistance and provides coherence to the text.

In *"The Department Is Very Male, Very White, Very Old, and Very Conservative": The Functioning of the Hidden Curriculum in Graduate Sociology Departments,* Eric Margolis and Mary Romero write of the struggles encountered by women of color graduate students in sociology and the effects of the "hidden curriculum." As a contribution to changing scholarship, Margolis and Romero argue that the women's stories, the authors' analysis, and the publication of the article are forms of resistance to the hidden curriculum and constitute "a lifting of veils to make visible what was hidden."

The goal of making visible that which is often obscured is also taken up by Cornel West in his interview with *HER* Editorial Board members Vitka Eisen and Mary Kenyatta and their discussion of heterosexism. West offers a vision of a democratic struggle that is inclusive of lesbian, gay, bisexual, and transgender people. He places heterosexism within the context of capitalism, thereby further establishing connections to other forms of oppression. He also reminds us that, as democratic educators, we continually have to examine the ways in which we may internalize, and therefore perpetuate, patriarchy and homophobia in our lives and our teaching.

In *Using a Chicana Feminist Epistemology in Educational Research,* Dolores Delgado Bernal outlines a feminist epistemological framework that is new to the field of educational research. This framework, which draws from the existing work of Chicana feminists, questions the notions of objectivity and a universal foundation of knowledge that are usually assumed in current research in education.

While Bernal recognizes the legacy of a feminist epistemology within the context of her work, Townsand Price-Spratlen discusses the role that Audre Lorde, W. E. B. DuBois, and Marlon Riggs have played in his own orientation toward "praxis" as a queer scholar of African descent. In *Negotiating Legacies: Audre Lorde, W. E. B. DuBois, Marlon Riggs, and Me,* Price-Spratlen describes his praxis formation as "negotiating legacies . . . an introspective process in which we attempt to learn the lessons of history by seeking to understand the contexts and contributions of our ancestors." In this chapter, Price-Spratlen provides an example to authors of how they may negotiate their own individual legacies of struggle and engagement with the society at large.

Finally, in *Latino Studies: New Contexts, New Concepts*, Juan Flores describes the historical and theoretical context for the study of Latino ethnicities. In discussing the changed context of Latino studies, Flores points to an interesting contradiction in the current movements for Latino and/or ethnic studies: while students at "elite" universities are marching and holding sit-ins for the creation of Latino studies departments, these departments are under threat of consolidation and dramatic budget cuts in the public universities that have housed them for decades. Additionally, the very nature of Latino studies has taken on a more global dimension that transcends particular Latino communities, such as Puerto Rican or Chicano studies.

Following the dual nature of many of the chapters in this section, while tracing the history of Latino studies, Flores is also calling for an opening of the theoretical space within Latino studies curricula, and the universities that house them, to allow room for the insights provided by feminist, postcolonial, and race theories, as well as lesbian and gay studies. This is, in fact, a critical dimension of the chapters in this part called "learning from struggles." The attempt to learn from struggle cannot be a static activity. We must engage with these authors, challenge their assumptions (and our own), and consider the contexts in which we live and work. Here is no "adventure in struggle" to counteract the ubiquitous "adventures in capitalism," but rather an invitation to perhaps "think different" and then, more importantly, to act differently as well.

Section One

national liberation

Nationalist Ideologies, Neighborhood-Based Activism, and Educational Spaces in Puerto Rican Chicago

ANA Y. RAMOS-ZAYAS

[Pedro] Albizu Campos [High School] is a school where the students want an education, without the gang violence, without racism; [it's] a place where you can find out about your background. This is good, because if you don't know where you come from, then you don't know where you're headed. My first impressions of this school were many, but what stood out the most was the different types of murals about people who had committed their lives and their hearts to give us, the next generation, the opportunities that they did not have. This school has changed me in many different ways. This school taught me to be me, and not what other people want me to be. This school helped me look at my community and say, "I can make a difference." I can be anything that I want to be, only if I put my mind to it, only if I want it. This school taught me about something that I'd never been taught before, and I realized that I needed to learn about my culture. I learned about how hard it was to come from the island of Puerto Rico or from Mexico and find a well-paying job to maintain a home, and to support children, in the land of opportunities, so to speak. (David Villalobos, 16)[1]

[Pedro Albizu Campos High School] is about keeping us away from the gangs in the community and getting into the activities of the community. It is a comfortable place to come to, where everyone takes the time to listen to your problems and tries to help you out. The teachers understand when you are having trouble with a certain question or problem. They would actually go over it until you finally got the hang of it. I was really messed up at Clemente [the other high school in the community]. I never really knew how an A would look on my report card until I came here. This school is a real good experience for me. There is a lot of activities to join, like [the march against the] *Sun-Times,* which I participated in. The Washington trip [to advocate on behalf of Puerto Ricans imprisoned for political reasons] was a lot of fun. This school is the best thing that has happened to me since I first started high school. (Lydia Vélez, 15)

Harvard Educational Review   Vol. 68 No. 2 Summer 1998, 164–192

In this article, I focus on the role of grassroots, pro-Puerto Rican independence activists in community-based educational projects in Chicago. Through this focus, I attempt to understand Puerto Rican education at the intersections of conflictive political narrative, notions of "community building," and nationalist identities, as I believe that schooling cannot be divorced from the political and socioeconomic forces governing neighborhood development. In the case of Chicago's Puerto Rican barrio, there is a powerful irony in the fact that a pro-independence ideology, which encourages critical appraisal of U.S. policies toward Puerto Rico and of the myth of the "American Dream," actually encourages high school students to pursue mainstream mobility routes, such as abandoning gangs, finishing high school, and enrolling in college. One would think that such nationalist ideologies and identity politics would instead create resentment and anger, and encourage program participants to reject mainstream U.S. institutions. However, the opposite seems to be the case: high-risk Puerto Rican youths — including gang members and teenage mothers — are being drawn into the alternative high school, peer counseling initiatives, and the community-building process sponsored by the pro-independence activists. I argue that it is precisely the identity politics behind the oppositional education programs that explains why these students defy the odds and remain interested in schooling.

This article is based on field research in northwestern Chicago, including a series of follow-up visits to the area. The sampling frame for this research consisted of employees and clients of not-for-profit and grassroots multiservice agencies, most of whom live in Humboldt Park, West Town, or Logan Square, all neighborhoods in this part of Chicago. These multiservice organizations included a continuing education program for adults and teen mothers; GED and ESL programs; a parental involvement project at the main local high school; and a local chapter of a national not-for-profit youth education agency. The ethnographic methodology was eclectic, including participant observation; informal and semistructured interviews; life history interviews; focus groups including youths and young adults; and textual analysis of journals, murals, and area markers, personal letters, grassroots publications and newsletters, and autobiographical writings by students at various educational and informal sites. Archival research was also done at the Chicago Historical Society.

First I present the historical background of militant Puerto Rican politics in Chicago, as well as the urban patterns that define the largest Puerto Rican community in the Midwest. Second, I examine the Pedro Albizu Campos High School (PACHS) and its umbrella organization, the Juan Antonio Corretjer Puerto Rican Cultural Center (PRCC). In particular, I look at how students, teachers, and staff conceptualize "struggle," nationalist identities, and community building. Finally, I explore the political and class dynamics involved in the interaction between pro-independence grassroots activists and barrio residents on the one hand, and white-collar Puerto Rican city officials, professionals, and the mainstream media on the other. I argue that an oppositional education (an education that centers on promoting social criticism) premised on political ideologies — including developing an understanding of struggle, nationalist pride, inequality/oppression in the United States, and community involvement — is a potentially powerful, yet largely untapped, philosophical resource for ethnoracial youth education and popular education programs.

HISTORICAL BACKGROUND:
PUERTO RICAN POLITICAL MILITANCY IN CHICAGO

Social and political awareness triggered by the civil rights movement in Chicago, coupled with early Alinsky-style community development efforts in Humboldt Park in the 1970s (Cruz, 1997), partly explains the distinctive politicization of Puerto Rican identity in Chicago.[2] The nationalist political militancy that has characterized the Chicago Puerto Rican community ever since resulted in part from the simultaneous arrival of Puerto Ricans in Chicago in the 1960s and community strategies developed during that time, as well as the continued neighborhood activism of the 1970s and 1980s.

The civic organizations of the early 1960s — particularly the "hometown clubs," made up of people from the same hometowns in Puerto Rico — had provided recreational and social structure to recently arrived Puerto Rican families (Padilla, 1987). After the Humboldt Park Riots of 1966 and 1977, both triggered by confrontations between the police and residents after the Puerto Rican Day parades, and the implementation of community action programs, more militant efforts emerged. The Young Lords Organization, among the most renowned embodiments of Puerto Rican political militancy in the United States, was founded in Chicago at this time, when a group of Puerto Rican high school dropouts and former gang members launched neighborhood-based programs by occupying and taking over local institutions.

In the early 1980s, the Chicago Puerto Rican community was at the center of political controversy in the United States and Puerto Rico. The Fuerzas Armadas para la Liberación Nacional (Armed Forces for National Liberation, or FALN), a clandestine group advocating political independence for Puerto Rico "by any means necessary," publicly admitted responsibility for a series of bombings in military facilities in both the U.S. and Puerto Rico in the late 1970s (Fernández, 1994). The fifteen Puerto Rican group members of the FALN, thirteen of whom were born or raised in Chicago, were eventually arrested and given lengthy sentences on charges of "seditious conspiracy to overthrow the U.S. government."[3] Reporters from Puerto Rico and all parts of the United States arrived in Chicago's Humboldt Park to interview the relatives of the youngsters involved in the FALN; some were hoping to resurrect a waning nationalist tradition, while others were curious to see who these "terrorists" were (Bruno, 1981).

The FALN redefined Puerto Rican politics and social networks in Chicago in several ways. Deep divisions developed between the prisoners' supporters and opponents and today remain a source of intragroup conflict among barrio activists in Chicago. Since the prisoners, prior to their incarceration, had developed grassroots programs that tended to the Puerto Rican poor (examined below) and were working poor themselves, many barrio residents and activists associated grassroots activism and militant nationalism with antipoverty programs in Humboldt Park. In some cases, these political divisions were understood along class lines. Most informants claimed that the militant activists were working-poor barrio residents; their opponents were perceived to be more white collar. However, there were exceptions in both camps.

In the 1980s, at the peak of FALN activity and FBI persecution, when most group members were still "underground," Puerto Rican residents of Humboldt

Park/West Town appeared divided. "Signs of 'FALN Welcomed Here' appeared on people's houses and cars," commented Lola Rivera, a Puerto Rican woman in her early thirties, whose uncle is an FALN prisoner (Rivera was named an "outstanding teacher of the year" at both the local high school and the Pedro Albizu Campos High School). Jaime García, an active statehood advocate, said he agreed with the FBI and other government agents that the FALN members were "terrorists" who "gave all Puerto Ricans a bad name."[4]

Puerto Rican *independentista* (advocating for independence), nationalist, and communist militancy has been traditionally marginalized from "official" narratives — that is, those conveyed by mainstream sources, such as media reports, textbooks, legal discourse, and so on — in "an attempt to create a unifying, non-conflictive history of 'the Puerto Rican people' . . . [in which] violence was the missing aspect of historical discourse" (Díaz-Quiñones, 1993, pp. 26–27). The marginalization of these events contributes to *la memoria rota* (the broken memory), which Díaz-Quiñones defines as "the rupture of the continuity in the Puerto Rican community, the memory deliberately negated by political power, or broken by official repression and cultural exclusion" (1993, pp. 11–12). However, in Humboldt Park, Puerto Rican nationalist history has been resurrected, modified, and incorporated into all aspects of barrio life. In fact, Puerto Rican nationalism and a militant history that view violence and armed struggle as sometimes necessary serve as ideological foundations for neighborhood development and educational projects. Nationalist narratives have been adopted as ideological foundations of alternative and/or oppositional social service programs in Humboldt Park. Barrio activists and residents see their socioeconomic condition as Puerto Ricans in the United States as analogous to the political relations between Puerto Rico and the United States; in both cases, narratives of colonialism and struggle are evoked. Hence, a Puerto Rican youth "struggles" with the consequences of poverty, just as Puerto Rican nationalists have historically "struggled" against U.S. political control of Puerto Rico. These analogies bridge community-building projects (such as the urban renewal project of Humboldt Park's commercial area, community health clinics, alternative education programs, and cultural events) with metanarratives of heroism and sacrifice drawn from Puerto Rican nationalist movements of the past.

ETHNOGRAPHIC CONTEXT: URBAN PATTERNS AND THREATS TO THE PUERTO RICAN COMMUNITY

Chicago's neighborhood-based urban pattern contributes to the strong associations between cultural groups and specific city areas.[5] In Chicago, the "Puerto Rican community" is coterminous with the Humboldt Park/West Town/Logan Square area, while the heart of the "Mexican community" is on the South Side (especially Pilsen, or "la Villita"), and African Americans are largely concentrated in the west and southwest sides of the city.[6] Awareness of this neighborhood-based ethnic distribution is essential to understanding the interethnic relations, territoriality, and nationalist manifestations among Puerto Ricans in Chicago.

Of the three adjacent neighborhoods that border the Puerto Rican community, West Town is the closest one to downtown Chicago and, hence, is a very desirable real estate area. Within West Town itself, structural differences are dramatic. Sections of West Town are considered "historic landmarks," with gray stone mansions similar to those in the most exclusive Chicago neighborhoods. These mansions are less than a couple of blocks away from abandoned factories, car repair garages and dealers, unpaved streets, and run-down houses that appear abandoned, but often are not.

Racial and social differences between Puerto Rican residents and non-Puerto Rican newcomers exacerbate group misperceptions. While many interviewees referred to the newly arrived residents of West Town as "yuppies," the White twenty-somethings moving into Wicker Park, the easternmost section of West Town, are far from being the clean-cut, high-paid professionals one associates with this label. More typical of Wicker Park residents is a style of numerous body piercings, tattooing, spiked and dyed hair, and worn-out clothes — what one informant wittily described as "the Harley Davidson meets Morticia Adams look." The area is advertised as perfect for artists, and, indeed, many aspiring young White artists have moved there. A proliferation of trendy coffee shops, art supplies stores, and New Age music clubs cater to the expanding Wicker Park artist population.[7]

"They are . . . they are like hippies or something," commented Alma Juncos, a middle-aged Puerto Rican woman who is a parent-volunteer at the local high school. "That looks so disgusting. Look at those tattoos, the tongue and nose earrings. That's self-mutilation!" "These White kids think that living in poverty is 'cool.' They wanna be friends with Blacks and Latinos and pretend they are homeboys and homegirls themselves," explained Tamika Miranda, a stylish Puerto Rican woman in her mid-twenties who works at a local Latino agency and attends law school at night. The general feeling is that these gentrifiers are privileged people who mock the evils of actual poverty by appropriating the discourse of the poor as their own. Because most of the young Latino agency workers and grassroots activists themselves grew up in poverty, they are particularly condemning of the romanticized version of a very painful reality of barrio life.

The influx of non-Puerto Ricans — particularly White artists, African American families, and Central American immigrants — into West Town, Humboldt Park, and Logan Square, respectively, has strengthened nationalist sentiments among Puerto Rican barrio residents and activists. The growing importance of making it known that "Humboldt Park is Puerto Rican" is partially evidenced by the symbols used to mark key sections of the neighborhood. The most recent addition to the numerous nationalist murals, statues, and streets named for Puerto Rican heroes consists of two fifty-ton Puerto Rican flags of steel erected on Division Street to mark both ends of Paseo Boricua, Humboldt Park's main commercial area. Neighborhood flyers explaining concepts like "gentrification," "ethnic cleansing," and "urban renewal" are frequently distributed to barrio residents, as activists encourage Puerto Ricans to "sell to other Puerto Ricans" and to "support Puerto Rican businesses."

Barrio residents know that their chances of moving to a "better area" are bleak, and that the threat of displacement into even more run-down areas looms on the horizon. Some residents see Humboldt Park, West Town, and Logan Square as leading venues for employment among Puerto Ricans of all socioeconomic and occupational levels, but these employment opportunities will vanish if the community disperses. Social service agencies are already contemplating relocation as their clients are displaced by other groups. Owners of small businesses that rely on the community for survival are threatened with extinction as well. Similarly, ambulatory businesses, like the unionized fritters cooks (*los fritoleros*) in Humboldt Park or the sellers of miscellaneous area souvenirs (e.g., Paseo Boricua T-shirts, stickers, Puerto Rican flags) on Division Street are also threatened by the changing composition of the neighborhood. These small and ambulatory businesses target a very specific, Puerto Rican population, and are unlikely to survive the changing ethnic composition of the area. Thus, new symbols, urban plans, and agendas to "Puerto Ricannize" Humboldt Park have been promoted by neighborhood residents and grassroots activists.

When the two steel Puerto Rican flags were unveiled on Division Street, many nationalist activists commented on how "these flags are the only monuments to the Puerto Rican flag there are in the world." Presumably, prominently displaying Puerto Rican nationalist symbols would prevent further gentrification and protect small Puerto Rican businesses in Chicago. "This is the use of nationalism to reclaim space . . . away from gentrifiers," argued a leading neighborhood activist and administrator of the Puerto Rican Cultural Center, one of the main grassroots organizations in the area, also founded by FALN members.

"LOS NACIONALISTAS" IN HUMBOLDT PARK: THE PUERTO RICAN CULTURAL CENTER, MILITANT NARRATIVES, AND NATIONALIST IDENTITIES

One cannot pass by the Juan Antonio Corretjer Puerto Rican Cultural Center (PRCC) without noticing the building. The bright colors of Puerto Rican revolutionary flags and quotations of "Viva Puerto Rico Libre," "Freedom to Puerto Rican POWs," and "No to Colonialism" written on the building walls are in sharp contrast with the underutilized gray factories and small walk-up houses surrounding the Center. The faces of several men and women — the FALN prisoners who founded the Center — hang on colorful poster boards on the walls of the building. The Juan Antonio Corretjer Puerto Rican Cultural Center is named after a celebrated Puerto Rican poet, activist, and member of Puerto Rico's Nationalist Party from the 1930s through the 1950s. The Cultural Center building was a Walgreen's photo lab before being rehabilitated in 1976 by a group of community activists who were advocates of Puerto Rico's independence from the United States. The hard work that transformed a deteriorated building into a comfortable, welcoming place is a source of great pride to the community.

The atmosphere of the Cultural Center is one of constant motion; people of all ages walking up and down the stairs, answering phones, calling each other out. The feeling that everybody knows each other well, combined with a sense of purposefulness in the building, evokes the need to be "doing something" or "working on something" at all times, as if a sign were hanging by the entrance door stating, "no lounging allowed beyond this point." In fact, most members of the Cultural Center spend long evenings and most weekends in this building — planning activities, printing flyers, designing projects, writing grants, cleaning and repairing, and even doing "overnight security" shifts to make sure the Center is always attended.

Approximately fifty or sixty staff and twice as many project participants — not including the residents who receive occasional services or attend specific activities (e.g., a museum exhibit, health clinic orientations, a City Hall demonstration) —

constitute the regular members of the Cultural Center. Most members, barrio residents, and youth who participate in the Center's projects live the daily torments of poverty, which serve as an unfortunate common bond among them.

The projects sponsored by the Cultural Center have emerged as specific needs have arisen in the community, rather than according to a planned strategy. For instance, the National Committee to Free the Puerto Rican Political Prisoners (NC) was founded to guide the campaign to liberate five nationalists, who were granted amnesty in 1979. Most recently, the NC has continued its efforts to gain amnesty for the fifteen Puerto Rican men and women — including the founders of the Cultural Center — still being held in U.S. federal penitentiaries.

The high incidence of HIV and AIDS in the Puerto Rican community, and the funding available for AIDS education, research, and treatment, led to the creation of the Center's Vida/SIDA health education program. Similarly, the need for safe child care prompted the development of the Consuelo Lee Corretjer Child Care Center. The Family Learning Center (FLC) represents a grassroots effort to involve parents in their children's education, and to advance their own educational development by pursuing high school degrees and job training. When the Chicago Park District refused to place a statue of nationalist leader Pedro Albizu Campos in Humboldt Park, the Center founded the Pedro Albizu Campos Museum of Puerto Rican History and Culture to house the statue. In an effort to "Puerto Ricanize" Division Street and deter further displacement of Puerto Ricans out of Humboldt Park, the Cultural Center created the BOHIO housing cooperative and bought three buildings in the Division Street area, one of which houses the Borikén Bakery and Café. These buildings are increasingly desirable real estate areas.

Awareness of nationalist Puerto Rican history and notions of "community building" are transmitted through popular education and social service programs aimed at high-risk students in Humboldt Park. One of the oldest and best-established projects of the Cultural Center is the Pedro Albizu Campos High School (PACHS), an alternative Puerto Rican high school. PACHS illustrates the intersection of popular education and community building in a nationalist context, and how learning among at-risk Puerto Rican youth takes place in controversial political settings.

Founded a year before the Cultural Center, PACHS — or "la Escuelita," as it is affectionately known — was created by a group of teachers and eleven Puerto Rican students who had been expelled from Murphy Tulley High School (now called Roberto Clemente High School). As Cultural Center activists and students proudly narrate, these students were expelled after organizing several strikes demanding a more culturally sensitive curriculum for the predominantly Puerto Rican student body, and refusing to salute the American flag, a pro-independence act of political defiance.

When their petitions for educational reform — including bilingual education and Puerto Rican history classes — went unheard, the eleven student leaders and other community activists, most of whom advocated Puerto Rican independence and belonged to pro-independence groups in the 1970s, rented the basement of a Presbyterian church in West Town and held Puerto Rican history and Spanish classes there. Once the Cultural Center was rehabilitated by some of the same students and community members in 1976, the high school moved to its present location on the second floor of that building.

Most of the students who come to PACHS are escaping gang activity or have been expelled from public schools because of too many absences, poor grades, or disciplinary problems.[8] When they arrive at PACHS, these students are one step away from dropping out of school altogether, if they have not already done so. "These kids have had lots of discouraging experiences with schools in general, [and with] racist teachers. [They have] been put down a lot. . . . Some others just come here because they want a school that teaches Puerto Rican history and culture," said Elena Colón, who teaches a Women's Studies and Health class, does individual counseling, and is in charge of most administrative work at PACHS.

Through its affiliation with the Cultural Center's other programs and with other community organizations, PACHS provides resources and information on a variety of issues outside the academic curriculum, such as health-related, legal, psychological, and financial problems. The school's long waiting list indicates that it has become a desirable option for many young people and their families. Director Melvin Rodríguez explains the increasing popularity of PACHS: "Students who fill out applications learn about us through friends or because they've had family members who have come here. Parents talk to parents, students talk to other students. They are all saying positive things about what we do here. Also, people know more about us through the work we do in the community."

"If even one, just one, student stops coming to the school, drops out, we have all failed," Rodríguez once said in a teachers' meeting, when frustration with one particular student had escalated. "Mondays are the worst days because we haven't seen students in two days and a lot happens in their lives, especially over weekends," one of the teachers explained. On this day, one student had just found out she was pregnant and needed guidance, another one had been raped, and yet another one had been arrested for writing gang signs on a wall and his mother did not speak enough English to get him out of detention. Like most Cultural Center members, the PACHS teachers are second-generation Puerto Ricans born in Chicago or brought to the Midwest as children; some are the sons and daughters of early steel mill workers (Bensman & Lynch, 1988). They have strong ties to Chicago's Puerto Rican barrio, where they grew up and still live, and have longstanding social and kinship networks. Fifteen-year-old Mark Anthony Rodríguez, a PACHS student, powerfully articulates the physical safety, cultural awareness, and emotional sustenance la Escuelita provides:

> This escuelita is a family that cares and supports you and will always be there to give you advice when you need it. They care so much about our education. Teachers and students treat each other like a big family. We can feel safe coming to this school because no one will shoot or shank you because they assume you are gang related.

Students' stories are poignant. Isis, a senior attending the Family Learning Center, a program for teen mothers and middle-aged students, recalls the support she received: "Melvin [PACHS's director] took food, clothes, everything to us when our house burnt down. We had lost everything. People from here helped us a lot." Whenever attendance drops below 85 percent, teachers commit themselves to making sure that the missing students show up to school, even if that involves giving students wake-up calls, rides to school, or literally dragging them out of bed.

Early in the school's admissions process, potential students realize that la Escuelita, besides being an alternative to gang violence, also supports explicit political stands and has its own philosophy, as student José Vega describes:

During the [entrance] interview, the teachers told me that Pedro Albizu Campos is a different school from other high schools. The reason was because the Escuelita had its own philosophy and a whole different environment from other schools. They also mentioned that the reason why this school exists is for the purpose of teaching and showing the youth about their culture, their past, their ancestors, and where we stand as Puerto Ricans in the world. Students attend here because they want to get away from the gang conflicts and want a better education where they feel safe.

NATIONALIST NARRATIVES AND CONCEPTUALIZATIONS OF "STRUGGLE"

A wooden sign at the school's entrance reads, "Dr. Pedro Albizu Campos High School, Excellence in Teaching Award, 1986." The sign is a souvenir of an incident frequently remembered at the Cultural Center as part of "the struggle," an occasion when the school's academic excellence award was rescinded because of its political history. In 1985, the Council for American Private Education (CAPE) and the U.S. Department of Education selected Pedro Albizu Campos High School as one of the exemplary private schools of the year. Shortly after the high school was notified of its award, a local television station aired a news series interspersing shots of the school with those of the trials of FALN members, suggesting that the school was a poor choice for the award. In response, the award was temporarily withheld, and a second team of observers was sent to assess whether the high school actually deserved the award. The award was reinstated, but suddenly rescinded again just five hours before the school's graduation ceremony, where the award was to be celebrated. "Eventually, after having it taken back the second time, they said they did want to give it to us. That's when we said we didn't want it anymore," explained a PACHS teacher. Feeling that they nevertheless did deserve an award for educational excellence, teachers and students at PACHS inscribed their own award on the plaque that now stands at the entrance to the school.

"Some people refer to us as 'Those communists down the street,'" joked Armando Medina, a Cultural Center activist, "but when they come to us for services and get to know us, see what we do in the community, they understand what we're about." Many neighborhood residents recognize that the Center is one of the few places that offers viable and affordable alternatives in adult education, high school and infant programs, and health and housing counseling. Yet, they are also aware of the Center's political history, including its clashes with the FBI and support of the FALN.

At PACHS, activists and students tell about the day in 1983 when the FBI raided the Center and apprehended its founders. At 5 A.M, over fifty FBI agents wearing black jumpsuits and raid gear marked "FBI" entered the Puerto Rican Cultural Center, alongside Chicago police officers and members of the Illinois Law Enforcement division. Astonished neighbors and students working in summer programs stood outside the building while the FBI searched for evidence that linked other Cultural Center activists to the FALN members. None was found, but substantial damage was done to the computer equipment and the Center's archives. As one informant recalls:

> [When] the FBI raided the building they caused a lot of damage. We thought we'd have to close down, but the community helped out in rebuilding the place. In the first day alone, we collected $3,000 through fundraising. Eventually we raised $15,000 among the people of West Town.

This has become one of the most repeated stories about the Center's history, and Cultural Center activists still recall the impact of the incarceration of the FALN members on neighborhood life. Although no evidence was found, the school and the Cultural Center were listed as sites searched for terrorist activity, which colored the community's perception of the Center for a long time thereafter.

The controversy around these political prisoners — were they heroes of the Puerto Rican independence movement or terrorists unappreciative of the United States' generosity toward Puerto Rico? — is central to militant politics and social activism in Chicago's Puerto Rican community. While the Center avidly portrays the political prisoners as heroes, this image is contested by the prisoners' opponents. Yet other residents advocate for the prisoners, stating that "they have been in prison too long." Their statements offer humanitarian rather than political reasons for their support; still others perceive this campaign and the activists as "dated," leftovers from the 1960s (Fernández, 1994).

Perceptions of the political prisoners are mixed, conflictive, and provocative. Opponents of the prisoners perceived them as terrorists who brought unwelcome violence to the community and created a bad reputation for all Puerto Ricans, who were considered "trouble" by surveillance agents. In contrast, the prisoners' supporters and barrio residents, who remember the prisoners as "one of us" and as cherished community activists, perceive the prisioners' actions as heroism, nationalism, and authenticity.

One of the most telling narratives about the prisoners was articulated by Doña Luz, the grandmother and legal guardian of Zaida, a troubled and impoverished PACHS student. Doña Luz and Zaida's house is on the street that marks the gang warfare zone between the Cobras and the rival Latin Kings gang. The bare cement floor of Doña Luz's house oddly contrasts with the ornate religious images on the walls. The pungent smell of the uncollected dumpster near the house infiltrates the tiny living room on a humid summer afternoon.

"I've had to raise this kid all alone," said Doña Luz, a tired, dark-skinned Puerto Rican woman in her late fifties, pointing to Zaida, who sits quietly listening. Then, in a voice impregnated with contained emotion, Doña Luz added:

> That's why I wanted her to go to la Escuelita [PACHS], because my own sons went there, and I'm always grateful for that opportunity. I remember how I used to cook for school activities back then [1970s and 1980s]. But, it's not the same . . . since Alejandrina [Torres, one of the prisoners] has been gone [to prison]. It's not the same. She used to come here all the time, helped my sons. She helped us so much. . . . She helped everyone so much.

Doña Luz sees Alejandrina as a "savior" of sorts, similar to those on her house's walls, a woman who acted as a sacred mediator for the poor. Doña Luz remembers Alejandrina for her efforts in community building and her humanitarian commitment to barrio residents.

In Humboldt Park, narratives and myths around the FALN members abound and are at the center of both barrio mobilization and conflict. As Lancaster (1988) argues, "Once told, these tales are nothing; recited a thousand times, they become folklore, myth, collective representation . . . they ultimately pass into mnemonic devices of class consciousness, the guideposts and blueprints of future praxis" (p. 133).

The teaching award incident and FBI raid serve as narratives that illustrate, as one teacher commented, "the significance of terms like 'struggle,' 'resistance,' and the 'sacrifices' of standing by one's beliefs." These narratives, along with the numerous public demonstrations on behalf of the FALN prisoners, against educational budget cuts and media misrepresentations of Puerto Ricans, create unique definitions of struggle. As Carmencita Martínez, an eighteen-year-old PACHS student, recalls:

> In my second year [at PACHS], all I did was experience things that were related to school. My first experience was when I went to protest with the school. We were protesting for the Puerto Rican POWs. We want them free! It was good. These protests have taught me that no matter what you want, you should always stand up for your rights. It showed me that if you want something you have to go out there and get it. It ain't going to be easy, but you will get it.

Hence, the politics behind education and community projects becomes explicit, implicitly encouraging students and parents to adopt these politics in their involvement with community projects.

While the Cultural Center values ideas of struggle and community building as signs of strength and resilience, for many students struggle implies daily dangers, poverty, and sacrifices that create conflictive attitudes toward the community-building process. For instance, Vanessa Acosta, a bright young woman who has struggled with poverty, gang activity, and sexual abuse, wrote in a class paper that she hoped to "get an education so that I can get my parents a house outside this community."

Nonetheless, notions of "giving back" are also solidified at PACHS and other projects of the Center. As Diana Sánchez, an upbeat seventeen-year-old PACHS student, powerfully conveys:

> I came [to PACHS] with very little knowledge about my people, my community, and my history. But I came out with enough to give people a good argument, and to know what I am talking about. I chose to pursue my college education and major in criminal justice. I would like to come back someday and help my people, and of course my Escuelita. In the four years that I have been here, we have struggled as a family to keep this school open, and we have luckily succeeded. If I had a wish, I would wish that the students, teachers, and staff would never have to struggle again.

Like Vanessa and Diana, students appreciate the process of community building in addressing some of their immediate social needs. However, in the long term, these younger Puerto Ricans hope to pursue mainstream mobility routes, such as higher education, to improve their socioeconomic condition and be able to move out of or give back to Humboldt Park.

For many Cultural Center members of all ages, joining the PRCC marked a personal transformation or a raised political awareness — a *concientización,* as PACHS director Rodríguez describes the process — that also contributed to a heightened sense of their Puerto Ricanness and ethno-nationalist pride. PRCC activists associate involvement at the Center with an enhanced sense of Puerto Ricanness through the forging of an ideological identity grounded on a knowledge of nationalist Puerto Rican history, literature, symbols, and neighborhood activism. Juan González, a sixteen-year-old PACHS student, explains:

> What I really liked [my freshman year at PACHS] was when the school took a trip to Colorado. On that very same day we marched for the Puerto Rican Prisoners of War. We marched for Oscar López; he was going to be transferred to a maximum[security] prison called Florence, where if you get locked up you can't associate with any prisoners. I thought that was messed up.
>
> I know if I would have gone to another school, I wouldn't have made it this far [to graduation]. . . . I like this school because they teach you about your heritage, and when you learn about yourself and where you come from, you would be so amazed that you'd like to learn more. The only thing I can say now is I'm proud to be a Puertorriqueño, not to mention, I feel very good knowing two languages.
>
> I'm going to miss this school a whole lot. . . . You will not find another school like this one. I like this school because it helps teenagers realize that gangs aren't the only option there is in this world. Some of the students that come to this school work with Vida/SIDA; they become peer educators. They go out into the community, and sometimes they give out condoms to people. The Latinos in the Humboldt Park community have the highest rate of having AIDS. That's why we go out into our community to help Latinos and prevent them from getting the disease.

Students learn firsthand that they have skills valuable to their community by participating in numerous community-wide activities — from producing flyers announcing community events, to creating floats or artwork, to recruiting sponsors for particular events and conceptualizing projects. Some of the events, like the Boricua Festival, "el Desfile del Pueblo," and the Pedro Albizu Campos Puerto Rican Week, take place once a year, while others (e.g., Vida/SIDA peer counseling and workshops) are ongoing throughout the school year. Like Juan González, other PACHS youth perceive schooling as a conglomerate of interconnected activities, which encourage community building, sociohistoric awareness, and enhanced ethno-political identity. These provide a more immediate stage on which to enact their notions of struggle.

PUERTORRIQUEÑIDAD AND BOUNDARIES:
THE "UNITY" CLASS

At PACHS, like in other nationalist projects sponsored by the Cultural Center, Puerto Ricanness is the leading factor in determining the level of access a participant is allowed. Support for (or at least sympathy with) the Center's political visions is perhaps a close second. Asked to become director of the school after just one year of teaching, Melvin Rodríguez recalls: "There were people better qualified than I was, but they were not Puerto Rican. I had the most important qualification: being Puerto Rican." For many of the Center's activists, the Puerto Rican independence movement and the community work at the Center legitimizes Puerto Ricanness as an ideological identity premised on nationality-based alliances, even when this requires the avoidance of more inclusive multicultural or pan-ethnic identities such as "Latinos," "Hispanos," or "minorities."

"I would like to have more Puerto Rican teachers, but some people don't want to work here. The pay is too low or they don't believe in the political work," commented an activist, who stressed the need to create a "unified all-Puerto Rican front" among teachers in the school to make sure that "Whites don't follow on their natural tendency to take over." Elena, another PACHS teacher and administrator, echoes this sentiment: "As colonized people, we have a tendency to go to the White faces for guidance. And the White faces have a tendency to want to take over. In this school, White people are challenged with a different power structure, which places Puerto Ricans in charge."

The White teachers who have been at the high school the longest accept, and even understand, the boundaries they are not supposed to transgress by virtue of their not being Puerto Rican. The recent arrivals, however, wrestle with the fact that they are expected to remain at the margin of the school and the neighborhood issues discussed in all-Puerto Rican spaces, like the Unity for Social Analysis class.

The Unity for Social Analysis class, or "Unity," as this town meeting-style class is commonly known, is one of the most obvious "Puerto Rican spaces" at PACHS. This is a class in which Puerto Rican students and teachers talk about issues affecting the school and neighborhood, resolve conflicts, and plan activities. The fifty Puerto Rican students and five teachers sit in a circle in the basement cafeteria. White Americans, even those who have been teaching at PACHS for years, do not attend Unity unless invited in advance. During the academic year of my fieldwork, none of the White teachers was invited and a Mexican female teacher was invited once.

Many Unity gatherings aim to address the social conditions affecting all Humboldt Park youth. When Miguelito, a sixteen-year-old boy with severe learning disabilities and incredible mechanical skills, pulled a knife on Michelle, a first-year student, the question of whether Miguelito should remain at PACHS was discussed in Unity. In a particularly moving Unity session, students expressed their concern for Miguelito's behavior. Daniel Pérez, a senior whose broad smile shatters his tough-guy appearance, analyzed the situation: "Miguelito, I know you have a lot of anger in you, but we're like a family here. We're here to help you. In this school. With Melvin and the teachers. Not out there in the streets." A general nod indicated other students' agreement with Daniel's words, which echoed one of the phrases the school adopted from Consuelo Lee Corretjer — "Live and Help to Live." The students themselves decided that Miguelito should stay in the school, seek counseling, apologize to Michelle, and, by Michelle's request, not even go near her for a while. Melissa Lebrón, a fifteen-year-old PACHS student, comments on this unique aspect of the Unity class:

> One thing that I found very weird was "Unity" class. I had never heard about a class like this before. Unity is a class where you could bring up issues or problems that you have with a student or teacher. I will never forget this school. This school means a lot to me. If it wasn't for this school on this planet, I think I would've been a dropout and doing nothing with my life.

Unity also serves to engage Puerto Rican students and teachers in the political life of the Puerto Rican community. Political and social discussions in Unity transcend the limits of Humboldt Park; they revolve around demonstrations against federal cuts in education, letter-writing campaigns to free the Puerto Rican political prisoners, and planning neighborhood festivals and fundraisers. Abstract ideas such as struggle, liberation, sacrifice, and Puerto Rican culture often shape the discourse of the Unity class. This is demonstrated by the comments of PACHS students Haydée Ramos and Guillermo Morales. Haydée states:

> Leaving this school [after graduating] will leave me with memories like Unity, a class where everyone sat in a circle and discussed the problems affecting the school, community, teachers, and students. One of the biggest struggles in and out of Unity is the release of the prisoners of war, POW. Activities like Paseo Boricua, Fiesta Boricua, Puerto Rican Parade were also planned in and out of the Unity class. As I graduate from my Escuelita, I will proceed with my education by attending Northeastern [Illinois] University and study[ing] for my social work degree. I chose social work because as a Puerto Rican woman I want to help my Latino community [lead] a successful life.

Guillermo comments similarly:

> I see that [at PACHS] we do a lot of things with the few resources we have. I learned about Puerto Rican history. I see our prisoners of war as Puerto Rican heroes, and I thank them for having the courage to give up their own freedom for la Patria. I will never forget Unity class. The times we used to just sit together in a circle and joke around will never go away.

Understandings of Puerto Ricanness among Cultural Center activists are complex. The Center implicitly connects Puerto Rican "authenticity" to political ideology. Thus, a pro-independence Puerto Rican is somehow perceived as "more Puerto Rican" than a pro-statehood Puerto Rican. Other aspects that designate a "real Puerto Rican" are even more rigid, based on Spanish-language mastery and place of birth, similar to those constructions of "Otherness" harbored by Puerto Rico's elite (Díaz-Quinoñes, 1993).

The same essentialism that Chatterjee (1993), Said (1978), and many authors of autobiographical Puerto Rican literature (e.g., Esteves, 1980, 1984; Laviera, 1981, 1985; Piñero, 1980; Thomas, 1967) magnificently articulate is described by Díaz-Quiñones:

It is very easy to fall into the same essentialism and orientalism of the imperial gaze, in the name of "national" identity. . . . Nationalist discourse negates the cultural superiority of the imperial power, but often appropriates the pretended occidental rationality and turns it into discourse of power. The essentialist, exclusionary thought persists. The judges continue to be the judges, impeccable. (1993, p. 80; translated by author)

Old and young activists alike draw strong connections between ethnic identity and political militancy. For many second- and third-generation Chicago Puerto Ricans, knowledge of Puerto Rican history, mythology, and literature is associated with "being a real Puerto Rican."[9] For these activists, the Center is a catalyst for personal and political transformations, as well as a vehicle to earn cultural authenticity. Many authors (Klor de Alva, 1988; Oboler, 1995; Safa, 1988; Sánchez-Korrol, 1988) have argued that the Latino label homogenizes the histories, migrations, and socioeconomic characteristics of the individual Latino groups. These internal distinctions are essential to assess the specific needs and challenges each nationality-based group, like the grassroots activists in Humboldt Park, faces. As Oboler argues,

Yet, it was precisely at this point [in the Mexican American/Chicano and Puerto Rican movements of the civil rights era] that the term "Hispanic" began to be heard. Once again, the racial, class, and gender heterogeneity and the very real ideological differences within their respective communities were to be deemphasized. At the same time, it served to obscure the specific historical roots of each group's respective experiences in the United States. In other words, both in a sense were once again thrown into invisibility, although this time under an umbrella term ostensibly aimed at strengthening awareness of "ethnic diversity" within the "national community."(1995, pp. 78–79)

In Chicago, white-collar Puerto Ricans ally as "Hispanics" or "Latinos" through their occupational affiliations, while barrio groups reject pan-ethnic labels and direct their services to specific local needs. In fact, many barrio activists point to "the problem of multiculturalism" and, in the case of Puerto Rican nationalist activists, tailor their social services to Puerto Ricans by resurrecting images of a Puerto Rican militant past. While the techniques embraced in Unity — developing conflict resolution skills, encouraging self-criticism, opening communication channels, defining a support system, etc. — are perhaps not unique to PACHS, one of the main goals of these biweekly gatherings consists of "creating a Puerto Rican space," grounded on notions of Puerto Ricanness as the main binding force. Unity is premised on nationalist understandings of Puerto Ricanness as the primary bond between the Cultural Center members, including PACHS teachers and students and the surrounding Puerto Rican neighbors.

CLEMENTE HIGH SCHOOL: EDUCATIONAL REFORM, POLITICAL CONFLICTS, AND "LOS PROFESIONALES"

Cultural Center activists do not limit their community involvement and notions of struggle to the multiple projects the Center sponsors in Humboldt Park/West Town. While primarily pro-independence, supporters of the Center — many of whom have extensive insight into areas of popular education, gang activity, housing issues, and other social services — are also involved in mainstream local institutions. Because these activists understand their sociopolitical commitment in light of youth and neighborhood development, many of them have actually become involved in other key (predominantly Puerto Rican) spaces, such as Clemente High School. In fact, some of the best Clemente High School teachers (those evaluated by students and coworkers as "superior") are sympathizers, volunteers, or core members of the Center. These teachers are familiar with successful educational alternatives through their connection with Center-sponsored programs like PACHS and its adult equivalent, the Family Learning Center.

Clemente High School, the third-largest high school in Chicago, is located at the easternmost end of the main commercial Puerto Rican area on Division Street. Most Puerto Ricans who grew up in West Town and Humboldt Park attended Clemente High School, and a large percentage of the student body is still Puerto Rican (1,281 of its 2,373 students and 29 of its 153 teachers are Latino), despite a changing population in recent years. A discussion of Clemente High School is significant here because the building marks a physical space in which Puerto Rican concentration is high, and because Clemente High School is a space in which intergenerational and interorganizational barrio concerns are articulated (Cruz, 1997; Padilla, 1987).

The polemic at Clemente High School can best be understood as a conflict between two broad groups: the Cultural Center's pro-independence activists, who are largely from working-class or working-poor backgrounds, on the one hand, and a small group of powerful white-collar Latinos, including pro-statehood and conservative commonwealth Puerto Ricans, on the other. At the neighborhood level, these political affiliations are embodied in the specific ward aldermen and congressmen each group supports.[10] Each group perceives Humboldt Park and the urban development projects in a different light. Many of the white-collar professionals are involved in real estate and would like to capitalize on the recent interest White artists and yuppies have demonstrated in the area. The grassroots activists, by contrast, have drawn up concrete agendas to rehabilitate buildings, prevent further Puerto Rican displacement, and to mark the barrio as Puerto Rican.

Hence, divergent political ideologies vis-à-vis the status of Puerto Rico and local politicians in Humboldt Park, coupled with the posture toward urban barrio development agendas, partially account for the antagonism between grassroots activists and some white-collar professionals. The white-collar professionals distinguish themselves from pro-independence activists, whom they consider "terrorists," by focusing on their more mainstream political ideologies as "law-abiding citizens." The grassroots activists, by contrast, draw upon their class-based identity as *la gente pobre* (the poor people) — rather than the white-collar, suburban identity of *los profesionales*, as these activists refer to their opponents — to create solidarity among Humboldt Park residents.

As many grassroots activists explained in their interviews, los profesionales are the tiny minority of lawyers, city officials, real estate agents, and other corporate professionals who advocate traditional mobility routes, like the ones they themselves followed. For many of them, the American Dream worked. They lived through the process of earning professional degrees, attaining upwardly mobile corporate jobs, and moving to the suburbs to avoid their painful associations with barrio life. Many of these people do not live in the barrio, though they grew up in Humboldt Park. Some of these Puerto Rican professionals fail to address the different socioeconomic contexts faced by younger generations, or the employment venues provided by nationality-based barrio institutions (Cruz, 1997). Moreover, a desire to raise real estate prices and appropriate PRCC-owned buildings located in increasingly desirable areas have also been cited as reasons to attack the Cultural Center (Cruz, 1997; Geovannis, 1998).

Los profesionales are not an abstract contingency, as the emergence of *El Pito* ("the whistle") shows. *El Pito*, a clandestine newsletter published by Cultural Center opponents and distributed throughout the neighborhood, aims to discredit nationalist activists. The newsletter consists of personal attacks on barrio activists who are openly pro-independence and on supporters of Congressman Gutiérrez and Alderman Billy Ocasio (both considered *macheteros* — a historical term for militant nationalists — by their opponents).

These political postures become concrete in the debates around Clemente High School reform, which partially shifted school governance away from the centralized Downtown Board of Education and into the hands of neighborhood activists, parents, and students. In the 1980s, Chicago underwent a citywide reform that aimed to decentralize the control of schools, passing it to local decision-making councils. Discretionary funds were allocated to participating public schools, which were encouraged to develop local school councils to administer these funds. Clemente's local school council, called the School Reform Council, was composed of parents, students, barrio residents, and activists in Humboldt Park. Clemente's local school council outlined the special services to parents, students, and the community at large on which it would spend the discretionary funds. The elements of the reform were summarized in four main categories: 1) awareness of Puerto Rican history; 2) socioeconomic development strategies for the school community and neighborhood (e.g., promoting notions of "self-sufficiency," institutional autonomy, grassroots-driven urban renewal projects); 3) emphasis on individual commitment to the community and activism through hands-on involvement (e.g., parents' involvement in the school); and 4) enhancing cultural pride through artistic presentations, conferences, museum exhibits, and so on. The Clemente School Reform Council undoubtedly shared community development values harbored by grassroots activists, since many of these activists were involved in the conceptual and implementational aspects of the reform. This pro-independence presence is noticed (and even praised) by the parents of many Clemente High School students.

Alma Juncos is the mother of three adolescent sons and a parent aide at Clemente High School. Alma learned of the Cultural Center through her son's involvement in Son Del Barrio, a popular student Salsa band, which is led by Pedro Vidal, a Puerto Rican man in his early thirties and a core member of the Center. Having moved from Puerto Rico to Chicago in the mid-1980s, Alma mentioned that she noticed a much higher independentista presence in Chicago than in her hometown in Puerto Rico. When asked to explain further, Alma replied:

> Well, quite frankly, I don't know [why there are so many independentistas].
> But, I know there are a lot of them. I'll tell you one thing. For what I've seen,

I've seen that independentista people help . . . and work. They are hard workers. And they create projects for the community. For instance, somebody told me, "Uff, Clemente . . . that's bad in there, because all the teachers are independentistas." And I tell them, "Well, if they are independentistas . . . they still are good people." Because I have no complaints about the teachers. And, if they are, that's their right. But I've seen that they strive, struggle. They are hard working. . . . I've noticed something. Let me tell you. The people whom I think are independentistas care for the well-being of Puerto Ricans. I've seen that. They want the well-being of Puerto Ricans. And they help their own. If a community exists here, it's because of them.

Like other Clemente High School parents, Alma Juncos is not directly involved in the Cultural Center, other than through the work she does as a parent participant in the Clemente school reform. Nonetheless, like many other Humboldt Park residents, Alma has friends or relatives who have participated in programs sponsored by the Center, and she recognizes that the nationalist activists advocate for barrio Puerto Ricans. This echoes Justino Ramírez, an ASPIRA worker,[11] "who points to his ironic predicament as a pro-statehooder who finds himself working alongside nationalists because they [the nationalists] are the ones involved in community work here . . . the ones who have a vision and an actual understanding of the community's needs."

Many Humboldt Park residents and social service agencies consider the Clemente reform a pivotal point in the Center's history, since "the cause of Puerto Rican independence" acquired grounding on the local issues affecting the community. Since Center members have unsurpassed levels of neighborhood activism and are experienced in the educational field — having designed and implemented highly successful youth and adult education programs — their participation is especially noticeable in the ideological bases of the Clemente school reform. Under the banner of "Live and Help to Live," a variety of community projects have been developed at Clemente High School.

The Clemente High School houses satellite programs for several Puerto Rican community agencies, such as ASPIRA's Parents Institute,[12] Vida/ SIDA's AIDS education clinic, etc. These programs, aimed at serving its students and their parents in the neighborhood, bring together white-collar workers at not-for-profit organizations, barrio residents, nationalist activists, local politicians, and Puerto Rican high school students.

In addition to opening Clemente High School to the community through cultural events and emphasizing parental autonomy through the Parents Institute, the reform included programs to raise sociohistorical awareness among the students. Among the projects the PRCC activists have helped create are painting murals of Puerto Rican historical figures; recording a CD of music with social messages by the Son Del Barrio salsa band; a proliferation of self-reflective classes based on autobiographical writing by students; and a trip to Madre Isla, a coffee plantation in a small mountain town of Puerto Rico run by a grassroots cooperative.

Since Clemente is one of the few local institutions that receives significant state funds, the ways in which the local school council used the funds were closely monitored by white-collar professionals, some of whom disapproved of how the council used the monies. White-collar real estate professionals, city officials, and the media became the active outside critics of school reform and the School Reform Council.

On a misty June morning, Roberto Clemente High School's administrators called a press conference to respond to a cover-page article that had appeared the previous day in the *Chicago Sun-Times*, entitled "Public School's 'Pathetic' Use of Poverty Funds" (1995). The article condemned the Clemente School Reform Council's use of Chapter I funds to give parents part-time jobs (through the Parents Institute); to finance student trips outside the country (to Puerto Rico and Mexico); to open a legal clinic to advise students and parents on migration-related issues, and drug and gang cases; and to hire two out-of-state consultants to develop a "culturally sensitive" curriculum. "Funds earmarked for the education of poor children had, on this account, been thwarted," the article claimed. Then it pointed out that the two consultants hired "have close links to the Puerto Rican pro-Independence Movement" and that "the funds also were used to establish satellites for Clemente [High School] at the Pedro Albizu Campos School and Cultural Center — two Chicago pro-Puerto Rican Independence institutions." The article ends by noting that "the FBI would not say whether it is investigating the local school council's spending" (p. 6).

Several issues, recurrent in most social reform efforts in Humboldt Park, are illuminated in the heated disagreements over Clemente High School reform as played out in subsequent press conferences, articles, and community meetings. First, the reform made Clemente High School into an important community space, where essential sociopolitical networks develop and ideas of "community building" are forged. Given its strategic location at the heart of the Puerto Rican commercial strip on Division Street and being one of the few significant connections between the local neighborhood and the city government, Clemente High School is perceived as "a Puerto Rican space" that is key to the educational and occupational advancement of barrio youths and residents in general. Efforts aimed at "creating a better Puerto Rican community" directly place Clemente High School at its center. Because of this, the possibility of turning Clemente into an elite magnet school (in light of the changing ethnic composition and gentrification in Humboldt Park/West Town) is resisted and regarded with suspicion by the community (Cruz, 1997).

Second, the Clemente High School reform conflict points to the class and occupational dimensions of political conflict among Puerto Rican leaders in the Chicago barrio. Attacks on Clemente High are perceived by neighborhood residents and activists as attacks on the Puerto Rican community, as well as on the community-building efforts of la gente pobre.

Distinctions between los profesionales and la gente pobre highlight class and occupational divisions. These distinctions are also based on a sense of commitment to Humboldt Park, which is associated with particular political stands vis-à-vis the status of Puerto Rico (i.e., the notion that independentista activists are more committed to the community). Because of its involvement in the Clemente High School reform, the Center became more visible, and heated attacks came from corporate Puerto Rican pro-statehood and pro-commonwealth professionals. Right after the press conference in June 1995, discussions occurred about who the author of the article was and who the people quoted in it were. "That [article] was initiated by los profesionales again!" expressed a furious Esteban López, a controversial nationalist leader and director of the Center. Whenever he mentions los profesionales, López never names names, yet other activists, parents, and students seem to know who he means.

Third, the Clemente High School conflict raises issues of "interventionism" around the question of whom the barrio residents and activists perceive as "legitimately" able to criticize the efforts of la gente pobre. As an informant commented, "It's not so much what is said about us, but who is saying it." Humboldt Park activists challenged those outsiders who criticized efforts without actively engaging in neighborhood projects, with the idea that "if you're not part of the solution, you're part of the problem." The sensitivity to negative media reactions and to comments by nonbarrio residents — particularly non–Puerto Ricans or Puerto Ricans perceived as lacking community commitment — is enormous in Humboldt Park.

In an essay entitled "They're at It Again!" Josslyn Laracuente, a sixteen-year-old PACHS student, echoes the sentiment of Puerto Rican youth whose lives have been transformed by the very activists under attack:

> I can't believe the school is still being attacked. People fear what they don't understand, people are afraid of change. People are just blinded by the money they have, they think they could buy everything they see. But you know what, they could take our homes, push us out, but they will never, never break our spirits, or change the reason that we are Puerto Ricans, so as much as they try we will never lose and they will never win.

Media representations of Humboldt Park activism overlook the achievement at Clemente High School in both standardized test scores and the dropout rate. The theme of a Son Del Barrio song — "los profesionales come from the outside to talk about our school; looking at the negative but never at the positive" — echoes Puerto Rican youths' attitudes toward these media depictions (Integrity, 1997). The polemic on Clemente High School and on the reform is seen as an attack on the efforts of la gente pobre, as well as on Puerto Ricanness. However, as distinctions between Puerto Ricans based on class, activism, place of residence, and political stand are compounded with local struggles over positions and resources, intragroup boundaries become more complex. Puerto Ricanness among activists is not the same when one looks into Puerto Ricanness in the corporate or real estate sectors. Among activists, nationalist ideologies create the space for community building, but this space is constantly being ideologically and financially challenged.

CONCLUSION

Some of the key philosophical components of the Center are a politicized cultural identity grounded in an awareness of alternative/militant Puerto Rican history, and a positioning of the self in a global sociohistorical context. Recognizing the obstacles, this requires a constant struggle for survival (resistance, unity, autonomy, and agency). These philosophical components also permeate other community forums in which the Center activists are involved, such as the Clemente School Reform Council. These politics and their potentially positive effects on disengaged Puerto Rican students merit further ethnographic and theoretical examinations. By becoming acquainted with political protest strategies and neighborhood politics, and by developing a critical appraisal of socioeconomic opportunity structures, these students gain new insights into their own predicaments and generate a unique sense of possibility.

Education research has overlooked the strong underlying currents that shape ethnoracial educational settings. Politics and local neighborhood contexts are inseparable from schooling. When these political undercurrents are used to heal students' sense of powerlessness and despair, they deserve attention. Regardless of one's political stand, the accomplishments of nationalist activists, precisely because of the explicitly political visions that ground their commitment, are undeniable.

Pedro Albizu Campos's words, *La patria es valor y sacrificio* ("The fatherland is valor and sacrifice"), appear on a framed poster at the PACHS as a reminder of the intersections of community activism and Puerto Rican nationalism. For Chicago's Puerto Rican activists, nationalist history is not a "history of defeat" (Díaz-Quiñones, 1993), but a history of continuous struggle, community building, and educational alternatives. In addition to recognizing the process by which an abandoned discourse regains pertinence, as well as the discursive transformations of a "migrant" Puerto Rican nationalism, it is essential to examine the concrete social, economic, and political shapes that these forms of politicization and historicization take in U.S. Puerto Rican barrios.

Nationalism is indiscriminately considered a negative term in much Western literature, since many violent acts have been committed in the name of nationalist integration. Grassroots activists in Humboldt Park hesitate to embrace a nationalist label, not because they feel the label does not apply to them, but because they are aware of the negative connotations nationalism has in contemporary literature.[13]

In Puerto Rico, debates over nationalism are often associated with the university intellectual elite. In Chicago, however, these debates take place at the grassroots level. Nationalism is not only an intellectual ideology, but also a concrete vehicle for social reform among some barrio activists. As Sánchez (1994) comments, "to be a nationalist in the island involves secret prestige, but to be a nationalist in New York involves public hostility" (p. 15). And, while the meaning attributed to being a nationalist in Puerto Rico and being one in the United States is different, being a nationalist in the U.S. Puerto Rican community of Chicago is also perceived as the ultimate "proof" of cultural authenticity — in particular, when measures such as place of birth and Spanish language aim to challenge one's nationalist identity.[14]

As illustrated by the Clemente High School conflicts, nationalist projects experience heated opposition, mostly from nonbarrio Puerto Rican residents, city officials, white-collar professionals, and business or real estate people. However, to the many community residents who receive social services provided by nationalist activists, and for the thousands of Puerto Rican youth who learn firsthand their impact on the community-building process, *los nacionalistas son los únicos que de verdad se preocupan por los suyos* ["the nationalists are the only ones who truly care about their own people"].

Nearly two years after the end of my fieldwork, the Cultural Center activists were once again the source of heated conflict among mainstream media and opponents of pro-independence Puerto Rican politics. As seen in this article, this is not the first time that Clemente High School has been challenged for its administration of Chapter I funds. However, questions around Clemente High School's funding become secondary to the anti-independentista overtones of the articles. Continual reference to the political ideologies and kinship networks of several Clemente High School teachers and administrators — in particular, the connection between these teachers and FALN prisoners — occupy center stage.

"The manufactured crimes at Clemente High School are being used by the School Reform Board to say, 'Look, we need to have all the authority downtown,'" warned Sheila Castillo, director of the Chicago Association of Local Schools Council (Cruz, 1997, p. 5). Grassroots groups like the Center have withstood criticism by the mainstream media and anti-independentista factions. Opponents of the nationalist activists have traditionally focused on the group's controversial politics and critical view of history, while ignoring its outstanding educational and community achievements.

Carmencita Martínez, a charismatic seventeen-year-old student at Pedro Albizu Campos High School, describes the impact of the nationalist alternative education program on her life. In a poignant autobiographical essay, like many others published in local publications, Carmencita narrates her life trajectory, from a six-year-old living in the dumpsters (quite literally) to a hopeful high school graduate. She points to PACHS's role in her life:

> The porch [where Carmencita and her family slept during their early years in Chicago] was filthy. It had dirty diapers everywhere. Some rats and the garbage were right next to us. There were times when one of my brothers or I had to stay up all night and watch, making sure the rats wouldn't bite any of us. . . . In the morning when we got up, we would have nothing to eat. My older brother and I had to go around the neighborhood and see what we could find. Sometimes we got lucky. There was a lady who would give my brother and I food. My mom couldn't see us live like that anymore, so she had to give my older brother and I away. She stayed with the two younger kids. But she couldn't live without us. One day she got up and decided to apply for public aid. As soon as she got her money, she found an apartment and got us back together. Our apartment didn't have any light, gas, food, or windows, but we lived there. We ate peanut butter all day and drank powder milk that the church would give us. All we had in the apartment was a chair and a curtain. . . . The school I attend now [PACHS] is helping me get where I want to go, and they're giving me all the hope and support I need.

In a community considered among the poorest of the poor, where Puerto Rican youth and barrio residents continue to drop out of high school, join gangs, and experience the most inhuman consequences of poverty, any successful social initiative must be considered carefully. The powerful presence of nationalist or pro-independence activism in Humboldt Park is undeniable. Equally undeniable is the sense of hope and possibility that students and barrio residents, like the ones who appear in this article, experience at Pedro Albizu Campos High School and other community development programs sponsored by nationalist activists in Humboldt Park.

NOTES

1. Elsewhere in this article, pseudonyms are used in compliance with informants' wishes as expressed at the time of the interviews. The names of the young people quoted here are their real names. Many of them wanted to be recognized for their participation and some actually published the autobiographical writing that appears in this article in school yearbooks and local newsletters.
2. Saul Alinsky was a Chicago community organizer who later created the Urban Institute for Community Organizations. In the 1960s, he and his followers aimed to teach organizing skills/techniques to residents of marginalized Chicago neighborhoods so that they could become grassroots organizers.
3. Like Black militants and other sectors of the New Left (Anderson & George, 1986; Evans, 1979), many Puerto Rican activists in Chicago suffered the surveillance and harassment of FBI, CIA, and Defense Department agents and infiltrators. Personal files recorded Puerto Rican barrio residents' activism and "communist tendencies" in the most meticulous ways (see Padilla, 1987). This charge insinuates that those charged were active in the planning and execution of these bombings.
4. The impact of the FALN on the lives of barrio residents has been neglected in studies that focus on the structure, history, and motives behind these groups (Fernández, 1994; Zwerman, 1995). Yet, attitudes toward FALN members and the barrio activists who support them continue to be a source of heated conflict attached to community resources and activism among Puerto Rican activists and residents in Chicago.
5. The proliferation of smaller Puerto Rican communities outside of New York City has been noticed since the 1950s (Jones, 1955; O'Brien, 1954; Siegal, Orlans, & Greer, 1954; Vivas, 1951), when Puerto Ricans developed heterogeneous migration patterns. However, little scholarly attention has been given to these communities, or even to significantly sized urban Puerto Rican areas outside the Northeast. As Backstrand and Schensul (1982) and Enchautegui (1992) emphasize, variations in geographical context and community size must be considered in order to adequately address the special needs prompted by shifting demographic characteristics of the Puerto Rican population in the United States. In their study of Puerto Ricans in Hartford, Connecticut, Backstrand and Schensul conclude that any study of Puerto Rican communities must examine the total environment, "not around the ethnic group, but around the interactive relationships relevant to the group's achievement of its goals" (1982, p. 29). This model advocates an understanding of the area's "carrying capacity" (i.e., the availability of resources in the environment), the skills, characteristics, and resources brought into the adaptation area, the cultural and community strategies used by the residents, the characteristics of other groups sharing the area, and "the shifting relationships between competition/cooperation as Puerto Rican strategies overlap or conflict with the strategies of other sectors" (p. 30).
6. Chicago has the fifth-largest and most diverse Latino population of any city in the United States. According to the 1990 U.S. Census, Mexicans in Chicago, representing 65 percent of the city's Latinos, are the largest Latino group of the twelve nationalities with a significant presence (more than 1,000 people in each group) in the city. Puerto Ricans are the second-largest Latino group, with over 120,000 people (22.6%), followed by Guatemalans (2.4%) and Cubans (2%). All these Latino nationalities combine to make up 20 percent of the city's total population (includes only the Chicago Standard Metropolitan Area) (Fornek, 1992).
7. In 1990, Puerto Rican concentration in West Town ranged from 10 percent to 29.9 percent, while Puerto Rican concentration in Humboldt Park ranged from 40 percent to 69.99 percent (based on 1990 Census Tract of the Humboldt Park area). Important literature has been published on the subject of race and class relations in the

context of gentrification (Anderson, 1990), urban renewal and homesteading (Von Hassell, 1996), and community dissolution as a consequence of residential desegregation (Molotch, 1972). The actual impact of these processes on the lives and identity of residents — who naturally view displacement as undesirable — fuels suspicion toward incoming Whites.

8. Most PACHS students live below poverty level in the Humboldt Park sections hit hardest by gang warfare, drugs, unemployment, and a plethora of severe social problems. Their families receive some form of government assistance, primarily through AFDC and Social Security. Although the school's 1994–1995 annual tuition was only $500, only 20 percent of the students were able to pay it in full; most students participate in school fundraising activities, work-study, or hold an after-school job to pay their tuition. No student has ever been turned down or expelled for being unable to pay, despite the school's precarious financial situation.

9. In her groundbreaking literary critique of Nuyorican literature, Acosta-Belén (1992) argues that Puerto Rican identity is configured, articulated, and mediated through the literature of the Puerto Rican migrant community in New York City. Acosta-Belén emphasizes that such literary expressions must be examined in regard to "the Puerto Rican national question and the subordinate socioeconomic position occupied by Puerto Ricans within U.S. society" (p. 980). She continues: "This literature provided to Puerto Ricans born or raised in the United States a means of cultural validation and affirmation of a collective sense of identity that served to counteract the detrimental effects of the socioeconomic and racial marginalization that Puerto Ricans have experienced in the metropolis" (p. 980).

10. In the case of the grassroots activists, the support is ideological, but not electoral; Center activists do not believe in the process of voting because of their nationalist stance.

11. ASPIRA is a national not-for-profit agency focused on educational issues affecting Latino/Puerto Rican youth. Local branches of the organization exist in the larger U.S. cities (e.g., New York, Philadelphia, Hartford, Miami, and Chicago).

12. The Parents Institute is a concrete effort to bring more Puerto Rican parents (especially single mothers living in poverty) into the work force by providing work space in their children's schools. The act of giving jobs to parents, perceived by barrio activists as an effort toward self-determination, self-actualization, and self-reliance, was criticized by the more conservative white-collar professionals and news reporters, who thought the reform's main aim should have been to raise standardized test scores and encourage students to move out of the community.

13. While nationalist movements have been examined in light of state fragmentation, collapse, and repression, internal group dynamics have been overlooked. Warren concludes that "much less attention is directed to the internal dynamics of these [new social] movements: to the particular ways participants create and consume culture through their activism, to the ways social relations (not just individual choice) mediate involvements, or to the ironies of identity politics in movements that foreground one of many identities relevant to activists" (1996, p. 25).

14. As Díaz-Quiñones explains, the "need to preserve identities" and maintain "real and symbolic places" gains strength precisely by being away from the Island, and in perceptions of "the past and the present reconciled in the construction of a new version of history" (1993, p. 49). When nationalist identity is essentialized so that only Island Puerto Ricans who can speak "proper Spanish" belong, nationalist agendas in U.S. Puerto Rican communities are challenged to seek new forms of self-identification that will reincorporate individuals into the Puerto Rican history from which they have been excluded.

REFERENCES

Acosta-Belén, E. (1992). Beyond island boundaries: Ethnicity, gender, and cultural revitalization in Nuyorican literature. *Callaloo, 15,* 979–998.

Anderson, A. B., & George, W. P. (1986). *Confronting the color line: The broken promise of the civil rights movement in Chicago.* Athens: University of Georgia Press.

Anderson, E. (1990). *Streetwise: Race, class, and change in an urban community.* Chicago: University of Chicago Press.

Backstrand, J. R., & Schensul, S. L. (1982). Co-evolution in an outlying ethnic community: The Puerto Ricans of Hartford, Connecticut. *Urban Anthropology, 11*(1), 9–37.

Bensman, D., & Lynch, R. (1988). *Rusted dreams: Hard times in a steel community.* Berkeley: University of California Press.

Chatterjee, P. (1993). *The nation and its fragments: Colonial and postcolonial histories.* Princeton, NJ: Princeton University Press.

Cruz, W. (1997). Witch hunt at Clemente High: Puerto Rican nationalism and Chicago politics. *Crítica (34/35),* 11–18.

Díaz-Quiñones, A. (1993). *La memoria rota.* Rio Piedras, PR: Ediciones Huracán.

Enchautegui, M. (1992). Geographical differentials in the socioeconomic status of Puerto Ricans: Human capital variations and labor market characteristics. *International Migration Review, 26,* 1267–1290.

Esteves, S. M. (1980). *Yerba Buena.* New York: Greenfield Press.

Esteves, S. M. (1984). *Tropical rains.* New York: African Caribbean Poetry Theater.

Evans, S. (1979). *Personal politics: The roots of women's liberation in the civil rights movement and the new left.* New York: Random House.

Fernández, R. (1994). *Prisoners of colonialism: The struggle for justice in Puerto Rico.* Monroe, ME: Common Courage Press.

Fornek, S. (1992, September 16). Latinos here are epitome of diversity. *Chicago Sun-Times,* p. 16.

Geovannis, C. (1998). *The charges against Clemente High School.* Chicago: Chicago Ink.

Jones, I. (1955). *The Puerto Rican in New Jersey: His present status.* New Brunswick, NJ: Department of Education, Division against Discrimination.

Klor de Alva, J. (1988). Latino sociocultural diversity in the United States. In E. Acosta-Belen (Ed.), *The Hispanic experience in the United States* (pp. 107–136). New York: Praeger.

Lancaster, R. (1988). *Thanks to God and the revolution: Popular religion and class consciousness in the new Nicaragua.* New York: Columbia University Press.

Laviera, T. (1981). *La carreta made a u-turn.* Houston: Arte Público Press.

Laviera, T. (1985). *Amerícan.* Houston: Arte Público Press.

Maldonado, E. (1979). Contract labor and the origins of Puerto Rican communities in the United States. *International Migration Review, 13*(1), 15–32.

Molotch, H. (1972). *Managed integration: Dilemmas of doing good in the city.* Berkeley: University of California Press.

Oboler, S. (1995). *Ethnic labels, Latino lives: Identity and the politics of (re)presentation in the United States.* Minneapolis: University of Minnesota Press.

O'Brien, R. (1954). *A survey of the Puerto Ricans in Lorain, Ohio.* Lorain, OH: Neighborhood House Association of Lorain.

Padilla, F. M. (1987). *Puerto Rican Chicago.* South Bend, IN: University of Notre Dame Press.

Piñero, M. (1980). *La bodega sold dreams.* Houston: Arte Público Press.

Public school's "pathetic" use of poverty funds. (1995, June 4). *Chicago Sun Times,* p. 1.

Said, E. (1978). *Orientalism.* New York: Pantheon.

Safa, H. (1988). Migration and identity: A comparison of Puerto Rican and Cuban migrants in the United States. In E. Acosta-Belén (Ed.), *The Hispanic experience in the United States* (pp. 137–150). New York: Praeger.

Sánchez, L. R. (1994). *La guagua aerea.* Rio Piedras, PR: Editorial Cultural.

Sánchez-Korrol, V. (1988). Latinismo among early Puerto Rican migrants in New York City: A sociohistoric interpretation. In E. Acosta-Belén (Ed.), *The Hispanic experiences in the United States* (pp. 151–161) New York: Praeger.

Seijo-Bruno, M. (1981). Son pobres y puertorriqueños. *Claridad,* "En rojo" section.

Siegel, A., Orlans, H., & Greer, L. (1954). *Puerto Ricans in Philadephia: A study of their demographic characteristics, problems, and attitudes.* Philadelphia: Commission on Human Relations.

Son Del Bario. (1994). *Echando Pa'lante.*

Thomas, P. (1967). *Down these mean streets.* New York: Alfred A. Knopf.

Vivas, J. (1951). *The Puerto Ricans of Cleveland: A challenge to community organization.* Unpublished masters thesis, Western Reserve University.

Von Hassell, M. (1996). *Homesteading in New York City, 1978–1993: The divided heart of Loisaida.* Westport, CT: Bergin & Garvey.

Warren, K. (1996). Reading history as resistance: Mayan public intellectuals in Guatemala. In E. F. Fischer & R. McKenna Brown (Eds.), *Mayan cultural activism in Guatemala* (pp. 121–145). Austin: University of Texas Press.

Zwerman, G. (1995, September). *The identity vulnerable activist and the emergence of post-new left armed, underground organizations in the United States* (Working Paper Series, No. 218). New York: New School for Social Research, Center for Studies of Social Change.

Women and Education in Eritrea:
A Historical and Contemporary Analysis

ASGEDET STEFANOS

In 1961, the Eritrean people launched a national liberation struggle in response to Haile Selassie's unilateral incorporation of Eritrea as part of Ethiopia. In 1970, a group of Eritrean activists formed the Eritrean Peoples Liberation Front (EPLF), which became the predominant organization to shape and forge the war of liberation. This struggle was enormously successful in mobilizing and uniting the Eritrean people. In 1993, against great odds and without the sponsorship of a major world power, Eritrea gained its national independence. Early on, the EPLF asserted that the liberation struggle must take the form of a national democratic revolution and took steps to establish forms of democratic organization in the liberated areas.[1] In addition, the EPLF claimed that there was an interrelated need for both national independence and an egalitarian social revolution and that the former could not be attained without pursuing the latter. In 1974, the EPLF made a major decision to admit women into its ranks and to mount a comprehensive series of policies to foster women's emancipation[2] in the society as a whole.

During the contemporary period (1961–1997), Eritrea and Eritrean women have been undergoing massive social changes. This article explores whether and to what extent Eritrean women have been achieving emancipation, and, if so, what role education has played in that process. It assesses the changes that have occurred for women in the realm of education, during the armed struggle and after national liberation, by examining systems of schooling and learning opportunities — both formal and nonformal — available to women, curricula and pedagogical methods, and supports to promote the EPLF's stated goal of gender equity in education.[3] This assessment of women and education in contemporary Eritrea draws from the policies, programs, and commentary of Eritrea's political leadership and, in addition, from the perceptions and experiences of a diverse sample of Eritrean women, who were interviewed in 1983 and 1997. In a Third World society, particularly one undergoing major social change, the impact of education on women can be grasped only in the context of evaluating conditions in other realms of their lives, including family life, the economy, and politics.[4] Consequently, this article analyzes these other spheres, particularly when developments within them have affected how women have responded to educational reforms.[5] In addition, it discusses whether the dynamics of the revolutionary process itself have facilitated or burdened the political leadership's campaign for gender equity

Harvard Educational Review Vol. 67 No. 4 Winter 1997, 658–688

in education and women's capacity to pursue opportunities for schooling and learning.

The analysis of women and education in Eritrea during the contemporary period needs to be situated in a broader historical context. Accordingly, this article provides an overview of the general social condition of Eritrean women and the forms of learning and degree of educational access available to them in both the period of precolonial traditional society and the eras of Italian (1889–1941) and British (1941–1952) colonialism.

WOMEN AND EDUCATION IN ERITREA IN TRADITIONAL SOCIETY AND UNDER COLONIAL REGIMES

Before and during colonialism, Eritrean women's status was severely subordinate in educational and sociopolitical spheres. However, Eritrean women's dependent position was not static. Depending on the particular contradictions posed by changing socioeconomic and political conditions, women created spaces for themselves within the existing structures to gain some degree of cultural and social autonomy and self-determination.

The history of women's education in Eritrea demonstrates that broad social factors and specific developments in education that were relatively emancipatory for men — liberating them from natural, social, or ideological restraints — often have had quite different, and even opposite, effects upon women. These disparities between women's and men's experience were rooted in the social forces that systematically created obstacles for women's educational equity.[6] For example, under the Italian colonial regime of the 1940s, Eritrean women, in contrast to men, did not significantly partake in the educational and economic expansion of the period.[7] Those women who found access to learning and urban employment got locked into the informal sector of the economy, turning domestic duties into economic activities. A major reason for the separation of the sexes in education was the colonialists' disregard for women and for their productive capacity. This stance reinforced the prevailing indigenous system of gender inequality in education.[8]

Eritrean Women and Education in Traditional Society

In traditional Eritrea,[9] women's status was established within two distinct semi-feudal socioeconomic systems — agricultural and pastoral — and two conservative religious value systems — Coptic and Muslim.[10] For both sedentary highlanders and pastoral seminomadic lowlanders, the family was a crucial unit of learning and cultural activities.[11] The family was hierarchical, patrilineal, and authoritarian, with strict sexual and generational divisions of labor.[12]

Traditional formal education was established for religious purposes. Secular education can be generally characterized as informal and nonformal education. Traditional learning patterns reflected the agricultural and pastoral life of Eritrea, and were suited to the needs of the people; education fitted the young for their roles in communal life. Skills and crafts were handed down, along with traditions, customs, and knowledge of the complex system of rights and duties that ordered the society. Education was usually rounded-off by initiation ceremonies or "regimental" training, marking the young person's entry into full adult status. Thus, traditional Eritrean education was functional and utilitarian with respect to the social and economic roles women and men were called upon to fill.[13]

Religious education, controlled by the Coptic Church for the Christian highlanders and by the Mosque for the Muslim lowlanders, tended to buttress the political and social preeminence of men. The aim of this education was to prepare males for religious vocations and, in a few cases, for secular occupations that required literacy. Clerical authority was supportive of the upper-rung social groups and conservative in its view of women's place in society. Theological schooling for girls was not deemed worthwhile because women were always excluded from the ecclesiastical hierarchy and from temporal duties of governance in their communities. The majority of Eritrean women remained nonliterate.

Girls received much of their education from their mothers, who focused on the "sacramental" duties associated with being a wife and mother. Women's exclusion from public roles and the strict sexual division of labor determined that girls needed to learn skills directly connected to household management, child care, and health care. The early training of either Christian highland or Muslim lowland girls also focused on a limited range of religious activities and the social codes of "proper" family relationships. They learned to be courteous and subordinate, and to defer to males, even those younger than themselves. They came to expect that, once they became matriarchs, they in turn would accrue power and status over younger female household members.[14]

Within the family, women were given chief responsibility for household management. At the young age of five or six, daughters began to assume an array of tasks, such as caring for siblings, gathering firewood, carrying water, milking sheep and goats, pounding dried grains for brewing, and churning milk into butter. Women also learned various crafts, including spinning cotton, weaving baskets, and decorating household items and their homes.[15]

Early marriage meant that most girls would leave their homes before becoming of significant labor value to their families. The future bride was selected by the groom's parents with an eye to the continuity of the family's lineage (bearing male heirs) and proper household management. Girls often married well before puberty, as early as ten to twelve years of age. Once married, the young bride acquired further training under the tutelage of her mother-in-law.

In the predominantly agrarian society, women participated actively in the economic sphere. Eritrean Highland women were essential to the economy, farming the land along with men. They cleared acreage, weeded, harvested, winnowed, tended livestock, and ground grain into flour. Despite their active economic role in agricultural production, Highland women's status was subordinate to men's within the rural economy. Men were the sole owners of agricultural produce, and the fruits of their wives' and daughters' labor was their undisputed property. Men made unilateral decisions in the distribution of surplus produce and had total control over formal bartering transactions.

By contrast, female labor was not necessary among the nomads, who raised only cattle, and women were under significant subjugation. The constant movement of the family in search of pastures meant an isolated and rough existence for women. They were totally secluded and covered up while traveling on camel back, and then restricted in a small tent at a temporary campsite where they prepared the family meal, pushing it under the tent for the men of the family to eat. These nomadic women's activities consisted of building the frame of the hut and staying out of sight in it except to care for small children, while men moved around freely with their cattle and sat in the open air socializing with other men. The complex interaction of ecological necessity and Islamic religious laws resulted in a stark asymmetry between the sexes.[16]

Eritrean Women and Education during Colonialism

Eritrean educational institutions under Italian colonialism had a pattern of deliberate exclusion of females and sex-differentiated schooling. Beginning in 1889, the Italians introduced a capitalist economy, heavy taxation, and expropriation of land, which increased pressure on men and women alike. When men migrated to cities, women were left behind in the rural areas.[17] Usually only males were employed in the cash crop plantations and in mines and urban factories. Thus, women were excluded from the cash economy and were dependent on men.

Under both Italian (1889–1941) and British (1941–1952) colonialism, there was no effort to educate or develop the skills of women, since it was considered unnecessary to secure political domination and economic exploitation. In addition, Western patriarchal conceptions of acceptable sex roles contributed to different educational opportunities for boys and girls.[18]

Italian colonialism brought limited modern education to Eritrea — male Eritreans received education up to a fourth-grade level.[19] A handful of state vocational schools were established to train boys as noncommissioned officers, artisans, clerks, male nurses, and plantation workers. There were also Catholic and Protestant missionary schools, which largely excluded females, that were designed primarily to garner Eritrean converts, and only secondarily to train subalterns for the colonial administration.[20] Postprimary education was minimal, since the Italians were concerned that higher education might inculcate in Eritreans an anticolonial outlook.[21] After almost sixty years of Italian colonization in Eritrea, only a small, predominantly male segment of the population could claim rudimentary schooling,[22] and only a minority with "assimilated status"[23] were given the opportunity to pursue their education.

Generally, the British were less stringent than the Italians in restricting educational opportunity. They oversaw a notable expansion of schools in villages and towns. The rewards of schooling were visible, and Eritreans' desire for education increased rapidly. They began to enter white-collar professions as teachers, lawyers, entrepreneurs, and newspaper reporters, fervently taking advantage of the new educational programs. Nevertheless, these limited educational opportunities were largely reserved for males.

Both the secular and missionary educational systems constructed by the Italians and British shared characteristic features of colonial education. They negated Eritrea's history and culture and claimed that history began with the civilizing presence of colonialists.[24] Placing no value on Eritrean customs and institutions, they introduced European standards of behavior and general outlook into the educational system. This pedagogical bias was the "de-Africanization of nationals."[25]

In the shift from traditional to colonial education, two factors remained constant: females were generally denied access to formal schooling, and educators sponsored deliberate patterns of sex-differentiated roles. Education, even literacy, was not considered useful for women as they performed their daily tasks.

The few schools established for girls were run by missionaries. Curricula focused on general literacy education and on subjects that upheld the stereotypical role of women, with home economics as the principal subject. The schools' curricula included domestic duties such as sewing, embroidery, and cooking. Learning these skills constituted a girl's vocational education and socialized her to become an industrious and obedient woman.

A major component of missionary schools for girls was the promotion of converts and implanting religious principles in Eritrean families by turning girls into Christian wives and mothers. While most Eritrean women had little or no chance for wage-earning, schooling for girls was valued by all because it could provide a better opportunity for securing husbands who had good educational and economic standing. An unmarried educated and/or Christian woman's choices were limited to joining a convent and working within a missionary structure as a single woman. Some women married fellow male converts or evangelists.

In large part, Italian and British rule exacerbated Eritrean women's economic subjugation and reinforced their exclusion from education. Increased economic activity in the urban areas and Italian land confiscation brought a migration of Highland men out of the rural areas. This shift of men from working on farms to working on cash crop plantations and in mines and urban factories placed additional pressure on women in the rural areas.

Women, who never were property owners, were also excluded from the cash transactions and technical innovations of the modern sector, since only Eritrean males engaged in business activities. This exclusion also increased women's economic marginality. Colonialists' cultural prejudice and patriarchal biases led them to ignore Eritrean women. Not having access to wage employment, women could not learn the new skills that paid jobs offered. Thus, conservative Western conceptions of gender roles and capitalism's sexual division of labor were grafted onto existing traditional features of Eritrean women's subordination. The result often combined the worst elements of these diverse forms of gender inequality.

When women moved to the urban areas that arose with colonialism, job opportunities for Eritreans in the modern sector were far broader for males than for females, and jobs were stratified by gender. In the colonial hierarchy, the Eritrean women held the lowest position — the few girls who had access to training and skills were only prepared for household labor and for the humbler occupations in the modern sector.

In the early Italian colonial period, most families lived apart — men in the cities and towns close to work, their wives and children in the villages. The wives lived on their husbands' remittances, together with whatever subsistence farming they could muster. Normally husbands visited their homes once or twice a year, usually around planting and harvesting season to work on the family plot. Many male workers found this a double burden and ceased returning to their villages, yet continued to send money to their spouses. Many men lived with other women in the city and thus became even more estranged from their wives in the countryside.[26] Some married women in the villages led a miserable and lonely existence under the control of their in-laws. They were mostly viewed as misfits and treated as lowly workers. They were expected to raise their children and to wait indefinitely for husbands who often never returned.

Unlike other European colonialists, the Italians left the traditional family code untouched. Accordingly, abandoned women had no legal recourse. However, the contradictions between the traditional and colonial economic systems inadvertently created possibilities for women. In response to their men's departure to plantations and the city, some women left their villages and went to cities looking for jobs. Also lured to the city were those few women who did not conform to the social norms of the traditional village and were viewed as outcasts — widowed women, women without dowries, and divorced women. The city offered these women wider horizons and a certain freedom to start a new life. Some entered the informal market of brewing, handicraft, selling foodstuffs, and laundry work, while others gradually worked their way into agricultural industries.

By the 1940s, some women began to enter light industrial sectors such as textiles, matches, and coffee factories, where they were paid lower rates than men and endured long hours and harsh treatment. Despite discriminatory wages and unhealthy working conditions, urban employment gave women an alternative to marriage and a chance to earn their own money. Some created opportunities for themselves by turning domestic labor into an economic activity, serving in Italian households as maids, cooks, and nannies. They boarded with Italian families and supported their parents, siblings, and extended families with their wages. Many of them decided to forgo marriage in order to lift their family members from poverty, expecting that in old age they would be supported by one of the many relatives they had helped.[27]

Existence in the city enabled some Eritrean women to exercise greater control over their social lives and their choice of male partners. Among these were a group of females who owned and ran bars. While a number of them offered sexual favors to Eritrean and Italian male customers, most were respectable small-business women who garnered extraordinary independence and were notable figures in the urban social milieu. They resisted the sexual advances of colonialists, and later on, many actively contributed to the national liberation movement. Generally, the urban areas provided anonymity and a certain measure of autonomy for women who were escaping the control of extended families and the village. It provided women with a rare opportunity to reinvent themselves. Sharing similar experiences, women residing in cities created networks and solidarity among themselves. The majority of these women were nonliterate.

WOMEN AND EDUCATION IN ERITREA DURING THE NATIONAL LIBERATION STRUGGLE AND AFTER INDEPENDENCE: POLICIES AND PROGRAMS

An examination of both the traditional period and the eras of Italian and British colonialism indicate that education was undervalued and constricted and that Eritrean women in particular were greatly impeded in pursuing schooling and all forms of learning. The contemporary period (1961–1997), which commences with the launching of the war for national liberation, represents a radical departure in that educational resources have been greatly expanded, and there has been a significant break with the longstanding prohibition against women pursuing educational opportunities.

Education was viewed by political leaders as integral to the national liberation struggle, and is currently valued by policymakers as a core element of nation-building. In the view of both the EPLF and the government, the broad educational arena relates to both formal and nonformal learning; to efforts at consciousness-raising, including those that occur outside of schools; and to all opportunities for building skills. The design of and strategy for education is linked to a larger social vision that is egalitarian, responsive to the interests of peasants and workers, independent, oriented to self-reliance, and able to mobilize effectively all human and material resources.

Educational goals and objectives that were pursued during the liberation struggle have been adopted and expanded by the post-independence government. The broad educational strategy has a range of core components. First, there has been an effort to highlight Eritrea's history and heritage, and thereby eliminate the colonized mentality. Second, education has been designed to expose elements of the traditional culture that retard social and economic transformation, such as disdain for certain vocations, religious zealotry, and superstition.[28] There is an emphasis on training people in the scientific method in the study of both nature and society. There is a commitment to ensure that education engages and is accessible to the vast majority of people, rather than to a small, highly specialized elite. Accordingly, nonformal schooling has been given equal status to formal learning; both are seen as critical to developing the resources of the independent nation. In addition, the curriculum is anti-elitist; all subject areas highlight the everyday experiences encountered by students and are rooted in the concrete challenges of local life. The cleavage between mental and manual labor is seen as a false dichotomy that promotes an undesirable divide between exalted thinkers and denigrated laborers. Accordingly, the educational system combines learning with productive work. The pedagogical approach promotes active learning and collective cooperation. Teachers are encouraged to play a role in designing educational materials and to act as colearners with, rather than transmitting agents to, their students. A great deal of emphasis is placed on peer learning, and students are involved in shaping educational experiences.[29]

In the mid-1970s, the EPLF recognized the need to engage the full and active participation of Eritrean women in the liberation struggle. With this recognition came a commitment that has continued beyond independence to establish educational equity between the genders. Education was recognized as crucial in transforming women and enabling them to redefine their private and public roles. It has been a critical avenue for developing the consciousness of a newly emancipated woman, for disarming the objections of men and mothers, and for providing skills that permit females to operate on an equal footing with males in the reconstruction of Eritrean society.

The strategy for integrating the masses of women into a new educational system included combating the material and attitudinal barriers to access.[30] A fundamental obstacle was the parental view that a girl's only goal was to prepare for and succeed in getting married and that female education was an unnecessary frill or, worse yet, a costly distraction. Aside from notions about male superiority, there was an economic basis to parents' opposition to education for girls: the need for children to help with the persistent demands of domestic and agricultural labor. While some parents anxiously ceded time for schooling to sons, they stiffened when it came to daughters. The EPLF recognized the need for an intensive political education campaign in the liberated areas to confront parental resistance to female education. In mass gatherings and individual meetings, the EPLF's political activists explained to elders and parents the value of making education available to all young people. They noted that gender discrimination in schooling undermined the liberation effort and sometimes sternly criticized those who withheld education from their daughters. The cadres organized communal assistance for those families who relied on their daughter's extra hands, and the school calendar was often planned to minimize interference with periods of peak agricultural activity.

However, once access to education was established in the countryside, girls often lagged behind in their school work, and their dropout rate was high. Parents would often turn up to retrieve their daughters for work "because something unexpected had come up."[31] During the national liberation struggle, the EPLF was not able to block fully such parental interference, but it did work to accelerate its ability to help village girls to move to base areas to pursue their education.

The EPLF's Revolution School, established in the base area in 1980, became a site for advancing approaches to education that promoted female emancipation and reduced male chauvinism. It attempted to combat sexual stereotyping in its structure, methods, and curriculum. At the Revolution School, girls and boys were equal partners in all aspects of school life. Both boys and girls engaged equally in academics, gymnastics, maintenance, cooking, fetching water from the well, and building construction.[32] The integration of both genders into all school activities was considered essential to ensure that girls were able to experience fully an emancipatory environment and to participate in new learning and training opportunities.

In contemporary educational settings, curriculum materials include new images of women, such as handling tools or military equipment.[33] School texts discuss women's relationship with family, their work outside the home, domestic chores, and parenting, eliciting discussion on the value of women's work and their place in society. They note women's achievements in the revolution, including their new roles as combatants, teachers, mechanics, and engineers.

There is little systematic statistical data to measure the impact of the EPLF's campaign to give girls access to school. A 1987 EPLF report indicated that 40 percent of Revolution School students were female — an extraordinary increase from girls' almost total exclusion from schooling.[34] However, there is little doubt that the Revolution School benefited from the singular energy and control applied to it by the Front, and that its achievements on behalf of girls were not representative of schooling throughout the liberated territories or the country as a whole.

With independence, the new government took on the massive responsibility of education throughout the nation and of developing an expanded educational system that continued to promote female emancipation. The preeminence of education as the means to advance national reconstruction and development was upheld. The Ministry of Education's policy guidelines committed the government to compulsory basic education, including instruction in local languages, and eventually ensuring universal access to schooling.[35]

OTHER REALMS: ALTERNATIVE VENUES
FOR LEARNING BY WOMEN

The EPLF and the post-independence government have launched a multiprong attack on impediments to women's emancipation. This campaign goes beyond reshaping the educational system to engage and be accessible to females. Substantial interventions have occurred in economics and politics, and, to a lesser degree, in the domain of family life. In each of these arenas, interventions from above have opened up a range of opportunities for women to develop consciousness, acquire new knowledge, and pursue skills once unavailable to them. The contemporary leaders of Eritrea view education and learning not as a discrete, segregated activity, but as an integral component of individual and collective socioeconomic initiatives and efforts. Accordingly, one must include women's advances in politics, economics, and domestic life as additional avenues for breakthroughs in female education and learning.

Adopting a classical Marxist perspective, Eritrean leaders have viewed the economy as the decisive realm in which to secure the liberation of the Eritrean masses as a whole, and of Eritrean women in particular. Economic transformation is perceived as key to overcoming the oppressive class relations and impoverishment that have victimized the vast majority of both men and women. It is believed that the mobilization and integration of women into the labor force is essential for successful economic development of the nation. In the leadership's view, women's full participation in economic life as wage laborers helps to dissipate their traditionally inferior social status and subjugation. Accordingly, during the liberation struggle and since independence, a range of interventions to overcome obstacles and prohibitions to women's economic activity have been launched. The national Constitution[36] asserts that women have a right to work in all economic sectors and that the principle of "equal pay for equal work" must be gender-free. A decisive intervention establishes women's rights to own and work the land in the countryside, and for nomadic women to own herds.[37] As a modern economic sector has been revived and expanded during the liberation struggle and since independence, women have gained entry into a range of wage-labor fields that under colonialism had been the preserve of men. Females work in rural poultry and vegetable cooperatives and state farms, in quarries and mines, in factories, and as part of maintenance and repair units. They have assumed front-line and administrative positions in the human service agencies proliferated first by the Front, and then later by the government. They have converted unpaid household activities into retail operations by selling foodstuffs, baskets, pottery, and processed hides. Women entrepreneurs, a recent phenomenon, have developed small-scale businesses, primarily in the service and retail sectors, owning and running restaurants, bars, groceries, and clothing stores.[38]

The Eritrean leadership also asserts that substantial interventions to open up the arena of politics to women are necessary if gender oppression is to be addressed and if women are to be mobilized for nation-building. While leaders regard economic rights as the fundamental lever for changing women's status, they have viewed political empowerment for women as key to energizing and guaranteeing the emancipatory process.

Beginning in 1974, women's political mobilization and integration became a major priority of the EPLF. It strove to eliminate the substantial obstacles to women's participation in political activity. During a succession of nationalist efforts prior to the EPLF, women had been relegated to highly circumscribed, marginal activity. The EPLF broke with this legacy. The Front, which prior to this point had been exclusively male, formally welcomed and recruited women to join its ranks as cadre, a step which concretely legitimized women's capabilities to play political roles.[39] In addition, the EPLF proclaimed women's right to vote and to run for office. Local organizers actively criticized men's resistance to this process. Under the EPLF's tutelage, women became a presence and had an active voice in the newly organized village and urban assemblies that were established in liberated regions.[40] One indicator of the political empowerment of women is that, at the point of independence in 1993, they represented 30 percent of the Front's membership.[41] However, despite its sustained push for inclusion of women in the political arena, the current government (and the EPLF) has never acknowledged a need for females to assume positions within the core national or regional leadership. There were no women in the EPLF's Central Committee and currently only a few women are in high government positions. None are viewed as key players in major policy decisionmaking.[42]

Women's political activism has, nonetheless, given them a major opportunity to exercise new skills. Previously confined to family life, women developed their capabilities as they increasingly spoke in public and participated in shaping group opinions and decisions in the transformed political arena. With their views about public matters now making a difference, women had new incentives to learn about and analyze regional and national issues. These activities were instrumental in breaking women's internalized view of themselves, upheld by men, that they were "naturally" weak, shy, indecisive, and deferential. The taboo on women being forceful and taking initiatives in public was weakened, and men began to face criticism for chastening and disciplining such women as "hard-headed" and "unruly."

A major EPLF initiative was to welcome women into the liberation army as active combatants.[43] Thus, women gained entry into the independence struggle's highest status and most revered role, which once again broke decisively with male prerogatives, stereotypes, and self-stigmatization. Women had won access to the decisive fulcrum of the national liberation effort.[44]

In the mid-1970s, the EPLF established a women's organization, the National Union of Eritrean Women (NUEW).[45] The Front chose women cadre to head NUEW and to frame its mission, which was to engage Eritrean women activists at the grassroots levels; to form consciousness-raising groups so that women could break with internalized stigma and become active supporters of the Front's strategy to open up educational, political, and economic arenas to women; and to confront male domination legitimized by traditional and religious attitudes. The NUEW has continued since independence, and its branches have become ardent supporters of government initiatives that specifically abolished male privilege and of policy initiatives that support areas seen as central to the support and development of women, such as education, health care, and child care. Overcoming the initial resistance to unorthodox, militant female cadres, NUEW members entered the cloistered sanctums of women's *wushati* (or women's room)[46] and became highly adept at incrementally organizing cautiously conservative women. The NUEW has vigorously recruited women supporters for the Front and post-independence government that Eritrean male leadership could not have recruited. Nevertheless, while the NUEW has had an independent sphere of activity and significant Front and government support, those in its top ranks have always been selected by the national (male) leadership, which has also defined its overall mission and mode of operation.

During the liberation struggle and since independence, Eritrean leaders have crafted policies and programs that affect the realm of family life. These interventions into the family represent an additional route by which consciousness has been shaped and obstacles reduced that bear directly upon females' ability to gain access to education and opportunities for new learning and skills. Legislation has been enacted that abolishes customary common laws that enshrined male control over women in the domestic realm. Laws were passed that gave women rights equal to men's to choose a marriage partner, pursue divorce, and own family property. At the same time, they have encoded the preeminence of secular law over practices emanating from Coptic Christian and/or Muslim religious tenets that had legitimized women's submissiveness and absolute male authority in family matters.[47] These laws have had an enormous impact on Eritrean women's self-esteem and stature as full participants in family matters, and have also strengthened their sense of themselves as social beings and members of the larger society who are motivated to pursue schooling and educational goals, as well as economic and political interests.

The government has recognized that women are, by custom, singularly and disproportionately responsible for domestic labor and child care, and that these burdens impede their ability to pursue education, learn job-market skills, or fully enter into wage labor. Efforts have been made to lessen women's household work by establishing child-care centers, communal laundries, and flour mills. Attempts have been made to educate men so that they accept rather than block women from pursuing these alternatives to tending to children's needs or domestic chores. At the same time, the Eritrean leaders have claimed that a large-scale development of institutional infrastructure to lessen women's burdens in family life is contingent upon significant economic modernization. This is an example of a classical Marxist orientation that views economic advancement of the masses as the key catalyst for overcoming women's oppression and male dominance. Accordingly, the Eritrean leadership has abstained from pursuing initiatives to directly intervene in male privilege and sexism within the family. There are no educational campaigns to pressure, enlighten, or teach skills to men so that they can perform more household tasks, care effectively for children, or gain new appreciation for daughters. No programs have been created to challenge a culture that frees men to pursue public leisure activities and entertainment with each other, while women tend to their homes separately. Further, the government has been highly cautious in the area of sexual practices that oppress women. It has only tentatively and sporadically questioned customs, such as female seclusion, polygamy, and female circumcision. It seems probable that relatively unchallenged male sexism within family life emboldens fathers and husbands to undercut government-sanctioned drives to expand female access to educational opportunity.

WOMEN'S PERCEPTIONS AND EXPERIENCES

Eritrean political leaders' goals and policies for advancing female opportunities in education need to be measured against the concrete aspirations and experiences of Eritrean women. This article seeks to establish a sense of grassroots perceptions and perspectives. A group of Eritrean women were interviewed about their encounters with education during the national liberation struggle and after independence.[48]

These women were drawn from a diverse range of ages, places of birth, ethnic groups, primary languages, religious affiliations, and educational levels (if any).[49] These women saw themselves as participating in the liberation struggle, and were aware of the post-independence government's goal of national reconstruction and development. They shared this perspective with the vast majority of contemporary Eritrean women and men. They represent both cadre and mass participants, the level and status of their activity varies, and there are significant differences in the degree to which they feel connected to (or distanced from) Eritrean leaders and nationally organized political efforts.

These women express the view that the decisive mid-1970s leadership decision to integrate women fully into national liberation and development was essential to insure the success of these efforts. They do not believe that the leadership's commitment to women's emancipation was inevitable, and they give male national leaders credit for this decisive break with the legacy of male supremacy. Genct, a single fifty-year-old civil servant with the Public Works Department in Asmara, says:

> Women's oppression is deep-seated and multifarious. . . . [Eritrean leaders] have embraced "the women's question". . . [which] has given women the opportunity to participate and to fight against their specific oppression. This is an important concession. . . . The [leaders] did not have to do that. . . . It is a daring act.[50]

These women define education broadly. When they discuss education, they include both nonformal and formal learning, focus on both knowledge acquisition and skill building, place great emphasis on consciousness-raising activities, and highlight the positive psychological and developmental effects of education as much as its practical benefits. They often depict the revolutionary process itself as a nonformal setting that promoted the intellectual growth of its female participants. These women view education as a core arena in which reforms have had a significant impact on Eritrean women's gains toward emancipation. They generally regard the effects of opportunities for women in education as more substantial and fundamental than changes in the economy — the public realm viewed as the decisive lever for gender equality by Eritrean leaders. Keddes, a college-educated woman from a middle-class family, characterizes education as "pivotal" in enabling women to pursue new rights and access to female participation in politics and economic life:

For women, education is a critical measure to deepen their awareness about and to develop the means of change in their personal lives. Also, through the acquisition of training and skills women can successfully move into public life that was previously inaccessible to them. I would also say that education is pivotal in transforming the entire society into an egalitarian social system and a productive economic entity.

Many women perceive education as necessary in order for women to recognize and understand the nature of their oppression and to overcome self-stigmatization and, thereby, to embrace and participate in emancipatory efforts. As Asma, a thirty-four-year-old Muslim woman from a peasant family, describes:

> Education [is] the major element in the creation of a new Eritrean woman. Education helps [women] to understand the need for that change, thus empowering us to become major protagonists in our own name.

Yelsu, a thirty-year-old Coptic Christian woman from one of the Highland regions, couples the depiction of education as the key to women's social liberation with the guarantee it provides that children — the future of the nation — will pursue educational advancement:

> Education of women is the sure way to promote the social position of women . . . but it [also] equips them to impart their knowledge and training to the children they bear and raise within the household. So the next generation would grow up with new attitudes and values.

Time and again, these women reflect on how their participation and achievements in education were unimaginable until the reforms advanced by the Eritrean leadership. They note the scarcity of learning opportunities available to girls, the economic pressures that prevented their participation in schools, and the traditional beliefs and attitudes against women's intellectual development. Leila, an ex-combatant from a nomadic peasant family, notes that in her village "it was unthinkable for a girl to be sent to school" or attain rudimentary literacy. Women from towns and cities indicate that there, too, girls who pursued schooling were extremely rare.

Women place great value on the institutionalization of a curriculum open to both genders in all its dimensions. They depict the constraints that had been previously placed on female students. Senayit, a thirty-eight-year-old front-line medic, states:

> Before, there was a differential between females' and males' educational goals. Girls who remained in school were urged to take home economics and homemaking courses. . . . I had wanted to study the sciences. I dreamed of being a doctor. . . . There was no way I could do this in the [traditional] school system.

A reformed pedagogical approach that focused on lessons drawn from everyday life and concrete experience, rather than on rote textbook learning, greatly benefited female students, who had been steeped in the detailed narratives and ruminations of an oral culture. Some women indicate that schools' inclusion of collective manual labor as part of the educational experience and equal regard for both intellectual and physical activities also benefited females, who even more so than males had been traditionally restricted to and associated with manual tasks.

Many women characterize education (and revolutionary activity in general) as a "great awakener" that has catalyzed enormous growth in both understandings of self and of a larger social landscape. Twenty-six-year-old Mamet, a former member of the Eritrean Liberation Army, says:

> There is no yardstick to measure the revolution's influence over my life. Now I have better understanding about myself and others. . . . Before I came here, my interest in life was geared exclusively towards family affairs. I did not know anything about my country and the world beyond.[51]

Zewdi, a thirty-six-year-old Catholic single woman from a working-class background, says:

> I have undergone immense changes since I joined EPLF [and] because of . . . my academic achievement. . . . Today I can understand about my surroundings and about the world. My horizon has broadened.[52]

Emancipatory reforms for females in education are linked with interventions to achieve gender equality in the economy and politics. Senayit observes that the introduction of a gender-equal curriculum could not benefit females if the job market had remained rigidly segregated by genders: "[Gender-based curricula] reflected the sex-segregated labor force where women received lowly jobs and were easily dispensed with. Girls were [routed] into vocations such as secretaries and seamstresses." Sarah, a forty-five-year-old college graduate who holds a professional position at the Ministry of Culture, notes: "Because of the limitation of women's role [in the economy], women did not have the incentive to continue their education."

The Eritrean government regards economic modernization as the key factor in enabling females to fully access education. National leaders believe that once the nation has financial capability to develop and distribute education resources and families have greater economic well-being, girls will be able to take fuller advantage of new educational rights and opportunities. In contrast to this official view, the women interviewed generally regard male dominance and sexist attitudes within the family as the major impediments to females' accessing and utilizing the reformed educational arena. Time and again, they delineate how traditional family beliefs and practices block female participation in schools and learning. Although they recognize this as a manifestation of patriarchy — the rule of the father — they note that mothers have helped reinforce the tenet that education is unnecessary and undesirable for girls.[53] Leila, a forty-year-old married Muslim woman, relates:[54]

> My father had some education but my mother did not go school. My parents felt that a girl should learn from her mother how to be a good housekeeper, mother and wife, and the man will take care of the activities outside the home. In fact I was told the Prophet Mohammed has said that women should concern themselves only with family activities. So, it was unthinkable for a girl to be sent to school.

Twenty-two-year-old Rishan states:[55]

> When I was a little girl, villagers had a tremendous curiosity and enthusiasm for
> education. The elders used to accept contributions from farmers and request
> that the Italian administration establish schools, but it was to send boys not girls
> . . . [by saying] contemptuously that "a female will always remain a female so
> why waste time educating her." Women have never been seen as having the abil-
> ity to cultivate their minds.

Mamet agrees: she says that even in the urban areas, parents always feel conflicted
about sending their daughters to school. Interviewees stress that families' opposition to female education is rooted in their view that the priority for daughters is to
help mothers with domestic chores and to be trained and socialized to become
obedient and dutiful wives. Families have viewed education as a source by which
girls can become defiant and morally corrupt. Yelsu explains:

> With better education girls may refuse to marry the men who already have paid
> the dowry; scholastic ambitions might tempt girls not to give their full attention
> to their "proper role" as wives and mothers; higher education may instigate giv-
> ing up one's culture and the traditional status accorded childbearing; and,
> moral danger may arise from imported values and new ways of life. . . . [My par-
> ents felt] they were being very liberal by allowing their daughters to go to
> school in the first place. However, as the girl gets older, they worry she may be
> interested in boys and before it is too late they consent to the first eligible suitor
> who appears. In my own case, they insisted that my education had improved my
> chances for a superior husband and that they could not understand why I re-
> jected him. They kept saying, "but he is from a good family, educated and well-
> off." They felt that I could not get a better suitor than him.

Given the weight that respondents place on the patriarchal family's traditional resistance to females' access to education, they are extremely heartened by the reforms in education that include pedagogical approaches that challenge male students' sexist sense of superiority, and that allow boys opportunities to work and
study alongside girls.

WOMEN'S PERSPECTIVES ON OTHER REALMS FOR LEARNING

When the women interviewed discuss national policies to achieve gender equality
in realms other than education — the economy, politics, and family life — they
note and value the increased power and material benefits that females won
through these reforms. At the same time, they stress that the emancipating policies in these realms also provided women with additional educational opportunities to develop knowledge, consciousness, and skills. Keddes readily links women's
new economic rights to own property, till the soil, sell products, and be wage laborers to changing relations with their husbands: "She can be an independent person
rather than an appendage to a man." She couples female economic emancipation
with the broader endeavor of women gaining a "foothold [into and] . . . learn[ing]
the skills of public life." She then asserts that to achieve all this, "a women needs to
have . . . education. Schooling would enable a woman to know what is possible and

to acquire training and skills." Many respondents often note the intellectual growth that occurs as women encounter new work opportunities. As Yelsu states: "Access to employment enabled women to gain not only personal earnings and economic security, but it also broadened their horizons towards new experiences and ideas that were previously inaccessible to them when they were isolated in their homes." These women stress that intensive education and consciousness-raising have been key in making men more accepting of female economic equality and in motivating women to pursue new economic opportunities. As Sarah says:

> Some conservative rural villages have accepted the notion of women's right to own land. But this happened after conducting a long and arduous political education and discussion with the entire village community and not the least with women themselves.

Leila describes vividly how things have changed for women:

> [When I was young,] it was forbidden for women to plough the land and engage in all kinds of activities like selling grains or vegetables . . . [our] society does not find it acceptable for women to do these things. [It] is considered an insult to her husband. . . . Even if she is an able-bodied woman and her husband is sick or she becomes widowed, she has to hire a field hand to do this specific job. This rule is something that no woman would dare break for she will be an outcast. . . . Now [women] are doing all these new things. We [women] are opening our eyes to a new way of life. Even our husbands are open to these new ideas. I only hope it remains like this when the war is over. . . . I like it better this way.

To these interviewees, women's full and equal participation in politics is a critical milestone in the movement toward gender equality. They often speak of their newly gained political understandings and activity as eventually producing a consciousness about their own oppression as women and the need to overcome it. Zewdi notes that, when joining the Front and commencing political activism,

> all I wanted is [to] stand on equal grounds with the enemy and avenge the misery and devastation it has brought to our people. I learned that there were other dimensions to struggling for national liberation, that we need to eradicate other types of oppression in our midst. There is prejudice, poverty, and illiteracy and there is also gender oppression. [Eventually] I ma[de] the connection between my political and my personal oppression. . . . Now, I consider it a bonus to exercise my rights, not only as an Eritrean but also as a woman.

Women embrace their admittance to the army because it not only allows them to exercise their patriotic fervor and desire for national liberation, but also because it is a decisive "testing ground" to demonstrate that their skills and tenacity are equal to men's. As Sarah explains, "In the course of the liberation struggle, no women fighters have deserted . . . whereas there were many men who deserted."

These women often see political activism as yielding more than political gains. To them, it also empowers women and creates a consciousness that females are able to forge their own destinies. Yelsu says that "the emancipation of women is not something that will be handed to us. We should earn it, through our own struggle." These women recognize that women's political participation results in enhanced power, but they also value political work because it also gives females opportunities to learn and to acquire new skills. Genet explains:

[As a top political organizer assigned to a rural village,] I find my work challenging and gratifying because I relate with different types of people and their issues. . . . [I] have a chance to upgrade [my] skills. . . . There are new issues and challenges that one runs into all the time. I am always learning.

The NUEW is perceived as guarantor of women's political space and its organizers are viewed as uniquely capable of opening other women's eyes to the nature and need to overcome female oppression. As Mamet relates:

We can go to the inner sanctum of women's *wushati* and talk to them. It's even better to have a meeting . . . there, because they become very animated and direct. . . . And joining an all-female organization does not violate their sense of propriety. . . . Through the local [NUEW] chapter, women can participate [fully] in public life.

The interviewees place great value on interventions to foster gender equality within the family. As Genet notes, "Women's oppression has thrived . . . in the privacy and quiet corners of people's homes."[56] Respondents credit the new egalitarian laws about marriage, family property ownership, and divorce with giving women privileges and autonomy that were once the exclusive preserve of their menfolk. At the same time, they stress that new, more emancipated family dynamics help women to speak up for themselves and to expand their abilities. Women now share with men decisions about family budgets. They have a greater voice in planning children's (male, as well as female) futures. They speak of a whole range of familial discussions and decisionmaking that their spouses now engage in with them "where there is respect for each other's views." Women who are widowed and divorced describe how egalitarian family laws enabled them to exercise new capabilities and rights to raise their children effectively.

INCREASED CRITICISM FROM BELOW AND INDICATIONS OF DEMORALIZATION: SHIFTS DURING THE EARLY POST-INDEPENDENCE YEARS

Fourteen years after the initial interviews, which were conducted during the liberation struggle in 1983 and four years into independence, the commentary of women respondents indicated much continuity in their attitudes and perspectives. All spoke with energy about the successfully waged liberation war, the welcome end of combat traumas and losses, and the myriad tasks and changes occurring since independence. Many have positions integral to national reconstruction, and some are associated with the government or with nonprofit organizations that receive state funding. All speak with pride about their individual participation in Eritrea's struggle for and achievements under independence. Most remark, without regret, that they have participated in experiences and activities that could not have been anticipated, given their gender and, for many, economic background. Many possess an intimate knowledge of regions of the country, ethnic groups, and second (and third) languages that were not connected to their own birthplaces, identities, and upbringings — a form of cosmopolitanism that was rare among most Eritreans twenty-five years ago and unimaginable for its constricted and cloistered females.

Nevertheless, the interviewees are generally far more critical of and pessimistic in 1997 about the Eritrean leadership's efforts toward gender equality and women's emancipation than they were in 1983 in the midst of the liberation struggle. There are more indications of bitterness, charges of bad faith, and evidence of alienation and demoralization. Ironically, many look back on the liberation war as "a better time" for women's rights and empowerment — "when we were living most heartily." Even so, these harsher appraisals do not just focus on the years since independence, but also on the decades of the liberation struggle itself. The respondents' critical commentary focuses on general aspects of Eritrean women's condition and does not concentrate in particular on female access to and pursuit of education. However, their insights are suggestive of how and why the drive to create gender equality in the educational realm may be losing momentum.

A large number of respondents characterize women as experiencing a range of difficulties and encountering frustrations and disappointments. They believe there is a resurgence of male reactions against women's gains during the liberation struggle and that Eritrean leaders either minimize this phenomenon or do not regard challenging it as a major priority. Eritrean women believe that the government's predominant focus is on economic modernization and that it has displayed a tendency to regard women's emancipation as a side issue or distraction. Many of these critics believe that leaders point too readily to disappointments in current international financial aid or the low levels of national resources as a rationale for why there is waning momentum for women's advancement. They assert that their leaders have long overvalued large-scale economic development as a contingency for gains in gender equality. These women have a revisionist view (often amending their own earlier appraisals) that during the liberation struggle there were gaps in the Front's pursuit of women's emancipation and that, with independence, for a variety of reasons, these deficiencies have intensified.

A large number of women are critical about what they regard as the government's relative abandonment of women activists — particularly those who were combatants in the liberation army. In the view of those women interviewed, the condition of the vast majority of female cadre is not an "insiders" issue. They regard the status of former women fighters and society's regard for them as a reasonable indicator of how the masses of Eritrean women — and the struggle for gender equality — are faring in post-independence Eritrea. Female members of the liberation army were largely rural peasants and working class (in contrast to the small number of female cadre who served in administrative noncombat positions, who were more educated and came from families with better economic circumstances).[57] While these respondents feel that all Front activists — both men and women — have not received as much care as they deserve, they feel this tendency has been harshest on females in general, and military personnel in particular.

They note that women fighters often had little or no education prior to joining the struggle, and that while many attained literacy during the liberation years, their further education was stymied by the imperatives of war. Many developed new skills during the struggle, but they were inadequately developed and are not well matched to the peacetime economy. Further, unlike upper-level female non-combatant administrators, the women fighters have few networks among men, which are critical to advancing in post-independent Eritrean society. To its credit, Eritrea has undertaken a massive demobilization of its army, recognizing that modernization is the work of civilians and that a permanent mobilization can undercut economic and political development. However, a significantly greater percentage of women than men have been demobilized[58] and this has accelerated the difficulties of former female members of the liberation army. As Sarah relates:

> The [demobilized] women have few marketable skills. . . . They live a miserable and impoverished life. They come and tell me that "you were right, we should have looked out for ourselves and acquired some education and useful skill. All we thought about was contributing to the revolutionary effort. Perhaps we were duped." Now, you see them in terrible shape, poorly clothed, unhappy, with *madia*[59] on their faces, walking the streets of Asmara.

Some respondents believe that women cadre faced covert and unsanctioned disaffirmation during the liberation years. They do not view this as having been imposed by male Eritrean leaders, but as a manifestation of chauvinist attitudes among Front members that were not effectively challenged either by the leadership or by women themselves. Noting that no women combatants ever achieved the three highest officer ranks in the army, Keddes said that the effect was to keep women locked in the ranks or lower leadership roles that, ironically, required more physically demanding activity:

> It meant women combatants had years of carrying heavy weapons and supplies, climbing difficult terrain. They sustained multiple injuries and eventually their performance stagnated or declined because age catches up on you. Even though there have been many skilled female combatants, they never rose beyond the rank of *hailee*[60] — we hit a "glass ceiling." We were told that the promotion required a higher level of training and educational background. Of course many of the females were peasants, who became literate after they joined and did not get beyond sixth-grade level of education. Due to their upbringing, they were viewed as having tremendous ability to withstand the physical hardship of guerrilla fighting. So the men said women were put where their labor is needed most. However, this was an excuse, since these factors do not limit peasant or working-class men from acquiring high status.

During the liberation struggle, many women activists had much exposure to a collective life, which despite its gaps in gender equality allowed women to work and live side by side with men, to perform tasks formerly reserved for males, and, in many instances, to have their effectiveness judged without bias. As they often say, "The revolution was a great equalizer." In this context, they abandoned the subservient and diffident stance that women had traditionally assumed. In today's civil society and economy, these women are often penalized for their "emancipated ways." Discussing demobilized women, Rishan notes that they often

> cannot get a job, because they are discriminated against. Even when they seek jobs like waitressing or store clerk position, employers say "we want women who

have pleasant smiles and look appealing." [More traditional] women break their gaze and smile, and can put up with occasionally verbal abuse from male bosses and coworkers. Whereas these women know their rights and expect fair treatment. So they are shunned.

Many parents of women activists have begun to castigate them for going on a wayward path and abandoning cherished traditions during the years of struggle. A number have one or two children or are childless, which is condemned as a symptom of failure. Many women note that there is currently a notable "conservative backlash" in civil society against "liberated females." For example, in towns and cities, there has been a resurgence of elaborate weddings, and women are returning to traditionally feminine dress and finery. Symbols of women's delicacy and submissiveness have regained renewed acceptability as well.

Women respondents also characterize a current resurgence of men's supremacist attitudes. They assert that Eritrean leaders have reduced their commitment to organized mass education and consciousness-raising around gender issues and that this emboldens men to behave chauvinistically. They believe that this trend is marked among many men who were active during the liberation struggle. For example, they note that the divorce rate among Front members is over 35 percent.[61] While some of these divorces can be viewed as an indicator of modernity, respondents believe that they are predominantly initiated by men, who pursue younger women as partners and largely abandon responsibility for the children from their first marriages. These women believe that one aspect of the "women's liberation" is that men have embraced open forms of irresponsibility that used to be condemnable. As Keddes explains, "Now that men have no monopoly over family property, they believe it is all right to leave a woman outright and then, only through the goodness of their hearts, would they assist former wives in raising their children."

ANALYSIS AND CONCLUSION

The twenty-three-year collective effort in Eritrea to address longstanding female oppression in general, and to eliminate women's exclusion from education in particular, has had substantial successes. Statistical data demonstrate that women have achieved significant access into the contemporary educational system that has developed during the past two decades. For example, in 1992–1993, 45 percent of primary school students and 28.5 percent of high school graduates were female. In addition, there were 3,085 women teachers representing 37 percent of elementary, 17 percent of middle, and 10 percent of high school faculties.[62] The magnitude of this achievement is appreciated when it is contrasted with Eritrea's traditional and colonial epochs, when women's involvement in education was viewed as largely unnecessary and undesirable. Nevertheless, while women now participate as students, teachers, and, to a lesser extent, policymakers, they are still in the minority. Further, after initial breakthroughs and successes, there is evidence of a leveling off of effort and success, as indicated, for example, by persistently high dropout rates for females and the government's inattention to the factors that promote that trend.[63]

National leaders have adopted comprehensive and creative policies to promote gender equity in education, which suggests the authenticity of their effort. During and after the liberation struggle, government officials have defined broadly the components of education, focusing not only on formal schooling and youth, but also on nonformal educational efforts, adult education, and on-the-job training as core elements of the new educational system. This has been advantageous for women, who have needed many and flexible opportunities for learning to overcome the diverse obstacles that had marginalized them historically. Nonformal educational programs have insured that, as women gain entry to education, it is not just a small, privileged minority who have become involved and that major deficits, such as pervasive female nonliteracy, are addressed. Adult education programs are available to the many middle-aged and elderly females who shouldered much responsibility for liberating the nation and stabilizing its independence. Adult education has also helped win parents' acceptance of the merits of schooling and their daughters' rights to become students. The official emphasis on consciousness-raising as a core component of education has been vital in motivating females to pursue educational opportunities and in lessening male opposition to gender equality in this realm. Educational policymakers' attention to skill development, and not simply to the acquisition of knowledge, has helped women grasp the relevance of education in enriched, concrete terms, in contrast to previous generations, who were led to view women's schooling as, at most, a transitory stepping stone to a more desirable husband.

The interviewees in this study testify to the efficacy and accomplishments of the contemporary effort to emancipate Eritrean women from the constraints that kept them from getting an education. They describe the radical departure of current educational policies from the legacy of female exclusion from schooling, delineate the manner in which institutional supports have facilitated their pursuit of formal and nonformal learning, and marvel at their significant individual advances in knowledge and skill. These women place great value on educational reforms undertaken in the context of a broad, far-reaching national campaign to overcome their oppression. They believe that their participation in new educational programs has often been catalyzed and strengthened by their involvement in the realms of politics, the economy, and domestic life. They are a living testimony to contemporary gains in educating women. From adolescents to grandmothers, from peasants residing in remote regions to inhabitants of the capital city, from those who have recently attained basic literacy to those who have attended college — Eritrean women collectively demonstrate an impressive level of intellectual curiosity, analytic adeptness, and confidence in the value of their own perceptions and opinions. They address a range of issues — national economic policies, power dynamics in local political organizations, the intricacies of male chauvinistic practices, the transmission of internalized stigma from mother to daughter, the effects of sexual mores — that were literally unimaginable as topics for women two decades ago.

I found evidence in my analysis of government documents, national newspapers, meetings with public officials, and 1997 interviews with Eritrean women that there is currently a loss of momentum and, perhaps, a reversal in the movement to fully integrate women into public life, including education. The majority of women are concerned and somewhat skeptical about the government's ability to sustain a commitment to advance women's rights and status. They note that leaders are increasingly preoccupied with economic development. They see evidence that high-level officials believe that to pursue vigorously "the women's question" distracts from the collective unity and sacrifice required for modernization. Women suspect that leaders are ceding a need for them to return to more traditional roles in order to stabilize a massive reconstruction effort. For example, respondents believe the government is complacent in not implementing the kind of infrastructural supports — such as day-care centers and laundry and cooking establishments — that are particularly vital to facilitate women's participation in educational, political, and economic activity. Women activists consistently place far greater emphasis than do government leaders on the need to aggressively confront male sexism and privilege within the family and the cultural beliefs that legitimize female subordination. The current official focus on economic development is viewed as intensifying the government's relative disengagement from the cultural struggle around women's emancipation. In addition, the rapid decline in mass consciousness-raising activities is viewed by women as a major setback in efforts to enhance women's self-esteem and to reverse male chauvinism. The interviewees believe that the government's posture has the effect — even if not intended — of lending support to a conservative backlash within society against gender equality and "the new emancipated woman." The social organization and culture forged within the Front during the liberation struggle allowed female and male members to live and work together in a way that was far more egalitarian than gender relations in the larger society. Respondents poignantly characterize women cadre as increasingly ostracized in public and private life, and view the government's inattentive support of former Front members, particularly females, as contributing to their isolation and demoralization.

Official speeches and policy documents demonstrate the government's narrowing focus on economic modernization and a dearth of new ideas and programs to push forward on women's liberation. A female official, selected by the government, who monitors programs directed to women, conveys current official complacency when she asserts that governmental structural interventions to ensure gender equality have been "largely achieved and now it is women's turn and responsibility to move forward on their own."[64]

In my own view, there are significant indications that government policymakers are turning away from an active campaign to eliminate women's oppression. I believe that longstanding weaknesses and fault lines in the Eritrean leadership's pursuit of gender equality have contributed to this shift. First, despite significant advances in the public arena, women were never able to break into the highest rankings of national political leadership, and this was never established as an emancipatory goal. Further, the NUEW has never been a fully autonomous organization. Those in senior positions of NUEW have always been selected by the top male leaders of the government (and formerly the Front), who also have defined its overall mission and sphere of operation. NUEW has never departed from or critiqued the agenda and priorities of the national leadership. The assertion that NUEW funding comes solely from nongovernmental organizations (NGOs) seems more a government strategy to inspire NGO support than evidence that the women's organization has a truly independent financial base. Despite an impressive record of substantial creativity in mobilizing women at the grassroots level, the NUEW has never established itself as an independent player that can pressure policymakers to attend to women's interests. The EPLF's initial embrace of women's emancipation was tied to a strategy to fully enlist marginalized groups into the liberation war. Eritrean leaders' commitment to gender equality has never been fully extricated from this pragmatic instrumentalism, and has thereby been vulnerable, especially once a major component of that commitment — the war effort — was no longer a factor.[65] While Eritrean activists have lessened their theoretical reliance on classical Marxism,[66] this orientation is still influential in the nation's political dialogue, and it systematically demotes women's oppression by making it a condition dependent on more basic social inequities.[67]

Many of the women interviewed discuss how they embraced the national revolutionary leadership, admired its success in forging independence, and were exhilarated by its sponsorship of women's emancipation. They speak of their devotion, their willingness "to hold nothing back and make every sacrifice" to the revolutionary cause. They often note that — given the legacy of women's subordination — females have "a duty" to be extraordinary in their performance and "to pass every test," as Zewdi put it. These themes, which are persistent, suggest that, in some sense, women switched their dutiful allegiance from the father — the domestic patriarch — to the liberating nation and its male leaders. It is understandable that strands of subservience remain in how women have positioned themselves in relation to the contemporary struggle to create a modern Eritrea. In my own view, women's vigorous criticism of the national leadership and its policies signals a major step forward in female assertiveness and independence. While the critical attitudes of these women activists are generated by setbacks to the struggle for gender equality, they represent a maturation of their capabilities and confidence in shaping public life.

Finally, Eritrea's current context and situation — nationally and internationally — promotes obstacles and challenges to a vigorous pursuit of women's rights and equality. The people of the nation have undergone a harrowing and traumatic struggle to achieve peace and independence. There is an understandable yearning for calm, amicability, and freedom from conflict. In this atmosphere, many — including former female activists — are zealously seeking the normalization of everyday life. This can result in a decline in the collective will and interest to pursue arduous battles against forms of female subjugation that have been entrenched for centuries. Even when they suffered from massive exploitation themselves, Eritrean men vigilantly guarded and preserved their dominance over women. Imperial powers chose not to tamper with or challenge these male prerogatives. It has been indeed "a daring act" and enormously courageous that contemporary Eritrean male leaders and women activists made women's rights and equality a major component of their vision and program for liberation and social revolution. In these early years of independence, Eritrea faces the monumental task of national reconstruction within an international political arena and world economy that largely marginalizes Africa and exempts itself from financial support to Third World societies.[68] This creates more pressures to blunt a sustained mobilization against women's oppression within Eritrea — a social struggle that will inevitably generate domestically pronounced tensions and opposition. It will take many more "daring acts" by both national leaders and Eritrean women to push forward the struggle for gender equality.

NOTES

1. "Eritrea: New Society Is Being Born," *Eritrea Information, 4,* No. 9 (1982), 12.

2. I have opted to use the term "emancipation," which is defined as a release from oppressive constraints. It is also the opposite of oppression, which is the imposition of unjust restraint on the freedom of individuals and groups. From these definitions it follows that there are conceptual connections between oppression and emancipation. The diverse Western feminist literature on women's liberation does not explicitly define the term, focusing instead on the question of *why* and *how* women are oppressed. However, feminists implicitly outline the concept of women's emancipation by suggesting different strategies to achieve women's liberation. For the purpose of this article, I conceived the term "emancipation" as a process of setting women free from restraint. Emancipation is not viewed as some finally achievable state or situation, but rather as the process of eliminating forms of oppression as they continue to arise. Thus, the domain of women and human liberation is constantly redefined and extended. Eritrean women's emancipation is therefore viewed from a perspective that presupposes a dynamic rather than a static view of society. Because of this, education is viewed as a critical element in changing Eritrean women's self-concept, autonomy, and options to participate in a democratic society. For further discussion, see Asgedet Stefanos, "African Women and Revolutionary Change: A Freirian and Feminist Perspective," in *Mentoring the Mentor: A Critical Dialogue with Paulo Freire,* ed. Paulo Freire, James Fraser, Donaldo Macedo, Tanya McKinnon, and William Stokes (New York: Peter Lang, 1997); Andrew Parker, Mary Russo, Doris Sommer, and Patricia Yaeger, eds., *Nationalisms and Sexualities* (London: Routledge, 1992); Seth Kreisberg, *Transforming Power: Domination, Empowerment, and Education* (Albany: State University of New York Press, 1992); Carmen Luke and Jennifer Gore, eds., *Feminisms and Critical Pedagogy* (London: Routledge, 1992); Albert Memmi, *The Colonizer and the Colonized* (Boston: Beacon Press, 1967).

3. See Rosemarie Buikema and Anneke Smelik, *Women's Studies and Culture* (London: Zed Books, 1993); Ann Diller, Barbara Houston, Kathryn Morgan, and Maryama Ayim, *The Gender Question in Education: Theory, Pedagogy and Politics* (Boulder, CO: Westview Press, 1996).

4. For a discussion on the EPLF's and the Eritrean government's education goals, see Ministry of Labor and Human Welfare Report, *Initial Report on the Implementation of the Convention on the Rights of the Child,* (Asmara, Eritrea: Government of the State of Eritrea, 1997), pp. 60–62. In addition, as works in critical pedagogy have pointed out, education can be an important site of ongoing contestation and control. Likewise, resistance theorists indicate colonial struggles are also a rejection of domination and an assertion of self-determination. So, both revolution and education are interdependent in asserting the possibility of human agency, or the belief in the individual's ability to make a difference, to bring about an egalitarian society. See Paulo Freire, *Pedagogy of the Oppressed* (New York: Continuum, 1970); Michael W. Apple, *Ideology and Curriculum* (New York: Routledge, 1990); Henry A. Giroux, *Theory and Resistance in Education* (South Hadley, MA: Bergin & Garvey, 1983); Paulo Freire and Donaldo Macedo, *Literacy: Reading the Word and the World* (Westport, CT: Bergin & Garvey, 1987); Paul Willis, *Learning to Labour* (New York: Columbia University Press, 1977).

5. The strategy of Eritrean education is to attack the structural constraints to women's access to education. See Asgedet Stefanos, *An Encounter with Revolutionary Change: A Portrait of Eritrean Women,* Diss., Harvard Graduate School of Education, 1988, p. 295; Sheila Parvyn Wamahiu, ed., *Girls' Education in Eritrea* (Asmara, Eritrea: Ministry of Education and UNICEF, 1996), p. 6.

6. See Jane Gaskell and John Willinsky, eds., *Gender In/forms Curriculum: From Enrichment to Transformation* (New York: Teachers College Press, 1995); Miriam David, *The State, The Family and Education* (London: Routledge & Kegan Paul, 1980).

7. For detailed discussion on women's access to formal education during Italian and British colonial rule, see Stefanos, *An Encounter with Revolutionary Change*, pp. 203–206.

8. Stefanos, *An Encounter with Revolutionary Change*, p. 205.

9. Here, the term "traditional" is used to differentiate between socioeconomic structures that predated colonization and those that took shape during colonialism. Economic development theorists use the term traditional to suggest "backward" in contrast to "modern." They characterize traditionalists as "rural, unproductive, consumptive, uneducated, irrational, uncompetitive, unmotivated, acquisitive." Modern is defined as "urban, productive, autonomous, motivated, literate, rational, punctual, efficient." See David McClelland, *The Achieving Society* (New York: Irvington, 1976, rpt.); Alex Inkeles and David H. Smith, *On Being Modern* (Cambridge, MA: Harvard University, 1974); Daniel Lerner, *The Passing of Traditional Society: Modernizing the Middle East* (New York: Free Press, 1958).

10. There was also a minority of Protestant and Catholic highlanders in traditional Eritrea. Stefanos, *An Encounter with Revolutionary Change*, p. 204.

11. There are nine distinct national/linguistic groups within Eritrea — Tigre, Kebessa (Tigrinya), Belen, Denkel, Sahho, Barya and Beza (Kunama), Ben Amir, and Beja. For a detailed account of the history of Eritrea and its sociocultural groups, see Stefanos, *An Encounter with Revolutionary Change*, pp. 70–186.

12. A people and socioeconomic system that do not fit into these broad categories are the Kunamas. They were both agriculturalists and pastoralists. They did not adhere to a monotheistic religion. Their society followed a matrilineal descent line. Social relations were relatively nonhierarchical.

13. Stefanos, *An Encounter with Revolutionary Change*, pp. 188–197.

14. These expectations were gleaned from my interviews with Eritrean women in 1983. See "Women's Perception and Experiences of Their Personal Status within the Family," Stefanos, *An Encounter with Revolutionary Change*, pp. 348–353.

15. Women carry singular responsibility for household management. Asma, an interviewee from a peasant background, stated: "I rarely saw my mother sitting down doing nothing. She always worked. The work within the home is solely hers. She prepared the daily family meal, raised her children, and took care of the sick and the old in the family. My father did not perform any duties within the home even when it is not farming season, because tradition did not permit him to do so. [However,] my mother was also expected to 'lend a hand' during planting and harvesting season," Stefanos, *An Encounter with Revolutionary Change*, p. 346.

16. Studies of pastoral societies are comparatively sparse and a focus on women even more rare. In order to have a fuller picture of Eritrean women, the differing structures and experiences of seminomadic women should be studied in their own right. Stefanos, *An Encounter with Revolutionary Change*, p. 193.

17. By the 1940s, one-fifth of the Eritrean population was urbanized. See Jordan Gebre-Medhin, *Peasant and Nationalism in Eritrea* (Trenton, NJ: Red Sea Press, 1989), p. 61.

18. Italy, like all other European colonial regimes in Africa, had Victorian sensibilities about women's position within its own society and so was less interested in women in the colonies. For an analysis of colonialists' view of African women, see Fanon's classic analysis of Algerian women's position during the French colonial period: Frantz Fanon, *A Dying Colonialism* (New York: Grove Press, 1965).

19. Italians had a separatist and functional view of education for Eritreans, which led them to a policy that government education can only go as far as the fourth-grade

level. Kennedy Nicholas Trevaskis, *Eritrea: A Colony in Transition* (London: Oxford University Press, 1952), p. 33.

20. The various Catholic and Protestant missionaries were fiercely competitive among each other, which was aggravated by the fact that in the Highlands, where their activities were based, Eritreans were conservative Coptic Christians who viewed conversion as ludicrous. Promises of schooling and health services were used as major inducements to enter the mission orbit and become a convert. Stefanos, *An Encounter with Revolutionary Change,* p. 203.

21. Trevaskis, *Eritrea: A Colony in Transition,* p. 33.

22. In contrast to a rigid policy of noncontinuation of schooling beyond fourth-grade level, mission schools allowed some Eritreans to pursue their education further. Trevaskis, *Eritrea: A Colony in Transition,* p. 34.

23. Children who were fathered by Italians were conferred Italian citizenship and were permitted to enjoy the full benefit of Italian education in segregated parochial schools. Stefanos, *An Encounter with Revolutionary Change,* p. 204.

24. Trevaskis quotes from an official confidential memo to Italian headmasters by Signor Festa, Director of Education in Eritrea, in 1938: "By the end of fourth year, the Eritrean student should be able to speak our language moderately well; he should know the four arithmetical operations within normal limits; he should be a convinced propagandist of the principles of hygiene; and of history he should know only the names of those who have made Italy great." Trevaskis, *Eritrea: A Colony in Transition,* p. 33.

25. See Asgedet Stefanos, *Women and Education in Guinea-Bissau: An Analysis of Theory and Practice,* Qualifying Paper, Harvard Graduate School of Education, 1981, p. 19. Also, see Amilcar Cabral, *A Return to the Source* (New York: African Information Service and PAIGC, 1973); Donna Landry and Gerald Maclean, *The Spivak Reader* (New York: Routledge, 1996); Homi K. Bhabha, *Nation and Narration* (London: Routledge, 1990); Stephanie Urdang, *Fighting Two Colonialisms: Women in Guinea-Bissau* (New York: Monthly Review Press, 1979).

26. Family life worsened during British and subsequently under Ethiopian regimes: "The colonialists' neglect of the rural areas has caused the disintegration of Eritrean families. Starting from the Italian period, male members migrated to cities in search of work. Years went by before their families saw them and many did not return. Sometimes men decided to move on rather than come back penniless. As the situation worsened, both men and women increasingly began to go further and further away from their homes, to the other African countries, the Gulf states, Europe and the United States." Stefanos, *An Encounter with Revolutionary Change,* p. 371.

27. It was not desirable for Eritrean women to become maids in Italian homes.

28. Traditionally, some occupations were viewed as not "proper." For example, there was a deep-seated prejudice against musicians, singers, leather-workers, jewelry-makers, and blacksmiths. These groups were shunned and intermarried among themselves. Stefanos, *An Encounter with Revolutionary Change,* p. 198.

29. As has been discussed, the barriers for girls to access education had been sturdy and longstanding. Prior to the liberation struggle, nonliteracy among Eritrean women was over 90 percent. Seyoum A. Haregot, *The First Year: Fourth Quarter Report, May-July, 1996* (United Nations Office for Project Services, Second-Phase — Support for Public Sector Management Programme, Project ERI/94/006), p. 33.

30. "Relationship between Society and School," *Eritrea Information,* 5, No. 3 (1983), 7.

31. "The Revolution School Achievement and Problems," *Eritrea Information,* p. 11.

32. Stefanos, *An Encounter with Revolutionary Change,* p. 298.

33. For example, there were themes of "mother's brigade," "mother's day," or "working mothers" and the portrayal of women in official iconography "with a gun in one

hand and a baby in the other" that were promoted as manifestations of interest in women's issues. However, there was no similar representation of men hailed as images of "fathers' work brigade" or "fathers with a child in one hand and a gun in the other." For a detailed discussion on this, see Stefanos, *An Encounter with Revolutionary Change*, p. 427.

34. "The Revolution School Achievement and Problems," *Eritrea Information*, p. 10.

35. Even though "basic education" (seven years of schooling) has been promoted as a requirement regardless of gender, the government has ceded that it has not created the educational capacity to make compulsory schooling a viable alternative. See Ministry of Labor and Human Welfare Report, *Initial Report on the Implementation of the Convention on the Rights of the Child*, pp. 64–73; Wamahiu, *Girls' Education in Eritrea*, p. 6; Department of Research, *Eritrea: Basic Education Statistics and Essential Indicators 1995/96* (Asmara, Eritrea: Ministry of Education, 1996).

36. See *Draft Constitution of Eritrea* (Asmara, Eritrea: Constitutional Commission of Eritrea, July 1996), p. 19.

37. Traditionally, property and livestock ownership had been an unassailable male prerogative. As the EPLF applied the principle of "land to the tiller" in liberated areas, it distributed land directly to refugees and landless peasants, a vast majority of whom were women. In post-independent Eritrea, the Land Reform Proclamation has provided equal access to female land ownership. See "National Democratic Program" in Stefanos, *An Encounter with Revolutionary Change*, pp. 446–447; *Draft Constitution of Eritrea*, p. 20.

38. The majority of women who are self-employed are found in the service and retail sectors, 38 percent and 39 percent, respectively, while only 18 percent are in manufacturing and less than 1 percent are in commercial farming. Haregot, *The First Year: Fourth Quarter Report*, p. 37.

39. The push for this shift came concurrently from below. Increasingly, in the cities and towns, females — particularly high school and college students — were becoming visible in organized nationalist clandestine activities. For a detailed discussion on women's political participation, see Stefanos, *An Encounter with Revolutionary Change*, pp. 279–285.

40. The Front's campaign for breaking with male political domination was clearly connected to its own needs for active supporters to wage the battle for national liberation under its leadership. The EPLF saw women, along with marginalized ethnic groups, landless peasants, and youth, as naturally more sympathetic to its egalitarian agenda and drive against traditional beliefs that upheld the status quo, than the men who had a grip on local and family privilege and power. For more information about the EPLF's view of gender equality, see Stefanos, *An Encounter with Revolutionary Change*, pp. 274–279.

41. The Minister of Education, His Excellency Osman Saleh, in his Opening Address to the Workshop on Girls' Education, in September 1996, Wamahiu, *Girls' Education in Eritrea*, p. 6.

42. In the executive branch, there are two women out of fourteen ministers — one is a Minister of Tourism and the other is a Minister of Justice; there are four women directors — of Postal and Communication, Central Personnel Administration, Social Affairs, and National Union of Eritrean Women. There are no women as provincial governors. While women constitute 31.3 percent of all government employees, they outnumber men in clerical and custodial services. Haregot, *The First Year: Fourth Quarter Report*, p. 37.

43. Women represented 20 percent of active combatants in 1983 and 30 percent in 1993. The inclusion of well-trained women into the army helped lessen the impact of the vastly larger number of troops under Ethiopian command. International journalists

regularly highlighted the numbers and performance of female EPLF fighters as a unique feature in Eritrea's independence struggle. They observed that the Front's iconic imagery of a woman with a gun in hand was not solely a symbol of new female assertiveness and freedoms, but rather a familiar happenstance in areas under Front control. Stefanos, *An Encounter with Revolutionary Change,* pp. 274–279.

44. In interviews, women combatants said that they fought to the death, partly because of what they knew about the atrocities that Ethiopian soldiers inflicted on female POWs. They felt that the sexism of the enemy soldiers made them more determined as fighters.

45. All rural and urban residents were organized into one of "five mass organizations according to social class or groups — women, youth, peasants, workers, and professionals." Stefanos, *An Encounter with Revolutionary Change,* p. 271.

46. Among settled agriculturalists, *wushati* is a small room within the hut that is reserved for women only. Male members older than five are by tradition prohibited from entering this room.

47. See Stefanos, *An Encounter with Revolutionary Change,* pp. 292–293.

48. In 1983, I interviewed twenty-four women in eleven towns and villages in the northeastern and northwestern regions of Eritrea. I returned to Eritrea in January 1997 to do follow-up interviews, and was able to locate eighteen women from my original study and to broaden my sample to eight additional women, some of whom held key positions in the new post-independence government.

49. The interview sample represented an age range of sixteen to sixty-five; single, married, divorced and widowed; Tigre, Kebessa, Denkel, Sahho, Kunama, and Belen nationalities; Coptics, Muslims, Catholics, Protestants, and various African religious orientations; nonliterate to college-level education; political activists and nonactivists; peasants, factory workers, medical doctors, and students.

50. During the national liberation struggle, Genet worked as a coordinator of refugee women in the village of Arrarib. She received her elementary education at a Catholic missionary school and had an arranged marriage at the age of fifteen. She subsequently resumed her schooling and got a certificate in business administration.

51. After military demobilization, Mamet invested the $4,000 [in U.S. dollars] compensation from the government in a cotton plantation project. Since the project was not well conceived, she along with many others lost her lifelong investment. She is presently unemployed. Her marriage failed, and she and her two small children are presently living with ex-combatant friends.

52. Zewdi works as a store clerk, after completing her high school level education.

53. As some respondents indicated, occasionally there were mothers and often brothers who were ardent supporters of their schooling.

54. Leila is of Sahho nationality. She and her husband own a gift store in Massawa.

55. Rishan, an ex-combatant, is presently working as a parking lot attendant in the capital city. Her parents are farmers and Coptic Christians from Kebessa. She was in fifth grade when she joined the liberation front.

56. Many respondents described vividly the low status of females within their families when they were children. Asma states, "In the family, a women is not considered an equal human being to a man. She is there to serve him. A father chooses her husband. . . . She is prohibited from leaving the house." Keddes adds, "In our home, our oldest brother assumed the second command to our father. . . . My mother deferred to him. Even my younger brothers had better rights than me. . . . Men do not want women to be independent. Even when they are oppressed themselves, men feel that women are their domain." Sarah, who is from a middle-class urban family, says, "My mother kept careful watch over me. When parents find a girl playing with her broth-

ers, she will be told to go inside the house and sit there or do something useful. If a girl protests, the explanation given by all mothers to their daughters is, 'boys can play and be rambunctious, but a girl must be quiet and stay in the house, and keep busy. Besides, a girl should not expect to be treated equally with boys.'"

57. In post-independence Eritrea, this same group of women currently occupy the mid-level administrative and moderately prestigious white-collar jobs. See Stefanos, "Appendix E: Biographical Charts," in *An Encounter with Revolutionary Change*, pp. 466–467.

58. Women representation in the military has been reduced from 30 percent to 10 percent. "Of those who were demobilized, only 14 percent had skills that can be translated into employment or income-generating activities." Haregot, *The First Year: Fourth Quarter Report,* p. 39.

59. Facial skin discoloration caused by stress.

60. The military hierarchy starts with being in charge of a *gujelle,* a unit of ten people; then *ganta* (composed of three *gujelles*); *hailee* (three *gantas*); *bottolini* (three *hailees*); *brigade* (three *bottolonis*), and finally *Kefle-Serawit* (three *brigades*). Sarah states "that up to the *hailee* level, the work is physically demanding — one has to be physically fit for guerrilla warfare, carrying heavy weapons and supplies, walking and climbing difficult terrain. In addition, one has to endure multiple injuries. But, once you become a *bottolini* leader, what is demanded is leadership ability based on your experience and training for strategic plans and supervising ancillary divisions such as medical, economic, and other units."

61. Interview with the director of *BANA* — Eritrean Women War Veteran Association.

62. Haregot, *The First Year: Fourth Quarter Report,* pp. 4–50.

63. In 1997, Mamet provided two relevant examples of government disinterest — the decline in mass consciousness-raising programs to deal with parental attitudes toward female education and the dearth of interventions to lighten domestic labor, which gets relegated to females and promotes removing girls from schools.

64. This same remark was offered by the three women officials who held top positions within the postrevolutionary government.

65. Asgedet Stefanos, *An Encounter with Revolutionary Change,* William Monroe Trotter Institute Research Report No. 33 (Boston: University of Massachusetts, 1996), pp. 72–74.

66. Like most Third World revolutions, Eritrea's approach to women's issues was influenced by an instrumental reading of two well-known texts: Frederick Engels, *The Origin of the Family, Private Property and the State,* ed. Eleanor Burke Leacock (New York: International Publishers, 1972), and V. I. Lenin, *The Emancipation of Women* (New York: International Publishers, 1966). In this approach, moving women into the public sector was viewed as key to solving women's problems. The privileging of the role of production over women's familial relations has been functional to the struggle for national liberation during armed conflict and the drive for economic development after liberation. The appeal for women to fulfill the general needs of the society legitimizes the reproduction of sexual divisions of labor both in the work force and in the home.

67. According to Senayit, recent official theoretical acceptance of a mixed economy "with heavy emphasis on privatization is not advantageous to women, who will have difficulty gaining a foothold in the free-for-all of individual entrepreneurship — where men's longstanding dominance in business will have unchecked reign."

68. Although the Eritrean government does not have any debt to service, its ability to raise funds has been severely hindered by its devastated economy and the overall poverty of its people. Eritrea is one of the poorest countries in the world, with a GDP

per capita below U.S. $120–$150, less than half the U.S. $300 average for sub-Saharan African countries. Ministry of Labor and Human Welfare Report, *Initial Report on the Implementation of the Convention on the Rights of the Child,* p. 5.

The Palestinian Uprising and Education for the Future

KHALIL MAHSHI
KIM BUSH

A popular uprising against colonial rule presents both a threat and a challenge to educators. They must abandon their traditional curricula and approaches to learning and respond to a community insistent upon meaningful change and relevance in the education of its children. The *intifadeh* — the Palestinian uprising against twenty years of Israeli military occupation — now in its second year, poses this challenge to educators who live in the West Bank and Gaza. They are currently working against tremendous odds to offer alternative forms of schooling (henceforth referred to as alternative, neighborhood, or popular schooling) while all schools are closed by military order. At the same time, they are attempting to prepare for a future when a Palestinian system of education can be developed. Whether we enthusiastically create alternative schools or change the system as a whole, the ties between school and community are strengthened. The intifadeh has erased traditional lines which divide educators and citizens, creating a laboratory for dramatic changes in all areas of education.

We would like to concentrate on an analysis of education. However, in order to clarify the issues involving the relationship between alternative schooling and the intifadeh, we offer a bare framework of major developments in the field before 1988. Palestinians directly involved at various levels of education are a major source of information for the analysis of the current situation. They are sometimes identified, but often the names and exact locations of popular schools must remain anonymous. Because of the nature of education in Palestine, there are no reliable statistics on popular schools and the extent of popular involvement. We must rely on conjecture in many cases, hoping that a more accurate history of the movement will be written when fear of reprisals is gone. We freely admit that more extensive research in the area is needed. This paper represents an initial analysis.

THE EDUCATIONAL SYSTEM: A HISTORICAL OVERVIEW

For nearly five hundred years, outside powers have imposed their systems of education on the Palestinian people. Under the Ottoman Turks (1517–1917), education was limited to either practical training or religious instruction. In reaction to these limitations on public Turkish education, private Muslim and Christian

Harvard Educational Review   Vol. 59 No. 4 November 1989, 470–483

schools evolved in various parts of Palestine. Schools grew up in mosques as a nationalist response to Turkish control, in one of the earliest instances of Palestinian popular education. "[A] new Arab nationalist consciousness was beginning to take root in reaction to Turkish political and cultural domination. This led to a revival of interest in Arabic language and literature and the establishment of Arab Newspapers and communal schools" (Graham-Brown, 1984, p. 16).

Under the British mandate (1917–1948), both Zionism and British imperial control threatened Palestinian culture. The British increased the number of schools for Palestinian Arabs in order to increase the number of educated Arabs in the civil service. It is generally acknowledged, however, that the schools that the British government funded for Arabs failed to meet the demand of even half of the non-Jewish population (Palestine Royal Commission, 1937, p. 337). Not only was education for Arabs underfunded, but it did not meet their specific cultural and political needs (Badran, 1969, p. 142; Tibawi, 1956, p. 205). The attitudes of most Palestinians toward schooling during this period are summed up by Dr. Khalil Totah: "The major grievance of the Arabs is . . . that they have no control over it [their education]. It would seem that Arab education is either designed to reconcile the Arabs to this policy [of establishing a Jewish homeland], or to make that education so colorless as to make it harmless and to endanger the carrying out of that policy" (Graham-Brown, 1984, p. 20). As in the era of Turkish rule, the failure of the British to provide an adequate educational system for Palestinians encouraged the growth of a nonsectarian nationalist movement. Despite the inadequate provision of government education by the British, the traditional value of education, especially formal schooling, has strengthened over time. Formal education was perceived as a means for securing a white-collar job with steady income, and to enhance social status, in a predominantly peasant society.

After 1948, the West Bank fell under the authority of Jordan, and the educational system underwent yet another change, still heavily flavored by the British. Gaza, on the other hand, was controlled by the Egyptians. Both Jordanian and Egyptian systems of education follow the British model of external examinations and an exam-based curriculum. The vast number of Palestinian refugees dispersed throughout the Arab world after 1948 have been served by the United Nations Relief and Works Agency (UNRWA), created by the U.N. in 1949. UNRWA schools were established in the West Bank, Gaza, Jordan, Syria, and Lebanon in every refugee camp, providing education from first through ninth grades. From the outset, educational advisors from the United Nations Educational, Scientific and Cultural Organization (UNESCO) helped the UNRWA system develop curriculum and train teachers. UNRWA schools generally follow the curriculum and educational system of the Arab country in which they operate.

This amalgam of local, Turkish, British, and Egyptian-Jordanian systems of education was further complicated after the Six Day War in June 1967, when Israel occupied Gaza and the West Bank. In effect, the pre-1967 curricula and educational system remained in place, but they were administered by the Israeli military authority. In 1982, as a first step toward creating an image of legitimacy for the continued occupation of the West Bank and Gaza and imposing limited self-administration on the Palestinian population, Israeli military authorities divided the Israeli military government into two parts. The Civil Administration was in charge of services and civil matters for the Palestinians. The Israeli army was to deal with security and military matters. Army officials who headed the different service departments in the military government remained in their posts after establishment of the Civil Administration. The Israeli plan to replace them with Palestinians from the West Bank and Gaza was never implemented, due to the resistance of the Palestinian population to the scheme of self-administration as an alternative to full national independence.

Education, as a service to the Palestinian population in the West Bank and Gaza, falls under the Civil Administration. Therefore it is completely controlled and supervised by Israeli authorities — a fact of great importance when we consider the Israeli reaction to the intifadeh. Thus, since 1948, three separate school systems have evolved: UNRWA, private, and government, each of which adheres to essentially alien curricula, in which Palestinian culture and history have been ignored or actively suppressed by the Israelis. Just as the Palestinians created popular institutions to preserve and transmit their culture during Turkish rule and British rule, they have also resisted integration under the Israelis. They have established educational and cultural institutions, and grassroots organizations to preserve and develop their national identity, nurture self-reliance, and resist dependence on the Israeli authorities. In a very real sense, one of the faces of the intifadeh is a determination to develop a national consciousness and to resist amalgamation into Israel or any Arab non-Palestinian country.

THE INTIFADEH: CAUSES AND GROWTH OF A MOVEMENT

On December 8, 1987, a car carrying four Gazans was rammed by an Israeli vehicle and all were killed. Few would have predicted that this event would spark a national uprising, now entering its second year and showing no sign of abating. Analysts have suggested many causes for the intifadeh, including obstruction of economic development, unjust taxation, economic hardship, denial of self-determination and human rights, repression, confiscation of land, and increasing Israeli settlement on Palestinian land. All of these reasons can be summed up as a refusal to live under foreign occupation any longer (Tamari, 1988). One might add to these, the extreme frustration of a very youthful population with few opportunities for meaningful work. The Palestinian population is overeducated for the undeveloped economic situation in the West Bank and Gaza. High school and university graduates end up in jobs that do not match their qualifications. They place blame on the occupiers, and on a system of education that is archaic and in many ways irrelevant to their needs and aspirations.

The intifadeh, which literally means "shaking off" in Arabic, has taken as many forms as the Israeli occupation itself. Although street action and resulting death and injury have attracted the most publicity, other forms of nonviolent action are just as important. For example, most Palestinians in the West Bank and Gaza have refused to pay taxes on property and businesses. All shops now close their doors at noon, honoring a "national" commercial strike. A campaign to boycott Israeli products has had significant impact on the occupier's economy. In a few villages, people discarded their identity cards as a symbolic rejection of military authority. These actions and many others symbolize the spirit of resistance of the Palestinians.

In conjunction with direct daily confrontation with the military, a movement based on extensive popular organization has been created. The Unified National

Leadership of the Uprising (UNLU) issues a bimonthly leaflet or directive commenting on important issues, outlining major tactical steps, and indicating dates for all-day strikes. With the exception of these directives (there have been thirty-six since the beginning of the intifadeh to date), the movement is decentralized and counts heavily on local initiative for new thinking and new forms of nonviolent direct action. This movement — essentially "headless" — poses the gravest threat to the Israelis because it is uncontrollable.

ISRAELI RESPONSE TO THE INTIFADEH

The Israelis have responded to the more visible forms of the intifadeh with direct military action, through their Border Police, active and reserve army, and the Shin Bet (local equivalent of the FBI). The record of their brutal repression is well known (see Al Haq, 1988b) but these methods have failed to stop the intifadeh. In addition to the use of tear gas, a wide range of weaponry, and frequent beatings, the Israelis have resorted to various forms of collective punishment, including house demolitions and sealings; preventive (called "administrative") detention; restriction of travel, communication and movement; and censorship.

Desperate to deprive the movement of its youthful energy and leadership, the Israelis have used their control over education as a way of pressuring the Palestinian population. Since February of 1988, most of the schools in the Occupied Territories have been closed, sometimes for a month, often for much longer. The official justification for school closures has been that schools have been the centers for organizing demonstrations and other direct actions. Palestinians and many Israelis, however, believe that the authorities are well aware of Palestinian reliance on education as a solution to their many problems, and that they have exploited this vulnerability by closing schools frequently and without warning as a collective punishment (see Cohen, 1989). This has resulted in West Bank schools being closed for more than thirteen of the past sixteen months since the beginning of the intifadeh. (Gaza schools have suffered from prolonged and repeated curfews, though they have not been officially closed as in the West Bank.) The matriculation exam that ninth graders take to qualify for entrance into high school was canceled in 1988–1989. Last year, the Jordanian Ministry of Education accepted a proposal by education officials in the West Bank to water down the Jordanian Tawjihi exam required for entrance into all Arab universities (as well as universities in the West Bank and Gaza). The students were made to sit for one session of the exam (the mid-year session) instead of two, thus covering only half of the curriculum required for the Tawjihi (or for grade twelve). The exam might not be administered at all in the West Bank in 1989. After continual harassment and arbitrary closures in previous years, all West Bank and Gaza universities have been permanently closed since 1987 (Al Haq, 1988a; Jerusalem Media and Communication Center, 1989).

The long-term results of controlling education to punish a population are too hard to measure. What happens to first and second graders who are acquiring literacy skills, then denied books and instruction? What are the sociopsychological consequences of being cut off from friends, and the socialization process that schools at all levels offer? How easily will math skills learned in the elementary grades be recovered after a year's absence? Will high school students who have used the streets as classrooms be able to return to the old style of authoritarian education? Some preliminary psychological studies have been conducted on the impact of the intifadeh. Experts, some of whom were interviewed for this article, describe a loss of literacy and numeracy skills, but a growth in self-reliance and self-esteem. One educator from a West Bank university spoke about the "reawakening" of the Palestinians. She recalled widespread depression and submissiveness on the part of both the educated and uneducated Palestinians in the mid-1980s, and her fear that they had given up. The events of December 1987 sparked a new determination to resist the occupation and to develop new Palestinian institutions. Her opinion is shared by many observers and participants in education, who view the intifadeh as the opportunity of a lifetime.

INTIFADEH EDUCATION: THE CHALLENGE

Critical analysis of the educational system in the West Bank and Gaza, and its relevance to Palestinian society, started at the beginning of this decade. Even before the intifadeh, a few efforts were made to introduce relevance in the educational system. These educators were arguing against the diploma-orientation of the system. Although they have remained a minority among educators in the West Bank and Gaza, the intifadeh has widened this circle and accelerated this process, as educators and laypersons are on notice that the time has come for significant changes in the entire educational system. Prolonged school closures have prodded everyone into action. This action has taken three very distinct forms. Schools have sought alternative forms of instruction as a temporary substitute for classroom-based education, which is now illegal. The pressure to provide ongoing education to the population has encouraged educators to consider different types of distance-teaching, including learning by correspondence, and the use of television and radio. Popular committees in nearly every community in the West Bank have started neighborhood schools as temporary replacements for government, UNRWA, and private institutions closed by the military. Neighborhood schools have opened the eyes of parents, educators, and especially students, to new forms of education. The intifadeh has increased the need for a national curriculum that reflects the new confidence Palestinians have developed in their culture and their own institutions. Clearly, the greatest challenge of the occupation and the intifadeh is to discard years of occupation education and start afresh. Long-term educational planning by a handful of Palestinians is producing some impressive alternatives, among them "Education for Awareness and Involvement," which we describe later in this article.

ALTERNATIVE MODES OF INSTRUCTION

At first glance, alternative modes of instruction adopted by schools in the Occupied Territories may appear to have no real impact on the system itself. After all, they are only substitutes for classroom instruction, In fact, the process of developing alternative modes of instruction has raised important issues about how students learn and how those traditional patterns might change.

The UNRWA schools adopted a Crash Plan in the spring of 1988 when it became apparent that schools were going to be closed for a long period. They attempted to streamline the curriculum by prioritizing learning objectives and cutting unnecessary materials from individual courses. Teachers prepared worksheets based on textbooks, but student participation was essentially voluntary, and the results were not very encouraging. UNRWA administrators and teachers are aware of the value of autonomous learning and cooperative effort (finding parallels with the Islamic Kuttab, in which students studied the Koran in ungraded classes and helped each other). But without at least some interaction between teacher and pupil, especially at the middle school levels, or the active intervention of parents-as-teachers, the UNRWA Crash Plans seem doomed to failure. More recently, UNRWA has proposed the development of television and radio instruction, using both Jordanian and Egyptian channels at certain hours during the day. They see this as an answer to short-term needs and a step toward long-term planning in adult education. Unfortunately, Palestinians have no control over radio and television stations in neighboring countries, and therefore little has been done with programmed instruction.

Most government schools have done little to provide self-study packets or to circumvent official closures. The Civil Administration, employer of all government schoolteachers, has tremendous leverage over them. In April 1988, all government schoolteachers in the Ramallah area were called to a meeting by the Civil Administration and reminded that any attempts to provide education to students would be considered illegal and grounds for immediate dismissal. Few teachers heeded the warning completely, but they acted very discreetly.

Private schools, with their greater freedom, have been able to experiment more with home-learning packets and have been slightly more successful. Some of these schools, like the Friends Schools in Ramallah (two Quaker schools, one hundred years old, renowned in Palestinian history and in neighboring Arab countries, and foremost among schools in the West Bank), have started by training teachers to write self-study materials. After a short training period led by an educator from one of the West Bank universities, teachers produced packets for all of their classes. These packets were based on existing student textbooks and have the following five components for each unit or chapter:

1. the learning objective of the unit measured in behavioral terms
2. the activities students must engage in to meet the standards, such as studying the contents of a chapter
3. additional assignments for further study and practice
4. self-evaluation tests, with answers provided
5. exercises to be turned in to the teacher for feedback and grading

In order to motivate students to work in a consistent and organized manner, packets specify the material to be covered during a period of time, at the end of which the students turn in the exercises for feedback.

Israeli military authorities have decided that the self-study packets provided by some of the private schools violate the school closure order. In fact, the army entered the Friends Boys School in Ramallah and stopped their distribution. The headmasters of this and other schools were summoned individually to the military headquarters and ordered to stop providing the packets to their students.

The use of self-study packets as an alternative mode of instruction during the intifadeh raised a number of important questions:

1. How could the packets be distributed to large number of students without attracting the attention of military authorities?
2. If, in order to avoid student gatherings, students are not required to turn in homework frequently, how can one ensure motivation, regular and steady work, and self-organization?
3. If homework is graded in order to motivate students, how does one ensure that they have done the work themselves without outside help?
4. What does one do with the grades? Are they used for credit and promotion to the next grade level? Will the educational authorities who are responsible for certifying accept these grades for official purposes, when the authorities are supervised by the Israeli Civil Administration?
5. When students are barred from school campuses by the army, how can they interact with teachers to get assistance when they encounter difficulties, especially when the use of radio, television, and newspapers is not possible?
6. How does one prepare self-study packets for students in lower elementary grades who have not yet perfected their reading and writing skills?

Experimentation with self-study packets continues. It appears that in the West Bank educational system, which is exam- and grade-oriented, students will not be motivated for self-study unless exams are given on a regular basis. Schools are trying to hold exams in areas where the closure order is not in effect, or at times and places where the authorities will not be able to stop them. Experience will enable educators to develop effective self-study programs.

West Bank and Gaza universities have been subject to greater harassment and more direct military confrontations than high schools. As a result, they have been reluctant to become actively involved in alternative modes of instruction. Nevertheless, some classes have continued to meet, especially for seniors (for many of whom graduation has been postponed up to three years). In order to cover the material, most of the professors have pared down their subject matter drastically and changed the mode of instruction from teacher-centered lectures to smaller discussion groups. Thus the universities, like the elementary, preparatory, and secondary schools, have begun the process of looking for effective forms of home or non-school-centered learning.

NEW FORMS OF EDUCATION: POPULAR EDUCATION IN NEIGHBORHOOD SCHOOLS

By March 1988, people began to realize that the intifadeh was going to last a long time. The Unified National Leadership of the Uprising issued a directive that called for a boycott of the Israeli Civil Administration and for the establishment of an independent alternative structure for the provision of services to the Palestinian population. People responded by reviving the Popular Committees first created and used in 1982, when boycotting the newly established Israeli Civil Administration. The newly established committees undertook a wider range of responsibilities and services in their neighborhoods. These included cultivating neighborhood gardens to ensure the supply of vegetables in case the Israeli army stopped supplies from entering; providing public cleaning and basic health services; centrally purchasing, storing, and distributing food supplies; setting up a guard system against the Israeli settlers, the army, and thieves; and collecting donations to provide assistance to those unemployed because of the intifadeh.

Popular Committees assumed responsibility for education when it became clear that the Israeli authorities intended to use school closure as a form of collective punishment. While some schools were attempting to offer alternative modes of instruction, Popular Committees began to organize neighborhood schools. Classes were held in houses, mosques, churches, and clubs. Sometimes classes were held in gardens not easily seen from the street. They were taught by anyone in the neighborhood who was educated and able to volunteer their time. In some cases, university or high school students taught younger pupils. Most often, parents, without any formal experience in education and teaching, taught classes. This movement of neighborhood schools came to be known as Popular Education. At least in the beginning, people, including those on the Popular Committees, saw these schools as temporary, necessary only until the intifadeh was "over" and life "returned to normal." As a result, popular education erupted spontaneously everywhere, and there was little, if any, central direction. Only during April and May of 1988 did neighborhood schools openly flourish.

In May 1988, the Israeli authorities outlawed Popular Committees and all their activities, including educational and cultural ones. According to this law, any person convicted of membership in the Popular Committees would face a sentence of up to ten years of imprisonment. The army started actively raiding neighborhood schools, partially sabotaging popular education. In addition to military raids, Israeli authorities reopened schools for short periods of time and then closed them again. Organizers of alternative schools were demoralized; led to expect that the educational scene would return to normal, all their efforts at creating an alternative system seemed unnecessary. The Popular Education Movement is now more clandestine, decentralized, and smaller. Since May 1988, popular education has continued underground, well directed and organized in a few areas and virtually nonexistent in others. Now neighborhood schools continue to meet in some communities, and women's committees in refugee camps have organized small classes taught by international volunteers. Even these classes, which service no more than three hundred students, are subject to constant harassment, interruption, and closure.

Because popular education lacked a central organizing body for the whole West Bank, neighborhood schools differed significantly from one another and from one geographical area to another. In some towns, a single committee would direct and supervise the neighborhood school movement as a whole. In such cases neighborhood schools would be almost identical in curriculum and in the number of lessons given per week. Teachers attended meetings for coordination and evaluation. Where there were no such supervising committees, neighborhood schools differed significantly from one another in numbers of periods per day and the number of days they operated each week. They also differed in the subjects they taught and in the curriculum they used.

The curriculum of neighborhood schools was very informal, but followed the official textbooks, the Jordanian Israeli-censored textbooks that students already had and all schools in the West Bank are required to use. These texts provided a foundation for teachers who needed them (or were accustomed to them), but were abandoned by others who wanted to strike out in new directions. Students were separated into grade levels or, in some cases, combined for practical purposes. Because classes were generally smaller, averaging ten students, students had the chance to experience new teaching methods in a radically different educational atmosphere. Neighborhood schools opened everyone's eyes to alternatives, although the curriculum remained essentially unchanged. Many teachers were forced to improvise and become more creative. For example, science teachers were forced to improvise and create "kitchen laboratories" using materials at hand of examples from the intifadeh (for example, a physics teacher discussed electrical conductivity by asking students why it was dangerous to remove Palestinian flags from power lines). In some neighborhood schools new classes were added, such as Palestinian drama and music, and more time was spent talking about national and political issues. Unfortunately, because of the unpredictability of the situation, most participants saw neighborhood schools as decidedly temporary, and did not put the effort into developing a truly alternative and relevant curriculum. Many students as well had a feeling that neighborhood schools were temporary and — in the formative period (April–May 1988) — did not take them seriously. They assumed that work in neighborhood schools would not be graded or accepted for credit and for promotion in their regular schools.

A number of problems and challenges face the popular education movement. Among these are the following:

1. How to sustain interest and a high level of participation when many people are fearful of official reprisals and frustrated by intermittent opening and closing of schools.
2. How to discipline students who are used to an authoritarian method of classroom management.
3. How to sustain seriousness and motivation among students who are accustomed to working only for exams and grades.
4. How to compete with the distractions in the community, like television programs, films, playing in the streets, and working for money.
5. How to develop similar standards among neighborhood schools if they are indeed the answer to the closure of schools for months or years.
6. How to assure that grades and exam results will be accepted for legal or accreditation purposes.

During the formative period of the popular education movement, many teachers and other educators considered these questions seriously. They were especially concerned about the lack of training and experience of teachers in neighborhood schools and the absence of uniform standards in those schools. With the help of a number of prominent educators from West Bank universities and other educational institutions, the General Federation of Employees in the Education Sectors in the Occupied Territories, which consists of representatives of all of the teachers' unions, organized a conference in May 1988 to address educational alternatives. The conference had very ambitious goals, the most important of which was to shape the enthusiasm of popular educators into an alternative school system of high quality. The organizers hoped that as a result of the papers presented and the ensuing discussion a set of guidelines for alternative schooling would be agreed upon and later published in a handbook for neighborhood schools. However, the detainment of members of the executive committee, the clampdown of the Israeli authorities on neighborhood schools, and the reopening of all schools in the West Bank hampered the efforts and efficiency of the Federation. This conference was the first, and possibly the only, step taken toward organizing the popular education movement. Now, almost a year later, those who attended the conference see it as a historic moment: for the first time, members from all levels of the educational community met together to determine the future course of education in the West Bank and Gaza. If one looks carefully, one will see that some of the lofty goals of that conference are being realized, slowly and subversively, in some schools and among some innovative educational thinkers.

NEW FORMS: EDUCATION FOR THE FUTURE

The concerns raised by many Palestinian educators at the conference (and by thousands who participated in the popular education movement) have been addressed by a few isolated but exemplary programs. Most of these started before the outbreak of the intifadeh, but the intifadeh has reinforced their vision and educational philosophy. All of these programs have a common desire to create genuine alternatives to the existing educational system. All of them seek to develop a new system relevant to Palestinian society and centering on the development of well-rounded human beings. These programs cover a wide spectrum of educational levels, from preschool through high school.

At the preschool level, educational psychologists and teachers are introducing activity-oriented programs and discarding passive content orientation. The intifadeh has catalyzed these basic changes, both because teachers have had to look for alternative forms to circumvent closures and intervention, and because the uprising encourages innovation. At Bethlehem University, Jacqueline Sfeir and the teacher trainees are developing programs that emphasize a "gadget-free" learning environment that will work equally well in small villages and in middle-class suburban communities. Villages have received these pilot programs in play-centered learning enthusiastically, but the middle-class communities, which are conditioned to view learning in terms of measurable results, have been more reluctant to embrace them. Dr. Sfeir noted how village women watched their children learning while playing and said, "This makes sense; maybe we can learn this way." Later they applied that lesson to their literacy classes. The preschoolers in the Bethlehem University program are the children of the intifadeh. The cornerstone of their education in preschool is problem solving and investigation. The rest of the educational system should follow this philosophy.

The Early Childhood Resource Center (ECRC) in East Jerusalem is building on the aforementioned ideas, but in a different setting. Recognizing the intifadeh as a rare opportunity to introduce meaningful change into the ways children are taught, the ECRC is developing a series of self-help booklets. One booklet helps parents to recognize and respond effectively to psychological problems that have grown out of the climate of violence of the intifadeh. As part of a community mental health program, it combines self-reliance with professional and paraprofessional help. Another, pitched to elementary school students, teachers, and parents in any educational milieu, encourages problem solving, cooperative learning, and reducing reliance on the teachers. This booklet resulted from the experience of many popular schoolteachers, incorporating their ideas for use of local resources and reduced reliance on formal schools.

These programs advocate comprehensive curriculum change, as well as a major transformation in teaching methodology on all levels. More important, they stress the need for the integration of school and community, and insist on education that is relevant to the current needs of the community. Only one pioneering project has responded to this challenge — "Education for Awareness and Involvement" (EAI) — the pilot project of a few private schools in the West Bank. It merits careful study because it contains the beginnings of a new Palestinian curriculum. The originators of EAI took a critical look at education in the West Bank and concluded that "it has become infected with the 'diploma disease': higher degree awarding has become the most important function of school education while the needs of about 90% of the students who never make it to university are not met" (EAI Brochure, 1988). In order to make education more relevant, they focus on five key areas:

1. transforming teaching methods from lecturing to learning by doing
2. making education more relevant to the world of work and production by including vocational training alongside academics
3. introducing career counseling and internship programs to students in upper secondary grades
4. including classes and activities more pertinent to the situation and developmental needs of the occupied palestinian territories as well as increasing awareness of their unique environment and culture
5. strengthening the ties between school and community through increased involvement in community service, the establishment of parents' committees, and parent involvement in the implementation of components of EAI

A pilot program was initiated in 1985 in the five Evangelical Lutheran Schools, and a year later in the Friends Boys School. These six schools have a total student body of about three thousand boys and girls from a wide range of socioeconomic backgrounds, from working to upper middle class. Now, nearly five years after the originators of EAI put the ideas together, the program has moved considerably toward implementing the five major goals identified above.

Teachers' committees were formed for each academic subject. These committees coordinated workshops on student-centered learning. They are presently developing activities to complement and enrich the official school curricula and textbooks. This whole approach is intended to help teachers develop self-confidence and become actively involved in a lifelong process of curriculum enrichment and development and to keep textbooks and curricula continuously relevant.

Vocational education workshops have been established in each of the participating schools. All seventh- through ninth-grade students are enrolled in two workshop periods each week. They also visit production and work sites to familiarize them with different careers in their community. Some of the schools participating in EAI have started student production in their workshops. The products, such as pottery and ceramics, are marketed through school fairs or in local shops. Some of the skills the students learn in vocational education classes, such as gardening and food preservation, have gained more importance during the intifadeh, making it easier for the schools to convince the parents of the value of the nontraditional, nonacademic components of EAI. As a result, individual schools are currently thinking of placing greater stress on vocational education and reviewing course offerings. Preliminary assessment of the vocational education component of EAI has exposed a lack of centralized curriculum and too great a reliance on traditional manual-training methods. A number of teachers who were interested or involved in academic counseling have been trained in the area of career counseling during the past three years. They are presently involved in setting up a career counseling office in each of their schools.

Materials that have been developed to increase student awareness of Palestinian society are currently used in some classes. According to Yacoub Qumsiya, chairperson of the follow-up committee of EAI, the intifadeh has done more than any formal course of study could ever have accomplished. In the words of a recent progress report, the last fifteen months have increased the "awareness of the students about their society and their readiness to participate in its development" (Azzouni-Mahshi, 1988). In addition, a two-year workshop for science teachers in Environmental Awareness and Protection has begun to study the natural environment of Palestine and to document the names of wild plants and animals. Again, the intifadeh has stimulated new interest in Palestinian culture and history, which should be developed in future classes.

Has any progress been made in improving ties between schools and communities? The intifadeh has interfered with progress in this area, although it has increased awareness of the importance of cooperation between the school and the community by making school education a preparation for life in the West Bank Palestinian community and, hopefully, in the future Palestinian state. EAI schools have not openly addressed the issues raised by popular education, but they have reinforced the belief that the community can and should be a very powerful force in shaping its own educational future.

Palestinian educators have rarely allowed themselves the luxury of dreaming about their own system of education, but EAI seems to be a step in that direction. It insists on basic changes in the teaching-learning process and in the curriculum. It has a program for realizing this goal. Four or five new schools will probably join the original ones, and others (all private) have shown an interest in the program. The originators still face some daunting challenges, such as giving students (especially veterans of the intifadeh) a real voice in determining their educational future, providing good political and economic education for future leaders, evaluating the overall effectiveness of EAI at the end of five years, and finding ways to make it work in all schools in the Occupied Territories, not just a selected few. The real test of the value of this innovative program is whether it is flexible enough to provide an educational model for the future.

Some would argue that innovative educational programs like that of the EAI and others mentioned above won't work without a fundamental change of attitude on the part of the Palestinian population as a whole. Munir Fasheh, a professor of education at Birzeit University, is researching new ways of learning. His approach complements that of EAI by promoting learning in situations where it is least expected. Fasheh contends that if people come to value learning outside traditional institutions, learning will become a community-wide and "infectious" process. Once again, the intifadeh has made the unexpected possible by throwing refugee camp dwellers and upper-middle-class businessmen into the same struggle. Both will have to change their attitudes about education fundamentally if they want to be prepared for the future.

CONCLUSION

The colonial heritage of the Palestinians has not only left them with an irrelevant system of education, but created a culturally dependent mentality. Whenever they have had the rare opportunity to decide what their children should study they copied ready-made programs from the West. The intifadeh has brought about a fundamental change in this attitude: people from all sectors of Palestinian society have come to realize the strength that comes from collective action. From this newly found sense of power has grown a confidence in their ability to promote major institutional change and to achieve national independence. They have come to realize that an educational system stemming from their own culture and responding to their particular needs is essential in the foundation of a future state.

The intifadeh has challenged Palestinians to change their attitudes about the process of learning and the existing system of education. But are the people of Palestine up to this challenge? In many interviews conducted for this article, one gets a contradictory sense of people wanting to return to life the way it was before this period of struggle and pain, yet also wanting to build a brand-new society. Palestinians have a similar attitude toward education. On the one hand, they want to return to school and pick up where they left off before the uprising started. On the other, they are experimenting with many new forms of learning. The uncertainties of the intifadeh have made people look for a few islands of security, and the educational system, in whatever form, represents one of them. If people are unwilling to settle for the old ways of learning and schooling, will they put the effort into making the substantial changes required? It is really too soon to know, but one is tempted to say that as the intifadeh continues, it will deepen the Palestinian resolve to take any risks necessary to build a new state and establish new institutions.

REFERENCES

Al Haq. (1988a). *Israel's war against education in the occupied West Bank*. Ramallah: Al Haq (Law in the Service of Man Series).

Al Haq. (1988b). *Punishing a nation*. Ramallah: Al Haq (Law in the Service of Man Series).

Azzouni-Mahshi, S. (1988). *Education for awareness and involvement. Progress report no. 1-1988*. Jerusalem: Evangelical Lutheran Church.

Badran, N. A. (1969). *Education and modernization in Palestine: 1918–1948*. Beirut: Palestine Liberation Organization Research Center.

Cohen, J. S. (1989, May 18). Education as crime. *The Jerusalem Post*.

Graham-Brown, S. (1984). *Education, repression and liberation: Palestinians*. London: World University Services.

Jerusalem Media and Communication Center. (1989). *Palestinian education: A threat to Israel's security?* Jerusalem: Author.

Palestine Royal Commission Report. (1937). London: Palestine Royal Commission.

Tamari, S. (1988). What the uprising means. *Middle East Report, 152*, 24–30.

Tibawi, A. L. (1956). *Arab education in mandatory Palestine*. London: World University Services.

Section Two

changing scholarship in academia

"The Department Is Very Male, Very White, Very Old, and Very Conservative": The Functioning of the Hidden Curriculum in Graduate Sociology Departments

The title of this article comes from an observation made by a woman of color, a graduate student in sociology. Like the exclamation "The emperor has no clothes!" this observation makes visible what students and faculty have tacitly agreed not to see. In this article, we examine graduate programs in sociology from the subjective position of women of color graduate students. In doing so, we uncover elements of the curriculum and professionalization processes that have long remained hidden. The students of color we interviewed for this study reveal in particular how the graduate school curriculum in sociology not only produces professional sociologists, but also simultaneously (re)produces gender, race, and other forms of inequality. No doubt there are women of color who obtained Ph.D.'s in sociology without these experiences, just as there are women who found the hidden curriculum so odious that they left graduate school. We interviewed women surviving graduate school who volunteered to discuss these issues in detail. They reported encounters that "stuck in their minds," which may not have been everyday occurrences but which left indelible marks. Taken together, they suggest patterns of interaction with intended and unintended consequences that make it particularly difficult for students of color, women, and students from working-class backgrounds to survive and thrive in graduate school. In revealing these aspects of the hidden curriculum, we hope to open a dialogue on graduate school socialization practices that go far beyond sociology departments.

Philip Jackson's (1968) concept of a "hidden curriculum" was developed through observations in K–12 public schools. He noticed that the peculiar disciplines and behavioral expectations that are found in classrooms and embedded in school practices do not necessarily further intellectual development. Jackson observed that grade schools give students credit for "trying," reward "neatness, punc-

Harvard Educational Review Vol. 68 No. 1 Spring 1998, 1–32

tuality and courteous conduct" (p. 33), and provide negative sanctions for the violation of institutional rules. At roughly the same time, Robert Dreeben (1968) looked at school culture and concluded that it taught students to "form transient social relationships, submerge much of their personal identity, and accept the legitimacy of categorical treatment" (p. 147). Building on the work of Elizabeth Vallance (1973–1974), Michael Apple and Nancy King (1977) analyzed how elements of the curriculum come to be "hidden" (pp. 33–34). Apple and King describe two aspects of the hidden curriculum that they term "weak" and "strong." The weak form consists of the connections to civil society that encompass the processes that transform children into social beings able to live and work together, form social institutions, and develop agreed-upon meanings. This is a Durkheimian concept of socialization essential to social life:

> It is nearly impossible to envision social life without some element of control, if only because institutions, as such, tend to respond to the *regularities* of human interaction. What strongly influenced early curriculum workers was a historically specific set of assumptions, common sense rules, about school meanings and control that incorporated not merely the idea that organized society must maintain itself through the preservation of some of its valued forms of interaction and meaning, which implied a quite general and wholly understandable "weak" sense of social control. (Apple & King, 1977, pp. 33–34)

The inseparable "strong" form of the hidden curriculum was part and parcel of the *Weltanschauung* (worldview) of these nineteenth-century curriculum developers:

> Deeply embedded in their ideological perspective was a "strong" sense of control wherein education in general and the everyday meanings of the curriculum in particular were seen as essential to the preserving of the existing social privilege, interests, and knowledge of one element of the population at the expense of less powerful groups. Most often this took the form of attempting to guarantee expert and scientific control in society, to eliminate or "socialize" unwanted racial or ethnic groups or characteristics or to produce an economically efficient group of citizens. (Apple & King, 1977, p. 34)

Critical theorists (Anyon, 1980; Apple, 1971, 1980; Giroux, 1981, 1983; Willis, 1977) instituted projects to make visible those overdetermined aspects of the hidden curriculum that operate to reproduce inequality. They conducted studies demonstrating how elements of the hidden curriculum (e.g., discipline) have not been applied uniformly, but are stratified according to social class, race, gender, and sexuality. Perhaps due to the influence of Marxism on critical pedagogy, most research on the hidden curriculum has focused on the public education system and on capitalism's reproduction of class stratification, rather than on gender, race, or other forms of inequality.[1]

The distinction between weak and strong forms provides a useful heuristic for analyzing the hidden curriculum in graduate programs because it differentiates the professionalization process essential to "becoming a sociologist" ("weak" form) from socialization processes that function to reproduce stratified social relations ("strong" form). The way in which these two aspects of the socialization processes in graduate schools play out in practice can be seen in the astute response of one woman in our study to the question, "Would you recommend this program to another woman of color?":

> If you're talking about a Black student who is interested in some level of discussion or something with other students, I couldn't recommend this program for her. If she were interested in the possibility that she might form some kind of mentoring relationship with the faculty, then I couldn't really recommend this program. . . . If she were looking for some satisfying level of social interaction with either faculty or students, I couldn't say that she would find it here. . . . If they just wanted to get a good education in sociology and learn a lot about theory, a generally good program, I'd say yeah, come to [this] university. But if they're looking for something else, a rounded-out good experience, not just the academic, but something that recognized racial/ethnic issues and offered some level of social interaction for minority students, then I couldn't say this would be the program.

In this quotation, the weak form of socialization is aimed at providing "a good education in sociology"; the strong form reproduces inequality through the exclusion of racial/ethnic issues from the curriculum and the absence of opportunities for "social interaction for minority students." After describing our study in the next section, we examine the weak form of the hidden curriculum and its function in the professionalization of women of color graduate students. Then we turn to the strong form and the reproduction of inequality.

THE STUDY

To obtain detailed descriptions of the "extracurricular" interactions between graduate students and faculty, as well as between students, we conducted open-ended interviews with twenty-six women of color graduate students enrolled in Ph.D. programs in sociology.[2] The participants were a subset of a sample of sixty-six women graduate students of color who had completed a survey in 1989 that was conducted for the Social Issues Committee of Sociologists for Women in Society (SWS), which had expressed concern that women of color graduate students and faculty were underrepresented in sociological associations, including SWS itself.[3] The initial aim of the study was to identify problems and barriers faced by these women, and to make recommendations to sociology departments, faculty, and professional associations. The original sample was constructed from the American Sociological Association's (ASA) list of minority fellows and augmented with additional names received in response to our inquiries to each of the graduate programs listed in the ASA's *Guide to Graduate Programs.* One hundred and sixty-five questionnaires were mailed out. A return rate of 40 percent resulted in a sample of sixty-six women graduate students of color. One item on the questionnaire asked respondents if they would be willing to be interviewed. We were able to locate twenty-six of these respondents, and interviewed them in 1991.[4]

This subset of twenty-six respondents, primarily shaped by their willingness to be interviewed, consisted of two Native Americans, eleven African Americans, five Asian Americans, and eight Latinas;[5] three of these also identified themselves as international students. These women were enrolled in graduate programs across the United States: ten were in graduate programs on the West Coast; ten on the East Coast; four in the South; and two in the Midwest. The women ranged in age from twenty-five to sixty-five, although half were between twenty-five and thirty-five. The women were in various stages of their graduate careers: three were still taking courses; seven were completing comprehensive exams; fourteen were in the dissertation process; and two had recently graduated. The sample included graduate students in both private and public institutions; however, the majority were enrolled in public institutions.[6]

Interviews were conducted by phone at the convenience of the respondents, and lasted from 45 to 90 minutes. The interview protocol was broad in scope, giving respondents space to define the issues they faced in graduate sociology programs. Interviews touched on a wide range of issues related to the graduate experience, including: formal and informal social structures of graduate programs; financial and mentoring support; relationships with faculty and other graduate students; research, publishing, and teaching opportunities; and other experiences that influenced decisions, choices, and career plans. They were transcribed and coded in general categories of mentoring, financial assistance, networking, reasons for selecting graduate programs, relationships with faculty and students, teaching and publishing opportunities, and the issues they identified as barriers to completing the Ph.D. Only after this process and an examination of emergent themes did it occur to us that the concept of "hidden curriculum" (Jackson, 1968) would provide a useful organizing principle. This concept allowed us to recognize the women's words as "thick descriptions" of, on the one hand, how graduate programs socialize students into the profession and the impact of the hidden curriculum, and, on the other hand, of students' resistance to and conflict with aspects of the professional role (Geertz, 1973). Clifford Geertz's term "thick description" refers both to the dense texture of accounts of social life and to the social scientist's interpretations and generalizations about life and culture. It is important to note that our investigation of sociology graduate students relies on the words of women specifically trained and interested in what C. W. Mills (1959) termed the relations between private troubles and public issues.

The following section explores professionalization in graduate education. We then identify distinct consequences of these processes for women of color, discuss the forms and structures of the hidden curriculum that women reported, and describe the socialization messages that emerge from various everyday practices in higher education. We conclude our analysis by focusing on resistance — not only the students' strategies for creating alternative professional identities and skills, but also the process by which resistance becomes an alternative socialization process.

PROFESSIONALIZATION: THE "WEAK" FORM OF THE HIDDEN CURRICULUM

When discussing graduate school, socialization is typically called professionalization, but as Jack Haas and William Shaffir (1982) note, the words mean the same thing. These scholars suggest one set of possible meanings:

Sociologists have . . . examined the process by which neophytes are socialized into the profession. This process, referred to as professionalization, includes several dimensions: developing and identifying with and committing oneself to the profession and a professional career; developing greater loyalty to colleagues than to clients; acquiring a certain detachment and routinization toward one's work; gaining formal knowledge and skills in order to make competent judgments; and developing a *pretense* of competence even though one may be privately uncertain. (p. 132)

Like other institutions, academia produces socialization in extracurricular interactions between students and faculty. In one of the few studies addressing the operation of the hidden curriculum at the university level, G. Bergenhenegouwen (1987) observes:

The hidden curriculum in university can be described as the whole of informal and implicit demands of study and study achievements that are to be met for someone to complete units of study. The teachers' informal demands are made partly consciously and partly unconsciously. (pp. 536–537)

Bergenhenegouwen provides four examples, all of which we consider weak forms:

To show a business-like and detached attitude with respect to the subject of study. If feelings, intuition and interest are allowed to play a role, this expresses insufficient distance and lack of a clear and a balanced view.

Students are supposed to work with theoretical constructions, use professional jargon and abstract concepts, etc.

Students are expected to "hold their own, by showing a confident attitude and giving little or no evidence of anxiety, nervousness or feelings of uncertainty in exams or interviews."

Students must learn to value "the satisfaction gained from achieving more and getting better results than others, which gives people also a sense of self esteem." (p. 537)

Self-reflective studies of graduate education in sociology have similarly emphasized aspects of the hidden curriculum that are related to the weak form. Although some researchers have contributed to the abstract body of literature called the "sociology of sociology" (Crothers, 1991; Egan, 1989; Plutzer, 1991), most of the studies have been "applied," focusing on the assessment/evaluation and improvement of graduate education and training.[7] In describing the socialization process in graduate programs, Charles Crothers (1991) argues that, as a group, students undergo "status degradation" as they are stripped of their past identities and treated as "baby sociologists."[8] The structure of graduate school acknowledges *only* academically gained and credentialed knowledge, thus privileging theory over practical social knowledge. Janet Malenchek Egan (1989) identifies the process as one of resocialization: "Currently lacking professional self-image and scholarly world view, it [professional socialization] alters the past rather than merely building on it" (p. 201).

While requiring a new professional identity of their students, graduate programs provide few formal mechanisms to help graduate students make the transition from being directed students (taking course work and passing qualifying exams) to being self-directed researchers who are developing professional or disciplinary identities.[9] In their study of professional self-concept among graduate students, Ronald Pavalko and John Holley (1974) note that research and teaching opportunities are important in insuring socialization toward professional identity. In another study of socialization in graduate and professional schools, Carin Weiss (1981) finds that, while informal interaction with faculty is significant in developing a high professional role commitment, graduate programs seldom make explicit that this is a component of the students' education, or that it is considered a faculty responsibility. In a study conducted by Julius A. Roth (1955), faculty advisors at the University of Chicago were asked about the conceptions of "good" and "poor" graduate students. Roth elicited descriptions of learning environments that "create a restricted culture in which students with certain characteristics will thrive, while others with negatively valued characteristics will run into repeated stumbling blocks" (p. 350).[10] For example, even if one measure of intellect was originality, "when a student's originality carried him outside the limits" of the dominant paradigm in sociology, she/he was more likely to be labeled "bizarre" than a potential sociologist. Roth's work suggests that women, working-class students, and students of color may be at a disadvantage if they lack the expected "cultural capital."[11]

A few studies address the impact of graduate school socialization on White women and working-class students, but not on students of color, particularly women of color.[12] In her study on self-concept and graduate school, Egan (1989) examines the same characteristics Roth (1955) identifies (assertiveness, confidence, independence, and being well-adjusted) and concludes:[13]

> In my definition, high self-esteem is contingent on a view of oneself as a competent, worthwhile person, deserving of acceptance and expecting to succeed. Individuals assess whether they possess these qualities according to the standards and the frame of reference provided by their culture. If this self-view is challenged by structural features of the socializing organization, the possibility exists for a lowering of individual self-esteem. (p. 201)

The actual locations and mechanics by which the hidden curriculum produces professional identity include: department culture, cliques or factions, group interactions in meetings or seminars, mentoring or apprenticeship relationships, the informal or formal allocation system for teaching and research assistantships, the selection of courses for teaching assistants to teach. For example, several female students reported that they were frequently assigned, or encouraged, to teach courses on the sociology of women, gender, or women's studies; students of color are assigned to teach courses on race relations or in ethnic studies programs.

In analyzing the transcripts of the sample of women of color in this study, other areas emerge: hiring and promotion practices, graduate student recruitment, allocation of department resources, required readings, and course offerings and requirements. The everyday practices surrounding these aspects of graduate student life serve to socialize students toward identifying with and committing themselves to professional careers as sociologists. Graduate programs socialize students to develop loyalty to and identify with the faculty and other sociologists while distancing themselves from undergraduate students and research subjects (Pavalko & Holley, 1974; Weiss, 1981). Students are expected to acquire a certain detachment, generally referred to as scientific objectivity, to conduct "value-free" sociology (Mirande, 1988). Formal and informal interactions between faculty and students — such as seminars, research assistantships, and office hours — assist students in gaining sociological knowledge and the skills to conduct research, teach, and write, and in becoming competent in the oral and written use of professional jargon.

The hidden curriculum receives powerful support from the premium placed on the concept of competition (Bergenhenegouwen, 1987; Egan, 1989; Kleinman, 1983) and isolation (Egan, 1989; Sherlock & Morris, 1967) that are so characteristic of graduate school. Even in its weak form, professionalization requires detachment and distance, the use of abstract concepts, assertive self-confidence, competition, independent work habits, and loyalty to colleagues — even at the expense of allegiance to one's community of origin. These things are taught in an informal and unregulated socialization process directed, in large part, by males from the majority culture who, until recently, have dominated the profession. For women and students of color, professionalization requires the adoption of attitudes and behavior patterns that are different from or antithetical to their culture of origin — requirements that make the path through school more problematic and perilous than it might be for a student who arrives equipped with the dominant forms of cultural capital.

Our interview subjects mentioned competition repeatedly. Graduate programs structure individualistic learning experiences that encourage competition for grades and scarce resources, including teaching and research assistantships. Access to resources frequently requires the sponsorship of a mentor, thereby making students compete for the attention of graduate faculty members. The following quotation from one of the graduate students interviewed suggests the relationship between being mentored and access to resources:

> That's the kind of thing [the application process for a Research Assistant position] where it depends on who you know. Who you hook up with. What's around. I mean, there's no formal way to do it at all. And it's been a problem. I constantly hear "Oh, so and so is working on this project and that project" and I think "God, that's really interesting. I would love to do that but how did they find out about it?" And that's part of the informal process.

Recognizing competition as a primary characteristic of the professionalization process, students described ways in which the faculty discourage a cooperative or team approach to learning and how the structures of the graduate program place students in constant competition with each other:

> The relations [between students] are very stressed. And also students are very competitive in my department because there is this informal ranking system. Because they're allowing more and more students into the program, they have less and less money to give to students. And so students really have to compete for money and that competition takes the form of who gets the highest scores

and who impresses a professor more. Things like that. And it can be quite nasty at times, but the department sort of encourages that because they rank students on a scale of one to ten. So each student has a rank. So it's just an ugly situation.

However, grades are not the only criteria for obtaining positive feedback from faculty. As Roth (1955) notes in his study, faculty advisors reward assertiveness, confidence, and independence because they perceive these personality traits as indicators of a "good" student. The following quotations illustrate the hidden structures of mentorship in graduate school and the students' self-perceptions that they seem to be lacking vital elements of cultural capital, such as aggressive networking and the expectation that professors are there to serve students — beyond teaching classes — by identifying opportunities to further students' careers: "Part of it may just be that I'm not the kind of person that asks a lot of other people"; "I didn't ask for it [guidance]. Although the couple times I asked for it [advice] the responses I got weren't very good. It was almost like — well, you're supposed to sort of just inherently know how to do this." Like other graduate students, these women of color consider the hidden structure of mentoring a problem, particularly in cases in which having a mentor is closely tied to obtaining teaching and research assistantships:

> It's just that there are people who have made very good connections with faculty and work with them and seem to get the benefits of having that connection.
>
> If you don't have a spokesperson or people that know your work and so forth there's no one there to stick up for you. Because you know the faculty meetings are closed. So you really need to develop a relationship with some of the people that you can work well with.

The absence of formal structures to assure that mentoring takes place leaves students to develop their own resources. This may have been appropriate when graduate education was essentially middle-class White males teaching other middle-class White males. At that time a certain homogeneity of cultural capital could be assumed, and if a student could not marshal that capital to network, find a mentor, and compete vigorously for a position, one might conclude that the "bizarre" student would not make a good sociologist. The old model implied "reproduction" of sociologists and mainstream sociology. This message was embedded in the everyday experiences of the women we interviewed: the "ideal type" of sociologist is a European American, heterosexual, middle-class male. White males, fathers of the discipline, became established historically as the ideal type, and this is maintained through various practices, including the exclusion of others. Not surprisingly, women of color encounter difficulty fitting into programs designed for students from different racial, class, and cultural backgrounds, and gender because they have little, if any, of the cultural capital that White, middle-class, heterosexual males possess. One respondent, who acknowledged that she did not have the same undergraduate training as other first-year graduate students, describes the frustration of not fulfilling her advisor's expectations, and hence being unable to solicit her assistance: "She just doesn't know how to deal with people that don't come in already perfect. And no one does."

So, the diverse student body of today, including both undergraduate and graduate students, produces a paradox: How can the hidden curriculum "reproduce" what does not yet exist — that is, women of color sociologists? Only by making the functioning of this curriculum visible can we overcome the hidden assumptions, failures, and gaps that have made it unnecessarily difficult or impossible for some students to survive graduate school.

REPRODUCING INEQUALITY:
THE "STRONG" FORM OF THE HIDDEN CURRICULUM

In addition to ignoring the differential implications that the weak form of the hidden curriculum has for a diverse student body, previous research has not examined the strong form. In Stanley Eitzen's (1989) proposal for a course entitled "Introduction to Graduate School," which was published in a special issue of *Teaching Sociology*, Eitzen discusses the status of women and minorities in the profession. However, he does not include guidelines or recommendations for dealing with racism and sexism, nor does he address ways to prepare White students to work and learn in a diverse university setting.[14] As yet, there are no detailed studies on the operation of hidden curricula in higher education or the (re)production of racial, ethnic, and gender hierarchies. The existing research has not taken a critical stance on "professional socialization," and as such the analyses do not recognize that, as in grade school, "professional socialization" takes place within a system of power and inequality and has strong aspects that have to do with the reproduction of inequality.

Analysis of the interview data in this study produces eight elements of the strong form of the hidden curriculum: stigmatization, blaming the victim, cooling out, stereotyping, absence, silence, exclusion, and tracking.[15] We will discuss each of these in turn, but two points must be made: first, all these elements of the curriculum may be hidden, but they are not *well* hidden. As Vallance (1980) observes, they may be visible to all, but lie "outside the confines of the explicit and formal curriculum" (p. 141). In the following sections, we illustrate the discussion with quotations from the interviewees, for whom much of what was intended to be hidden was painfully obvious. Second, as critical theorists note, the term "reproduction" does not capture the elements of resistance open to students (Apple, 1980; Giroux, 1981, 1983). This is especially true in sociology, where one of the core values being reproduced is critical inquiry. We shall return to these themes later.

Stigmatization

Women of color frequently get their first view of the strong reproduction of inequality when they are recruited and admitted into graduate programs. Many women reported that classmates, office staff, and faculty stigmatized them as "affirmative action" students rather than identifying them in terms of their specific interests in sociology. The affirmative action classification makes race and/or gender the determining factor in social interaction, and occasionally relegates students of color to positions of affirmative action "mascot":

> Coming in as a woman of color — there was always that stigma that you were an affirmative action student; that you got in because they LET you in, that you did

not GET in . . . like this is OUR Indian student. And . . . even some of the secretaries and some of the other people would refer to me as OUR Indian student.

I remember one guy coming up to me about my second year. He said, "Geez, so you must be the affirmative action case." I said, "What the hell do you mean?" I happen to have seen his transcript from Princeton, which was a C– or a C transcript. My transcript was an A transcript. So I just said, "No. As a matter of fact, my transcript is better than some of yours [White students]."

Intense competition for admissions, assistantships, grants, and fellowships ignite a hostile environment for students of color when they compete for scarce resources with White students. When universities implement affirmative action programs and policies in a racially hostile environment, students of color constantly find their qualifications called into question. The following account illustrates how competition between students within a racially charged environment plays out by pitting White students against students of color who are perceived as less competent:

One [White] student put a note in a professor's mailbox with an article written in the *New York Times* by a conservative. And the argument was, "Well, these minority students are just so ill prepared for universities. That's why there's so much racial conflict because the better prepared White students have to deal with these stupid Black students and then they come in and try to ask for equality and then you give them scholarships on top of that — that's what the whole problem is." So this student in our department thought those of us [students of color] who were sitting around "bitching" for equity fell into this category.

Anne Pruitt and Paul Isaac (1985) depict ways in which White faculty maintain hostile environments through social interaction with graduate students of color. They argue that the behavior of graduate faculty helps set the tone in the department and establishes norms and values governing student interactions, describing precisely an element of the operation of the hidden curriculum:

Often the expectations and attitudes of white faculty lead minority students to feel stigmatized. Some students feel that they would not be enrolled except for affirmative action requirements. They feel that they must continue to prove themselves. Dissertation topics that focus on minority issues are not well received. White faculty commonly characterize such interests as unworthy, an attitude that, when added to the usual environmental pressures, makes graduate school intolerable. (Pruitt & Isaac, 1985, p. 534)

Blaming the Victim and "Cooling-Out"

Early researchers explored two elements of the hidden curriculum in higher education: blaming the victim and "cooling-out" (Hearn & Olzak, 1981; Ryan, 1976; Young, 1974). Blaming the victim refers to social interactions that socialize students to define themselves as the problem, rather than exploring the structural causes for their experiences within the institution. This ideology requires students to see their experiences as unique and particularistic, rather than linked to the culture and social structure of higher education.

"Cooling out" refers to socialization messages that encourage students to lower their expectations and to identify situations they once protested as "normal" and unchangeable (Young, 1974). Students who have been "cooled-out" can be redirected to appropriate tracks that reflect their social and economic backgrounds. Burton R. Clark (1960) drew attention to the importance of cooling-out in higher education as a way to address the problem created in a democratic society that is caught in the "inconsistency between encouragement to achieve and the realities of limited opportunity" (p. 139). Clark (1960) argues that cooling-out is the function of moving unpromising students toward more realistic alternatives rather than having them fail. However, when this cooling-out process is applied to a diverse or working-class student body, the nontraditional student served by an open admissions policy comes to be defined as the problem. By analyzing the formal and informal structures that discourage politically committed and active students from pursuing their original research agendas, T. R. Young (1974) developed an interpretation of the cooling-out process that is linked to the development of a distant and detached professional identity. Students we interviewed reported that they were discouraged from pursuing sociology of race, conducting research involving their racial or ethnic groups, and applied or action research. The advice an advisor gave to one graduate student was not unique: "If you're interested in communities or ethnic studies, then you're going to be ghettoized and you're going to be perceived in a certain way." The metaphor of the "ghetto" underlines the incompatibility of this kind of research and the development of a professional identity and academic career.

Blaming the victim and cooling-out functions offer significant insights into the reproduction of inequality in higher education. The hidden curriculum serves the cooling-out function by inculcating a certain detachment from racism and social injustice. For example, one student explains how she began the process of cooling-out by defining unequal learning conditions as acceptable and matching her expectations to those conditions: "I haven't expected very much and I haven't gotten very much. And I have just taken it as 'that's the way it is.'" Another way of developing detachment from racism is to define the observation and naming of racism as a personal weakness — that is, as being oversensitive to the issue. As one student concluded, "If you took issue with everything that happened, you would be filing a grievance every single day. And so I thought, 'Well, who cares, it's just that I was really taking it personally.'" Acquiring "professional distance" implies becoming blind to the personal experience of inequality, as well as to larger social issues. The process encourages women of color to stop identifying their community of orientation and shift loyalties to faculty and other graduate students in the profession. Acquiring "professional distance" and developing a "professional identity" is a function of graduate school generally. However, the process impacts women of color, particularly women of color from working-class or poor backgrounds, in different ways. As previously noted, professional identity incorporates White, male, heterosexual, and middle-class attributes and values; thus, the fewer similarities the student shares with the ideal type, the more there is at stake for that student.

Cooling-out functions of the hidden curriculum are also apparent in the women's descriptions of the higher status of theoretical work, in comparison to applied research. One woman offered a description of the process and criticized the disadvantage experienced by students with a political commitment and agenda:

> Very often women of color are interested in doing the kind of research that has some real policy implications and that's really oriented toward problem-solving issues. And at the program in [this] university it's the kind of research that's almost disdained and it's almost looked down upon. They [students of color] thought they were jeopardized and placed in a whole different category because their work wasn't understood. Whenever it had to do with race or ethnicity, then it wasn't seen as valuable or as important. People [faculty in the department] have been very kind about my little research project here, but I know that it's not the kind of thing — I mean they place a much higher value and premium on things that are purely theoretical.

Her characterization of the tension involved in pursuing applied research within her graduate program is consistent with William Mayrl and Hans Mauksch's (1987) analysis of the ASA survey that concludes, "The bulk of graduate education involves talking about sociology rather than doing sociology" (p. 17). While the cooling-out functions are not exclusive to women of color, to students of color, or to women students, the point is that the less cultural capital a student brings to the graduate setting, the more impact the process has on that student's educational experience.

Stereotyping

Our use of the term "stereotyping" is twofold. First, it refers to the social construction of groups in terms of race, class, ethnicity, age, gender, etc., and to the attribution of simplistic, often inaccurate, gross generalizations of group behavior. These stereotypes may be positive, as when Asians are seen as a "model minority," or negative, as in the perception of Blacks as less intelligent. Inaccurate and misleading images such as these are constructed in popular prejudice, trafficked in the mass media, reproduced in school texts and curricula, and purveyed by social scientists employing dubious measures of central tendency to compare one group's aptitudes and achievements to another. Our second use of stereotyping is analogous to the ecological fallacy in which aggregate measures are applied to analysis at the individual level, applying gross generalizations of group behavior to individuals. On an individual level, these group characteristics become central elements in prejudging an individual's capacity or the meaning of her/his actions.

A number of works examining the experiences of discrimination in academia have critiqued notions of professionalism and the professional role as constructs for the analysis of class, gender, race, sexuality, and age bias (e.g., Aisenberg & Harrington, 1988; Barnes, 1986; Granfield, 1992; James & Farmer, 1993; Padilla & Chávez, 1995; Trask, 1993; Williams, 1991). While not focused specifically on the hidden curriculum, these critiques pose significant questions about equity in the process of professional socialization. The literature on women of color identifies two conflicts with the professional role — internalization of negative stereotypes and internalization of a norm. In the first conflict, Latina and African American women encounter students and colleagues who have internalized negative stereotypes about Latinas and African Americans. A few students described relationships with European American faculty that never developed beyond stereotypes: "My main frustrations with her [mentor] is that she just really doesn't know who I am. I mean, for someone who worked with her for so many years, it's like she has no idea who I am." For instance, a student in our study described her interaction with her mentor as limited to an ethnic, racial group category rather than including individual characteristics. Michele Foster (1991), for example, demonstrates that African American teachers encounter the results of the negative portrayal of African American women in literature and the media by having their intelligence and competency under constant scrutiny. In an earlier report on African American women in academia, Yolanda Moses (1989) points out that stereotypes and racial biases intensify when Whites feel "threats to their own sense of economic entitlement" (p. 14). The second conflict stems from professional roles that assume a race norm that is White and frequently male. Thus, in her study of African American women professionals, Cheryl Townsend Gilkes (1982) finds that professional identity is shaped and supported by a "commitment to the norms and values of the dominant [White, middle-class] society" (p. 290). Deborah Carter et al. (1987–1988) similarly find that African American women faculty confront cultural conflicts embedded in expectations and standards established by White males:

> Their personal lives extract a loyalty to their culture that is central to acceptance by family and friends. At the same time, they must struggle with their own identity as women in a society where "thinking like a woman" is still considered a questionable activity. At times, they even experience pressure to choose between their racial identity and their womanhood. (p. 98)

Haunani-Kay Trask's (1993) account of racism at the University of Hawaii highlights a conflict with the chair of her department arising from her inclusion of "sections on racism and capitalism as basic American institutions and ideologies" instead of units on the family and Christianity:

> Intellectual, political, even stylistic differences became the source of heated conflict between us. Her belief that there existed a correct way — a culturally correct way — of speaking and behaving made it clear to me how white hegemony in Hawai'i and on the campus would mean a tight constraint on *my* cultural behaviors. I was to start acting, as we say in Hawaiian, as *ho'ohaole*, someone who behaves like a white person. I was shocked, bemused, furious, and depressed. Very depressed. (p. 213)

As these accounts demonstrate, the hidden criteria for constructing professionalism include stereotypical attitudes, values, and expectations that may require women of color to deny their culture and to fit into a male model of behavior. One woman recalled the Puerto Rican students' discomfort with the required reading materials assigned in a department seminar because they involved the denial of their culture and the distortion of the Latino experience to fit a cultural determinist model: "We [Puerto Rican students] are not comfortable with that course. We don't like to be insulted that way." Having been assigned readings on Puerto Rican communities based on Oscar Lewis's (1965) "culture of poverty" thesis, the student found little reference to the social, political, or historical factors contributing to current levels of poverty, high school dropout rates, and unemployment.

Absence

The hardships graduate students experience due to the competitive culture of graduate school and the lack of a cooperative learning environment are intensified for women of color who are frequently isolated as the only women of color in a program or in an entering cohort. This position forces them to become the "lone voice" speaking from their standpoint — a kind of loneliness and isolation that differs from that of the "lone scholar" (Becker, 1982; Hood, 1985) or of individualism (Kleinman, 1983). The paradoxical uniqueness of being both isolated and a spokesperson for one's group is captured in the following:

> I'm like the first black African American student I guess that they've had in the past eleven years now. They do get a lot of foreign students but not Americans. In fact, as far as American minority students go, as far as I can tell there are none other than me.
>
> The first time I walked into the campus, one of the secretaries — who turned out to be a really nice person in the long run — she just kind of had this startled look, "Can I help you?" In the kind of way when somebody thinks you're going to rob them and they figure they better help you before you help yourself. She kind of looked and saw this Black woman standing there and usually the only other Black person to come to the building is the woman who sweeps the floors. I thought, "Oh boy, this is a really a good start." The second thing that shocked me was, they have these wonderful pictures lining the stairwell of every graduate since 1901. The first Black woman I saw in that lineup graduated the year I got there. So I was Black woman number two or Black woman number three. I thought, "Good god, I didn't realize it was this bad."

Many of these women had experienced being in a seminar when the topic of race arose and all eyes turned to them, the one African American in the room. Being the only woman of color in a department, seminar, or social event often carries the expectation that they can represent the voice of their community or, in fact, speak for all women of color. The most common example students gave of this was being asked to participate on panels in the department, university, and at professional conferences. In all of these cases, they were the only one representing a specific voice.

Being the only woman of color within her environment also means rarely being able to have one's norms and values validated through interaction with faculty or other graduate students. Without the opportunity to interact with other women of color graduate students, a student lacks access to a support group that might validate her experiences as a minority female graduate student in a predominately White male institution, as this student described:

> I never see them [other women graduate students of color] and I never talk to them. They're just not around at all. I think they had such a horrible experience that they just stay off campus and come in only when necessary.

Moreover, the absence of faculty of color in Ph.D. programs, coupled with the reluctance and difficulty that White faculty have in mentoring students of color, exacerbates the situation for these students. Women of color who attempt to establish mentoring relationships with faculty of different cultures, class backgrounds, and/or genders, often find unexpected complications. One respondent noted the difficulty students of color had interacting with a faculty member whom the White students considered supportive and progressive:

> This guy is an Anglo male and he cannot even relate to me. He's a very nice person. He has tried. He cannot even talk to me and not feel uncomfortable. Every time we sit and talk he's all jumpy. He can't deal with me being different. And the only explanation I can get, you know — I'm not White. That's the only reason why — because I don't see any other. We have the same interests. I like all the things he likes, I read, I know what his field is. But, when I approach him or anything he's so uncomfortable that it makes me feel uncomfortable. I don't want to be next to him. I see my friends who are Anglo, they get along [with him]. . . . I know he is not racist. I know that it's not that. He cannot deal with me. Culturally I don't know what he thinks I come from or, I don't know, it's weird. So I think that it helps in graduate school to be White.

Another student explained:

> It would be one thing if there were no women of color on the faculty and a woman of color could still get a mentor — that's sort of one problem. But neither of these things are happening. One, there's no one who is going to mentor us and two, there are no women of color on the faculty. So the two sort of compound one another.

The underrepresentation of faculty of color, particularly women, in Ph.D. programs underscores the racial "fit." The following "inventory" of a department makes the point:

> The department has between forty and forty-five graduate students and about ten to fifteen faculty persons. It's a very conservative department. All professors are White men, except for about two women. Only one tenured female faculty. One junior faculty that's Black. One minority woman who is on leave and she's a junior faculty. So the power structure of the department is very male and very White and very old and very conservative.

Since the faculty in Ph.D. programs are predominately European American and male, women of color graduate students are confronted with images and role models that are unattainably different, and they are constantly reminded of those differences. The following quotation from a Latina student illustrates how conscious she is of the differences between who she is and the "ideal type" represented by the faculty in the department. It also highlights the range of differences that is created by the lack of diversity among the faculty in graduate programs:

> First, I think the professors kind of feel that we are different to them. It's true. I have different ideas. I have a different language. I was involved in political things and they were not. You know, I mean we are totally different. I am a woman. I have an accent. It's totally different.

Deafening Silences

Various policies and practices establishing graduate curricula produce and reproduce knowledge while simultaneously reproducing inequality. By not incorporating the writings of scholars of color or acknowledging the importance of the study of race relations, Ph.D. programs maintain an implicit hierarchy of knowledge. Consequences of this hierarchy materially affect academic careers by limiting access to prestigious and lucrative university or research positions, publishing opportunities, and professional recognition. Hidden curricula socialize students to norms that devalue certain kinds of research questions and approaches. The most common observation that arose in the interviews was a deafening silence — the absence of race and gender in the curriculum.[16] The following discussions of course offerings reflect a common description of graduate curricula given by the women interviewed:

> There are no courses [on gender]. There's one course on the family that a woman professor has taught. After that, the courses have not been offered since she left, which was about a year and a half ago. Courses for women in particular as far as either family, women in society or women and work, there have been no courses on that. So I would say for women there have been no courses particularly geared to them. For minorities on the other hand, there have been a few courses on minorities, ethnic minorities, and social stratification . . . but there are really no courses that particularly deal with minority women.
>
> We're still pretty conservative and mainstream. The department does not pay much attention to race and ethnicity and I was very frustrated in terms of their curriculum. In order to take a course on race and ethnicity I had to go outside the department to study those things. It was always a residual category or a category that didn't have any critical place [in sociology].

Even though some women were enrolled in programs that identified race or gender as areas of concentration, not one of the women reported programs that required courses that focused on these topics. Regardless of a department's claimed specialization in these areas, students found that such courses were not always available at the graduate level or were offered on an irregular basis. As one student noted, "They have some courses listed in the catalog but they just don't offer them. So when you look at it you're sort of deceived. You have to actually look at what they have been offering." Another student summed up this aspect of what might be hidden in the curriculum: "The department looks a lot better on paper than it is in reality."

Maintaining traditional sociology as *the* graduate curriculum is accomplished by not requiring courses on the sociology of race and gender and limiting the number of graduate seminars in these areas. Required courses in theory and methods are similarly silent on race and gender and are restricted to narrow sociological traditions. Students commented on their instructors' inability to incorporate the experiences of groups of color and women in their sociological analysis. They noted as well the absence of authors of color in the required readings assigned to courses:

For example, one class I took on gender focused on theoretical issues. The readings that we did — I think there were five or six required books — and none of these books, not any sections of these books, really focused on the black female experience although it was a class in gender. . . . Another example, an aging class that I took — very little focus on race. . . . If you are looking at comparative historical or theoretical stuff and the focus is on the major social thinkers, there's not even an opportunity to bring up issues that necessarily relate to racial minorities. So there's a lot of invisibleness in the overall program.

These practices constitute a hidden curriculum that socializes students to the norms and values surrounding traditional sociology and the academic structure. The success of this socialization is apparent in one student's comparison of nongender courses as "meatier" and higher status for students seeking teaching assistantships. In her article on Black women sociologists in academia, Gloria Jones-Johnson (1988) identifies the significant norms and values embedded in the curriculum:

Unfortunately, sexist, racist, cultural-bound and middle-class assumptions held by faculty result in the omission of the perspective of women of color, biased teaching, limited learning and myopia in sociological pedagogy. Sociological knowledge has assumed both a masculine and white perspective. (p. 315)

Programs that offer neither regularly scheduled graduate courses in race relations nor an integrated curriculum socialize students to a traditional perspective. The silence of race and ethnicity in the curriculum inculcates students with significant beliefs and values of what constitutes legitimate knowledge and fields to study. That which can be spoken of and made visible is legitimate, that which is invisible and "dare not speak its name" is ipso facto illegitimate. The message is that U.S. sociology (that is, sociology from a White, male, middle-class, and heterosexual perspective) is *the* legitimate form of sociology — others are either illegitimate or less valuable forms of knowledge. As one student concludes:

I mean it was like saying that all the thinking in the world comes from Europe. People in other parts of the world don't have ideas. Your experience as a person of color isn't really reflected in what you study and what you learn.

Breaking the silence is a violation of the unspoken rules of the hidden curriculum. Several women told us that professors and other students responded to requests for more seminars on race, an integrated curriculum, and the inclusion of readings by scholars of color as uncivil behavior:

Even amongst graduate students, it was rude to bring up the topic of racial discrimination or what to do about race or what to do about the high attrition rate. I mean, it was just — it was really irrelevant.

There is still, on an informal basis, this sense that you're sort of being rude if you bring up race, issues of race. You know, you shouldn't be talking about these things.

First of all, I was sticking my neck out and telling people things they didn't want to hear. I mean, I think the whole topic of race is very, very touchy. And I was told a couple weeks after I'd given the talk, in a one-to-one conversation with a White male, that basically all the White males are afraid to say anything. . . . I felt frustrated even after the fact, because I felt like, you know, I'm glad you're coming and telling me this, but that's no solution either, for you all just to decide, "We're going to pout and sulk and we're not going to say anything."

Faculty and graduate students frequently respond with deafening silence to comments about race in class or they tend to avoid students who bring the topic of race into public discussions. When faculty treat students' comments on race as rude behavior, students learn that requests for an inclusive curriculum or concern about race are viewed by faculty as importunate, not professional behavior.

Exclusion

If sociology were defined as the sum of what has been published, the discipline would probably be one of the most cosmopolitan and innovative fields in the academic world. In fact, it is this openness that attracts many students. But from the perspective of the graduate student, sociology is defined in the local venue of individual sociology courses and departments where the hidden curriculum enforces local definitions. Students who are vocal about discussing issues of equity, racism, and sexism within the department, the university, and the discipline are sanctioned by exclusion or ostracism. For instance, in the most extreme case reported, an advanced doctoral student served on a conference panel on the status of women of color in the discipline. Her advisor was in the audience and took personally critical comments the student made about the culture and social structure of graduate education in sociology. The advisor felt this was an assault on her and the department and refused to work with the student for a year, delaying the student's progress on her dissertation. Students who persistently address issues of inequality risk being labeled activists, driven out of sociology, and, in some cases, pushed into interdisciplinary programs.

Similarly, students who express an interest in studying their own ethnic community are sometimes discouraged, ridiculed, or considered poor students. As one noted:

We were all going around introducing ourselves and saying what we were doing. So when my turn came I said my name is such and such and my dissertation is going to be on the labor force participation of Latinas in [a certain] city. And the same professor just cracked up. He said "What? Latinas? Is that sociology?"

Numerous students reported being advised not to do research on their own communities:

One of the things the faculty told us is don't get in that field, especially if you're a Chicana scholar. Don't get into issues that deal with gender and the family because you're ghettoizing yourself. You're not going to be marketable.

The recollections of this graduate student and others who were advised not to do research on their own communities suggest, rather than demonstrate, a chilling effect of the hidden curriculum. Similarly, some sociology faculty conveyed to some students the perception that African American studies, Chicana/o studies, and the other ethnic studies programs were beyond the pale, being either an intellectual ghetto outside of the mainstream of the discipline or an actual ghetto where one would damage one's "marketability" in sociology. These quotations intimate the impact that the hidden curriculum might have on future interactions with graduate faculty. Certainly a student does not have to heed a faculty member who advises against a certain line of research; nevertheless, going against the grain in this way makes it difficult to find members to sit on your committees, to garner letters of recommendation, and sometimes to receive recognition from the department. Students adhering to the advice of the hidden curriculum help to maintain traditional sociology and the narrow boundaries of the discipline. Thus they move into the mainstream of sociology rather than staying at the margins, living their academic lives in the ghetto.

The interviewees noted that their interests in race and gender were discouraged or stigmatized, whereas the interests of other students often received favorable responses from the faculty. One woman, told by her advisor that she risked not being considered as a serious scholar if she continued research on race and gender, pointed to the different way faculty treated a White male student who pursued research on gender and race. Such research suddenly became a legitimate area of study. This woman clearly perceived that there was a lack of consistency in the way faculty dealt with the issue of researching one's own community. As in many social interactions, her perception was informed as much by what she did not hear as by what was made explicit.

> They [faculty] were telling me that it [the study of her ethnic group] was too subjective and I should learn and do more things, be more objective and cover a broader area, and write about other people in other groups rather than just my own. But I never once have heard one of the foreign students who were doing their own country ever told that. They were doing the same thing I was doing. So it was okay for them to do it. And I really felt a little prejudice there.

Unlike White students who conducted research on White populations and communities, women of color were more likely to be treated as unable to distance themselves and maintain the appropriate professional detachment necessary to study their own communities. Students of color pursuing topics directly tied to their ethnic communities must establish a delicate balance to avoid exclusion from mainstream sociology and "banishment" to ethnic studies. Issues of "professional distance" are raised in ways that White sociologists studying White communities never experience. One woman bitterly remembers the statement of one of her committee members at the start of her oral comprehensive examination:

> "You know I finally figured out what's wrong with you . . ." And I was kind of stunned. And I said, "Oh well, what?" And he said, "You are too much like an Indian and not enough like a sociologist." Well, my jaw dropped and I was speechless. And he went on to say, ". . . and if you don't straighten up you know what's going to happen? We're not going to allow you to teach sociology. We're going to put you down in Ethnic Studies and Native American Studies or something

like that for the rest of your life." Isn't this interesting, that this is my exam in race relations and this is the first question or remark that I faced.

The message is clear: to be Native American is not compatible with being a sociologist.

The tendency of some faculty to place race relations outside the boundaries of sociology serves to reproduce mainstream sociology. The hidden curriculum that many of the women encounter in their graduate programs reclassifies and marginalizes the study of race (and in some cases gender) into domains of ethnic studies and women studies. One student concluded, "My hunch would be that my work would be much more welcomed in, say, ethnic studies or women's studies than sociology."[17] Because interdisciplinary programs like ethnic and women's studies offer only a B.A. or a master's degree, the study of race and gender is further labeled as inferior to traditional sociology.

Tracking

Like the term hidden curriculum, tracking is another concept borrowed from education research that is usually applied to the analysis of K–12 public schooling. Sometimes called ability grouping, it refers to the common practice of using test scores, school performance, and sometimes input from counselors to classify students into groups such as honors, college preparatory, general, business, or vocational tracks. Tracking is thus a critical sorting and selecting mechanism that creates differential access to higher education. Track assignment tends to be correlated with social class, race/ethnicity, and, in the case of math and science, with gender (Mortenson, 1991; Oakes, 1985). Similarly, in graduate school, the strong form of the hidden curriculum not only socializes, but also functions as a kind of tracking system providing differential access to the best research opportunities, postdoctoral fellowships, and publishing opportunities, as well as to jobs in prestigious institutions. One student's interactions with her mentor made her feel that she was being directed toward lower status occupations within the discipline:

> Personally she [the mentor] makes a lot of assumptions about me that I find insulting, like maybe I'm destined to teach at a community college instead of a university. She always is the one that takes on a woman of color as an advisee and it doesn't matter what your interests are. Our joke is that basically we're her colonized people because I mean it's like she doesn't really know who we are. But she has us and it's sort of like little badges on her shoulders that she works with students of color.

RESISTANCE AND ALTERNATIVES

While it is important to recognize the powerful nature of the hidden elements of curriculum in reproducing race, class, and gender inequality, and in reproducing a particular structure of sociology as a discipline and academic department, it is equally important to recognize and give full weight to the ability of students to resist and refuse, both individually and collectively.

Resistance theory has become an important strand of critical pedagogy, developing in part to explain why working-class students and students of color leave the education system (Everhart, 1983; Willis, 1977), and in part to provide teachers a more hopeful subject position as "cultural workers" or "transformative intellectuals" (Freire, 1985; Giroux, 1988). The women we interviewed had in many respects avoided the first form of resistance.[18] Though generally from working-class backgrounds, they had persevered and reached the lofty heights of graduate school. They spoke of a number of resistance strategies that they employed to survive and to transform what they perceived as an oppressive social order. These accounts are particularly interesting because they give us a glimpse into the furnace in which critical pedagogies are forged.

The women's resistance took a number of forms. They struggled to maintain ties to their communities of origin and to keep a focus on social action, despite the powerful socialization messages to adopt "value-neutral" or "objective" social science perspectives. They challenged sociological research on their own communities. They pointed out contradictions in sociological theory and practice. They adopted paradigms, theories, and concepts from the discipline both to criticize the discipline and to analyze their own situation as citizens, as graduate students, and as scholars of color. They employed their own perspectives to refute sociological findings, departmental practices, and individual faculty interactions with students. They simultaneously developed a number of proactive resistance strategies. The women described attempts to bring in guest speakers and visiting scholars to broaden the curriculum, and they went outside the department to take classes in ethnic and women's studies to remedy perceived deficiencies in the curriculum. They fought within the department for equity in the allocation of resources, and within individual seminars for more inclusive literature.

In his article, "I Never Had a Mentor: Reflections of a Chicano Sociologist," Alfredo Mirande (1988) reflects on the irony of the graduate socialization process that required him to be detached and distant from his research and teaching interests, as well as from the commitment and motivation that led him to sociology:

> My interest in sociology was first sparked by a sociology class which I took as a junior in high school, although I was to learn, subsequently, that, like many others, I had entered sociology for all of the "wrong" reasons. My initial conception of the discipline was that it entailed the study of society with the aim of alleviating societal ills, social inequality, and racism. In graduate school, however, I learned that what I thought was sociology was social work and/or political activism, not sociology. Sociology, according to my mentors, was the detached scientific study of society; objective, value neutral, and universal. (p. 356)

The women we interviewed articulated similar linkages between political and social commitments:

> The reason I chose sociology was that after I got out of high school I worked for some social welfare organizations. One of them I worked for was a federally funded program that was called "Model Cities." I became very excited about the idea of making social and structural changes that made a difference in people's lives.

The impetus behind these women's decisions to pursue a Ph.D. in sociology often accounts for their resistance to mainstream sociology. Students who entered graduate programs with specific interests in research topics related to their communities resisted adopting distant and aloof professional roles. They manifested their resistance by challenging research and theories about communities of color that they perceived as blaming the victim. As noted earlier, one student described the reaction of the Puerto Rican graduate students to a course using Lewis's "culture of poverty" paradigm to explain the Latino community as insulting. Unlike the detached sociologist, these students were powerfully motivated by community identity and loyalty. For example, one Black woman challenged the interpretation of Black residential patterns presented in a study discussed in the seminar. Her professor argued that the researcher's false assumptions were not grounds to discredit the study:

> That's the difference between him and me. He's White and accustomed to reading things like this that White people write about Black people all the time, and he buys into these mythologies. Well I don't buy that. Because as an African American I've decided I'm going to define myself and not going to be confined by White people's definitions any more. I said, "You don't have to take this article out but at least put a disclaimer on this." He tried to say he didn't know enough about urban sociology to say that was false. I said, "I don't know enough about urban sociology to disclaim the rest of the article, but I know enough about Black people to say that the premise is false."

When students compare the literature and rhetoric on diversity with the actual practices in their departments, they notice contradictions between theory and practice. These contradictions highlight what they perceive as their own contradictory position both in the department and in the discipline. Thus, though sociology departments universally claim a commitment to issues of diversity, when students arrive they frequently perceive that "diversity" means that their physiological presence in the institution is all that is important. Their individual perspectives, community backgrounds, and analyses that shed light on issues of diversity are less valued. In a dialectical reversal, instead of applying mainstream sociological knowledge to the analysis of their community, students turned their community backgrounds into perspectives from which to criticize department practices:

> I think that there's a real lack of living up to what we say we stand for. Like we're concerned about race and gender and social class. But the everyday operation of the program, what we teach, doesn't reflect that. I think the classes that we teach should bring out the perspective of people of different races and social classes and you don't find that. I think that in putting together the course readings it should be incumbent on teachers to find that research out there, no matter how sparse it might be, that brings in the minority perspective and brings in the class perspective. I don't see that done very much.

Another form of students' resistance was the application of a sociological analysis to their own everyday experiences in graduate school. As their sociological imaginations developed, students became more aware of the social dynamics in the hidden curriculum that reproduce social inequality. Developing a critical perspective helped students identify contradictions and avoid internalizing conflict as a personal failing. In the following discussion, a student of color reflects on the privileged position held by another member of her cohort:

> I'd go home and think, you know, is it just me? Is it just that I'm really competitive? Is it just that maybe I don't have anything to say? And it wasn't until my third year when I was doing a writing seminar where we would evaluate one another's work and I actually looked at this person's work and realized, no, I wasn't all wrong. You know, a lot of what he was saying was really fluff and it wasn't rigorous. But the fact that he'd been given the floor over and over and over again had [validated him]. . . . It really pissed me off because there was this incredible irony of being in sociology and having the professor and graduate students there ignore the social dynamics of the classroom and how they were affecting us. And I felt frustrated because people who I thought should have been up in arms about it just sort of, you know, blamed themselves or talked about, you know, their own fears about being in graduate school and they didn't look at the sociological implications of what was going on in the department.

Students recognized that the field is changing and research in the area of race and gender has had an impact on the discipline. In evaluating the kind of training they were offered in the program, students identified the limitations and tried to broaden narrow definitions of traditional sociology. For instance, one woman who had first-hand experience with sociology outside the United States noted the shortcomings of a department where the emphasis was solely on quantitative and positivistic approaches:

> It's very much numbers. No critical analysis. No critical thinking. No profound analysis of matters. It was basically this is variable A, variable B — make association among them and that's it. That's not the kind of sociology I like. I went to school in [another country] and I went to a Catholic university there. And it was much more critical. And much more European also. We did study Merton and all the functionalist North American sociology; but we also studied a lot of other schools of thought. Here it was like we rarely saw something different. It was very conservative quite frankly. Very, very conservative.

Students were aware of the growing interest in race and ethnicity in disciplines outside sociology. Resistance to the dominant paradigms frequently involved taking actions to change the curriculum. One strategy was to bring in outside speakers and organize colloquia. Sometimes it was necessary to protest the spending of funds to duplicate what was already offered in the curriculum.

A common resistance strategy was to seek out and enroll in classes outside of their department where they could find the new literature and approaches to the study of race and gender: "I was very frustrated in terms of their curriculum. In order to take a course on race and ethnicity I had to go outside the department." Ethnic Studies, Women's Studies, and International Studies were identified as important adjuncts to Ph.D. programs in sociology. Unlike their home departments, these interdisciplinary programs were more receptive to critical theory, alternative paradigms, and social action research. They were not perceived as undercutting students' interests in race and gender.

An interesting example of someone developing creative alternatives was a student who found that the competition in the department made access to grant information difficult. She developed her own database and made it available to other students of color in the program:

> What I did in my third or fourth year was basically to get together with some of the other minority students who were interested in this and gave them all my [grant and fellowship] files. Basically I said to them, go copy as much as you need to copy, because they were starting from like below ground zero. So I shared my information with them and basically every conference we go to that has anything with grants, I put it in their boxes. So it's kind of a one-way flow from me to them. And I've been doing that now for about three years with them. I also clip and put things in my other colleagues' mailboxes. If I think it's a grant that's for women's issues [related to particular areas] I put it in their boxes.

Several of the women advocated taking more aggressive action in demanding equity in the department, particularly in the allocation of teaching and research assistantships. Others offered incoming women of color students advice on obtaining all the assistance needed to succeed in the competitive and hostile environment of the department: "Push for a better offer. Do not just accept a department's offer but try to get what you need to survive in graduate school."

CONCLUSION

The consequence of the hidden curriculum in graduate school is that it reproduces mainstream or traditional sociology. As Michael Apple (1980) wrote, the reproductive function "posit(s) a mirror image relationship between the norms and values taught in school and those 'required' in the economy" (p. 47). Clearly, reproduction by itself is an inadequate concept that allows little room for change in the discipline and ignores the students' ability to resist. As we have seen, forces external to the discipline — that is, court-ordered integration and requirements for gender equity, affirmative action legislation, and open enrollments — have brought new students and new ideas into universities and sociology departments. These newcomers chafed under the hidden curriculum, found its demands discriminatory, and rejected much of its discipline when it did not clearly relate to furthering their intellectual development or practical skills. In bringing their sociological imaginations to bear on their own experience in graduate school and seeking alternatives, their resistance helped change sociology, not just in theory and methods, but in the functioning of the hidden curriculum. In a very real sense, the women's telling of their stories, as well as our analysis and publication of them, is part of this resistance. It is a lifting of veils to make visible what was hidden.

There is much more work to be done on these issues. While it is far beyond the scope of this article, we might assert that the creation of new academic departments, including Women's Studies and Ethnic Studies, and the development of academic theories and paradigms including elements of feminism, critical race theory, and critical pedagogy, were as much resistance to the hidden curriculum in mainstream departments as they were attempts to open the official curriculum to include women and people of color and those from working-class backgrounds.

Strategies for achieving educational equity in higher education require an understanding of the barriers and obstacles presented by the hidden curriculum. The graduate students we interviewed indicate that it is essential to closely examine informal structures of control, including the treatment of race in the curriculum, the validation of paradigms deemed "appropriate" or "mainstream," intellectual support for specific ideas and perspectives, the awarding of teaching and research assistantships, mentoring, the stigmatization of students of color as "affirmative action cases," the maintenance of double standards, and the privileging of certain cultural capital and perspectives at the expense of others. Perhaps even more than academic performance, these factors stratify educational opportunities for students of color and may force these students to leave the discipline or higher education.

Given the current attacks on affirmative action programs and the continuing underrepresentation of people of color on higher education faculties, faculty of all races and genders need to recognize and root out the strong elements of the hidden curriculum in college and graduate school. If we are to preserve a diverse student body, we must help individual students survive and thrive in school. To accomplish this task, it is important to divest graduate programs of the vestiges of the inappropriate and discriminatory practices that lie hidden in the curriculum and professionalization processes.

NOTES

1. For instance, see Paul Willis's (1977) influential work, *Learning to Labour: How Working Class Kids Get Working Class Jobs.*
2. Qualitative methods are particularly appropriate for studying the operation of the hidden curriculum. As Elizabeth Vallance (1980) noted: "The state of mind required by inquiry into the hidden curriculum is by definition open to unknowns and attuned to the subtle and irregular qualities of schooling. Much the same can be said of qualitative inquiry methods" (p. 138).
3. As one of two sociologists of color serving on the Social Issues Committee of SWS in 1989, Dr. Romero volunteered to conduct a survey of women of color graduate students. The survey on women of color faculty was never completed. Preliminary findings were presented at the 1990 SWS annual meeting. Findings were also presented at the meetings of the American Sociological Association, the Society for the Study of Social Problems, and Research on Women in Education. The paper presented at Research on Women in Education, "Is That Sociology?: The Accounts of Women of Color Graduate Students in Ph.D. Programs," was later published in Dunlap and Schmuck (1995, pp. 71–85).
4. This was not a random sample. Excerpts are provided here from interviews with a self-selected group of women of color graduate students of sociology. These are extremely articulate, thoughtful women who chose to study sociology, in many cases because of an interest in race, ethnicity, and gender, and a commitment to social justice and social change. They are reflecting on educational experiences that were painful and difficult. Are the incidents they discuss typical? Are there counter examples? There is no way to answer such questions.

5. The sample is fairly consistent with the national data on women of color receiving doctorate degrees in 1991–1992. Of the 1,550 women of color, 53 were Native American, 497 were Asian American, 647 were Black, and 353 were Hispanic (*Chronicle of Higher Education*, 1995, p. 40).

6. In order to assure anonymity, a further breakdown of sample characteristics is not possible, since there are so few women of color graduate students in sociology. All names and places have been changed or omitted.

7. Several national and regional sociological associations have conducted studies on the status of women in the profession. The Committee on the Status of Women of the American Sociological Association (ASA) has written the following reports: "The Treatment of Gender in Sociology" (1985), "Equity Issues for Women Faculty in Sociology Departments" (1985), and "Recommendations on the Recruitment and Retention of Women Sociologists" (1986).The Pacific Sociology Association (PSA) also published several reports on the status of women (Araji & Ihinger-Tallman, 1988; Kulis & Miller, 1988; Nigg & Axelrod, 1981). Students of color, particularly women of color, have not received adequate attention (Blackwell, 1983; Exum, Menges, Watkins, & Berglund, 1984).

8. Laura Rendón (1992) also comments on the devaluation of past experience and knowledge in education.

9. See Bernard C. Rosen and Alan P. Bates (1967) for comments on the attempt to train students to be independent in an authoritarian social structure.

10. In a more recent article, Eric Plutzer (1991) identifies how sociology faculty determine which students are "most likely to succeed" and which are potential failures. His findings suggest that sociologists administer graduate programs in an irrational fashion that counters the established sociological knowledge, and act on a belief in predestination — that is, "some graduate students are members of the elect and predestined for success" (p. 302).

11. "Cultural capital" is a concept with a history in sociology dating back to nineteenth-century Weberian descriptions of the social world as composed of status groups. The concept was further developed in the conflict theories of Randall Collins (1975). George Farkas (1996) summarized the cultural capital perspective as the recognition that "educational and earnings stratification . . . [result] from credentialing systems wherein the cultural hegemony of middle- and upper-class groups operate through school and workplace reward systems that are only loosely, if at all, tied to actual productivity" (p. 10). In short, the cultural abilities and knowledge of poor, racial/ethnic, and female persons are less valued and rewarded by schools that function not only meritocratically, but also as gatekeepers to privileged status groups. An important study by Annette Lareau (1987) demonstrated how, even when schools seek parental input, the cultural expectations of middle-class teachers clash with cultural capital held by working-class and poor parents. Differences in cultural capital make it difficult or impossible for productive interaction to take place. For example, in his 1988 article "I Never Had a Mentor: Reflections of a Chicano Sociologist," Alfredo Mirande states, "I also had to develop verbal aggressiveness, since this was clearly a valued trait in graduate students" (p. 358).

12. For instance, see Crothers (1991), Egan (1989), and Plutzer (1991).

13. Egan's article is a theoretical view of the self. She writes, "My use of a structural focus leads to descriptions of universities and graduate departments that belong to an 'ideal type'" (p. 201).

14. Recently two sociological journals have devoted special issues to graduate education: *American Sociologist* (1989) and *Teaching Sociology* (1991).

15. In general, we employed the "grounded theory" techniques of Barney Glaser and Anselm Strauss (1967) and Strauss (1987). Initially we performed a content analysis,

coding the transcript using an open coding scheme. Next we examined the emerging categories and used axial coding to further develop the categories. However, we did not aim at a pure form of grounded theory research. The entire enterprise was informed by the fact that we, and apparently many of our research subjects, are conversant with much of the literature of sociology, including Marxism, feminism, conflict theory, and symbolic interactionism. Together and separately, the authors have specialized in issues of race relations and gender, social class and the labor process, critical race theory, sociology of education, critical pedagogy, and the specific literatures on cultural capital and the hidden curriculum. Previous investigations in these areas helped make visible and highlighted the categorical nature of the examples and stories offered by the graduate students.

16. Of course, the lack of integration in the curriculum exists throughout higher education and is *not* exclusive to the discipline of sociology. Describing her undergraduate experience at Barnard, June Jordan (1981) expresses the plight many students of color still find today in academia: "No one ever presented me with a single Black author, poet, historian, personage, or idea, for that matter. . . . Nothing that I learned, here, lessened my feeling of pain, and confusion and bitterness as related to my origins: my street, my family, my friends. Nothing showed me how I might try to alter the political and economic realities underlying our Black condition in white America" (p. 100).

17. Ph.D. programs in ethnic studies and women's studies did not exist in the institutions that many of these women attended. Therefore, the women remained enrolled in sociology programs. They also remained committed to becoming sociologists and transforming the discipline.

18. Of course, many students of color drop out of graduate school, or leave sociology for other programs, and it would be interesting to interview them. In the current study, however, we only interviewed those who had persisted and were succeeding in sociology.

REFERENCES

Aisenberg, N., & Harrington, M. (1988). *Women of academe: Outsiders in the sacred grove.* Amherst: University of Massachusetts Press.

American Sociological Association. (1985). *Equity issues for women faculty in sociology departments.* Washington, DC: Author.

American Sociological Association Committee on the Status of Women in Sociology. (1985). *The treatment of gender in sociology.* Washington, DC: Author.

American Sociological Association. (1986). *Recommendations on the recruitment and retention of women sociologists.* Washington, DC: Author.

Anyon, J. (1980). Social class and the hidden curriculum of work. *Journal of Education, 162,* 67–92.

Apple, M. W. (1971). The hidden curriculum and the nature of conflict. *Interchange, 2,* 27–40.

Apple, M. W. (1980). The other side of the hidden curriculum: Correspondence theories and the labor process. *Journal of Education, 162,* 47–66.

Apple, M. W., & King, N. P. (1977). *What do schools teach?* In R. H. Weller (Ed.), *Humanistic education* (pp. 29–63). Berkeley, CA: McCutchan.

Araji, S. K., & Ihinger-Tallman, M. (1988). *The status of women in the Pacific Sociological Association region: A report from the Status of Women Committee.* Paper presented at the Pacific Sociological Workshop, Las Vegas, NV.

Barnes, D. R. (1986). Transitions and stresses for Black female scholars. In S. Rose (Ed.), *Career guide for women scholars* (pp. 66–77). New York: Springer.

Becker, H. S. (1982). *Art worlds*. Berkeley: University of California Press.

Bergenhenegouwen, G. (1987). Hidden curriculum in the university. *Higher Education, 16,* 535–543.

Blackwell, J. E. (1983). *Networking and mentoring: A study of cross-generational experiences of Blacks in graduate and professional schools*. Atlanta, GA: Southern Education Foundation.

Carter, D., Pearson, C., & Shavlik, D. (1987–1988). Double jeopardy: Women of color in higher education. *Educational Record, 68/69,* 98–103.

Chronicle of Higher Education. (1995). *The almanac of higher education, 42* (Supplement to issue No. 1). Washington, DC: Author.

Clark, B. R. (1960). The "cooling-out" function in higher education. *American Journal of Sociology, 65,* 569–576.

Collins, R. (1975). *Conflict sociology*. New York: Academic Press.

Crothers, C. (1991). The internal structure of sociology departments: The role of graduate students and other groups. *Teaching Sociology, 19,* 333–343.

Dreeben, R. (1968). *On what is learned in school*. Reading, MA: Addison-Wesley.

Dunlap, D. M., & Schmuck, P. A. (Eds.). (1995). *Women leading in education*. Albany: State University of New York Press.

Egan, J. M. (1989). Graduate school and the self: A theoretical view of some negative effects of professional socialization. *Teaching Sociology, 17,* 200–208.

Eitzen, D. S. (1989). The introduction of graduate students to the profession of sociology. *Teaching Sociology, 16,* 279–283.

Everhart, R. B. (1983). *Reading, writing and resistance*. Boston: Routledge & Kegan Paul.

Exum, W., Menges, R. J., Watkins, B., & Berglund, P. (1984). Making it to the top: Women and minority faculty in the academic labor market. *American Behavioral Scientist, 27,* 306–324.

Farkas, G. (1996). *Human capital or cultural capital*. New York: Aldine DeGruyter.

Foster, M. (1991). Constancy, connectedness, and constraints in the lives of African American teachers. *NWSA Journal, 3,* 233–261.

Freire, P. (1985). *Teachers as cultural workers*. Boulder, CO: Westview Press.

Geertz, C. (1973). *The interpretation of cultures*. New York: Basic Books.

Gilkes, C. T. (1982). Successful rebellious professions: The Black woman's professional identity and community commitment. *Psychology of Women Quarterly, 6,* 289–311.

Giroux, H. (1981). Hegemony, resistance, and the paradox of educational reform. *Interchange, 12,* 3–26.

Giroux, H. (1983). Theories of reproduction and resistance in the new sociology of education: A critical analysis. *Harvard Educational Review. 53,* 257–293.

Giroux, H. A. (1988). *Teachers as intellectuals*. Granby, MA: Bergin & Garvey.

Glaser, B. G., & Strauss, A. L. (1967). *The discovery of grounded theory: Strategies for qualitative research*. Chicago: Aldine Press.

Graduate education [Special issue]. (1989). *American Sociologist, 16.*

Graduate education [Special issue]. (1991). *Teaching Sociology, 19*(3).

Granfield, R. (1992). *Making elite lawyers*. New York: Routledge.

Haas, J., & Shaffir, W. (1982). Ritual evaluation of competence. *Work and Occupations, 9,* 131–154.

Hearn, J., & Olzak, S. (1981). The role of college major departments in the reproduction of sexual inequality. *Sociology of Education, 54,* 195–205.

Hood, J. (1985). The lone scholar myth. In M. F. Fox (Ed.), *Scholarly writing and publishing: Issues, problems and solutions* (pp. 111–124). Boulder, CO: Westview Press.

Jackson, P. W. (1968). The daily grind. In P. W. Jackson (Ed.), *Life in classrooms* (pp. 33–37). New York: Holt, Rinehart & Winston.

James, J., & Farmer, R. (Eds.). (1993). *Spirit, space, and survival: African American women in (White) academe*. New York: Routledge.

Jones-Johnson, G. (1988). The victim-bind dilemma of Black female sociologists in academe. *American Sociologists, 19,* 312–322.

Jordan, J. (1981). Note of a Barnard dropout. In J. Jordan (Ed.), *Civil wars* (pp. 96–102). Boston: Beacon Press.

Kleinman, S. (1983). Collective matters as individual concerns, peer culture among graduate students. *Urban Life, 12,* 203–225.

Kulis, S., & Miller, K. A. (1988). Are minority women sociologists in double jeopardy? *American Sociologists, 19,* 323–339.

Lareau, A. (1987). Social class differences in family-school relationships: The importance of cultural capital. *Sociology of Education, 60,* 73–85.

Lewis, O. (1965). *La vida: A Puerto Rican family in the culture of poverty.* New York: Random House.

Mayrl, W. W., & Mauksch, H. O. (1987). The ASA survey of graduate programs: Some problems with unproblematic responses. *American Sociologist, 18,* 11–18.

Mills, C. W. (1959). *The sociological imagination.* New York: Oxford University Press.

Mirande, A. (1988). I never had a mentor: Reflections of a Chicano sociologist. *American Sociologist, 19,* 335–362.

Mortenson, T. G. (1991). *Equality of higher educational opportunity for women, Black, Hispanic and low income students.* Iowa City, IA: American College Testing Program.

Moses, Y. T. (1989). *Black women in academe.* Washington, DC: Association of American Colleges Project on the Status and Education of Women.

Nigg, J., & Axelrod, M. (1981). Women and minorities in the PSA region: Results of the 1979 Survey. *Pacific Sociological Review, 24,* 107–128.

Oakes, J. C. (1985). *Keeping track.* New Haven, CT: Yale University Press.

Padilla, R. V., & Chávez, R. C. (Eds.). (1995). *The leaning ivory tower: Latino professors in American universities.* Albany: State University of New York Press.

Pavalko, M. R., & Holley, J. (1974). Determinants of a professional self-concept among graduate students. *Social Science Quarterly, 55,* 462–477.

Plutzer, E. (1991). The Protestant ethic and the spirit of academia: An essay on graduate education. *Teaching Sociology, 19,* 302–207.

Pruitt, A. S., & Isaac, P. D. (1985). Discrimination in recruitment, admission, and retention of minority graduate students. *Journal of Negro Education, 54,* 526–536.

Rendón, L. (1992). From the barrio to the academy: Revelations of a Mexican American "Scholarship Girl." *New Directions for Community Colleges, 80*(4), 55–64.

Rosen, B. C., & Bates, A. P. (1967). The structure of socialization in graduate school. *Sociological Inquiry, 37,* 71–84.

Roth, J. A. (1955). A faculty conception of success in graduate study. *Journal of Higher Education, 26,* 350–356, 398.

Ryan, W. (1976). *Blaming the victim.* New York: Random House.

Sherlock, B. J., & Morris, R. T. (1967). The evolution of the professional: A paradigm. *Sociological Inquiry, 37,* 27–46.

Strauss, A. L. (1987). *Qualitative analysis for social scientists.* New York: Cambridge University Press.

Trask, H-K. (1993). *From a Native daughter: Colonialism and sovereignty in Hawai'i.* Monroe, ME: Common Courage Press.

Vallance, E. (1973–1974). Hiding the hidden curriculum: An interpretation of the language of justification in nineteenth century educational reform. *Curriculum Theory Network, 4,* 5–21.

Vallance, E. (1980). The hidden curriculum and qualitative inquiry as states of mind. *Journal of Education, 162,* 138–151.

Weiss, C. S. (1981). The development of professional role commitment among graduate students. *Human Relations, 34,* 13–31.

Williams, P. J. (1991). *The alchemy of race and rights: Diary of a law professor.* Cambridge, MA: Harvard University Press.

Willis, P. (1977). *Learning to labour: How working class kids get working class jobs.* Farnborough, Eng.: Saxon House, Teakfield.

Young, T. R. (1974). Transforming sociology: The graduate student. *American Sociologist, 9,* 135–139.

Cornel West on
Heterosexism and Transformation:
An Interview

In the fall of 1995, deep in the midst of shaping and developing a special issue, several *Harvard Educational Review* Editorial Board members had the opportunity to hear philosopher and scholar Dr. Cornel West speak at the Harvard Graduate School of Education. They enthusiastically reported back to us that in his talk, West, who is Professor of Afro-American Studies and of the Philosophy of Religion at Harvard, drew explicit and repeated connections between White supremacy, patriarchy, and heterosexism. At the time, we were searching for an article that would illuminate the deep ties between different forms of oppression in the United States. We envisioned an article that would serve as a bridge from the diverse topics represented within the special issue to broad systems of power, privilege, and domination. Inspired by Dr. West's articulation of the above issues, as well as by his focus on democratic struggles for liberation, we asked him if he would be willing to be interviewed for our special issue.

Dr. West agreed, but he expressed concern that, as a heterosexual, he not displace "any of the gay, lesbian, or transgender voices." He went on to say:

> For me it is a privilege and really a blessing to be part of the issue, because the issue that you're raising is very important. But as you know, it's important as well that one not come in from the outside, as it were. It is important not to push aside any of the voices that come from inside of the movement itself.

It was precisely his respectful concern that compelled us to request an interview with Dr. West. In addition, we found it very powerful, particularly in light of our largely heterosexual readership, that a heterosexual activist and scholar would repeatedly take a strong position against heterosexism. When cast in a way that made clear that this was an opportunity to reach out to other heterosexuals and say to them, "If you're serious about being a democrat or a radical, then this piece of our struggle is essential," West readily agreed to participate.

In this interview with HER Editorial Board members Vitka Eisen and Mary Kenyatta, Cornel West offers a vision of a democratic struggle that is inclusive of lesbian, gay, bisexual, and transgender people. He places heterosexism within the context of capitalism, establishing connections to other forms of oppression. He also reminds us that, as democratic educators, we continually have to examine the

Harvard Educational Review   Vol. 66 No. 2 Summer 1996, 356–367

ways in which we may internalize, and therefore perpetuate, patriarchy and homophobia in our lives and our teaching. West shares some of his personal struggle facing his own homophobia, and he emphasizes the importance of so-called straight people joining their gay and lesbian brothers and sisters in the effort to dismantle heterosexism and other systems of oppression.

We've often heard you speak about the connections among homophobia, patriarchy, and racism. Why do you talk about these issues, and how do you see them linked? And would you also talk about some of the personal challenges you face as a heterosexual Black man, in taking such a vocal stance against heterosexism?

My own understanding of what it means to be a democrat (small d), partly what it means to be a Christian, too, but especially what it means to be a democrat, is that you're wrestling with particular forms of evil.[1] It seems to me that to talk about the history of heterosexism and the history of homophobia is to talk about ways in which various institutions and persons have promoted unjustified suffering and unmerited pain. Hence, the questions become: How do we understand heterosexism? Why is it so deeply seated within our various cultures and civilizations? We could talk primarily about America, but we can talk globally as well. I think it fundamentally has to do with the tendency human beings have to associate persons who are different with degradation, to associate those who have been cast as marginal with subordination and devaluation. So in order to be both morally consistent and politically consistent, I think democrats have to focus on particular forms of unjustified suffering across the board, be it patriarchy, vast economic inequality, White supremacy, or male supremacy. It's just a matter of trying to be true to one's own sense of moral integrity.

You've taken a very visible, very public stance against heterosexism and homophobia. Are there personal challenges for you in taking that stance?

Well, no doubt, no doubt. Any time you offer a serious critique of the systems of power and privilege, be it compulsory heterosexuality, be it White supremacy, or what have you, you're going to catch some hell. There's no doubt, both within the Black community and the Black church, as well as outside, that I tend to catch hell on this issue. There's no doubt about it. But for me, it's fundamentally a matter of trying to highlight the moral ideals that serve as a basis of the critique of homophobic behavior, heterosexism as a whole, as well as their political consequences. I don't think that one can actually engage in serious talk about the fundamental transformation of American society — that is, the corporate elites, the bank elites, the White supremacists, the male supremacists, as well as the heterosexists — without talking about hitting the various forms of evil across the board. The interesting thing is that some of the critiques almost have to take an *ad hominem* form. A person might think, wait a minute, why is he so concerned about homophobia? There must be something going on in his personal life, and so forth.

[1] The term "democrat" (small d) refers to the political philosophy rather the political party.

My view is that I have to recognize deep homophobia inside of me, because I grew up in the Black community, in the Black church, on the Black block, and there's a lot of homophobia in all three sites. So I'm quite candid about the internal struggle that I undergo because of my own homophobic socialization. How do you deal with the feelings of either threat or fear — and, I think, for many homophobes — outright hatred? I don't think I ever, even as a young person, hated gay brothers or lesbian sisters. I think I did associate it early on with something that was alien. And I've often, even in movies, seen lesbian love as very different. I think that, in a patriarchal society, for a man to see two women involved in lesbian activity is less threatening than seeing two men involved in gay activity. When I've seen gay activity on the screen, for example, it does hit me viscerally as very alien and different. That's where my moral struggle comes into play, in terms of acknowledging that difference from my perspective, but not associating it with degradation or disgust. Rather, it is just a particular mode of human expression that I have been taught to associate with degradation. I simply acknowledge it as different, but I don't have to make that connection with degradation, per se. And in doing so, I have been honest with myself. In an interesting way, people say, well, you're so interested in this issue, maybe you've got a secret life or something. And I say, you know, if one is gay or lesbian, one should be proud of it. There's nothing to hide in that regard, it seems to me. And if one isn't gay or lesbian one may just acknowledge that others make certain kinds of choices and have different orientations, and so forth. So-called straight persons can go on about the business of living and still fight an anti-homophobic struggle along with gay and lesbian comrades.

Your earlier comment about the homophobia you witnessed growing up in the Black community reminds me that there's a certain lore about communities of color — not all communities of color, but particularly religious communities of color — that suggest that there is more overt homophobia within these communities than in dominant White communities. Can you speak about this perception? How much of this lore is an attempt on the part of the Right to force divisions where there might be alliances?

Yeah, that's a tough question. That's a very tough question, because degrees of intolerance and tolerance and degrees of hatred and openness are very difficult to measure. I know when I was growing up in the Black community, most people knew that, let's say, the brother who played the organ in the church was a gay brother. People would say, oh, that's so and so's child. You know, he's that way. And they'd just keep moving. There wasn't an attempt to focus on his sexuality; he was an integral part of the community. It wasn't a matter of trying to target him and somehow pester him or openly, publicly degrade him. Those who said he's "that way" didn't believe that way was desirable, but they just figured that's just the way he was, that's just his thing, you know. But one of the ways in which he chose to function was to be part of his community. People knew it, but he just didn't make a big deal out of it.

For me, however, it's very important that even closeted sexuality be something that's seriously interrogated, because it can lead toward a kind of internalized homophobia within gay or lesbian persons themselves. I think you get some of that in the great James Baldwin, in his struggles over whether he wants to be gay in iden-

tity or to highlight his particular sexual orientation as a public feature of his identity. And that's a tough question. But when I was growing up that tended to be the
attitude.

I had always thought that even though homophobia was thick, it was dealt with
in such a way that it did not disunite the Black community because this was a community under siege, dealing with institutional terrorism, Jim Crow, Jane Crow, and
so forth — you had to accent commonality. At the same time, we have seen an increase in so-called gay bashing and lesbian bashing in the country as a whole, including the Black community and other communities of color. Here, of course, as
you get a slow shattering of community, in this case the Black community, then a
lot of the paranoid dispositions become more salient and more visible. One of
those forms is violence against gays and women, and this is also the case when we
consider violence against sisters in the Black community. We've always had that,
but we've seen also an exponential increase in this violence as the community dis-
integrates. So I'm a little reluctant to say that homophobia is actually more rampant in the Black community than it is in the larger White community. My hunch
is that it runs pretty deep in both. But in the past, it was cast in such a way that it
was subordinate to the survival of the Black community as a whole. As that community now undergoes a very, very deep crisis, if not slow dissolution, we see the
scapegoating of the most vulnerable: Black women, gays, and lesbians.

*With highly charged political and moral issues such as sexuality, how do democratic edu-
cators balance a respect for diverse community values with respect for their own democratic ideals, particularly where community values may run counter to them?*

I think it's a tough call. Partly it's just a matter of a certain kind of practical wisdom
because I don't think there are any abstract principles that would allow us to make
various judgments in each case. There are going to be tensions any time you're
dealing with very rich notions of individuality. And by individuality I don't mean
the rugged, ragged, rapacious individualism of American capitalism, but of free
choices that people make that help them make and remake themselves as persons
within a community. Individuality within a community always has a certain kind of
tension. I think as democrats, as radical democrats, it's very important that we
keep alive a subversive memory of critique and resistance; and therefore, when we
talk about sexuality, we understand it as a particular discourse, a particular institutional practice over time and space that has reinforced certain systems of power
and privilege. At the same time, there's a tradition of resistance against that system
of power and privilege.

Foucault and others have pointed out that the very construct of homosexuality
itself comes from the medical community (you know, Westphal's work in 1870),
and, as such, is constituted as a disease, and of course, as a crime, legally and politically.[2] This is a shift from the discourse of sodomy, which was viewed as a sin against
nature. Now this is a very important move because it's an attempt by a set of elites
to exert a certain kind of control over how people view their bodies, what they do
with their bodies, what the state does with their bodies, and how those bodies are

[2] Michel Foucault credits Carl Westphal's 1870 article "Archiv für Neurologie" with presenting the
first medical categorization of homosexuals as a "species" in *History of Sexuality: An Introduction* (New
York: Vintage, 1978/1990), p. 43.

scarred and bruised, internally and externally. But this shift is also connected to other systems of power and privilege, White supremacists, the rule of capital and so on.

What you actually have then is an attempt to keep alive a certain subversive memory for a democrat. For me it's impossible to be a democrat and not have a very deep sense of remembrance of the freedom fighters who came before and what they were up against. What was the nature of the systemic oppression that they were responding to? And at the same time you've got a number of these different traditions, each with its strengths and its weaknesses. You've got the Black freedom struggle that has historically focused on White supremacy; it has not said enough on issues of vast economic inequality, and has hardly said enough when it comes to homophobia and heterosexism. Then you've got a gay/lesbian freedom struggle that has focused primarily on heterosexism and homophobia, and at times has not said enough about White supremacy. I think in the U.S. context there's always tension when it comes to the legacy of White supremacy, which cuts through every tradition of resistance and critique. That's why somebody like Audre Lorde for me was, and in memory is, such a towering figure. It's so rare to have such a deep artist, on the one hand, and a sophisticated political activist on the other. She was also a progressive humanitarian who could speak to the depths of human suffering and pain that cut across the various forms of oppression and create a common space, a radical democratic common space. That doesn't happen too often, it doesn't happen often at all. To think through the notion of difference in such a way that it becomes a source of strength, rather than a set of obstacles and impediments that reinforce our own paranoid disposition, is rare. We all have the paranoid dispositions. For me the important thing, as a Christian, is to recognize that the evil is inside each and every one of us, in part because of that treacherous terrain called history that has shaped us, and socialized us, and acculturated us. Consequently, it's not ever a matter of one group feeling as if they don't have some White supremacy, male supremacy, or homophobia inside of them. Because we've been socialized in the White supremacist, patriarchal society, those residues are there no matter how liberated one thinks one actually is. It's a perennial struggle, and that's one of the reasons why there has to be a collectivity. You have to organize and mobilize to keep each other accountable. That's part of the democratic ethos within radical democratic groups, because we have to prefigure, in some way, the kind of society that we're talking about within our own movement. The only way we deal with these evils inside of us is to keep each other accountable. I'm not sure we ever fully eliminate them. Audre Lorde says, look inside and then name the forms of oppression working therein, and, at the same time, never be paralyzed by them, never be debilitated by them. She's so honest about her internal struggle against oppression.

What do you see as the limits of identity politics and the struggle for democratic ideals, and what are the strengths? How can people mobilize across and through identity politics?

I think identity politics, on the one hand, are inescapable and, on the other hand, still too limited. It's inescapable primarily because we have such underdeveloped class-based politics in America. The power of corporate and bank elites is such that it has made it very difficult for fellow citizens to believe that class-based politics can be sustained in a way that these politics would actually meet head-on the tremendous entrenched power of the rule of capital. Consequently, a person falls back on her/his own particular ethnic, racial, sexual identities as a way of sustaining some critique against this deeply conservative society, in which the rule of capital is almost a precondition for democracy to flower and flourish. On the other hand, we have a society that has been so deeply rooted in White supremacy that it makes it very difficult to talk about class-based politics without talking about just how central race and racism have been in the constitution of American identity, culture, and society.

You get a lot of reductionist formulations from the left about this issue. The argument goes: it's really a class issue, it's got to be just a class issue. To engage in that reductionist formulation is partly an attempt to sidestep the challenge of race when we've had this long history of race-based slavery and race-based Jim Crow.

And so I think identity politics have lost sight of a class-based analysis, which makes it impossible for people to conceive of a fight for the fundamental democratic transformation of American society toward more egalitarian distribution of goods and resources. It's impossible to conceive of that fight without beginning with one's own conception of one's pain and suffering as it relates to the most visible scars. The most visible source of those scars for people of color are White supremacists. For women, it has been patriarchy. For gays and lesbians, it has been heterosexism and homophobia. While beginning there, I think one ultimately has to reach a space where there's some overlapping consensus regarding the way in which these various systems of oppression operate. In the economic sphere, you have to have coalition because the powers that be are so strong that individuals will be crushed. We've seen that over and over and over again. For example, any time a gay or a lesbian activist attempts both to accent the critique of heterosexism and homophobia and then to link them to other oppressions, the powers that be become even more hostile. That is true of the Black movement, and it is true of the feminist and womanist movement. Democracy — radical democracy in all of its forms — tries to accent the variety of institutional and individual forms of evil and constitutes the most formidable threat to the powers that be. Very much so. And the powers that be are quite serious. No doubt about that. They've got a lot of resources at their disposal to crush people. No doubt.

The question about identity politics is linked to a question about destructive divisions between liberation struggles for people of color and liberation struggles for gays and lesbians. The hierarchy of oppressions — "my oppression is worse than your oppression" — gets in the way of coalition building. What can be done to foster coalition?

I think the fundamental issue is the difficulty of forging bonds of trust between various communities of resistance. The reason why it's difficult to generate those bonds of trust is, I think, precisely because, at the psychocultural level, the forms of fear and insecurity and anxiety associated with others come from the prevailing systems that socialize us in a way that reinforces the fears and anxieties and insecurities associated with the "other"; for example, gay, lesbian, Black, brown, red, and so forth. The powers that be know that as long as there are no bonds of trust or very, very weak bonds of trust, there won't be any effective coalition-building or any substantive alliances among communities of resistance. And they're right. The only way bonds of trust can be forged is when you have enough courageous activists, so-called leaders and so-called followers, who are willing to violate the prevailing lines of demarcation that are in place. But to violate and transgress those lines of demarcation means that those persons have to struggle deeply within themselves to wrestle honestly with their own insecurities and the anxiety that they associate with other people. There's a certain kind of existential honesty and intellectual candor that must go with political courage, both with leadership and so-called "followership," if we're ever going to forge the kinds of bonds of trust necessary to create the coalitions that can present at least a substantive challenge to the powers that be. There's still no guarantee even after the bonds of trust are forged — they've got armies and tanks and a whole lot of other things — but at least the chances are better.

What does that candor look like?

The candor? Well, it's painful, it's very painful. When I start with the homophobia in me, it's painful. One is ashamed of oneself in terms of how one has been socialized. How does one attempt to overcome it? I would think in White brothers and sisters, when they actually look at the White supremacy in them, it's got to be painful if they're serious democrats, if they're serious about struggle. You overcome it by not just wrestling with it, but also by fusing with others in a context that will keep you accountable in such a way that you will remain vulnerable and, hence, open for growth and development, rather than simply debilitated, paralyzed, and therefore frozen. I think this is true in a variety of the different contexts that we've talked about: the patriarchy inside of us, the class arrogance inside of us, and the homophobia inside of us.

All of that requires a certain level of political courage. So where's the base?

That's very true. I think the political courage is based on a profound commitment. If you're fundamentally committed to dealing with the suffering and pain, you will be willing to put yourself through some processes. One sign of commitment, for me, is always the degree to which one is willing to be self-critical and self-questioning, because that's a sign that you're serious about generating the conditions for the possibility of overcoming the suffering that you're after. Commitment is fundamentally about focusing on the suffering and trying to overcome it, trying to understand where it comes from, its causes, its effects. At the same time, it is about trying to prepare oneself to sacrifice and to serve in such a way that one attempts to overcome the suffering.

In addition to that, there is a serious intellectual dimension, and that has to do, again, with historical consciousness and that dangerous memory, that subversive memory. Because one of the ways in which one views oneself in process is to realize that you're part of a larger process and tradition that has been going on, and that persons who have raised the same kind of questions you raise struggle in their own ways. You can see it in their lives, their growth, their development, and their conscienticization. It is a complex and a perennial process, but it's worth it. I think one of the things that we have to convey is that even given all the pain and suffering associated not just with being victimized, but also with being agents against that victimization, is that there's also a deep joy and ecstasy in struggle. It is a desirable way of being in the world because it does, in fact, give you a sense of meaning and purpose. It gives you a sense of camaraderie, connectedness, and relatedness. And a decadent civilization such as our own suffers from what Arthur Miller called the disease of unrelatedness, where people quest for relations and intimacy, and suffer a lack of community and solidarity. It's just a spiritually impoverished way of being in the world. My good friend Stanley Hauerwas says that capitalism tends to produce rather s-h-i-t-t-y people, and he's absolutely right. He's absolutely right. Non-market values of love and care and service and laughter and joy run counter to that seriousness of maximizing personal preferences and maximizing profits. It's just a very impoverished way of being human, you see. I think that one of the things we democrats, radical democrats, have to acknowledge is this joy and ecstasy in pain-ridden struggles. So you get this fascinating juxtaposition of the joy and the pain and the despair and the hope all linked together. But that's what it begins with anyway.

Living out paradox . . .

That's exactly right. Living in time and space, and that's where for me, the Christian perspective comes in, you see. To my mind, the best of Christianity has been that of a quest to be an existential democrat. See, what the Palestinian Jew named Jesus was all about was, "I'm going to overturn various forms of hierarchy that stand in the way of being connected with you compassionately." You see? And so the common eating, wherein all hierarchies of cuisine are called into question. Everybody come. Everybody use your hands. The same was true of free healing.

The ruling elite in the Roman Empire had to put him to death for a political crime. Why? Because he went straight to the temple. The temple was the center of life. And he turned the tables on the money lenders. Why? Because this market activity, this buying and selling, was getting in the way of a loving, compassionate, sympathetic, empathetic relation with human beings. And you know, he knew he was in trouble; he was in deep trouble. He's got the Roman elites. He's got the top slice of Jewish aristocracy, he's violating their laws and he's speaking to their working classes, right there in the midst of the exploitation of the peasants occurring there across the board, among Jews and non-Jews. So you get this particular Jewish figure who comes in and reforms a dominant tradition of Judaism, provides a critique of the Roman Empire, and ends up on a cross. And his followers come up with a narrative that says that cross is based on his blood that flows, which is that pain and suffering. But love still seems to be piercing through, even at a moment when it seems God is silent and the good is impotent. It still seems to pierce through. And for democrats, existential democrats, that's all we have. The question is: How do we keep that love piercing through our communities in our attempts to create full solidarity? To keep alive traditions of resistance and critique, so that from Stonewall in June 1969, a high moment, a transformation of consciousness, a certain tradition has been kept alive that had been inchoate, but now it's consolidated in a new kind of way, you see.[3] There's this wonderful book by Robert Goss, called *Jesus Acted Up,* that talks about this conception of God, love-making, and just doing, in light of this tradition that I'm talking about.[4] It's one of the most powerful statements that I've read that links my own conception of what it means to be an existential democrat and a radical democrat from the Christian point of view, to the context of the gay/lesbian liberation movement. But Christians have no monopoly on this. The questions are: How do I endure compassionately? How do I continue to bring critique to bear in a loving way with no naive utopian notions that somehow things are going to get better without struggle, or that somehow struggle itself can produce perfectibility, but still be sustained in the midst of very, very dark and difficult times? And, of course, secular traditions have as much access to that compassionate love as religious traditions do, just as religious and secular traditions also bastardize and reinforce systemic oppression.

So how do you reconcile your Christianity with the contemporary Christianity that says love the sinner, hate the sin, when sin is read as "queer"?

Well, you do have to go back to the various claims to authority that are invoked. That means going back to the scripture, going back to the church fathers, and looking at all of the various ways in which the richness of Christianity has been so thoroughly debased and bastardized in the name of promoting forms of unjustified suffering. For example, in the scripture itself, when one actually looks at the nine references to so-called homosexuality or sodomy, most of them allude to male, same-sex sexual activities — there is only one reference to female. And part of these references are to tribal proscriptions, and part of them refer to male prostitution within Canaanite cults vis-à-vis Judaism. But, at the same time, there are deeply patriarchal, as well as homophobic, elements shot through those who wrote the text. That homophobia has to be teased out as well, in light of the claims of mercy and the claims of justice that are also in the text. As such, the text itself, of course, is polyvalent; it is ambiguous in that regard. For example, the Apostle Paul is concerned about lust and concerned about dehumanized relationships — no matter whether gay or lesbian, or so-called straight. This makes good sense. You want to treat each other as ends rather than means. There's no doubt about it. But, on the other hand, Paul himself is shot through with deeply patriarchal and homophobic sensibilities, being the person he was in his particular time. Now, of course, what's interesting is that most of the religious Right, and the religious persons who use scripture to justify homophobia, don't like to admit that Jesus is not only silent on the issue, but he goes about engaging in forms of touch and intimate relation, not sexual that we know of, but in intimate relation in the best sense of sensual, across the board, from Mary to Lazarus, you see. People have said, well, if homosexuality is such a burning issue, how come Jesus doesn't say anything about it? Because if he did, it would have been at least constituted within the writ-

[3] Patrons of the gay and lesbian Stonewall bar in New York City revolted against ongoing police harassment in June of 1969. This rebellion is commonly used to mark the birth of the contemporary lesbian and gay liberation movement in the United States.

[4] Robert Goss, *Jesus Acted Up: A Gay and Lesbian Manifesto* (San Francisco: HarperCollins, 1993).

ings of the synoptic gospels, you see. And that's very upsetting, very upsetting indeed to right-wing Christian brothers and sisters!

You could catch hell for this one too.

If Jesus was proclaiming a certain kind of love-centered state of existence that is impinging upon the space and time in which we live, impinging upon history, and if this issue of homosexuality and homoeroticism was such a fundamental sin, he certainly would have highlighted it. And so again, what we get, as in so many other cases, is an attempt to project various conceptions of the gospel that followed after the life and death and resurrection of Jesus, in an attempt to reinforce the very thing that he himself was fighting against. That goes from empire, to vast economic inequality, to the good Samaritan. My God, people don't realize how subversive that was in his day. That's like treating "niggers," and gays and lesbians, and so forth as if they're really part of the family. Now you see, that's just too big a challenge for most Christians who are holding on to such thin and impoverished conceptions of the gospel. And yet, if Jesus would come back and say that the good Samaritan in the latter part of the twentieth century was treating these so-called niggers, and treating these gays and lesbians, and treating these poor White brothers, whom you associate with trash, as part of the family, he would then reveal the depths of their idolatry. He would show that, in fact, what they're really tied to is a set of idols rather than that blood that flowed at that cross from the body of Jesus. It is a very important dialogue in which I think people like Peter Gomes and others have played a very important role: highly visible persons of integrity, who bring critique to bear on this particular form of evil.[5]

The last question that we have for you is, what do you think a lesbian and gay struggle brings to the struggle for a radical democracy?

There's a new dimension that gay brothers and lesbian sisters bring to the struggle, and that is a conception of the erotic linked to bodies that forces us to accent the cultural as well as the political and economic dimensions of our radical democratic movement. You see, America itself, of course, begins with indigenous peoples being dispossessed of their land, the subordination of indigenous peoples, and hence an attempt to create a Puritanically based conception of a nation with a city on a hill that's special and exceptional. Since the very beginning, Americans have been very, very uneasy with their bodies, and have associated the erotic with the different, the other, the alien. That attempt to escape from one's body and to be open to the variety of different pleasures that can flow from that body has always been associated with anarchy and disorder. This Puritanical culture cuts across race and class and region in America; and even though it has undergone a fundamental transformation, it's still around. Even when you had a Marxist-based movement, they didn't want to talk about the erotic; the Communist Party was often as Puritanical as the YMCA. The big difference was that they allowed for so-called cross-racial relations, which was subversive, culturally subversive. But it still wasn't as subversive as allowing the erotic itself to play a fundamental role. It is

[5] The Rev. Peter Gomes is Minister in Harvard Memorial Church and Plummer Professor of Christian Morals at Harvard Divinity School.

partly because the erotic itself has this Dionysian energy that overflows beyond the rational. In that regard, the erotic offers a much deeper critique of radicalisms that are linked to the Enlightenment. To be a serious gay and lesbian activist, or to have learned from gay and lesbian liberation movements, is to engage at this level of a critique of Enlightenment sensibility thinking that it's all about rational control and a rational project. I'm not trashing reason, or trashing the rational. However, the erotic forces us to acknowledge that our radicalism ought to be much more open and much more self-critical. Now there's a sense in which the Black movement brought this to bear as well, with the crucial role of the body, partly as a result of an African culture that is much less uncomfortable with the body than a Puritanical one. But, even the African and Afro-American traditions did not accent the degree to which the erotic could be found in same-sex relationships. And that, to me, is a crucial contribution, and also to someone like myself, a challenge, a crucial challenge. Here again, Audre Lorde and others have noted the ways in which the erotic can be empowering and ennobling, enabling and ennobling, and can actually release in us energies that, I think in the end, are indispensable for struggle because they also become forces for hope in a situation in which there is not a lot of hope.

The interesting question is the relationship between the ethical and the erotic. The erotic without the ethical can become just thoroughly licentious in the most flat hedonistic sense. But the erotic fused with the ethical means there is respect for the other, and that respect for the other also means being attentive to the needs of the other given their erotic energies. These kinds of issues seem to me to be fundamental ones because, of course, they affect every relationship. I mean, even in friendships that are nonsexual, there's an erotic dimension. And as teachers of students we know there's an erotic dimension, but it has got to be severed from any use of power for subordination, sexual pleasure, sexual manipulation, and so forth. But if one is honest in one's own humanity and is concerned with a qualitative relation with any significant other, I think one has to acknowledge that there is an erotic dimension. And it's precisely this dimension, among others, but especially within this dimension, that I think gay and lesbian movements have made a major, major advance in radical thought and in radical action.

Thank you so much for contributing to this special issue on lesbians, gays, bisexuals, and transgender people and education. We acknowledge your courage and integrity, and we appreciate your commitment to a democratic struggle for social transformation that includes lesbians, gays, bisexuals, and transgender people as well as all other oppressed people.

Using a Chicana Feminist Epistemology in Educational Research

DOLORES DELGADO BERNAL

> Schools . . . presuppose and legitimate particular forms of history, community, and authority. . . . The question is what and whose history, community, knowledge, and voice prevails? Unless this question is addressed, the issues of what to teach, how to teach, how to engage our students, and how to function as intellectuals becomes removed from the wider principles that inform such issues and practices. (Giroux, 1992, p. 91)

Epistemological concerns in schools are inseparable from cultural hegemonic domination in educational research. The way educational research is conducted contributes significantly to what happens (or does not happen) in schools. In education, what is taught, how it is taught, who is taught, and whose fault it is when what is taught is not learned are often manifestations of what is considered the legitimate body of knowledge. For Chicanas, this is not merely an epistemological issue, but one of power, ethics, politics, and survival.[1] Employing a Chicana feminist epistemology in educational research thus becomes a means to resist epistemological racism (Scheurich & Young, 1997) and to recover untold histories.

In this article, I describe a Chicana epistemological perspective by providing an example of my research, which places Chicanas as central subjects and provides a forum in which Chicanas speak and analyze their stories of school resistance and grassroots leadership. I draw from the strong traditions of Black, Native American, and Chicana feminists in an attempt to articulate a Chicana feminist epistemology in educational research that reflects my history and that of the women I write about, a unique history that arises from the social, political, and cultural conditions of Chicanas. Most feminists of color recognize that gender, race, class, and sexual orientation — not gender alone — determine the allocation of power and the nature of any individual's identity, status, and circumstance (Collins, 1986; hooks, 1989; Hurtado, 1989; Pesquera & Segura, 1993). Therefore, "endarkened" feminist epistemologies are crucial, as they speak to the failures of traditional patriarchal and liberal educational scholarship and examine the intersection of race, class, gender, and sexuality.[2] Endarkened epistemologies in general, and Chicana feminism in particular, inform my perspective.

Harvard Educational Review Vol. 68 No. 4 Winter 1998, 555–582

I first review briefly the failure of traditional mainstream educational scholarship and liberal feminist scholarship to provide a useful paradigm to examine the realities of working-class Chicana students. Second, I outline characteristics of a Chicana feminist epistemology by drawing from the work of Chicana scholars in various disciplines. Next, I use the work of Anselm Strauss and Juliet Corbin (1990) to describe four sources of what I call "cultural intuition" — that is, the unique viewpoints Chicana scholars bring to the research process. In doing so, I provide examples of my own cultural intuition as it relates to my research. In the last sections of this article, I clarify what I mean by a Chicana feminist epistemology and cultural intuition by describing an oral history study that examined a specific example of Chicana students' oppositional behavior as an act of school resistance and grassroots leadership (Delgado Bernal, 1997).[3] I demonstrate how, although not specifically articulated at the time of my study, my research was guided by my own cultural intuition and a Chicana feminist epistemology.

THE FAILURE OF LIBERAL EDUCATIONAL SCHOLARSHIP

Gender, ethnic, and class oppression contribute to the unique position of working-class Chicana students, yet liberal educational scholarship has failed to provide a useful paradigm to examine this intersection. For example, theories that attempt to understand how schools replicate the social relationships and attitudes needed to sustain the existing relations in a capitalist society have traditionally focused on White, working-class male students and ignored the role of female students (Bowles & Gintis, 1976). The goal of school resistance literature has been to better understand the role of agency in the process of social reproduction; however, most early studies are also grounded in a traditional, patriarchal epistemology that focuses on White working-class males and does not fully explain the resistance of female students (MacLeod, 1987; Willis, 1977). Theories of cognitive development (Piaget, 1952, 1954) still espoused in many teacher education and educational psychology programs are normed on the behaviors of White middle-class male students, and ignore or are misapplied to students of any other identities. Historically, traditional mainstream educational scholarship has not addressed the influence of gender, race/ethnicity, class, and sexuality on education policy and practice.

Most liberal feminist scholarship has also failed to provide a useful paradigm to examine the gender, ethnic, and class oppression that contribute to the unique positions of working-class Chicana students. Liberal feminist scholarship gives primacy to the domination of patriarchy without seriously addressing how institutional and cultural differences based on sexism, racism, and classism create a different range of choices and options for Chicanas (Zambrana, 1994). Another problematic position of liberal feminist scholarship is the notion that an analysis should begin with the commonalities of women's experience. By only looking at commonalities based on gender and omitting issues of race/ethnicity or class, one may overlook how institutional and cultural structures constrain and enable different groups of women differently. For example, very little is known about the educational mobility of women of color in general, and Chicanas in particular. Until recently, the educational paths of Chicanas were rarely explored. Today there are studies that have investigated the barriers to education experienced by Chicanas

(Gándara, 1982; Segura, 1993; Vásquez, 1982), the marginality of Chicanas in higher education (Cuádraz, 1996), and in the college choice and resistance of Chicanas (Talavera-Bustillos, 1998). These studies go beyond the commonalities of women's experience and examine how family backgrounds, school practices, male privilege, and class and ethnic discrimination shape Chicanas' educational experiences and choices. More specifically, Denise Segura (1993) found that teachers' and counselors' actions channeled Chicanas into nonacademic programs offering a lower quality of instruction, which restricted their range of life chances and options. Segura and other Chicana scholars address the shortcomings of liberal educational scholarship by embracing a Chicana feminist epistemology that examines Chicanas' experiences in relation to an entire structure of domination. Although it is impossible in this article to describe all the nuances of a Chicana epistemology or its evolution, in the next section I outline some of the defining characteristics of a Chicana feminist epistemology.

A CHICANA FEMINIST EPISTEMOLOGY

The relationship between methodology and a researcher's epistemological orientation is not always explicit, but is inevitably closely connected. Sandra Harding (1987) makes a distinction between epistemology, methodology, and method that is helpful in defining a Chicana feminist epistemology. "Method" generally only refers to techniques and strategies for collecting data. Although early feminist arguments defended qualitative approaches to studying and understanding women's lives over quantitative approaches, feminists today have reconsidered the false dichotomy of qualitative and quantitative methods (Maynard, 1994). Though quantitative methods are limited, both methods have been used in Chicana feminist research (e.g., Delgado-Gaitan, 1993; Flores-Ortiz, 1991; Pardo, 1990; Pesquera & Segura, 1990; Soldatenko, 1991), and as numerous educational researchers and feminists have pointed out, both methods have been used to objectify, exploit, and dominate people of color (Fine, 1994; Kelly, Burton, & Regan, 1994; Lather, 1991). A decision of whether to use qualitative or quantitative methods primarily depends on the topic and the research questions asked. Therefore, what becomes crucial in a Chicana feminist epistemology goes beyond quantitative versus qualitative methods, and lies instead in the methodology employed and in whose experiences and realities are accepted as the foundation of knowledge.

Methodology provides both theory and analysis of the research process, how research questions are framed, and the criteria used to evaluate research findings (Harding, 1987). Therefore, a Chicana methodology encompasses both the position from which distinctively Chicana research questions might be asked and the political and ethical issues involved in the research process. Liberal feminists have argued that what distinguishes feminist research from other forms of research is "the questions we have asked, the way we locate ourselves within our questions, and the purpose of our work" (Kelly, 1988, p. 6). However, these feminists (as well as mainstream scholars and Chicano male scholars) have too often failed to ask questions that analyze the interrelationships between classism, racism, sexism, and other forms of oppression, especially from Chicanas' perspectives. Liberal feminist research has insisted "on its political nature and potential to bring about change in women's lives" (Maynard, 1994, p. 16), yet this research has not addressed the lives of Chicanas.

Instead, it has been Chicana scholars who have challenged the historical and ideological representation of Chicanas, relocated them to a central position in the research, and asked distinctively Chicana feminist research questions, all important characteristics of a Chicana feminist epistemology (e.g., Alarcón et al., 1993; de la Torre & Pesquera, 1993; Flores-Ortiz, 1993; Mora & Del Castillo, 1980; Pérez, 1993; Romero, 1989; Zavella, 1993). By shifting the analysis onto Chicanas and their race/ethnicity, class, and sexuality, scholars are able to address the shortcomings of traditional patriarchal and liberal feminist scholarship (Castañeda, 1993; Castillo, 1995; Pardo, 1998; Pérez, 1993; Ruiz, 1998; Trujillo, 1993), thereby giving voice to Chicana experiences and bringing change to their lives. For example, Yvette Flores-Ortiz (1998) points to the need for and begins the process of creating a Chicana psychology. She points out that "the theory and practice of psychology have subjugated Chicanas by measuring their development, personality, and mental health against a male white upper-class model" (p. 102). Even feminist psychology that challenges patriarchal assumptions subsumes Chicanas under the variable of gender, and leaves them appearing deficient or dysfunctional when compared to White middle-class women. Flores-Ortiz's theoretical framework for a Chicana psychology relocates Chicanas to a central position and is informed by her twenty years as a clinical psychologist and her experience of immigration to the United States. Lara Medina's (1998) research documents the voices of how twenty-two Chicanas learned to substitute "patriarchal religion with their own cultural knowledge, sensibilities, and sense of justice" (p. 190). Her research challenges the spiritual and ideological representation of Chicanas in religion by asking how Chicanas re-create traditional cultural practices and look to non-Western philosophies as part of an ongoing process of spirituality. These and other Chicana scholars embrace and further develop a Chicana feminist epistemology by researching the lives and experiences of Chicanas, and framing their research questions in ways that give voice to these women. Inés Hernández-Avila (1995) speaks candidly about the importance of this kind of scholarship, and though a Chicana feminist epistemology may be unsettling for those operating within traditional research epistemologies, she affirms its importance in the academy:

> When I and other Native American women are central as subjects — as sovereign subjects — we often unsettle, disrupt, and sometimes threaten other people's, particularly many white people's, white scholars', white women feminists' sense of self as subjects. That may not have been my or our primary motivations, but it is necessarily inherent in Native women's claiming our right to speak for ourselves. (p. 494)

Epistemology involves the nature, status, and production of knowledge (Harding, 1987). Therefore, a Chicana epistemology must be concerned with the knowledge about Chicanas — about who generates an understanding of their experiences, and how this knowledge is legitimized or not legitimized. It questions objectivity, a universal foundation of knowledge, and the Western dichotomies of mind versus body, subject versus object, objective truth versus subjective emotion, and male versus female. In this sense, a Chicana epistemology maintains connections to indigenous roots by embracing dualities that are necessary and complementary qualities, and by challenging dichotomies that offer opposition without reconciliation. This notion of duality is connected to Leslie Marmon Silko's (1996) observation of a traditional Native American way of life: "In this universe there is no absolute good or absolute bad; there are only balances and harmonies that ebb and flow" (p. 64).

A Chicana feminist standpoint also acknowledges that most Chicanas lead lives with significantly different opportunity structures than men (including Chicano males) and White women. Patricia Hill Collins (1986) points out that Black feminists (similar to Chicana feminists) rarely describe the behavior of women of color without paying attention to the opportunity structures shaping their lives. Thus, adopting a Chicana feminist epistemology will expose human relationships and experiences that are probably not visible from a traditional patriarchal position or a liberal feminist standpoint. Within this framework, Chicanas become agents of knowledge who participate in intellectual discourse that links experience, research, community, and social change. Adela de la Torre and Beatríz Pesquera (1993) comment on this tradition, which places Chicanas as speaking subjects:

> Rooted in the political climate of the late 1960s and early 1970s, our scholarship, like other currents of dissent, is a Chicana critique of cultural, political, and economic conditions in the United States. It is influenced by the tradition of advocacy scholarship, which challenges the claims of objectivity and links research to community concerns and social change. It is driven by a passion to place the Chicana, as speaking subject, at the center of intellectual discourse. (p. 1)

While acknowledging the diversity and complexity of Chicanas' relationships and experiences, we must also recognize that, as an indigenous/mestiza-based cultural group, our experiences are different from those of African Americans and Native Americans in the United States. A Chicana feminist epistemology is informed by and shares characteristics of endarkened feminist epistemologies (e.g., examinations of the influence of race, class, gender, and sexuality on opportunity structures), but is different from the "Black Feminist Thought" of Collins (1991) or the intertribal discourses of Elizabeth Cook-Lynn (1996) and Marmon Silko (1996). A unique characteristic of a Chicana feminist epistemology is that it also validates and addresses experiences that are intertwined with issues of immigration, migration, generational status, bilingualism, limited English proficiency, and the contradictions of Catholicism. In addition, through the process of naming dynamic identities and diverse cultural/historical experiences, these issues have been studied and written about by numerous Chicana feminists in a much different way than most Chicano male scholars (e.g., Alarcón, 1990; Anzaldúa, 1987; Castillo, 1995; Medina, 1998; Sandoval, 1998; Trujillo, 1998).

For example, concepts such as mestiza, borderlands, and Xicanisma are unique to a Chicana epistemology. A mestiza is literally a woman of mixed ancestry, especially of Native American, European, and African backgrounds. However, the term mestiza has come to mean a new Chicana consciousness that straddles cultures, races, languages, nations, sexualities, and spiritualities — that is, living with ambivalence while balancing opposing powers. Gloria Anzaldúa (1987) states that "the new mestiza copes by developing a tolerance for contradictions, a tolerance for ambiguity. She learns to be an Indian in Mexican culture, to be Mexican from an Anglo point of view. She learns to juggle cultures" (p. 79). Within a Chicana feminist epistemology, borderlands refers to the geographical, emotional, and/or psychological space occupied by mestizas. Anzaldúa believes that those individuals who are marginalized by society and are forced to live on the borderlands of dominant culture develop a sixth sense for survival. Therefore, Chicanas and other marginalized peoples have a strength that comes from their borderland experiences. Xicanisma, a term introduced by Ana Castillo (1995), describes Chicana feminisms that are developed from and carried out to "our work place, social gatherings, kitchens, bedrooms, and society in general" (p. 11).

Rather than use an epistemological framework that is based solely on the diverse social histories of other women of color (e.g., Black feminist thought) or the social history of the dominant race (e.g., liberal feminist thought), a Chicana feminist epistemology offers a standpoint that borrows from endarkened feminist epistemologies and is grounded in the unique life experiences of Chicanas. For example, in educational research it is important to remember that Chicana students experience school from multiple dimensions, including their skin color, gender, class, and English-language proficiency. Castillo (1995) reflects on the trauma a Chicana may experience in regard to bilingualism:

> She was educated in English and learned it is the only acceptable language in society, but Spanish was the language of her childhood, family, and community. She may not be able to rid herself of an accent; society has denigrated her first language. By the same token, women may also become anxious and self conscious in later years if they have no or little facility in Spanish. (p. 39)

Bilingualism is often seen as un-American and is considered a deficit and an obstacle to learning. Prohibiting Spanish-language use among Mexican schoolchildren is a social philosophy and a political tool that has been and continues to be used to justify school segregation and to maintain a colonized relationship between Mexicans and the dominant society (Delgado Bernal, 1999). In my own research, I learned how Vickie Castro, a Los Angeles Unified School District board member, was physically separated from peers as a young girl because of the devaluation of Spanish:

> I do recall my first day of school. And I did not speak English. . . . I just recall being frightened and I recall not knowing what to do and I recall being told to just sit over there in the corner. And there was one other little girl and we were just scared out of our minds. (Castro, 1994, pp. 2, 3)

Historically, many Chicana and Chicano students have been segregated and stigmatized, with their perceived language deficiency used as justification. Students today continue to be segregated based on their limited English proficiency. In June 1998, California voters passed Proposition 227, the English Language Education for Immigrant Children initiative. The initiative does away with all bilingual education and English-language development programs that do not meet its rigid 180-day English-only approach.[4] It promotes stigmatization by allowing local schools "to place in the same classroom English learners of different ages but whose degree of English proficiency is similar."

To ground one's research within the experiences of Chicanas means that we deconstruct the historical devaluation of Spanish, the contradictions of Catholicism, the patriarchal ideology that devalues women, and the scapegoating of immigrants. Indeed, the everyday lives of Chicanas demonstrate that they are often at the center of these struggles against cultural domination, class exploitation, sexism, and racism. A Chicana feminist epistemology is therefore grounded in the rich historical legacy of Chicanas' resistance and translates into a pursuit of social justice in both research and scholarship.

A Chicana feminist epistemology that is based on the lives of Chicanas and is dedicated to achieving justice and equality combats what James Joseph Scheurich and Michelle Young (1997) call epistemological racism. As they define it, epistemological racism arises out of the social history and culture of the dominant race and is present in the current range of traditional research epistemologies — positivism to postmodernism and poststructuralism. Traditional research epistemologies reflect and reinforce the social history of the dominant race, which has negative results for people of color in general and students and scholars of color in particular. A Chicana feminist epistemology arises out of a unique social and cultural history, and demonstrates that our experiences as Mexican women are legitimate, appropriate, and effective in designing, conducting, and analyzing educational research. A Chicana cultural standpoint that is located in the interconnected identities of race/ethnicity, gender, class, and sexuality and within the historical and contemporary context of oppressions and resistance can also be the foundation for a theoretical sensitivity (Strauss & Corbin, 1990) that many Chicana scholars bring to their research.

FOUR SOURCES OF CULTURAL INTUITION

The disciplines of Black and other ethnic studies and women's studies have opened the way for multiple theoretical and epistemological readings in the fields of educational research. A major contribution of these fields is that feminists and scholars of color (and those of us who identify as both) have argued that members of marginalized groups have unique viewpoints on our own experiences as a whole. (Dillard, 1997, p. 5)

I argue that Chicana researchers have unique viewpoints that can provide us with a perspective I call "cultural intuition." A Chicana researcher's cultural intuition is similar in concept to Strauss and Corbin's (1990) "theoretical sensitivity" — a personal quality of the researcher based on the attribute of having the ability to give meaning to data. Their construct of theoretical sensitivity indicates an understanding of the subtle meanings of data, and that "one can come to the research situation with varying degrees of sensitivity depending on one's previous reading and experience with or relevant to the data" (p. 41). They argue that theoretical sensitivity actually comes from four major sources: one's personal experience, the existing literature, one's professional experience, and the analytical research process itself. Having outlined in the last section important characteristics of a Chicana feminist epistemology, I propose that these four sources contribute to Chicana researchers' cultural intuition and are the foundation of a Chicana feminist epistemology in educational research. However, my concept of cultural intuition is different from theoretical sensitivity because it extends one's personal experience to include collective experience and community memory, and points to the importance of participants' engaging in the analysis of data. In the next sections, I briefly describe the four sources and how each contributes to my cultural intuition as a Chicana researcher. The sources do not include all possibilities, yet they provide a framework that facilitates an understanding of cultural intuition and therefore a Chicana feminist epistemology in educational research. My hope is that this framework helps demonstrate what forces shape a Chicana feminist epistemology without limiting the nuances that must be addressed in future work.

Personal Experience

First, one's personal experience represents a very important source of cultural intuition and is derived from the background that we each bring to the research situation. As many feminists contend, the researcher is a subject in her research and her personal history is part of the analytical process (Maynard, 1994; Stanley & Wise, 1993). Through past life experiences, individuals acquire an understanding of certain situations and why and what might happen in a particular setting under certain conditions. This often implicit knowledge helps us to understand events, actions, and words, and to do so more confidently than if one did not bring these particular life experiences into the research (Strauss & Corbin, 1990). For example, my life experiences as a Chicana, a student, and a participant in protest politics such as campus and community demonstrations and boycotts helped me to understand and analyze my data. The oral histories I collected in my study of Chicana student activists (Delgado Bernal, 1997) were not heard as merely random stories, but as testimonies of authority, preemption, and strength that demonstrate women's participation and leadership in school resistance. In other words, my personal experiences provided insight and a cultural intuition from which to draw upon during my research.

However, personal experience does not operate in a vacuum. To extend Strauss and Corbin's (1990) notion of personal experience, I argue that personal experience goes beyond the individual and has lateral ties to family and reverse ties to the past. Personal experience is partially shaped by collective experience and community memory, and as Marmon Silko (1996) states, "an individual's identity will extend from the identity constructed around the family" (p. 52). Through the experiences of ancestors and elders, Chicanas and Chicanos carry knowledge of conquest, loss of land, school and social segregation, labor market stratification, assimilation, and resistance. Community knowledge is taught to youth through legends, *corridos*,[5] storytelling, behavior, and most recently through the scholarship in the field of Chicana and Chicano Studies. As a child, my own family experience included learning through my grandmothers' stories, which were sprinkled with religion and mysticism, and my father's stories about the urban challenges of his childhood. As an adult, I began interviewing and recording the stories and knowledge that my family members shared with me. This knowledge that is passed from one generation to the next can help us survive in everyday life by providing an understanding of certain situations and explanations about why things happen under certain conditions. Sara Lawrence-Lightfoot (1994) discusses the unique knowledge that comes from the intertwinement of collective experience and intuition in African American communities:

> The development of this understanding is not rational — it comes from "the gut"; it is based on experience and intuition. There is the idea that this suspicion is passed down from the ancestors who teach the next generation the subtle dangers — through act and deed — who instruct their offspring in how to walk through treacherous minefields, who show them jungle posture. (p. 60)

Lawrence-Lightfoot writes of the "ancestral wisdom" that is taught from one generation to the next, and calls it "a powerful piece of our legacy" that is "healthy" and "necessary for survival." Likewise, Marmon Silko (1996) writes of how the Pueblo people have depended on the collective memory of many generations "to maintain and transmit an entire culture, a worldview complete with proven strategies for survival" (p. 30). For Chicana researchers, ancestral wisdom, community memory, and intuition influence one's own personal experiences. And it is personal experience that provides one source of cultural intuition from which to draw upon during research.

Existing Literature

Another source of cultural intuition is the existing literature on a topic. Technical literature includes research studies and theoretical or philosophical writings, while nontechnical literature refers to biographies, public documents, personal documents, and cultural studies writings (Strauss & Corbin, 1990). Having an understanding of this information provides some insight into what is going on with the events and circumstances we are studying. The technical literature may be used to stimulate theoretical sensitivity by providing concepts and relationships that are checked against actual data. For example, in my study of Chicana student activists, my readings of endarkened feminist theories, school resistance theories, and the sociohistorical politics of Chicano schooling offered me a particular cultural intuition into the phenomenon I was studying by providing possible ways of approaching and interpreting data. My readings of descriptive materials, such as newspaper articles, also enhanced my cultural intuition by making me sensitive to what to look for in my data and helping me generate interview questions.

Professional Experience

One's professional experience can be yet another source of cultural intuition. Years of practice in a particular field often provides an insider view of how things work in that field (Strauss & Corbin, 1990). This knowledge, whether explicit or implicit, is taken into the research and helps one to understand differently than if one did not have this experience. My experiences as a bilingual teacher, a teacher educator, and my work with education programs in Latino community-based organizations have all contributed to the way I understand and analyze my data in educational research on Chicana students. Indeed, Strauss and Corbin (1990) would argue that due to my professional experience I can move into the educational environment and gain insight into the lives of Chicana students more quickly than someone who has never worked in a school setting with Chicana students: "The more professional experience, the richer the knowledge base and insight available to draw upon in the research" (p. 42).

Analytical Research Process

Finally, the analytical research process itself provides an additional source of cultural intuition: "Insight and understanding about a phenomenon increase as you interact with your data" (Strauss & Corbin, 1990, p. 43). This comes from making comparisons, asking additional questions, thinking about what you are hearing and seeing, sorting data, developing a coding scheme, and engaging in concept formation. As one idea leads to another, we are able to look more closely at the data and bring meaning to the research. For example, in my study of Chicana student activists, my increased awareness of concepts, meanings, and relationships were influenced by my interaction with the interview data (e.g., transcribing, reading transcriptions, listening to taped interviews, and coding interviews). In addition, my awareness was also increased by including the women I interviewed in the analytical process of making sense of the data.

Extending Strauss and Corbin's analytical research process, I suggest that including Chicana participants in an interactive process of data analysis contributes to the researcher's cultural intuition. Pizarro (1998) calls for "a new methodological approach to research in Chicana/o communities" (p. 57) that includes participants as equals at all stages of the research. "This requires that researchers and participants deconstruct the epistemology of the participants and use it as the basis for the entire project" (p. 74). In the latter half of this article, I describe in detail how using a focus group strategy allowed me to incorporate the epistemological perspectives of the Chicanas I interviewed. This process allowed me to go beyond a simple feedback loop, and bring meaning to the data based on an interactive process.

Of course, researchers must be careful to not let any of the four sources block them from seeing the obvious or assume everyone's personal and professional experiences are equal to theirs. Early in my research, I learned that the women in my study were very diverse and the life experiences they shared with each other were very different from my own personal experiences. For example, all eight of these women shared the following similarities: they were second- or third-generation Chicanas, first-generation college students, grew up in working-class neighborhoods on the east side of Los Angeles, and were student activists in 1968. As a third-generation Chicana and first-generation college student, I grew up in the suburbs of Kansas City, was in preschool in 1968, and was not introduced to political activism until my early twenties. Therefore, my personal experiences did not automatically designate me an "insider." I, like any researcher, had to be concerned with how I was approaching and interpreting my subject's stories of activism. As hooks (1989) states, we have to consider the purpose and use of our research:

> When we write about the experiences of a group to which we do not belong, we should think about the ethics of our action, considering whether or not our work will be used to reinforce and perpetuate domination. (p. 43)

While I do not argue for an essentialist notion of who is capable of conducting research with various populations based on personal experiences, I do believe that many Chicana scholars achieve a sense of cultural intuition that is different from that of other scholars. Sofía Villenas (1996) indirectly addresses this issue as she examines her own emerging and changing identity as a Chicana researcher. In doing so, she asks what constitutes an insider to a community of research participants and asserts that it is based on "collective experiences and a collective space" at multiple levels, rather than on a singular identity (p. 722). Villenas explains how her practice in the field as a Chicana educational ethnographer cannot be explicated in the same manner as White, middle-class researchers' relationships with their research participants. She therefore argues for a process by which Chicanas "become the subjects and the creators of knowledge" (p. 730), essentially advocating for the use of a Chicana feminist epistemology in educational research.

Likewise, Dillard (1997) speaks of cultural intuition in her discussion of theoretical and conceptual standpoints of Black women educational researchers. She poses that the insights from being and living as African American researchers opens up possibilities for the research community to see phenomena in new ways. And she views these standpoints of Black women as achieved rather than inherent in one's singular identity:

> While we will argue vehemently that Black women as a cultural group "theorize" and embody extensive life experiences which, while diverse, shape a coherent body, what we advance here is the notion that, in educational research, such theoretical and conceptual standpoints are achieved; they are not inherent in one's race, class, sex, or other identities. (pp. 5–6)

A Chicana researcher's cultural intuition is achieved and can be nurtured through our personal experiences (which are influenced by ancestral wisdom, community memory, and intuition), the literature on and about Chicanas, our professional experiences, and the analytical process we engage in when we are in a central position of our research and our analysis. Thus, cultural intuition is a complex process that is experiential, intuitive, historical, personal, collective, and dynamic.

Having defined cultural intuition and a Chicana feminist epistemology, I now attempt to illustrate what these concepts mean in educational research. In order to provide a concrete example of this conceptual discussion, the next section describes a research project I worked on over several years. As I describe the oral history project, it is important to point out that I only became attentive to my own cultural intuition and the epistemology I brought to the research after I completed the project and had time to reflect on the research process. Though my theoretical framework was shaped by the school resistance theories in the sociology of education literature and interdisciplinary critical feminist theories, my self-reflections have allowed me to (re)interpret my epistemological framework from a Chicana feminist standpoint.[6] I now realize that the way I asked my research questions, designed the methodology, collected the data, and arrived at conclusions was greatly influenced by my cultural intuition. Even where the individual and focus group interviews were held, my need to include the women in the data analysis process was unknowingly driven by a shared epistemology we all brought to the research. Therefore, it was both my cultural intuition and my epistemological orientation that served to resist dominant epistemologies and recover an ignored history of Chicana students.

RESISTANCE AND RECOVERY THROUGH AN ORAL HISTORY RESEARCH PROJECT

In 1968, people witnessed a worldwide rise in student movements in countries such as France, Italy, Mexico, and the United States. In March of that year, over ten thousand students walked out of schools in East Los Angeles to protest the inferior quality of their education. The event, which came to be known as the East L.A. Blowouts, focused national attention on the K–12 schooling of Chicanas and Chicanos and also set a precedent for school boycotts throughout the Southwest (Acuña, 1988). Though their stories are often excluded in written historical accounts, my research demonstrates that Chicanas played crucial leadership roles in these mass demonstrations and were intimately involved in the struggles for educational justice. As an educational researcher and a Chicana, I was interested in the women's voices and their unique experiences that had previously been omitted from the diverse accounts of the Blowouts. My historical-sociological case study, informed by my own achieved cultural intuition and a Chicana feminist epistemology, posed the following research question: How does pivoting the analysis onto key Chicana participants provide an alternative history of the 1968 Blowouts? This research question itself is distinctively Chicana, especially when compared to previous research that has examined the Blowouts. Chicano and White males have studied the event from a perspective of protest politics (Puckett, 1971), a spontaneous mass protest (Negrete, 1972), internal colonialism (Muñoz, 1973), the Chicano student movement (Gómez-Quiñones, 1978), and a political and social development of the wider Chicano movement (Rosen, 1973). Indeed, none of their historical accounts locate Chicanas in a central position in the research or address the many factors that restricted or enabled Chicana students to participate. My study, in contrast, examined how women interpret their participation in the Blowouts nearly thirty years later, and how their participation is important to an understanding of transformational resistance, grassroots leadership, and an alternative history of the Blowouts (Delgado Bernal, 1997, 1998).

To gain new perspectives and interpretations of the 1968 Blowouts and Chicana school resistance, my primary methods of data collection were in-depth, semistructured oral history interviews with eight key female participants from the Blowouts, a two-hour semistructured focus group interview, and phone interviews. Following a network sampling procedure (Gándara, 1995), I interviewed eight women who were identified by other female participants or resource individuals as "key participants" or "leaders" in the Blowouts. In scheduling these interviews, I allowed ample time, realizing that the length of each interview would vary. The interviews took place when and where it was most convenient for each woman — in their homes, their mother's home, or at work. I created an interview protocol with open-ended questions in order to elicit multiple levels of data that would address my research questions (see Appendix 1). Though the interview protocol was used as a guide, I realized that as the women spoke of very personal experiences, a less-structured approach allowed their voices and ways of knowing to come forth. I also asked probing questions to follow up on responses that were unclear or possibly incomplete in order to understand how the women interpreted the reasons and ways in which they participated in the Blowouts.

The oral histories were not merely heard as random stories, but as testimonies of authority, preemption, and strength that demonstrate women's participation and leadership in school resistance. My life experiences as a Chicana provided a source of cultural intuition that helped me both to listen to and to hear the interviewees. For example, in six of the eight individual interviews, religion was discussed in terms of Catholic values, contradictions of Catholicism, or spirituality. I understood Rosalinda Méndez González's feelings of disillusionment and betrayal when she passionately talked to me about the contradictions of her Catholic upbringing and the influence it had on her activism. Having been exposed to these contradictions myself, and still identifying as a "cultural Catholic" (Medina, 1998), I heard her story as a very personal one. She remembers:

> And then from my Catholic upbringing we were taught about compassion and charity, and how Jesus healed the ill and took care of the poor, and all of that. . . . And I go to college and find out that every religion in the world claims the same thing, that they're all the only true one, and that all of them have committed atrocities in the name of God, in the name of their religion, that the Catholic church tortured people and killed people in the name of God. (Méndez González, 1995, pp. 14, 78)

After conducting individual oral history interviews, I corresponded with each woman twice. The first time I sent a complete copy of the interview transcript with a letter describing their role in the analysis of the data. The following is a portion of that letter:

> I've decided to send transcriptions back to the women I've interviewed so that you each have a chance to see my initial interpretation. I believe it's important that you have an opportunity to reflect and respond to what you said in the interview. This will not only strengthen my analysis, but it allows each woman to interact with and "dialogue" with her own interview. The interview transcription with comments and questions in the margins is the one I'd like for you to review. These comments and questions are specific to areas that I'm curious or not quite clear about (that is, other women commented on the same issue, or I've since thought of a related issue). If possible I'd love for you to respond in writing on the transcription and/or a separate page. Please bring this copy and your comments with you to the focus group interview. At that time, we can further address any areas you'd like to elaborate on or additional questions I may have. The second clean copy is for you to hold on to — an interesting keepsake. (see Appendix 2)

Closer to our meeting, I wrote the women informing them where we would be holding the group interview and the agenda for our meeting. Here is a portion of that letter:

> Well, the date of our group interview is drawing near and I wanted to send you this update. On Saturday, February 17th we will hold our event in East Los Angeles' Self-Help Graphics from 4:00 to 7:00 P.M Tomás Benitez, assistant director of Self-Help (and Mita Cuaron's husband) was able to secure space for us in the art gallery. The art gallery will be particularly special given the beautiful ex-

hibit, La Vida Indigena, and the fact that the interview will be filmed. . . .

The agenda for the actual group interview will follow a semi-structured format. That is, based on your responses in the individual interviews, I will identify a few topics I would like to ask the group to respond to. In addition, I would also like each of you to bring up any blowout-related issues or events that are particularly interesting to you. . . . I'm not as interested in reconstructing the "Truth" of what happened as I am interested in your individual experiences and their similarities and differences. (see Appendix 3)

When we met for the two-hour focus group, all but one of the women had read and reflected on their transcripts prior to the group meeting, and three of them returned their transcript with responses to my queries actually written in the margins. Their comments ranged from yes/no responses and name spelling corrections to several emotional sentences elaborating on their activism and a paragraph explaining why someone considered herself a leader. The written reflections were of course helpful to my analysis, as they provided me with additional information and clarified specific points from the individual interviews. The impact of the written reflections, however, was small in comparison to the lessons I gained from the subsequent group dialogue. My real interest in conducting a focus group interview was to incorporate the explicit use of group interaction to produce data and insights that might have been less accessible otherwise (Krueger, 1988).

I now realize that the focus group process seemed natural to me partially because of the cultural intuition I brought to the research project. I was used to my grandmothers' storytelling in which absolute "Truth" was less important to me than hearing and recording their life experiences. It was my familiarity with and respect for ancestral wisdom taught from one generation to the next and a regard for collective knowledge that allowed me to approach the research project with complete respect for each woman's testimony of school resistance. Indeed, the women shared their community knowledge through a form of storytelling in which all the women talked about their resistance by invoking stories about their families, quoting their parents, and mentioning where their parents were born. To make a point about democratic ideals and the right to question authority, Rosalinda contrasted her upbringing and socialization with that of her mother's a generation earlier:

> I remember when I was a kid growing up in Texas and going to school and being taught these things about democracy and how different my response was from my mother's response. My mother was born and raised in Mexico, in Chihuahua. And if you spoke up against the government, the next day your body would be found. . . . And she was terrified of standing up for her rights or speaking against any authority figure, and that included teachers. (Focus Group Interview, 1996)

The interaction among the participants also produced new information and differing viewpoints. For instance, several women were reminded of something based on another woman's recollections and made comments such as, "I was listening to Mita talk and I hadn't thought about it till right now . . .". The group interaction also allowed them to compare and contrast their experiences with each other. Three of the women come from politically progressive families who had been concerned with justice struggles for many years, and one of them stated, "I was born into this family of struggle, protest, rebellion, [and] . . . equal rights." In contrast, the other women spoke of coming from a more "traditional family." Whatever their personal family experiences were, they all agreed that during the time of their activism there was a knowledge or "gospel" in Mexican homes in East Los Angeles that did not question the Church or schoolteachers' absolute authority: "The church, whatever they say and the teachers, whatever they say." The women's interactions were a form of storytelling in which they were able to compare and contrast their memories and experiences. Their group dialogue also provided me with invaluable lessons in relation to the data analysis process.

LESSONS FROM THE FOCUS GROUP

Prior to the focus group interview, I sorted data by integrating key themes that emerged from the women's individual oral histories with the existing literature. During the focus group, I presented four themes related to the women's school resistance and asked them to respond to my preliminary interpretations of how these themes shaped their student activism: dual identity, patriotism, dimensions of leadership, and awareness/agency. Presenting my preliminary findings to the women was one way of including their knowledge and a means of avoiding "authenticity of interpretation and description under the guise of authority" (Villenas, 1996, p. 713). Indeed, my cultural intuition and the women's knowledge helped shape my final analysis.

For example, I was originally attempting to interpret the women's behavior within the common duality of "good girl" and "bad girl" discussed and critiqued by a number of Chicana authors (Anzaldúa, 1987; Castillo, 1995; Hurtado, 1996; Trujillo, 1993). These imposed constructions of Chicanas' identity are couched in women's sexuality and in what is perceived as acceptable and unacceptable behavior. The two polarized roles of Virgin Mary and whore exemplify the ultimate "good girl" and "bad girl." Aida Hurtado (1996) states that these are "social locations that are given cultural space to exist" (p. 50). During the individual interviews the women talked about their "good schoolgirl" behavior in terms of being "college-bound," "real straightlaced," "a star student," "head cheerleader," and in the "goody-goody camp." Yet in the same breath they discussed their very bold resistant behavior that was considered "bad activist student" behavior and deviant by most of society. The women wrote articles for community activist newspapers regarding the poor conditions in their schools, stood up to accusations of being communists, provided testimony about the inferior quality of their education to the U.S. Commission on Civil Rights, and were arrested by police and expelled from school because of their activism. Because shifting from "deviant (and therefore defiant) locations . . . to culturally sanctioned locations is . . . difficult" (Hurtado, 1996, p. 50), I was interested in how they were able to move between these social locations. Therefore, I asked the women how the social, cultural, and sexual realities of their lives were manifested in the duality of "good schoolgirl" and "bad activist student."

The women expressed a belief that my preliminary analysis was slightly off target. In fact, they believed that rather than moving between these two social locations, they were engaging in the same type of behaviors as "good schoolgirls" and as "bad activist students." It was the perceptions of their behaviors that changed. Their good schoolgirl behavior of speaking up in class, asking questions, and offering leadership to sanctioned student organizations was acceptable behavior (and even encouraged). However, when they practiced these same behaviors during the school boycotts, they were perceived as deviant. Their behavior had not changed — others' interpretation of their behavior had. In other words, they helped me to see that their "good schoolgirl" behavior that was so openly rewarded by good grades, student council positions, and respect from teachers was the exact same behavior that was unfairly punished when they used it to protest the inferior quality of their education. Their insight contributed to my reorganization of themes and altered my preliminary analysis.

In another case, the women confirmed my preliminary analysis regarding the complexity of gender's influence on their different dimensions of leadership. For example, during the oral history interviews, women made statements ranging from "Nobody ever said that you couldn't do this because you were a girl" to "I know that the females were not the leaders," and from "Being a female was not an issue, it was just a non-issue" to "I'm sure I knew that there was sexism involved . . . but we probably didn't talk about it." During the focus group interview the influence of gender continued to be perceived in a somewhat nebulous way. The diversity of statements found within interviews, between interviews, and at the focus group interview led me to conclude that there was no one distinct and precise viewpoint on gender's influence. Rather, the women's individual and collective thoughts on gender represent the indeterminate and complex influence of gender within a structure of patriarchy — a system of domination and unequal stratification based on gender.

Including these women in the analytical process of making sense of the data helped shape my research findings and was an important source of my own cultural intuition. Just as importantly, their participation in this process made them not just subjects of research, but also creators of knowledge — an important characteristic of a Chicana feminist epistemology. Thus, contrary to patriarchal historical accounts of the 1968 East L.A. School Blowouts, a Chicana feminist standpoint exposes human relationships and experiences that were previously invisible.

CONCLUSION

The issue of subjectivity represents a realization of the fact that who we are, how we act, what we think, and what stories we tell become more intelligible within an epistemological framework that begins by recognizing existing hegemonic histories. . . . [Thus], uncovering and reclaiming of subjugated knowledges is one way to lay claim to alternative histories. (Mohanty, 1994, p. 148)

How educational research is conducted significantly contributes to what and whose history, community, and knowledge is legitimated. A Chicana feminist epistemology addresses the failure of traditional research paradigms that have distorted or omitted the history and knowledge of Chicanas. Though similar endarkened feminist epistemologies exist in specific segments of women's studies and ethnic studies, acknowledging a Chicana feminist epistemology in educational research is virtually unprecedented. And yet, a disproportionate number of all Chicana and Chicano Ph.D.'s receive their doctoral degrees in the field of education (Solorzano, 1995). Without an articulated Chicana epistemology or an acknowledgment of cultural intuition within the field of education, these scholars are restricted by cultural hegemonic domination in educational research.

Therefore, one of the major contributions of this article is an emerging articulation of a new epistemology in educational research. This epistemology gives license to both Chicana and Chicano education scholars to uncover and reclaim their own subjugated knowledge. It also allows them to place some trust in their own cultural intuition so that they move beyond traditional areas of research situated in existing paradigms that overlook the particular educational experiences of Chicanas or Chicanos. To illustrate this point, consider the experience of Chicano scholar Octavio Villalpando when he conducted his doctoral dissertation research. Villalpando's (1996) investigation yielded very significant quantitative evidence demonstrating that Chicana and Chicano college students benefit substantially from affiliating primarily with other Chicanas and Chicanos during college. These benefits were particularly noteworthy for Chicano students, spanning a range of several important postcollege outcomes. Although these are significant findings in the field of higher education, they could not be completely explained by preexisting higher education paradigms. Villalpando's analysis might have been taken further had he been able to access his cultural intuition (Villalpando, personal communication, 1998). A Chicana feminist epistemology gives Chicana and Chicano education scholars some freedom to interpret their research findings outside of existing paradigms, and hopefully develop and propose policies and practices that better meet the needs of Chicanas and Chicanos.

Given the significant and growing Chicana and Chicano student population, particularly in the Southwest, it certainly is not my intent to suggest an end to all educational research on Chicanas that is not conducted by Chicana scholars. Indeed, I hope that others will read this article and think about their own epistemological framework and that of the Chicana and Chicano communities they research. Borrowing from a Chicana epistemology may help all scholars to raise more appropriate research questions and avoid asking questions based on a cultural deficit model or incorrect stereotypes. Chicana sociologist Mary Pardo (1998) provides an insightful example of a White woman colleague who asked an inappropriate question based on stereotypes rather than the knowledge base of the East Los Angeles Chicanas she was reporting on. During Pardo's research, she and her colleague were having a meal with women from Mothers of East Los Angeles (MELA), a group of working-class community activists. Her colleague asked the group how they might mobilize around a hypothetical case of false imprisonment of an alleged youth gang member. Pardo describes why silence engulfed the room:

> Her question about the alleged gang member reflected the media assumption that gang activity constituted the most significant problem facing Eastside Los Angeles residents. But the women from MELA were long-time, stable home owners, most of whose children had already graduated from college. They had . . . directed collective efforts at getting summer jobs for youth. . . . Rebuilding a neighborhood park and opposing the prison and toxic-waste incinerator consumed most of their time. (p. 12)

A new epistemological approach in educational research has the potential to avoid these type of inappropriate questions and focus on questions that may expose important school issues and community experiences that are otherwise not visible.

A major tenet of cultural intuition and a Chicana feminist epistemology is the inclusion of Chicana research participants in the analysis of data. This allows Chicana participants — whether they are students, parents, teachers, or school administrators — to be speaking subjects who take part in producing and validating knowledge. A focus group interview is one data collection strategy that helps Chicana scholars and non-Chicana scholars include the epistemology of their research participants in the analysis of data. The example I provide in this article demonstrates how focus groups can be paired with an oral history methodology to include Chicana participants in the interpretation of data. In addition, it seems that focus groups can be effectively used with other qualitative and quantitative research methods and methodologies such as school ethnography, student interviews, survey research, and classroom observations. In the future, we must look for additional strategies that provide opportunities for Chicanas and Chicanos to participate in the construction of knowledge and research that is dedicated to achieving social justice. Hopefully, "an analysis of the Chicana/o experience can . . . assist us in forging a new epistemological approach to academic life and can help us uncover a methodology that is true to and helpful in the struggle of these people as it 'creates' a new knowledge base" (Pizarro, 1998, p. 72).

NOTES

1. "Chicana" is a cultural and political identity composed of multiple layers and is often an identity of resistance that we consciously adopt later in life. "Chicana is not a name that women (or men) are born to or with, as is often the case with 'Mexican,' but rather it is consciously and critically assumed and serves as a point of redeparture for dismantling historical conjunctures of crisis, confusion, political and ideological conflict" (Alarcón, 1990, p. 250). The term Chicana is used to discuss women of Mexican origin and/or women who identify with this label. While many of the issues addressed in this article apply to Chicano males and other Latinas and Latinos, the focus here is on Chicanas.

2. Cynthia Dillard (1997) proposes that "endarkened feminist ideology described as inherently cultural, positional, political, strategic, relational, and transformative is offered as possible criteria and catalyst for future educational research. In contrast to our common use of the term 'enlightening' as a way of expressing the having of new and important insights, we use the term endarkening to suggest epistemological roots of Black feminist thought which embody a distinguishable difference in cultural standpoint" (pp. 3–4). I use endarkened in a similar way, and include not only Black feminist thought, but the feminist thought of all women of color.

3. In this study, school resistance was defined as students' acknowledging problems in oppressive educational settings and demanding changes.

4. Proposition 227 requires that "all children in California public schools shall be taught English by being taught in English." This requirement counters educational research that demonstrates that English immersion is one of the least effective ways to teach children with limited English proficiency the English language. The proposition also requires local schools to place students in English immersion classrooms for up to one year, based on their degree of English proficiency (Article 2). Parental ex-

ception waivers for the English immersion requirement may only be granted to parents who personally visit the school to apply and whose children meet certain requirements, including children who already know English, are over ten years old, or have special needs (Article 3).

5. The *corrido* is a Mexican ballad and is one means of oral tradition in which history and culture are preserved and shared through song. Corridos often tell stories of the struggles and resistance of Mexican people.

6. My self-reflections have been greatly influenced by earlier and recent Chicana scholars and writers. Unfortunately, much of the early work by Chicanas is difficult to find and has often gone unrecognized — indicative of the Eurocentric culture of academia. In the 1980s there was a reemergence of Chicana scholarship that not only repositioned class and ethnicity in relationship to gender, but also addressed the many aspects of sexuality. In the last few years the work of several progressive Chicana scholars has been particularly influential in helping me develop an articulation of Chicana feminist epistemology in educational research (Castillo, 1995; de la Torre & Pesquera, 1993; Hurtado, 1996; Pardo, 1998; Ruiz, 1998; Trujillo, 1998).

REFERENCES

Acuña, R. (1988). *Occupied America: A history of Chicanos.* New York: HarperCollins.

Alarcón, N. (1990). Chicana feminism: In the tracks of "the" native woman. *Cultural Studies, 4,* 248–256.

Alarcón, N., Castro, R., Pérez, E., Pesquera, B., Sosa-Riddell, A., & Zavella, P. (Eds.). (1993). *Chicana critical issues.* Berkeley: Third Woman Press.

Anzaldúa, G. (1987). *Borderlands, la frontera: The new mestiza.* San Francisco: Aunt Lute Books.

Bowles, S., & Gintis, H. (1976). *Schooling in capitalist America.* New York: Basic Books.

Castañeda, A. (1993). Sexual violence in the politics and policies of conquest: Amerindian women and the Spanish conquest of Alta California. In A. de la Torre & B. Pesquera (Eds.), *Building with our hands: New directions in Chicano studies* (pp. 15–33). Berkeley: University of California Press.

Castillo, A. (1995). *Massacre of the dreamers: Essays on Xicanisma.* New York: Plume.

Castro, V. (1994, December). [Transcribed interview conducted by Susan Racho with Vickie Castro]. Unpublished data.

Collins, P. H. (1986). Learning from the outsider within: The sociological significance of Black feminist thought. *Social Problems, 33*(6), S14–S32.

Collins, P. H. (1991). *Black feminist thought: Knowledge, consciousness, and the politics of empowerment.* New York: Routledge.

Cook-Lynn, E. (1996). *Why I can't read Wallace Stegner and other essays: A tribal voice.* Madison: University of Wisconsin Press.

Cuádraz, G. (1996). Experiences of multiple marginality: A case study of "Chicana scholarship women." In C. Turner, M. García, A. Nora, & L. Rendón (Eds.), *Racial and ethnic diversity in higher education* (pp. 210–222). New York: Simon & Schuster.

de la Torre, A., & Pesquera, B. (Eds.). (1993). *Building with our hands: New directions in Chicana studies.* Berkeley: University of California Press.

Delgado Bernal, D. (1997). *Chicana school resistance and grassroots leadership: Providing an alternative history of the 1968 East Los Angeles blowouts.* Doctoral dissertation, University of California, Los Angeles.

Delgado Bernal, D. (1998). Grassroots leadership reconceptualized: Chicana oral histories and the 1968 East Los Angeles school blowouts. *Frontiers: A Journal of Women Studies, 19*(2), 113–142.

Delgado Bernal, D. (1999). Chicana/o education from the civil rights era to the present. In J. F. Moreno (Ed.), *The elusive quest for equality: 150 years of Chicano/Chicana education*. Cambridge, MA: Harvard Educational Review.

Delgado-Gaitan, C. (1993). Researching change and changing the researcher. *Harvard Educational Review, 63,* 389–411.

Dillard, C. B. (1997, April). *The substance of things hoped for, the evidence of things not seen: Toward an endarkened feminist ideology in research.* Paper presented at the annual meeting of the American Educational Research Association, Chicago.

Fine, M. (1994). Working the hyphens: Reinventing self and other in qualitative research. In N. Denzin & Y. Lincoln (Eds.), *Handbook of qualitative research* (pp. 70–82). Thousand Oaks, CA: Sage.

Flores-Ortiz, E. (1998). Voices from the couch: The co-creation of a Chicana psychology. In C. Trujillo (Ed.), *Living Chicana theory* (pp. 102–122). Berkeley: Third Woman Press.

Flores-Ortiz, Y. (1991). Levels of acculturation, marital satisfaction, and depression among Chicana workers: A psychological perspective. *Aztlán, 20*(1/2), 151–175.

Flores-Ortiz, Y. (1993). La mujer y la violencia: A culturally based model for the understanding and treatment of domestic violence in Chicana/Latina communities. In N. Alarcón et al. (Eds.), *Chicana critical issues* (pp. 169–182). Berkeley: Third Woman Press.

Focus Group Interview. (1996, February). [Videotaped interview conducted by Dolores Delgado Bernal with study participants]. Unpublished data.

Gándara, P. (1982). Passing through the eye of the needle: High-achieving Chicanas. *Hispanic Behavioral Sciences, 4,* 167–179.

Gándara, P. (1995). *Over the ivy walls: The educational mobility of low-income Chicanos.* Albany: State University of New York Press.

Giroux, H. A. (1992). *Border crossings: Cultural workers and the politics of education.* New York: Routledge.

Gómez-Quiñones, J. (1978). *Mexican students por La Raza: The Chicano student movement in Southern California 1967–1977.* Santa Barbara, CA: Editorial La Causa.

Harding, S. (Ed.). (1987). *Feminism and methodology.* Milton Keynes, Eng.: Open University Press.

Hernández-Avila, I. (1995). Relocations upon relocations: Home, language, and Native American women's writings. *American Indian Quarterly, 19,* 491–507.

hooks, b. (1989). *Talking back: Thinking feminist, thinking Black.* Boston: South End Press.

Hurtado, A. (1989). Relating to privilege: Seduction and rejection in the subordination of White women and women of color. *Signs: Journal of Women in Culture and Society, 14,* 833–855.

Hurtado, A. (1996). *The color of privilege: Three blasphemies on race and feminism.* Ann Arbor: University of Michigan Press

Kelly, L. (1988). *Surviving sexual violence.* Cambridge, Eng.: Polity Press.

Kelly, L., Burton, S., & Regan, L. (1994). Researching women's lives or studying women's oppression? Reflections on what constitutes feminist research. In M. Maynard & J. Purvis (Eds.), *Researching women's lives from a feminist perspective* (pp. 27–48). Bristol, PA: Taylor & Francis.

Krueger, R. A. (1988). *Focus groups: A practical guide for applied research.* Newbury Park, CA: Sage.

Lather, P. (1991). *Getting smart: Feminist research and pedagogy with/in the postmodern.* New York: Routledge.

Lawrence-Lightfoot, S. (1994). *I've known rivers: Lives of loss and liberation.* New York: Penguin Books.

MacLeod, J. (1987). *Ain't no makin' it: Leveled aspirations in a low-income neighborhood.* Boulder, CO: Westview Press.

Marmon Silko, L. (1996). *Yellow woman and a beauty of the spirit: Essays on Native American life today.* New York: Touchtone.

Maynard, M. (1994). Methods, practice and epistemology: The debate about feminism and research. In M. Maynard & J. Purvis (Eds.), *Researching women's lives from a feminist perspective* (pp. 10–26). Bristol, PA: Taylor & Francis.

Medina, L. (1998). Los espíritus siguen hablando: Chicana spiritualities. In C. Trujillo (Ed.), *Living Chicana theory* (pp. 189–213). Berkeley, CA: Third Woman Press.

Méndez González, R. (1995, October). [Transcribed interview conducted by Dolores Delgado Bernal with Rosalinda Méndez González]. Unpublished data.

Mohanty, C. T. (1994). On race and voice: Challenges for liberal education in the 1990's. In H. A. Giroux & P. McLaren (Eds.), *Between borders: Pedagogy and the politics of cultural studies* (pp. 145–166). New York: Routledge.

Mora, M., & Del Castillo, A. R. (Eds.). (1980). *Mexican women in the United States: Struggles past and present.* Los Angeles: University of California, Los Angeles, Chicano Studies Research Center.

Muñoz, C., Jr. (1973). *The politics of Chicano urban protest: A model of political analysis.* Unpublished doctoral dissertation, Claremont Graduate School.

Negrete, L. R. (1972). Culture clash: The utility of mass protest as a political response. *Journal of Comparative Cultures, 1,* 25–36.

Pardo, M. (1990). Mexican American women grassroots community activists: "Mothers of East Los Angeles." *Frontiers: A Journal of Women Studies, 11,* 1–7.

Pardo, M. (1998). *Mexican American women activists: Identity and resistance in two Los Angeles communities.* Philadelphia: Temple University Press.

Pérez, E. (1993). Speaking from the margin: Uninvited discourse on sexuality and power. In A. de la Torre & B. Pesquera (Eds.), *Building with our hands: New directions in Chicana studies* (pp. 57–71). Berkeley: University of California Press.

Pesquera, B. M., & Segura, D. A. (1990). *Feminism in the ranks: Political consciousness and Chicana/Latina white collar workers.* Paper presented at the annual meeting of the National Association for Chicana and Chicano Studies, Albuquerque, NM.

Pesquera, B. M., & Segura, D. A. (1993). There is no going back: Chicanas and feminism. In N. Alarcón et al. (Eds.), *Chicana critical issues* (pp. 95–115). Berkeley, CA: Third Woman Press.

Piaget, J. (1952). *The origins of intelligence in children.* New York: International Universities Press.

Piaget, J. (1954). *The construction of reality in the child.* New York: Basic Books.

Pizarro, M. (1998). "Chicana/o Power!" Epistemology and methodology for social justice and empowerment in Chicana/o communities. *International Journal of Qualitative Studies in Education, 11*(1), 57–80.

Puckett, M. (1971). *Protest politics in education: A case study in the Los Angeles Unified School District.* Unpublished doctoral dissertation, Claremont Graduate School.

Romero, M. (1989). Twice protected? Assessing the impact of affirmative action on Mexican American women. *Journal of Hispanic Policy, 3,* 83–101

Rosen, G. (1973). The development of the Chicano movement in Los Angeles from 1967–1969. *Aztlán, 4,* 155–183.

Ruiz, V. (1998). *From out of the shadows: Mexican women in twentieth-century America.* Oxford, Eng.: Oxford University Press.

Sandoval, C. (1998). Mestizaje as method: Feminists of color challenge the canon. In C. Trujillo (Ed.), *Living Chicana theory* (pp. 352–370). Berkeley, CA: Third Woman Press.

Scheurich, J. J., & Young, M. D. (1997). Coloring epistemologies: Are our research epistemologies racially biased? *Educational Researcher, 26*(4), 4–16.

Segura, D. (1993). Slipping through the cracks: Dilemmas in Chicana education. In A. de la Torre & B. Pesquera (Eds.), *Building with our hands: New directions in Chicana studies* (pp. 199–216). Berkeley: University of California Press.

Soldatenko, M. A. (1991). Organizing Latina garment workers in Los Angeles. *Aztlán, 20*(1/2), 73–96.

Solorzano, D. G. (1995). The baccalaureate origins of Chicana and Chicano doctorates in the social sciences. *Hispanic Journal of Behavioral Science, 17*(1), 3–32.

Stanley, L., & Wise, S. (1993). *Breaking out again.* London: Routledge.

Strauss, A., & Corbin, J. (1990). *Basics of qualitative research: Grounded theory procedures and techniques.* Newbury Park, CA: Sage.

Talavera-Bustillos, V. (1998). *Chicana college choice and resistance: An exploratory study of first-generation Chicana college students.* Unpublished doctoral dissertation, University of California, Los Angeles.

Trujillo, C. (1993). Chicana lesbians: Fear and loathing in the Chicano community. In N. Alarcón et al. (Eds.), *Chicana critical issues* (pp. 117–125). Berkeley, CA: Third Woman Press.

Trujillo, C. (1998). La Virgen de Guadalupe and her reconstruction in Chicana lesbian desire. In C. Trujillo (Ed.), *Living Chicana theory* (pp. 214–231). Berkeley, CA: Third Woman Press.

Vásquez, M. (1982). Confronting barriers to the participation of Mexican American women in higher education. *Hispanic Journal of Behavioral Sciences, 4,* 147–165.

Villalpando, O. (1996). *The long term effects of college on Chicano and Chicana students: "Other oriented" values, service careers, and community involvement.* Unpublished doctoral dissertation, University of California, Los Angeles.

Villenas, S. (1996). The colonizer/colonized Chicana ethnographer: Identity marginalization, and co-optation in the field. *Harvard Educational Review, 66,* 711–731.

Willis, P. E. (1977). *Learning to labour: How working-class kids got working-class jobs.* Aldershot, Eng.: Gower.

Zambrana, R. (1994). Toward understanding the educational trajectory and socialization of Latina women. In L. Stone & G. M. Boldt (Eds.), *The education feminism reader* (pp. 135–145). New York: Routledge.

Zavella, P. (1993). The politics of race and gender: Organizing Chicana cannery workers in Northern California. In N. Alarcón et al. (Eds.), *Chicana critical issues* (pp. 127–153). Berkeley, CA: Third Woman Press.

I am indebted to the many Chicana scholars, activists, writers, and artists who have influenced my (ongoing) epistemological journey and helped me to better understand my cultural intuition. I am particularly grateful to Adaljiza Sosa-Riddell, Daniel Solorzano, Octavio Villalpando, and Harvard Educational Review Editorial Board members Romina Carrillo and Matthew Hartley for their invaluable insights and suggestions on this article. I take responsibility for my interpretations and, because producing knowledge must be part of an ongoing conversation, I welcome comments and constructive criticism.

APPENDIX 1

Sample of Interview Questions

1. Do you remember what it was that moved you to initially get involved in the Blowouts?
2. Specifically, in what ways were you involved in the planning and implementation of the Blowouts or its aftermath?
3. Think about your mindset as a high school student (or college student): how aware would you say you were of the school situation and the political issues of the Blowouts?
4. In retrospect, how much do you think your participation in the Blowouts was motivated by an awareness of inequities, a desire to change a dominant schooling structure, the excitement of the movement, and/or something else?
5. With hindsight, what do you think the initial stimulus was for your awareness of school problems? (Were you ever a participant at Camp Hess Kramer?)
6. Do you think there was anything special or different about the reasons or ways that male and female students got involved in the Blowouts?
7. Were you involved in organizing tasks, getting different groups of people to work together, and/or in developing a political consciousness in other students? Can you describe this involvement?
8. How aware or involved were you with any of the community newspapers, such as La Raza or Inside Eastside? Did you write, edit, distribute, or read any of these newspapers? If yes, how frequently?
9. Would you say you offered some type of leadership? If yes, how would you describe that leadership? If no, can you explain why you don't consider your participation leadership?
10. In retrospect, did sexism or patriarchy shape your involvement? If so, how? Did it also shape your involvement in a positive (negative) way?
11. Was your awareness of gender inequities a motivation to participate in the Blowouts, or would you say it was more an issue of race, class, or something else?
12. Did your parents (or home life) restrict or encourage your involvement? Can you describe how you were restricted or encouraged? Do you remember the ways in which the involvement of your girlfriends was restricted or encouraged?
13. Did your religious beliefs or those of your family restrict or encourage your participation in any way?
14. Can you talk about the involvement of "Mexicano" or "Spanish Speaking Students" as they were called then?
15. In a lot of social movements there are sometimes sentiments or actions that could be classified as conservative; in your opinion, did you see any of that in connection with the Blowouts? (That is, during the 1920 and 30s, union movements purposely excluded Mexican and Black workers; the early feminist movements ignored women of color and working-class women.)

APPENDIX 2: SAMPLE CORRESPONDENCE

Dear Cassandra:

I'm glad we connected last week and were able to talk. I'm especially happy that you'll be able to make it to the focus group interview on Saturday, February 17 at Self-Help Graphics. By the end of the month, I should be sending a letter out to everyone that includes the time, agenda, and directions to our meeting. In the meantime, I wanted to send you copies of your interview transcription.

I've decided to send transcriptions back to the women I've interviewed so that you each have a chance to see my initial interpretation. I believe it's important that you have an opportunity to reflect and respond to what you said in the interview. This will not only strengthen my analysis, but it allows each woman to interact with and "dialogue" with her own interview.

The interview transcription with comments and questions in the margins is the one I'd like for you to review. These comments and questions are specific to areas that I'm curious or not quite clear about (that is, other women commented on the same issue, or I've since thought of a related issue). If possible I'd love for you to respond in writing on the transcription and/or a separate page. Please bring this copy and your comments with you to the focus group interview. At that time, we can further address any areas you'd like to elaborate on or additional questions I may have. The second clean copy is for you to hold on to — an interesting keepsake.

Finally, as individuals we don't usually read transcriptions of what we've said. And though it can be very interesting, our voices sometime sound different in writing. It's important not to be too concerned with the grammar or specific style of a presentation, as I will edit these in its final form. What I am specifically interested in is the big picture; my research has to do with history and the participation of females in the 1968 East L.A. blowouts. One of the best ways to learn about this topic is through the oral histories of participants. Thanks again for allowing me to learn history from you in this manner.

I look forward to seeing you back in East L.A. on February 17th with the other women I've interviewed. If you have any questions feel free to give me a call.

Abrazos,

APPENDIX 3: SAMPLE CORRESPONDENCE

Dear Women of the Blowouts:

Well, the date of our group interview is drawing near and I wanted to send you this update. On Saturday, February 17th, we will hold our event in East Los Angeles' Self-Help Graphics from 4:00 to 7:00 P.M Tomás Benitez, assistant director of Self-Help (and Mita Cuaron's husband) was able to secure space for us in the art gallery. The art gallery will be particularly special given the beautiful exhibit, La Vida Indigena, and the fact that the interview will be filmed.

The following seven women have confirmed their attendance and will make up our interview group: Celeste Baca, Paula Crisostomo, Mita Cuaron, Rosalinda Méndez González, Tanya Luna Mount, Rachael Ochoa Cervera, and Cassandra Zacarias. With such an interesting strong group of women (none of whom were at a loss for words during the individual interviews), I thought it might be a good idea to spend the first 30 minutes socializing and catching up! Some light refreshments will be provided.

The agenda for the actual group interview will follow a semistructured format. That is, based on your responses in the individual interviews, I will identify a few topics I would like to ask the group to respond to. In addition, I would also like each of you to bring up any blowout-related issues or events that are particularly interesting to you. What makes this different than your individual interviews is the new information, differing viewpoints, and recurring issues that are generated from the group interaction. I'm not as interested in reconstructing the "Truth" of what happened as I am interested in your individual experiences and their similarities and differences.

A small volunteer camera crew led by Xochitl González (Rosalinda's Méndez González's daughter) and Alfredo Heredia (a cousin of Sal Castro's) will be filming the interview. I'm asking that each of you bring any photos, artifacts, or newspaper articles that you may have related to the blowouts. For example, Tanya found a blowout button; Mita has some photos and her mosaic art piece; and Celeste has the 1968 Lincoln Yearbook. If anyone has the picture of Bobby Kennedy with some of the blowout students, I'd really appreciate you digging it up and sharing it with the group. We will have a table set up so that we can actually document on film the items you bring. Finally, most of you have had a chance to review the transcript of your individual interview. Please bring the transcript copy and any additional responses or comments you might have written down.

I look forward to seeing each of you at 4:00 on Saturday, February 17. (Feel free to come early and enjoy the art exhibit.) I have enclosed the address and directions to Self-Help Graphics. If you have any questions feel free to give me a call or an e-mail if you're connected to cyberlandia.

Abrazos,

Negotiating Legacies:
Audre Lorde, W. E. B. DuBois,
Marlon Riggs, and Me

TOWNSAND PRICE-SPRATLEN

A power of the possible
Lies in reminders
Of past choices of greatness

Pictures help us
Pictures and words
Of Saints
Audre, William and Marlon
Their words
Written and spoken
These are the substance of a legacy left
The shaping of both present and future

A power of the possible
Lies in reminders
Of past choices of greatness

Their ability
To see so clearly
To raise questions, seeking answers
To produce with brilliance
And commitment
These three warriors
The substance of a legacy left

Pictures help us
To remember
— Townsand Price-Spratlen

As a first-year assistant professor of sociology, I realize that my primary goal is to be an effective educator. My effectiveness as an educator rests, in part, on my ability to seek out and build upon the powerful contributions of those who have walked this pathway long before I did. A part of what is required is the process of building

Harvard Educational Review Vol. 66 No. 2 Summer 1996, 216–230

a proactive personal and professional identity. This requires associating myself with examples of excellence, including historical figures and their good works. It is a process of "negotiating legacies" — that is, learning the lessons of history by seeking to understand the contemporary and historical contexts and contributions of our ancestors.

Among the key elements in building identity is striving to understand the primary characteristics that define our group affiliations. We are all many things at once, and some of what we are may seemingly contradict other parts of our identity.[1] For example, as a gay man of African descent, I, like many others, live out what may appear to be antagonistic truths. The apparent antagonism rests in a dysfunctional prioritizing of identities represented in the question, "Which are you, African American or gay?" To act as if these things are not always simultaneously true — and both worthy of loving affirmation — is to fall victim to the socially constructed antagonism between them.

My intent here is to consider a critical work of each of three individuals whose efforts have contributed greatly to my sense of self, my desire to achieve in both work- and nonwork-related settings, and my understanding of the responsibilities of an educator. Through Audre Lorde's *The Cancer Journals* (1980), W. E. B. DuBois's *The Souls of Black Folk* (1903/1953), and Marlon Riggs's *Tongues Untied* (1989), I continuously try to internalize greatness, negotiating their legacies one choice at a time.

NEGOTIATING LEGACIES

Among the tasks that lie before us as educators is to move our students and ourselves toward what Paulo Freire (1970) calls "the practice of freedom." A first step is building and reinforcing a link between external information and the individual student. A second step is for the student to extend this link and thereby learn to make proactive choices to bring about constructive social change. Negotiating legacies is critical to this practice.

As previously stated, negotiating legacies is an introspective process in which we attempt to learn the lessons of history by seeking to understand the contexts and contributions of our ancestors. It is a process of personifying the label "role model" by discovering expressions of our best self in the choices of others.[2]

The specific legacies we choose are often a product of our group affiliations, or of the "master variables" in sociological research, including race, ethnicity, age, gender, marital status, and socioeconomic status. Lorde, DuBois, and Riggs were all individuals who, for me, challenged the static perception of group affiliation by investigating the intersections of multiple selves within themselves. These authors recognized, in fact celebrated, one's affiliation with multiple groups. They considered gender, sexuality, race, religion, and class to be equally worthy points on a circle of identity, rather than placing them in a hierarchy of relative importance. Riggs, for example, suggested that a hierarchy of identities, which contradicts celebrating the intersection of multiple selves, is problematic, since all characteristics can be "nurturing and nourishing of your spirit. You can embrace all of that lovingly and equally" (Simmons, 1991b, p. 191). According to Simmons, queer intellectuals of African descent are being challenged to address questions of identity by providing "an understanding and a vision of homosexuality motivated by our love, not our anger" (p. 216). Negotiating legacies is one response to this identity challenge. We all can learn from reaching out to evaluate the lives of those who have previously nurtured their intersections within, and have left us pieces of their personal journeys.

Fundamental to the process of negotiating legacies is not being overwhelmed by the choices of those who moved with greatness or by the responsibility to then act with the knowledge acquired. The goal of the practice of freedom, as I understand it as an educator, is to "do what you can where you are."[3] In learning the lessons of history, both teacher and student are "challenging demons" — any individuals, acts, perceptions, or whispers from within and without that affirm negativity, inadequacy, or personal insecurity. Success in this process requires the ability to operate independently (and communally) with confidence and skill that is often developed through following the examples of others (Edwards & Polite, 1992). By "statin', debatin', and celebratin'" the ideas and ideals we value most, special legacies and special people worthy of the label "role model" arise.

SPECIAL LEGACIES

All legacies are not created equal. For reasons unique to any given person, some legacies are more important than others. For me, the lives and works of Lorde, DuBois, and Riggs constitute the cornerstones of a trinity of excellence. While each author produced a body of work worthy of serious study, three classics stand out in my mind. Through these works, I have come to understand the spiritual symmetry they provide.

Lorde, DuBois, and Riggs effectively merged art, education, and activism, teaching their lessons by living lives of daily "praxis." That is, they each recognized the importance of linking introspective reflection — an evaluation of their ideology and their day-to-day action — to the choices they made in order to live well. Their praxis orientations are perhaps best illustrated by the question posed by Audre Lorde, "What are the particular details within our lives that can be scrutinized and altered to bring about change?" (1984, p. 122). By refining this link throughout their lives, their moments of praxis created culture and included "self-determination (in contrast to coercion), intentionality (in contrast to reaction), sociality (in contrast to privatism), creativity (in contrast to sameness), and rationality (in contrast to blind chance)" (Young, 1978, p. 91). Each of these authors was of African descent, and each acknowledged openly the intersections within them, spending much of their lives proactively merging these sometimes disparate dimensions of themselves. Each was a reluctant warrior, willing to share their quiet strength with others while being true to both the bounty of their blessings and the sorrows of their pain. Speaking within and across communities, they seldom lost sight of their uniqueness, of their ability to give voice to individual and personal concerns, of their expression of thoughts, hopes, fears, and desires shared by many outside of themselves. They challenged oppression, the historical continuum of domination and servitude, because they were spiritually and "psychologically able to experience things and each other, outside of the context of violence and exploitation" (Marcuse, 1969, p. 25). Their goal was not to disappear within some melted mass, but rather to acknowledge the self-celebration in seeking common ground.

Each author entered my life at a time of critical need, helping me to merge my personal and professional identities. Reflecting upon their legacies enabled me to celebrate and affirm different elements of myself without losing sight of my wholeness. Audre Lorde was a poet, mother, womanist-feminist, and academic of Grenadian descent; she was proudly an activist and lesbian. W. E. B. DuBois was an accomplished social scientist, father, pan-Africanist, professor, magazine editor, and organizational developer, a man of mixed racial ancestry who merged nationalist and integrationist traditions in African American social thought. Marlon Riggs was a filmmaker, partner/lover, culture critic, and academic; he was proudly gay and a quiet activist. Individuals of immense strength and vision, each transcended tragedy, recognizing that their private struggles were both personal and public. These three great authors warmly celebrated their praxis orientations.

SACRED TRUTHS: AUDRE LORDE

Published in 1980 by Spinster's Ink, *The Cancer Journals,* as the title suggests, chronicles Audre Lorde's battles with, and triumphs over, her first bouts with breast cancer in the late 1970s. In it she stated, "Visions of the future I can create have been honed by the lessons of my limitations. Now I wish to give form with honesty and precision to the pain faith labor and loving which this period of my life has translated into strength for me" (Lorde, 1980, p. 15).

Lorde's *Journals* takes us through extremely personal elements of her journey with disease, effectively placing these elements in a sociocultural context of introspection, the family, the medical profession, and the capitalist imperative of cultural denial and inadequacy. In 1984, when I studied Lorde's *Journals,* it was immensely empowering for me to read of her triumphs over tragedy. "It was very important for me, after my mastectomy, to develop and encourage my own internal sense of power" (p. 73). Through her words I recognized anew the reciprocity of power that is a fundamental element of the relationship between author/artist and reader/observer. That reciprocity was the power that Lorde gained from documenting her postmastectomy realization, the power that I then gained from reading her words, and the power that her legacy gained from having inspired me. When I read her statement, I realized that it is essential for me to affirm my own ability to create change when I am being exposed to any significant challenge. It is this relationship of shared inspiration that is the foundation of negotiating legacies, be it in the classroom as an educator, in civic activities, or in conversations with a friend.

Having kept a journal since the age of thirteen, I was fascinated to see the value of journalizing presented so affirmingly through the eyes of emotional, physical, and spiritual pain. Through the pages of Lorde's *Journal,* I was introduced to a lesbian of African descent who faced cancer and found expressions of her best self from within that experience. Though she lost her right breast, Lorde recognized that loss is "different from," not "less than." She emphasized that missing history is *not* a weakness, be it a lost breast, or some other dimension of a past self. Too often, the worst expressions of denial come from those closest to empathy (i.e., other cancer survivors vesting extreme faith in the illusion of prosthesis). Facing death, celebrating a loving reciprocity, acting on duty and carpe diem (seize the day) are synergistic, not antagonistic, processes.

A woman of profound vision, Lorde emphasized the need to understand the potential divisiveness and potential strength in differences, showing us that anything that can act to divide can also be the foundation upon which greater understanding is built. As an educator, she effectively merged art and academia, celebrating stolen moments, time away from day-to-day responsibilities, in her journal. Born of Grenadian parents, Lorde was the personification of cross-cultural truths.

Audre Lorde inspired me to challenge the assumption of a disjuncture between my efforts as a positivist social scientist, journal keeper, and creative writer. These paths are not contradictory and can, in fact, be complementary. Lorde helped me to understand better the healing potential that the pages of a journal provide. I have been brought back to sanity on many a day by writing in my journal when an uncomfortable meeting or class, realization of flawed data, or a frustrating period of data analysis made insanity appear to be a much more viable option.

Speaking truth to power, literally and figuratively, is perhaps what Audre Lorde did best. Her legacy inspires me to challenge the silences of being closeted in my workplace and other areas of my life by adhering to the heterosexist conveniences of "passing" for straight and reinforces the importance of defining my surroundings in self-affirming ways. As a result, my office walls are a collage of images that celebrate the primary identity labels and the intersections they create: African American, queer, male, educator, writer, middle class, student of history.

Most importantly, Audre Lorde's legacy nurtures, in fact demands, that I challenge my own bigotries and move toward more than just perceptions of and actions toward individuals and groups whose experiences and identities are different from my own. She is my spark to a level of personal honesty, to the task of being true to myself and my vision as often as possible. This shapes the lessons I plan and present, the words I speak, the faith and hope that I possess, and my every interaction with others. Because of the brilliant strength of her legacy, I continually strive to "feel more deeply, value those feelings more, [so that I] can put those feelings together with what I know in order to fashion a vision of and pathway toward true change" (Lorde, 1980, p. 63).

To educators, Lorde's words illustrate that the power of community often gains strength by touching a power within each of ourselves. By reaching out with others, we can often make better sense of the "confusions of living" (p. 47). Her words speak of finding strength where she thought she had none, and are thus a living individual and cultural testament to Frederick Douglass's admonition that "power concedes nothing without demand." Her words and her life are profound examples of how to challenge any manifestation of oppression. She is an example of contradicting the contradiction: gay in a "straight" world; a woman in a "man's" world; a person of color in a "white" world. *Journals* is the telling of lesbian truths through the strong poetic eyes of a brilliant woman of African descent. It is one powerful piece of a legacy I will be negotiating for some time to come.

SACRED TRUTHS: W. E. B. DuBOIS

Originally published in 1903, DuBois's *The Souls of Black Folk* is a collection of essays and stories in which he reflects on societal injustice, historical figures, personal circumstances, and the forms and functions of leadership. The book is, in large part, a speculative assessment of the problems and potentials of the twentieth century from the pen of a well-educated, northern-born, biracial, African American scholar. DuBois was born in 1868 and raised in Great Barrington, Massachusetts. He completed his Ph.D. at Harvard University in 1894, two years before the *Plessy v. Ferguson* U.S. Supreme Court decision, which galvanized the "separate but equal" statute and gave legal teeth to the imposition of Jim Crow laws throughout the South. *Souls* was published when the vast majority of African Americans lived and worked a half-step above chattel slavery in the agrarian South. Hailed by Roy Wilkins, former executive secretary of the NAACP, as "one of the great books of our century" (promotional liner note of 1961 Fawcett Publications edition), *Souls* is a work of fundamental importance, with its blend of fiction, social criticism, and cultural commentary. Its title alone is both an acknowledgment and a celebration of the process of faith in the empowerment of African American people.

Souls provides an agenda for proactive choice-making in our collective struggle to move people of African descent, and American culture as a whole, toward a broader justice. It stands as a painful illustration that current discussions of a "leadership vacuum" in African America are not new, that there exists a rich tradition of disparate voices suggesting collective alternatives and directions. *Souls* is a text of immense foresight. In the chapter "Of the Dawn of Freedom," for example, DuBois chronicles the rise and fall of the Freedmen's Bureau.[4] Today we can see how attacks on the Bureau parallel more recent attempts to stunt government initiatives toward broader justice, such as affirmative action. DuBois creatively links social science and personal essay/reflection, cultural criticism and leadership critique. He provides a literary framework for using Afrocentric autobiographical reflection as a springboard for sociocultural analysis and an assessment of intergroup relations that other authors have adopted beautifully. Examples of this framework can be found in the works of Essex Hemphill in *Ceremonies* (1992), or Eddy L. Harris in *South of Haunted Dreams* (1993).

Souls includes what is perhaps DuBois's greatest single work, a brief chapter entitled "Of the Passing of the First Born," in which he struggles to understand the personal meaning and professional context of the death of his newborn son. With its interdisciplinary merging, *Souls* is indicative of DuBois's entire career. Over the course of his life, he completed a diverse set of vocational and avocational pursuits, including his work as an empirical sociologist, his later works of fiction, his work in prejudice and race theory, his efforts as a propagandist, his brief return to academia, and, finally, his self-exile in Ghana, a homeland that was not his place of birth.

I was introduced to the legacy of DuBois through conversations with my parents, and through the speeches of Dr. Bobby Wright, a Black nationalist psychologist and writer. Although I was trained as a sociologist, I went through graduate school without being assigned a single work by DuBois. This is especially problematic, given that he authored well over one hundred articles, a detailed set of lengthy sociological studies of African American life, and twenty-three books, many of which provided the basis for later sociological work.

Souls offers an excellent example of the educator as "propagandist," in that it provides a thorough, historical, and uniquely African American definition of the personal process of education as the practice of freedom. In the book's fourteen essays, DuBois provides what Freire calls a "social praxis . . . helping to free human beings from the oppression that strangles them in their objective reality. It is therefore political education, just as political as the education that claims to be neutral, although actually serving the power elite" (1985, p. 125). Illustrating the importance of being informed by a cross-cultural, interdisciplinary approach, *Souls* presents the professional benefits of a personal exploration of the meaning of identity politics. One line in particular still rings true as we approach the twenty-first century: "The problem of the twentieth century is the problem of the color line" (p. 23). *Souls* remains true to its title, celebrating the value of seeking out spiritual answers to "vocational" social scientific questions.

DuBois's legacy has directly impacted my worldview and my approach as an educator in several ways. First, and perhaps most simply, becoming familiar with his life has reinforced a healthy skepticism about whose works are defined as central to the canon of my discipline. This skepticism has led me to be more inclusive in the content of my teaching and to value a wider diversity of contributions. For example, when I presented an overview of the field of urban sociology in my graduate seminar, I began by discussing *The Philadelphia Negro* (1899), DuBois's classic work that predates the "Chicago School" of urban analysis by nearly a generation.[5] I also mentioned to my students how urban sociology, or any discipline, can simply ignore significant contributions of people who don't fall conveniently within the color-coded and often racist boundaries used to define the "seminal works" of an area of study.[6]

Second, beginning with my graduate training, the enormity of DuBois's legacy and my celebration of it affirmed my legitimacy or sense of belonging, even if others around me did not value his legacy as I did. This was especially important when some faculty members responded to me as if I did not belong to the academy. With that doubt removed, I was able to get on with the tasks at hand, striving to make the contributions that I value most, and building on the firm foundation of DuBois's legacy.

Third, DuBois's legacy leads me to continue to seek progressive change through the platform provided by academia — even though DuBois left academia in disgust, no longer valuing the potential contribution of a socially scientific accounting of racial dynamics. Perhaps with time, I, too, will lose faith in the potential of academia, and choose to make contributions through organizational development or some other outlet. But I doubt it. The limitations of a progressive agenda from *any* platform, be it academia or someplace else, rest in the intransigence of benefits acquired through race/White privilege that sustained oppression perpetuates.

Finally, I am constantly inspired by DuBois's legacy of determination to create and sustain a functional balance between my goals as a researcher and educator, and the duty and responsibilities of acting on the many blessings that I have been given. For DuBois, that meant participating in organizational development as a self-defined propagandist, as one of the key figures in the initial establishment of the Niagara Movement, and in the establishment of *The Crisis* magazine through the NAACP.

In the pursuit of this balance during graduate school, I worked to establish and sustain a level of excellence in the classroom, while helping to organize and participating in two organizations, Brother-to-Brother and the African American Graduate Student Association (AAGSA). Brother-to-Brother's intent was to enhance a sense of community among gay and bisexual men of African descent in the Seattle area by addressing political, spiritual, health/wellness, and social concerns. AAGSA focused on the needs of African American graduate and professional students, with an emphasis on building social and vocational networks and addressing political concerns on the University of Washington campus.

DuBois's legacy has instilled in me the desire and intention to continue the pursuit of academic excellence, coupled with organizational participation and community mobilization activities. This is what DuBois's call to action demands.

SACRED TRUTHS: MARLON RIGGS

Completed by Marlon Riggs in 1989, *Tongues Untied* is a videographic exploration of the substance, meaning, and contemporary challenges of the lives of gay men of African descent. Part biography, part poetry, part essay, it is a developmental exploration into the dynamics of identity and identity formation. The film provided me with my first visual image of the potential blending of race consciousness with an awareness of class status and a celebration of the "gay spirit." *Tongues* challenges the prevailing sentiment of homophobia within African America, unapologetically affirming an Afrocentric, gay identity.

Born into a military family in Fort Worth, Texas, in 1957, Marlon Riggs completed his B.A. at Harvard University in the mid-1970s. He later completed an M.A. at the University of California at Berkeley, specializing in historical documentary filmmaking. Riggs completed numerous projects prior to *Tongues,* including the Emmy Award–winning *Ethnic Notions* (1986), which evaluated historical representations of people of African descent in the mass media and advertising. *Tongues Untied* is an illustration of a gay educator of African descent who rises to the challenge of proactive necessity, as he describes it below, and expresses his abilities by openly presenting the lessons to be learned through autobiographical truth. Choosing not to hide behind a heterosexist veil to experience "success" as a filmmaker, Riggs acknowledges the responsibility of praxis that involved using his vocational skill to contribute to progressive change. In an interview entitled "Tongues Untied" he states:

> My feeling is that there are imperatives in one's life. I think people during the 1960s, more so than now, realized what that meant. There are some things you've got to do. You don't know all the answers. You don't know all of the consequences — you've got to do something because you know it's right. There is no alternative. You cannot sit in silence. You cannot maintain neutrality. You know it's right and you've got to move. (Simmons, 1991a, p. 191)

Tongues Untied, a work of uncompromising honesty, depicts some of the pain and the anguish that marks the lives of many African American gay men. In addition, it illustrates that the acknowledgment of sadness and loss is not a weakness, but a strength that affirms that we are not alone as we live our lives. The resulting unity of struggle can also move us toward transcending oppressive forces, individuals, and institutions. *Tongues* reaffirms the connection between individual and group destiny, recognizing that this destiny is to be fashioned of intersecting groups, being gay and being of African descent. It raises questions of gay cultural dynamics in an African American context, including the role of "signifying" and dance in negotiating interactions. For example, a portion of the film considers the practice of snapping one's fingers as a physical exclamation point following a verbal exchange. In a tone that humorously mocks social science, Riggs illustrates a menu of snap style alternatives that were most popular in the late 1980s. While this signifying had been done in veiled terms by people of the Harlem Renaissance (e.g., Countee Cullen, Langston Hughes, the Harlem Drag Balls, etc.), Riggs provides contemporary illustrations of the gay cultural dynamics (e.g., his own developmental processing, participating in Gay Pride marches) and relates them to the process of living in the age of AIDS.

The battles and debates that ensued in 1990 and 1991 over the airing of *Tongues Untied* on PBS exemplified the ambiguities of negotiating personal intersections on a public stage. An example of this was the discomfort in the African American community about *Tongues*'s meaning, relevance, importance, and value. The film also exemplifies the victories in the battles over funding artistic expression through the National Education Association, raising questions about the often unpleasant mixture of the politics of culture with the culture of politics.

Tongues challenges stereotypes of sexuality, sexuality education, group affiliation, and heterosexist norms. By illustrating the personal complexities of macrolevel struggles through its portrayal of the "gay movement" as an individual as well as a social process, it presents the artistry of a sociological imagination. Riggs affirms the sociocultural lessons of a music lyric and the deep emotional implications that a classic song hurtfully provides. For example, the film ends with the song, "You Can Do What You Want to Do." The lyrics emphasize the need to search for and find one's own voice amidst a chorus of cultural roles from which we choose, and to question the underdeveloping restrictions these roles in life often impose. Many life-affirming options lie before us, beyond the boundaries that heterosexist norms provide. "Playing it straight" (i.e., being gay, but leading a nongay life) literally and figuratively is one such role used by many to silence the personal complexities that arise when we move beyond the boundaries that bigoted norms demand. The abusive consequences of living within these boundaries should be challenged — strongly, frequently, and in many different ways. "You Can Do What You Want to Do" suggests that we seek out and create new roles and options, that we live them, celebrate them, and not be swayed into a return to silence by accepting the restrictive roles dictated by those bigoted norms. *Tongues Untied* stands as a proud example of how to carry out the day-to-day promise and practice of an educator's call to action.

Pedagogically, the film presents the educational contributions of many voices, the value of autobiographical elaboration, and the potential for effectively merging the two. The work of many other writers, artists, and activists are represented in the film, including Essex Hemphill, Blackberri, and the late Joseph Beam. Sharing his HIV-positive status with the viewer, Riggs ties his status to the proactive necessity of community affiliation, a recognition of the process of facing death, the ancestral power of those who have gone before us, and the strength of purpose that power provides for the living. Riggs's *Tongues Untied*, like Lorde's *The Cancer Journals* and DuBois's *The Souls of Black Folk*, is a work of uncompromising brilliance by an educator/artist/activist performing at the peak of his craft.

BRIDGING DISTANCE 101

In the summer of 1994, while a postdoctoral research fellow at Pennsylvania State University, I first used the lessons of praxis taught to me by these three great truth-tellers while teaching an introductory sociology course. Using *Sociology: Experiencing Changing Societies* (Kammeyer, Ritzer, & Yetman, 1994) as the textbook, I had the class view *Tongues Untied* as an introduction to a discussion of chapter seven, "Sexual Behavior from a Sociological Perspective." I felt a great deal of apprehension about showing the film in class because, as Audre Lorde pointed out, "the transformation of silence into language and action is an act of self-revelation and that always seems fraught with danger" (p. 21). I realized that the dangers, however real, were basically fears of the hypothetical, fears that overvalued remaining silent and the veil of "objective" presentation that the silence affords.

Having full responsibility for a course for the first time, I felt that my teaching skills were being placed in a fishbowl, subject to maximum scrutiny. For me, the fears were quite personal. Fear of getting bad teacher evaluations. Fear of having a student make a formal complaint about me within the department. Fear that having shown the film could be used as an excuse to dismiss me as little more than a cheerleader for Left-leaning causes who lacked a grasp of the material that a potential faculty member needs. Fear that academic opportunities would no longer be presented to me. I imagined being defined as "unemployable within academia," as an individual much more effective at sensationalizing topics than presenting substantive content to students coherently. "See," the critics inside my head would respond, "give him full charge of a course and he turns it from Intro Sociology into an Afrocentric Queer Nation meeting. We don't need that kind of junk in a university setting!"

My fears, while to some degree rational and well founded, were also flawed in many ways. Besides magnifying negative possibilities and not seriously considering positive ones, my fears did not take into account my position of authority — I was the instructor, which gave me all of the legitimacy I needed to transform my silence and show the film. The identities and worldview of all instructors constantly shape their presentation of a given topic. In organizing a course, a key question that must be addressed is, "How can this topic be effectively presented?" The film represented my use of discretion in answering that question. By showing the film, I made a choice consistent with the praxis of negotiating legacies: I changed my silence into language and action through learning the lessons of history and by celebrating Riggs's contributions, while still addressing the central issue of sexual behavior from a sociological perspective.

I sat near the back of the classroom and watched the thirty-five, mostly White students watch, listen, and react. While most sat in stillness, two reactions stand out in my memory. First, a young White man responded with audible revulsion when an image of two African American men kissing affectionately came across the screen. Second, at the end of the film, as I turned on the lights, I saw the tear-filled eyes of a young African American man. As he wiped his eyes, he shared with me a cautious smile, and, by doing so, gave me all the affirmation I needed for choosing to show the film. The class discussion that followed was safe, neutral, annoyingly noncommittal. Little anger was exhibited, and no vehement disagreement was expressed.

Showing the film and facilitating the discussion that followed was an act of negotiating legacies, of celebrating the contributions of my ancestors and illustrating a link between external information, the individual student, and action. I had hoped for a more lively discussion, one in which the brutal honesty of personal bigotries were at the center, one in which small steps were made in moving from the security of personal bigotries to a greater appreciation of the benefits of broader social justice, and the role that individuals can play in its realization. This appreciation seldom, if ever, results from a single group discussion, and the likelihood of movement toward such a view sharply declines when a space for brutal honesty is not created and maintained. I was annoyed at my inability to create such a space, and also that no students volunteered to create such a space among themselves.

The following day, an older student, a White fortyish mother of three, asked to talk with me alone outside the classroom. Prefacing her remarks by citing Marian Wright Edelman, she spoke of the need for "moral fiber" in the classroom, a "spiritual initiative" by educators, and "a return to the celebration of family." I agreed with her, and then challenged her on her perceptions of inclusion and definitions of these phrases. Out of a class of thirty-five students, only two students were willing to share in ways that had meaning for me; the older White woman, and a young African American man who was moved to tears by Riggs's brilliance.

These two interactions illustrated that at least two students were affected by the film's images in a very personal way, and that they were willing to break down the distance between the content of classroom information and their individual lives. The White woman's response challenged my authority and use of course content. This is a part of Friere's "practice of freedom," the praxis of being a student. That these two students would exhibit these skills in a class I was teaching in reaction to a film that means so much to me made both interactions especially enjoyable.

COMMON THREADS

Despite the different historical times of their contributions and their very different backgrounds and vocational disciplines, the three individuals featured in this article share some commonalities. As previously mentioned, throughout their lives and in the three works discussed, Lorde, DuBois, and Riggs all challenged the static perception of group affiliation by investigating various intersections within their own lives. Specifically, they acknowledged the multifaceted character of personal identity, and they led lives that embraced the multiple elements of their own identities. By doing so, they acted on a long-celebrated declaration of the responsibility of African Americans to "lift as we climb," while recognizing the need to define the "we" with forethought and care.

Through their strength, intellect, and commitment, Lorde, DuBois, and Riggs showed that praxis is far more than a theoretical construct. Leading by example and living lives seemingly void of bombastic grandness, they gave meaning to the process of the practice of freedom in everyday life by explicitly demanding the examination of their individual relationship to community — a community that was neither static nor homogeneous. Their examples show that we must ask and answer questions of identity in order to better understand our individual and collective roles in bringing about progressive social change.

Lorde, DuBois, and Riggs led lives that creatively challenged the prevailing authority. They recognized that the platform from which they as educators spoke allowed for some latitude in their efforts to break down institutional bigotries. They constantly self-scrutinized their own wholeness (Africanness/lesbianness/Americanness/gayness/classness/genderness) and, through their ongoing celebration of the written and spoken word, turned that scrutiny into legacies of excellence. They were all autobiographers, journal keepers, seekers and tellers of truth. As educators, they recognized that the classroom is only one dimension in a multidimensional strategy of change.

Each sought out, found, and redefined the critical symmetry between art and the scholarly presentation of information. In its positive mode, this information, like all propaganda, "is necessary to create social reality since social reality does not emerge unless there is conviction, belief, trust, and faith" (Young, 1978, p. 94). Each of them acknowledged and, by working both within and outside of the boundaries of the academy, to some degree transcended the limitations of the "community of scholars" that composed higher education. Each communicated with a broad audience, reaching beyond the scope of their personal circumstances to build a meaningful partnership between vocation and avocation and, in so doing, appealing to a diverse audience.

Each was touched by tragedy. We lost Audre Lorde to cancer, and Marlon Riggs to AIDS. And though W. E. B. DuBois died of old age at ninety-five, the death of his first-born son had a profound impact on the remaining sixty-two years of his life. Each was willing to question the meaning of pain or tragedy in their lives, the consequences that pain or tragedy brought about, and the challenges to isolation that the public nature of private battles can allow. Living daily the lessons that working for justice teaches, each seemingly gained and acted on what Audre Lorde articulated so beautifully: "I feel more deeply, value those feelings more, and can put those feelings together with what I know in order to fashion a vision of and pathway toward true change" (1980, p. 63).

SYMMETRY THAT REMAINS

Nearly thirty years ago, University of Michigan historian Harold Cruse stated that "the radical wing of the Negro Movement in America sorely needs a social theory based on the living ingredients of Afro-American history" (Cruse, 1967, p. 557). Negotiating legacies is a process that contributes to the development of that theory by bringing together the praxis orientations of historical greatness. Each of the legacies of this special trinity — Lorde, DuBois, and Riggs — will continue to inform and inspire me as I respond daily to the tasks that lie before me. Complex and diverse, and sometimes overwhelming, these legacies are an acknowledgment of self-celebration. They provide a call to action and motivate me to realize my best self. Together they inspire me to strive to merge the seemingly disparate elements of my identity: African American and gay, educator and propagandist, scholar and artist — the celebration of simultaneous truths.

Audre Lorde, W. E. B. DuBois, and Marlon Riggs now rest as creators of history, people who triumphed. They will remain symbols of greatness and excellence, of achievement and opportunity. The process of negotiating their legacies allows me to seek out the spiritual significance of past thought through the focused lens of those who saw so clearly, and to share that clarity through their consciousness, creed, and work. At its core, negotiating legacies involves learning the lessons of being proactive through the expressions of excellence of those we most value and respect.

NOTES

1. A detailed discussion of the complexities of identity formation is beyond the scope of this article.

2. For a variety of reasons, the concept of the role model has come under attack recently. For example, some critics point out the potential for an inappropriate magnification of the importance of the "other" in the process of self-definition, extending from an abusive hierarchy of human worth that negates a more humane perception of human equity (Duneier, 1992). However, the potential pitfalls do not outweigh the positive benefits of using role models in identity formation. Indeed, imitating has been a part of identity formation for centuries.

3. This is from a statement made by the character Billy Kwan (played by Linda Hunt) in the film *The Year of Living Dangerously* (McElroy & Wier, 1993).

4. During the period of Reconstruction in the 1870s, the Freedmen's Bureau was a government-sponsored organization created to assist newly freed African Americans in their social and political adjustments to citizenship.

5. The development of the field of urban sociology is typically traced to a group of sociologists affiliated with the University of Chicago during the period 1915–1940. "Robert Park, Ernest Burgess, and their colleagues and students advocated a scientific sociology that could help make sense of the complex social milieu of an industrial society" (Lee, 1988, p. 201).

6. For an elaboration of this point, see Ralph Wiley's (1993) engaging reflections on "identity and purpose."

REFERENCES

Cruse, H. (1967). *The crisis of the Negro intellectual.* New York: William Morrow.

DuBois, W. E. B. (1899). *The Philadelphia Negro: A social study.* Boston: Ginn.

DuBois, W. E. B. (1953). *The souls of Black folk.* Greenwich, CT: Fawcett. (Original work published 1903)

Duneier, M. (1992). *Slim's table: Race, respectability, and masculinity.* Chicago: University of Chicago Press.

Edwards, A., & Polite, C. K. (1992). *Children of the dream: The psychology of Black success.* New York: Anchor.

Freire, P. (1970). *The pedagogy of the oppressed.* New York: Seabury Press.

Freire, P. (1985). *The politics of education: Culture, power, and liberation.* South Hadley, MA: Bergin & Garvey.

Harris, E. L. (1993). *South of haunted dreams: A ride through slavery's old backyard.* New York: Simon and Schuster.

Hemphill, E. (1992). *Ceremonies: Prose and poetry.* New York: Plume.

Kammeyer, K. C. W., Ritzer, G., & Yetman, N. R. (1994). *Sociology: Experiencing changing societies.* Boston: Allyn & Bacon.

Lee, B. A. (1988). Urban sociology. In E. F. Borgotta & K. S. Cook (Eds.), *The future of sociology* (pp. 203–223). Newbury Park, CA: Sage.

Lorde, A. (1980). *The cancer journals.* San Francisco: Spinster's Ink.

Lorde, A. (1984). *Sister outsider: Essays and speeches.* Freedom, CA: Crossing Press.

Marcuse, H. (1969). *An essay on liberation*. Boston: Beacon Press.

McElroy, J. (Producer), & Wier, P. (Director). (1993). *The year of living dangerously* [Video]. Culver City, CA: Culver City Home Videos (Originally released by Metro-Goldwyn-Mayer, 1982)

Riggs, M. (Producer, Director). (1986). *Ethnic notions* [Film]. San Francisco: California News Reel.

Riggs, M. (Producer, Director). (1989). *Tongues untied* [Film]. San Francisco: California News Reel.

Simmons, R. (1991a). Tongues untied: An interview with Marlon Riggs. In E. Hemphill (Ed.), *Brother to brother: New writings of Black gay men* (pp. 189–199). Boston: Alyson.

Simmons, R. (1991b). Some thoughts on the challenges facing Black gay intellectuals. In E. Hemphill (Ed.), *Brother to brother: New writings of Black gay men* (pp. 21–228). Boston: Alyson.

Wiley, R. (1993). *What Black people should do now: Dispatches from near the vanguard*. New York: Ballantine Books.

Young, T. R. (1978). *Red feather dictionary of socialist sociology*. San Francisco: Red Feather Institute.

The author would like to thank Ronald Chennault for his help and supportive feedback in preparing this manuscript. Thanks also go to the three brilliant people who shined so brightly while on this earth, and who are celebrated in this article. Each of them left us with a powerful legacy of triumph. Because of them, the path on which we, the living, will take our next steps is far more clear.

Latino Studies: New Contexts,
New Concepts

JUAN FLORES

Latino Studies has been in the news of late. The most visible student protests of recent years on college campuses throughout the country have been directed at securing commitments from university administrations to establish programs in Latino and Asian American Studies. The office takeovers, hunger strikes, and angry teach-ins represent a clamor for new programs, faculty, courses, and resources in these neglected areas of social knowledge. This movement is making the news not because of any alarming tactics or massive participation, but because the demands are being lodged at the loftiest postsecondary institutions in the country, the Ivy League schools. After a twenty-five-year history of such programs at public urban universities such as the City University of New York (CUNY) and San Francisco State University, the call for Latino Studies and Asian American Studies has been raised, and can no longer be ignored, at Columbia, Princeton, Cornell, the University of Pennsylvania, and most of the other Ivies.

There is, of course, always another face to such news, a more somber mobilization frequently hidden from public view. While Latino and Asian students at elite institutions are busy facing down deans and fasting in their tents, the iron hand of fiscal constraints and shifting ideological priorities is at work slashing, reducing, and consolidating existing Latino and Asian American Studies programs and services at nearby public colleges and universities. For example, in the spring of 1996, the president of CUNY's City College announced that the departments of Africana, Latin American and Hispanic Caribbean, Asian American, and Jewish Studies were being downgraded into programs, under the umbrella of Ethnic Studies. Though CUNY President Yolanda Moses claims that she only intends to "strengthen" instruction in these fields, the signal is clear from City College — a mere twenty Harlem blocks from the hunger tents at Columbia — that programs focusing on the experience of oppressed and historically excluded groups are under the gun as likely candidates for "consolidation." After all, President Moses was herself acting under strong fiscal and political pressures within CUNY, and her decisions were very much in tune with the tenor of the times set by Republican state and city administrations.[1]

The real news, then, is that Latino Studies and the nascent (or re-nascent) movements to institutionalize the study of African American, Asian American, and other group experiences, are caught in a crossfire. As interest in Latino Studies

Harvard Educational Review Vol. 67 No. 2 Summer 1997, 208–221

grows at Harvard, Black and Puerto Rican Studies are threatened at Hunter. The conjuncture is actually one of clashing priorities, a collision between the expressed educational needs of an increasingly non-White student population and the conservative inclinations of many social and educational power brokers. What appears to be a threshold at one institution is, at the same time, a closing door at another; all attempts at curricular innovation are met with equally strong moves toward intellectual retrenchment and wagon-circling. This eminently contradictory climate sets the immediate context for the struggle over Latino Studies.

NEW CONTEXTS

An alert reading of prevailing and countervailing winds in the academy is a necessary starting point for an assessment of Latino Studies and parallel movements for educational change. The calls for inclusion, focus, and self-determination, and the reluctance with which these calls are met by entrenched faculty and wary administrators, reflect larger social contentions, in which the issues at stake are not courses and professors but food, shelter, and citizenship. Like Asian American Studies, Latino Studies has its historical raison d'être in the unresolved historical struggles over immigration, racism, and colonialism. The proliferation of students of color, and the contestatory nature of their presence in higher education, attests to the importance of these issues to the attendant curricular challenges. The attacks on minority admissions, as manifested by Proposition 209 in California, are at the political crux of the broader intellectual issue. As such, Latino Studies needs to be understood as a social movement, as an extension within the academy of the movements against racism and on behalf of immigrant rights afoot in the wider society. Only then can one see that the emergence of Latino Studies holds the promise of legitimation enjoyed by the empowered gatekeepers of academic discourse. Demographic, economic, and political changes, and the resolute efforts to stem their tide, thus undergird the widespread appeals for changes in educational institutions and their curricula.

Equally important is the need for historical memory. Today's Latino students, and much of the faculty, were very young or not yet born when coalitions of Black, Chicano, Puerto Rican, Asian, and Native American students first claimed their intellectual spaces at the universities in the late 1960s and early 1970s. There is an awareness, of course, that all this happened before, and that many of the present demands closely echo those that inaugurated the varied ethnic studies programs still in place, however precariously, in the 1990s. But a sense of continuity, and an understanding of the disjunctures, has been blurred with the passing of an entire generation and the dramatic geopolitical changes of the intervening years.

One of the most obvious differences between earlier and more recent university movements is that very few of the earlier initiatives went by the name of "Latino Studies." By and large they were called "Chicano Studies" or "Puerto Rican Studies," corresponding directly to the vocal, spirited, and politically grounded struggles of the Chicano and Puerto Rican communities for justice and liberation. There were exceptions, such as "Raza Studies" at San Francisco State, where the Latino student constituency was largely non-Chicano, or "Chicano-Boricua Studies" at Wayne State, where comparable numbers of Mexican American and Puerto Rican ("Boricua") students joined forces. However, for the most part, the forebears of the present-day Latino Studies efforts tended to be focused on specific national groups, and the "communities" to which they were accountable were nearer at hand, both geographically and culturally.

Much of this difference in nomenclature, and in relative distance from the communities, may be attributed to the ebb and flow of historical movements for change. The previous generation of Latino students and faculty activism coincided with a time of radical challenges to persistent colonial oppression on a global, national, and local scale. Militant opposition to the Vietnam war, defense of the Cuban Revolution, and the Black and Brown Power movements informed the rhetoric and strategic vision of Chicano and Puerto Rican Studies at their inception. That charged revolutionary aura does not surround the Latino Studies agenda in our time, though further ebbs and flows may eventually reconnect the university-based struggle to such systemic types of social confrontation.

The point of this historical view of Latino Studies is neither to romanticize nor to reject the past, but to help save us from reinventing the wheel. Drawing lessons from the past must not blind us to new insights and approaches, or to the possibility that conditions today may in some ways be even more propitious for the establishment of Latino Studies than they were a generation ago.

The main shift that has occurred between the present context of Latino Studies and its previous manifestation twenty-five years ago is perhaps best summed up in the words "global" and "globalization," with all due caution to what Robert Fitch has aptly called "globaloney."[2] The economic restructuring of world capitalism that took off in the mid-1970s, along with the telecommunications revolution, has created radically new levels of interaction and interconnectedness among populations. The growing mass migrations generated by these changes are also affected by them, and in their circular and transnational character they differ markedly from the migratory experiences of the early 1970s.

The diversification and geographic dispersal of the Latino population is the most visible evidence of these changes in the present-day Latino Studies context. In addition to the largest groups, Mexican American and Puerto Rican, there are now sizable immigrant communities in the United States from most Latin American countries. As many of these diasporas, notably the Mexican and the Puerto Rican, have fanned out across the country, the demographic landscape, as well as the political and cultural setting, has been further altered for U.S. Latinos.

This "globalizing" of the Latino presence is, of course, clearly evident at U.S. colleges and universities. On most campuses the Latino student body is diverse, often a mix between one large group — Mexican American, Puerto Rican, Cuban, or Dominican — and Latinos from a variety of other backgrounds. In some areas where there is a preponderance of one national group, it remains necessary, and feasible, to mount and sustain programs focusing on that group — such as departments, programs, and research centers in Mexican American, Puerto Rican, or Cuban Studies. But at most sites — including those in which students are calling for programs — Latino Studies makes sense, not only bureaucratically, but also because of the increasingly transnational nature of the student population and of their communities, as well as the geopolitical relations in which they find themselves.

It is not only the pan-ethnic or diverse Latino demography that explains — and perhaps justifies — the shift from a Chicano or Puerto Rican to a Latino Studies framework. The student constituency and subject matter of Latino Studies have not only become more multigroup in the sense of numerical diversity; rather, because of global and hemispheric restructuring, exemplified recently by such moves as NAFTA and the Caribbean Basin Initiative, the Latino communities in the United States are far more intricately tied to economic and political realities in their countries and regions of origin than ever before. Pan-Latino necessarily implies "trans-Latino," a more rigorously transnational unit of Latino Studies analysis than even the staunch "Third World" and anti-imperialist perspective of Latino Studies in its foundation.

NEW CONCEPTS

This sociohistorical context generates conceptual approaches for what remains essentially the same object/subject of study: the experience of Latin American and Caribbean peoples in the United States. With all the caveats, and fully recognizing that the very terms "Latino" and "Hispanic" are imposed labels — ideological hoodwinks aimed at tightening hegemony and capturing markets — the "Latino" concept is still useful, if not indispensable, for charting out an area of contemporary intellectual inquiry and political advocacy.[3] It builds on and complements the perspectives, curricular orientations, and programmatic structures of established Chicano and Puerto Rican Studies programs. The concept of "Latino Studies" allows for some space to mediate issues of inclusion and solidarity sometimes strained in nationality-specific situations; for example, what to do about the Central Americans, Dominicans, Colombians, and "other" Latinos who may not feel they fit into, say, a Chicano-exclusive notion of "La Raza." Such strains persist, of course, and it is still often difficult in many settings to get Puerto Ricans, Chicanos, and Ecuadorians, for instance, to come to the same "Latino" meetings, or to the same "Latino" dances.

In addition to the "global" economic and political shifts and their impact, the period since the first wave of Latino Studies has also witnessed significant new developments in social theory and methodology, or at least new emphases in thinking about issues of race, ethnicity, coloniality, nationality, gender, sexuality, and class. The altered historical field has made for a changed discursive field, much of it occupied by questions of cultural and group identity. If the early 1970s articulation of Latino Studies was guided by a rallying cry of cultural nationalism — boisterous and contestatory but also parochial and unreflexive — a current understanding of Latino experience is necessarily informed by insights and approaches developed by feminist, postcolonial, and race theories, as well as lesbian and gay studies. The presumed seamlessness and discreteness of group identities characteristic of earlier Latin perspectives have given way to more complex, interactive, and transgressive notions of hybrid and multiple positionalities.

Theorizing about gender and sexuality has done a great deal to dissolve the sexist and heterosexist conception of Latino group unity and inclusion, and to complicate the meanings of Latino claims and affirmation. Latina, Chicana, and Puertorriqueña areas of political activism and intellectual work have involved changes in prevailing ideas of Latino history and culture, and have helped bring into the foreground testimonial and ethnographic methods of social research. Revamping the canonical — straight male — notion of "Latino identity" with a view toward

contemporary theories of sexuality leads not only to new political stances and possibilities, but beyond that to new kinds of knowledge about cultural history, and
even a new, more variegated relation to theoretical practice. A striking account of
this interface of Latino and sexual identities and its intellectual consequences was
voiced recently by Oscar Montero, a Cuban American professor from CUNY, at
the 1996 conference of the East of California Network of the Association of Asian
American Studies. "It goes without saying," Montero states, "that 'Latino' and 'homosexual' signal different histories and different stories, unevenly deployed.
Bringing the two together creates a lopsided image, but perhaps a useful one. The
experiences of the body justify the mask, and this mask wants to question the received metaphors for defining identity: Latino by birth, queer by choice. Latino by
choice, queer by birth. What matters is that having taken a stance, linking with this
mask the two identities, a reader, a critic, a student, can turn to the salient works of
his or her tradition and read them anew, availing herself of whatever theories
might do the job."[4]

The contemporary Latino construct, and the intellectual project of Latino
Studies, is laced with this open, multidimensional disposition toward theory, and
must also incorporate critical understandings of processes of "racialization" and
"translocality." In addition to differentiation along the lines of gender and sexuality, the specific identity positions of "Black Latinos" and of mixed Latino backgrounds — Puerto Rican and Dominican, Mexican and Salvadoran — have drawn
increasing attention and have done much to sunder more or less monolithic and
essentialist assumptions of inherited conceptualizations. Angie Chabram, the
noted Chicana feminist and cultural studies theorist, has staked out new grounds
for a critique of traditional Chicano (and even Chicana) perspectives by reading
the new-found significance of her other, "repressed" Puerto Rican half. In her essay "Chicana! Rican? No, Chicana-Riqueña!: Refashioning the Transnational Connection," Chabram writes forcefully of the residual identity left by her absent
Boricua father, as filtered through her rooted Chicana mother, and their jarring
repercussions on her Chicanismo:

> It does not cease to amaze me that it was *she* who nurtured a sense of Puerto
> Ricanness in me — she who had all the right to be a nationalist following the
> purist dictates associated with this politics, for she was a Chicana, she was not
> mixed in my way with the Riqueña. In retrospect, it occurs to me that what she
> presented me with throughout one of the trajectories of our lives as mother
> and daughter was a pedagogy of Chicanas/os, a mode of knowing Puerto Rico
> from inside of Chicana/o, a way of speaking across fractured ethnicities, a way
> of initiating a dialogue among and between different ethnic groups.[5]

Chabram draws from these lessons a way of "countering our presumed singularity
with our historically verifiable pluralities, the ones that are intersected, and . . . engage positions from diverse fields of contestation"; she builds on her personal experience to summon "a strategic location from which to refashion a transnational
connection to ourselves and one another, and to contribute to a widening of imagined communities and spheres of contestation."[6]

Opinions will vary as to the utility and relevance of an explicitly postmodern
frame and vocabulary for these new lines of theoretical inquiry, and some reluc-

tance is surely due to hasty applications of "postcolonial" models to situations, like those of Chicanos and Puerto Ricans, which would still seem to be emphatically colonial in both historical trajectory and present condition. The term "multicultural" itself is another recent coinage that Latino Studies should treat with caution, since in its most prevalent usage it echoes the grave inadequacies of its ideological predecessor, cultural pluralism. Yet, while Marxist and other anti-imperialist intellectual and political traditions remain pertinent to a liberatory analysis of Latino reality, these new insights from multicultural and postcolonial theory are invaluable because they allow us to span the full range of Latino positionalities under the complex transnational conditions of our time. Whatever we may think of the vocabulary, reflections on questions of "hybridity," "liminality," "transgressivity," and the like, and the new intellectual horizons they signal, are clearly germane to any contemporary work in Latino Studies.[7] They complement, and add philosophical range to, what has been the guiding metaphor of Latino Studies: "la frontera," or the border.

It is the idea of the "nation," and of national culture and identity, that has entailed the recent rethinking that is perhaps most pertinent to a new discursive field for Latino Studies. Both Chicano and Puerto Rican Studies have relied, for their foundational narratives, on the national concept, whether that concept referred to historical home countries or internal colonies in U.S. barrios. Latino social experience was conditioned and defined by the hierarchized interaction of nations, and cultural identities were first and above all national identities. The boundedness and relative uniformity of their original territories went largely unquestioned, particularly in demarcating each Latino group from an "American" nationality, mainstream or otherwise. The guiding theoretical premises were adopted directly from thinkers like Frantz Fanon, Amilcar Cabral, and of course Lenin, with Black nationalism, Pedro Albizu Campos, and even José Vasconcelos and Octavio Paz being more immediate intellectual sources.[8]

Nationality is still no doubt the main binding principle and sensibility for each of the Latino groups, as evidenced at the annual Puerto Rican Day Parade, *Cinco de Mayo,* and other celebrations. Indeed, it is important to insist upon this persistence of specifically "national" affiliation in countering the tendency of U.S. social science and public policy to reduce Latinos to an "ethnic" group experience, with its implicit analogy to the prototypical story of immigrant incorporation. Yet despite the non-assimilationist thrust of most Latino discourse, the idea of the nation as the ontological locus of difference and opposition to the hegemonic Anglo "Other" has been seriously revised from many theoretical angles and Latina/o subject positions.

Here again, the varied feminist and queer critiques have been most incisive in their exposure of the "brotherhoods" of nations and their ideologically grounded foundational narratives. For contemporary Latino Studies, this undermining of the nation concept as hetero-masculinist mask extends to the diasporic communities spun off from the "home" nations in the course of global and regional reconfigurations. The nation also continues to be dissected and deconstructed along the lines of race and class, dimensions that were already strongly etched in the earlier stage of Latino Studies. Yet even the strident Third World, anti-imperialist stance of the early 1970s did contain some serious gaps, which subsequent theoretical work, especially on race, does much to fill. Updating the class critique of the nation is less visible within Latino Studies since the Marxist analyses published around 1980 (such as the Center for Puerto Rican Studies' *Labor Migration under Capitalism* and Mario Barrera's *Race and Class in the Southwest*),[9] though some fruitful lines of thinking have emerged from an application of "subaltern studies."[10] It is as though, with the abruptly changing economic geography of the past decade, historical reality has lunged far ahead of social theory: no new sociological terminology has surfaced that can account for the class relations resulting from the radical changes in the socialist world and the intricate transnational alignments and restructurings of present-day capitalism.

None of these critical assaults on the nation as hegemonic ploy has spelled the final demise of the concept of nation. It continues to be a central social category in the intellectual agenda of Latino Studies, and in the struggle of Latino national groups in the United States. But these assaults have resulted in a radical rethinking of the meaning of nationality, and in a recognition that the concept of nation is reliable as a political principle and rallying point only in its interaction with these other forms of social differentiation and liberatory movements.

The reinterpretation of the concept of nation that informs today's Latino Studies hovers around the idea of "imagined communities" as formulated by Benedict Anderson in his frequently cited book of that title.[11] In his formulation, the nation as a fixed and primordial territory of inclusion/exclusion becomes a malleable, fluid, permeable construct, a group given form by shared imaginaries. The idea of "imagined communities" lends itself well to the conceptual terminology of Latino Studies today because it helps to describe the "national" experience of Latino diasporas in all its ambiguity. The sense of belonging and not belonging to the nation — driven home to Nuyoricans (Puerto Ricans born and raised in New York) and Chicanos when they "return" to their "native" lands — confirms that nationality can not only be imagined, but actually created as a social reality by the force of the imagination. The paradox of being "nationals" in a thoroughly "transnationalized" economic geography — Latinos as "transnations" or translocal nationalities — is captured well with a loose, dynamic, and relational concept like "imagined communities." This concept is certainly more adequate than the essentialist and mechanical categories of the "national question" that influenced much of Latino Studies in its earlier stage.

Some theorists used to refer to this "question" of nationality and nationhood, true to Marxist-Leninist vocabulary, as the "national-colonial question." Indeed the renovation of the concept of nation and national culture begs the question of coloniality and, for Latino Studies, the pertinence of "postcolonial" theory. When Latino Studies programs were founded, nobody spoke of a "postcolonial" condition or era. On the contrary, colonialism and anticolonial struggle were precisely the terms around which that and simultaneous movements were defined. In the United States, at least, the postcolonial discourse is definitely a child of the intervening years, gaining ground in theoretical debates only in the past decade or so. Imperialism — which became a buzzword during the same period — is surely one of the subtexts. But the pressing question from the perspective of Latino Studies is whether Puerto Rico and the Southwest at some point ceased occupying a colonial position, and, if so, when and how. More particularly, can the experience of diasporic migrants from former colonial nations serve as a model, or analogue, for that of transnational communities like those of U.S. Latinos? The insights of theorists like Homi Bhabha and Gayatri Spivak are of some explanatory value, as is the critique of Anderson's "imagined communities" by Partha Chatterjee and others.[12] However, for the purpose of identifying the conditions faced by Puerto Rican, Mexican American, Dominican, and other Latino peoples in the United States, and the economic and political domination of their home countries, the term "postcolonial" seems to be jumping the gun at best. Even those most bent on minimizing the collision and incompatibility between Latino and other U.S. nationalities cannot fail to detect the signs of some kind of systemic social subordination, call it colonial or otherwise, and independent of any proposed remedy.[13]

PROSPECTS AND PROMISES

While the activist relationship of Latino Studies programs to their social contexts and communities is weaker now than in its founding years, the theoretical field of Latino Studies is now wider and more complex. The implementation of this rich intellectual agenda is also more complex, and certainly as challenging as in the years when Latino and other ethnic studies programs were first set in place. Today's ideological and fiscal obstacles are the most obvious challenges to Latino Studies, and must be faced without the momentum of the civil rights movement to build on. But even more pragmatic questions of institutional location and leverage present problems that were not faced when building ethnic studies was still a matter of filling a vacuum.

Currently, there are ethnic and minority studies programs that have been in place for many years on many campuses, including, of course, Chicano, Puerto Rican, and, more recently, Cuban and Dominican Studies. There are professional associations; academic research centers and networks; policy institutes; journals, scholarly and otherwise; and a proliferation of Web sites all devoted to ethnic and minority studies. Within the academy there are also emergent disciplines and areas (such as ethnic, cultural, and multicultural studies) and groundswells of change in already established interdisciplines and area studies (communications, comparative literature, and American, Latin American, and Caribbean Studies), all of which run parallel with or border closely on Latino Studies. It is important to constantly rethink the relation of a reemergent area like Latino Studies to the traditional disciplines, like history and anthropology, where some of the best work about Latinos is being produced, and most of which are also in flux or in a state of crisis.

What the best "fit" for Latino Studies may be in the present and shifting structure of the U.S. academy is clearly an enigma, especially as none of these umbrellas or potential federations is guaranteed to feel like home in a suspicious, reluctant, and sometimes dog-eat-dog institutional environment. Like Latino Studies itself, all of these abstractions from the specific historical experiences of the composite groups tend to dilute and distort those experiences, and to set up new exclusions and reductions. Furthermore, each of these transdisciplinary rubrics has its own trajectory and baggage that is often at odds with the guiding tenets of Latino Studies. Think of Latin American Area Studies, for instance, or even American Studies, which in their founding intentions were so consonant with the interests of U.S. and Anglo hegemony.[14] Special caution should be observed in dealing with new confections that sometimes go under the name of "Hispanic Studies," but that are often no more than opportune creations of Spanish departments desperate to shore up their ever-waning student appeal, while retaining their doggedly Hispanophile ideological conservatism. It would seem that nothing short of an autonomous, free-standing university Department of Latino Studies could promise a location conducive to the confidence needed to carry forward an adequate instructional and research project.

While departmental status may stand as a goal or desideratum for Latino Studies, a pragmatic and flexible approach is probably advisable under the present political conditions. Whether and how Latino Studies may be folded or built into some larger configuration would seem to be a case-by-case kind of decision, depending on the relative strength and compatibility of existing programs and alliances. Ethnic Studies, for example, might be right, provided there is a strong accent on questions of race and social oppression, and providing that the area is moving from a focus on strictly domestic issues of group difference and rights into the international arena. Some affiliation within American Studies could also work, as scholars and students in that area deepen their critical analysis of the field's reactionary and chauvinist origins and expand its horizons toward something like "Americas Studies."

With certain intellectual and political provisos, Latino Studies could also find a hospitable and productive place in relation to Latin American or Cultural Studies. An issue of central importance, though, that is often obscured in this quest for a larger floor plan, or theoretical rubric, is the relation of Latino Studies to African American Studies, on the one hand, and to Women's Studies on the other. The circumscription of the "Latino" concept in terms of ethnicity, geography, and language culture tends to cordon off Latino Studies from full engagement of issues of gender, sexuality, and "racial" identity.

If certain key theoretical principles of methodology and research practice are clear, the main immediate goal at some institutions may be getting a foot in the door, at others standing firm in defense of the spaces that have already been created, however flawed. For in the longer view, the objective is not limited to securing those spaces and opportunities, but extends to advancing new knowledge and new ways of understanding what knowledge is for and about. Latino Studies will become ghettoized and easy prey for closure or consolidation if it is divorced from this wider intellectual and social project, both at the university and in the larger community.

In this respect, and with all the contextual and conceptual changes, contemporary Latino Studies has much to learn from, and reaffirm in, its own history. In founding meetings and declarations, Chicano Studies and Puerto Rican Studies set forth certain principles of research and educational practice that continue to underlie the Latino Studies project today.[15] To extrapolate from the many goals and methods proclaimed, these founding plans called for knowledge production that was interdisciplinary in its methodological range, collective in its practice, and tied to the community. The primary methodological aims of bridging the divide between humanities and the social sciences remains the order of the day, with areas like ethnic and cultural studies and communications moving the discourse from "inter" in the direction of "trans-," "post-," and even "antidisciplinary." Collective research practice is still an obvious necessity, if only because of the volume and scope of this supposedly narrow and particularist object of study. We are now more aware that collective work means more than coauthorship or tight-knit study groups; rather, coordinations and collaborations at many levels, from anthology readers and conference panels to on-line cothinking, are indispensable to cover the ground and live up to the multiple challenges posed by recent theorizing. For one instance, the close attention to multiple positionalities in the analysis of socio-cultural experience reinforces the need for the coordination of diverse research and teaching perspectives.

As for the ties of Latino Studies to "community," that tenet would seem to hold more strongly than ever, because of the relative distance of much academic work — Latino and other — from the external "Other," but also because there is an immense ideological stake in keeping Latino higher education and Latino communities apart, and even at odds. The notion of "community," of course, has also been subjected to critical deconstruction and demystification. Though the concept of "imagined communities" is useful in displacing the concept of "nation" in the traditional sense, the very vagueness and mantra-like resonance of "community" can render it as meaningless as the oft-stated sanctities of the "national family."

Still, an affiliation, reference, and accountability to Latino people and social realities remains a sine qua non of Latino Studies. It is not a matter of studying the community/communities as something outside of and separate from ourselves. Socially, many of us are a part of and from these communities, and it is in this sense of intellectual work that the political is also personal. With all due caution with regard to fallacies of authenticity and a politics of "experience," Latino Studies does affirm the need for (for lack of a better word) "indigenous" perspectives on the reality "under study," perspectives that are generally ignored, or colonized, in much academic and journalistic coverage of Latino life.

For all its sensitivity to differences within the "Latino community," and its critical rejection of imposed group labels, Latino Studies also needs to reflect continually on the real or constitutive unities within and among the Latino population as a whole. The history of Latinos is already in mid-narrative, and even if we don't propose to "imagine" the "Hispanic" community as a "nation" in formation — the latest book on the subject is actually entitled *Hispanic Nation*[16] — some form of pan-group amalgam is always at least potentially on the horizon. Though it is important to view *lo Latino* ("Latinoness") from the optic of the particular national groups, the social and cultural perspective of each group also evokes some relation to a Latino "ethnoscape" of transnational dimensions.[17]

But even to consider such prospects, to trace historical congruences and study practical interactions, requires not only new curricula, but also new attitudes about mounting curricular strategies adequate to the task. It also requires a space very different from that provided by many universities in the present climate. Oscar Montero, cited earlier, summons this broader discursive and institutional agenda in his closing remarks:

> New curricula cannot succeed by mere inclusion of emergent discourses, after the fashion of eighteenth-century encyclopedists. It must incorporate a point of view, or a series of points of view, a different dialectic, and in the long haul, perhaps a different kind of university.[18]

NOTES

1. The events at City College are reported in the *New York Times,* March 19, 1996, p. B4, and in the *Chronicle of Higher Education,* March 29, 1996, p. 18. Reporting on the strike at Columbia University appears in the *New York Times,* April 15, 1996, pp. B1, B3.

2. The use of the word "globaloney" to refer to the obfuscation of local, national, and regional realities and contradictions by imposing a "global" or "transnational" framework occurs in Robert Fitch, *The Assassination of New York* (London: Verso, 1993).

3. See Juan Flores, "Pan-Latino/Trans-Latino: Puerto Ricans in the 'New Nueva York,'" *Centro Journal, 8,* No. 1/2 (1996), 170–186, and "The Latino Imaginary: Dimensions of Community and Identity," in *Tropicalizations: Transcultural Representations of Latinidad,* ed. Frances R. Aparicio and Susana Chávez-Silverman (Hanover, NH: University of New England Press, 1997).

4. Montero's remarks were published as "Coalitions/Collisions: Notes from a Latino Queer," in *Common Grounds: Charting Asian American Studies East of California,* ed. Robert Ji-Song Ku (New York: Hunter College/Columbia University), p. 45.

5. Angie Chabram, "Chicana! Rican? No, Chicana-Riqueña! Refashioning the Transnational Connection," in *Multiculturalism: A Critical Reader,* ed. David Theo Goldberg (Oxford: Blackwell, 1994), p. 284,

6. Chabram, "Chicana!" pp. 290, 292.

7. These terms and concepts occur frequently in the writings of "postcolonial" theorists like Homi Bhabha, Trin Minh-Ha, and Gayatri Spivak. See, for example, Homi Bhabha, "The Third Space: Interviews with Homi Bhabha," in *Identity, Culture, Difference,* ed. Jonathan Rutherford (London: Lawrence and Wishart, 1990), pp. 207–221. See also Juan Flores's essay, "Broken English Memories," *Modern Language Quarterly,* 57 (1996), 381–395.

8. See Frantz Fanon, *The Wretched of the Earth* (New York: Grove Press, 1963); Amilcar Cabral, *Return to the Source: Selected Speeches* (New York: Monthly Review Press, 1973), pp. 39–56; Pedro Albizu Campos, "Observations on the Brookings Institutional Report" and "Concept of the Race," in *The Intellectual Roots of Independence,* ed. Iris M. Zavala and Rafael Rodríguez (New York: Monthly Review, 1989), pp. 171–182; José Vasconcelos, *La Raza Cosmica* (Los Angeles: Centro de Publicaciones, 1979); Octavio Paz, "The Pachuco and Other Extremes," in *Labyrinth of Solitude* (New York: Grove Press, 1985), pp. 9–28.

9. History Task Force (Centro de Estudios Puertorriqueños), *Labor Migration under Capitalism: The Puerto Rican Experience* (New York: Monthly Review Press, 1979); Mario Barrera, *Race and Class in the Southwest: A Theory of Racial Inequality* (Notre Dame, IN: Notre Dame Press, 1979).

10. See, for example, Kelvin Santiago, "Subject People," in *Colonial Discourses: Economic Transformation and Social Disorder in Puerto Rico, 1898–1947* (Albany: State University of New York Press, 1994).

11. Benedict Anderson, *Imagined Communities: Reflections of the Origin and Spread of Nationalism* (London: Verso, 1983).

12. See, for example, Partha Chatterjee, *The Nation and Its Fragments: Colonial and Postcolonial Histories* (Princeton: Princeton University Press, 1993), pp. 3–13. See also Homi Bhabha, ed., *Nation and Narration* (London: Routledge, 1990). Also, Gayatri Spivak, "Can the Subaltern Speak?" in *Colonial Discourse and Post-Colonial Theory,* ed. Patrick Williams and Laura Chrisman (New York: Columbia University Press, 1994), pp. 66–111.

13. See Bertell Ollman and Edward Vernoff, eds., *The Left Academy: Marxist Scholarship on American Campuses* (New York: Praeger, 1986); Noam Chomsky et al. (eds.), *The Cold War and the University: Toward an Intellectual History of the Cold War* (New York: New

Press, 1997). On Latin American Studies, see Mark T. Berger, *Under Northern Eyes: Latin American Studies and U.S. Hegemony in the Americas, 1898–1990* (Bloomington: Indiana University Press, 1995).

14. See, for example, Linda Chavez, *Out of the Barrio: Toward a New Politics of Hispanic Assimilation* (New York: Basic Books, 1991), esp. chapter 10, "The Puerto Rican Exception." See also Flores, "Pan-Latino/Trans-Latino."

15. An account of the struggle for Chicano Studies, including the original "Plan de Santa Barbara," may be found in Carlos Muñoz, *Youth, Identity, Power: The Chicano Movement* (London: Verso, 1989). On Puerto Rican Studies, see María Sanchez and Antonio Stevens-Arroyo, eds., *Towards a Renaissance of Puerto Rican Studies: Ethnic and Area Studies in the University* (Highlands Lakes, NJ: Social Science Monographs, 1987). See also, Frank Bonilla, Ricardo Campos, and Juan Flores, "Puerto Rican Studies: Promptings for the Academy and the Left," in *The Left Academy: Marxist Scholarship on American Campuses,* ed. Bertell Ollman and Edward Vernoff (New York: Praeger, 1986), pp. 67–102.

16. Geoffrey Fox, *Hispanic Nation: Culture, Politics, and the Constructing of Identity* (New York: Carol, 1996).

17. The term "ethnoscape" and theory of transnational identity linkages is set forth in Arjun Appadurai, "Disjuncture and Difference in the Global Cultural Economy," in *Colonial Discourse and Post-Colonial Theory,* ed. Patrick Williams and Laura Chrisman (New York: Columbia University Press, 1994), pp. 324–339.

18. Montero, "Coalitions/Collisions," p. 46.

About the Authors

Deirdre Almeida is Assistant Professor of Education at the University of Massachusetts, Amherst, School of Education. Her professional interests center around Native American/indigenous education, curriculum and learning, school improvement, and women's education. She is author of "What Exactly Is It That You Teach?: Developing an Indigenous Education Program at the University Level" in *Cultural Survival Quarterly* (1998), and "Indigenous Education: Survival for Our Children" in *Equity and Excellence in Education* (1998).

Dolores Delgado Bernal is Assistant Professor at the University of Utah in Salt Lake City. She is interested in the socio-historical context of Chicana/o education, Chicana resistance and life histories, and oral history research methodology. She is author of "Chicana/o Education from the Civil Rights Era to the Present" in *The Elusive Quest for Equality: 150 years of Chicano/Chicana Education* (edited by J. F. Moreno, 1999), and "Grassroots Leadership Reconceptualized: Chicana Oral Histories and the 1968 East Los Angeles School Blowouts" in *Frontiers: A Journal of Women Studies* (1998).

Kim Bush is a teacher at the Friends Boys School in Ramallah, West Bank. He is trained as a historian specializing in African history. His primary professional concern is education for refugees, both those spontaneously settled and camp dwellers. He was formerly a high school teacher in Quito, Ecuador, and in Los Olivos, California. (Editors' note: This information is from 1989, when we originally published his article. No further information is available.)

Liveda C. Clements is a Cash Control Specialist at Mellon Trust in Medford, Massachusetts. She is a 1998 graduate of Boston University, where she had a major in political science and a minor in economics. She is interested in creative writing. (Editors' note: This information is from 1998. No more recent information is available.)

Sandra Del Valle is Associate Counsel of the Puerto Rican Legal Defense and Education Fund located in New York City. Her areas of interest are bilingual education and language rights. Her most recent publication is "La Politica del Idioma en los Estados Unidos: Una Visión Histórica y la Necesidad de un Nuevo Paradigma" ("Language Policy in the United States: A Historical Vision and the Need for a New Paradigm") in *Revista de Ciencias Sociales* (1998).

Munir Jamil Fasheh is Director of the Arab Education Forum at Harvard University's Center for Middle Eastern Studies. He is the founder and former director of the Tamer Institute for Community Education in Jerusalem. His primary professional interest is in creating learning environments, particularly for youth. He is author of "Talking about What to Cook for Dinner When Our House Is on Fire: The Poverty of Existing Forms of International Education" (1985) and "Community Education: To

Reclaim and Transform What Has Been Made Invisible" (1990), both in *Harvard Educational Review*. He is also the author of six books in Arabic.

Juan Flores is a Professor in the Department of Black and Puerto Rican Studies at Hunter College, and in the doctoral program in sociology at the Graduate Center, City University of New York. He is interested in Puerto Rican and Latino culture, and the sociology of culture and ethnicity. He is author of *From Bomba to Hip Hop: Puerto Rican Culture and Latino Identity* (in press) and of *Divided Borders: Essays on Puerto Rican Identity* (1993).

Jeff Howard, President of The Efficacy Institute in Lexington, Massachusetts, is interested in driving greater student achievement through mobilization of effort. He is author of "You Can't Get There from Here: The Need for a New Logic in Education Reform" in *Daedalus* (1995), and "The Third Movement: Developing Black Children for the 21st Century" in *The State of Black America* (1993).

Mieko Kamii is Associate Professor of Psychology and Education at Wheelock College in Boston, as well as Director of the Center on College, School, and Community Partnerships. Her research interests include children's cognitive development and learning, and teachers' professional development and learning. She is author of "Standards and Assessment: What We've Learned Thus Far" in *The Web* (1996), and "Cultural Divide" in *Fieldwork: An Expeditionary Learning Outward Bound Reader* (edited by A. Mednick and E. Cousins, 1996).

Stacey J. Lee, Associate Professor in the Educational Policy Studies Department of the University of Wisconsin-Madison, is interested in the ethnic identity and school achievement of Asian American students. Her previous publications include *Unraveling the "Model Minority" Stereotype: Listening to Asian American Youth* (1996).

Khalil Mahshi is Director General–International and Public Relations of the Ministry of Education in Ramallah, Palestine. His professional focus is national educational planning. He is author of "School Education in Palestine: From Collapse to Empowerment" in *Revista de Educación* (1998), and coauthor of "Education for Awareness and Involvement" in *Education with Production* (Mahshi et al., 1987).

Eric Margolis is Assistant Professor in the Division of Educational Leadership and Policy Studies at Arizona State University. A sociologist of education, he works in the areas of youth at risk, HIV/AIDS, and visual sociology. His recent publications include "Class Pictures: Representations of Race, Gender and Ability in a Century of School Photography" in *Visual Sociology* (1999), and "AIDS Research/AIDS Policy: Competing Paradigms of Science and Public Policy" in *Research in Social Policy* (1998).

Robert Parris Moses is President of the Algebra Project, which he founded. A mathematics educator, curriculum developer, and teacher trainer, his goal with the Project is to establish a pedagogy of mathematics that expects and encourages every student to succeed at algebra in middle school, and supports their efforts to do so. He is currently teaching at the Lanier High School in Jackson, Mississippi.

Sonia Nieto is Professor of Language, Literacy, and Culture at the University of Massachusetts, Amherst. Her research interests center around multicultural and bilingual education, the education of Latinos in the United States, and Puerto Rican children's literature. Her publications include *Affirming Diversity: The Sociopolitical Context of Multicultural Education* (2000) and *The Light in Their Eyes: Creating Multicultural Learning Communities* (1999).

Antonia Pantoja is former President and a current member of the Board of Directors of PRODUCIR, Inc., which is located in Canovanas, Puerto Rico. She is interested in community economic development, racism in Puerto Rico and in general, and in the development of a competent, ethical Puerto Rican leadership.

Wilhemina Perry is a Consultant to PRODUCIR, Inc., in Canovanas, Puerto Rico. Her major professional interest is community economic development.

Townsand Price-Spratlen is Assistant Professor in the Department of Sociology at Ohio Sate University. His major professional interests include urban sociology, internal migration, and community viability. He is coauthor of "The Geography of Homelessness in the United States" in *Population Research and Policy Review* (with B. A. Lee, 1999), and author of "Between Depression and Prosperity? Changes in the Community Context of Historical African American Migration" in *Social Forces* (1998).

Ana Y. Ramos-Zayas is a Postdoctoral Fellow with the Harvard Children's Initiative in Cambridge, Massachusetts. Her research concerns are cultural nationalism, Puerto Rican/Latino studies, and cultural and social capital. She is author of *"La Patria es Valor y Sacrificio": Cultural Nationalism, Pedagogical Spaces, and the American Dream in Puerto Rican Chicago* (in preparation).

Mary Romero is a Professor in the School of Justice Studies at Arizona State University. Her research and teaching interests are gender and race relations in education and labor. She is author of *Women's Untold Stories: Breaking Silence, Talking Back, Voicing Complexity* (1999) and *Challenging Fronteras: Structuring Latina and Latino Lives in the U.S.* (1997).

Asgedet Stefanos is Assistant Professor at the University of Massachusetts, Boston. Her professional interests center around education and pedagogy, African studies, and women studies. Her publications include "Angles of Vision: Teaching Multi-Disciplinary and Inclusive Courses" in *Achieving against the Odds: Teaching and Learning at the University of Massachusetts at Boston* (edited by T. Sieber and E. Kingston-Man, in press), and *An Encounter with Revolutionary Change: A Portrait of Contemporary Eritrean Women* (1997).

Tyrone A. Sutton is Publisher of *Street Scholar* magazine. His professional interests are writing, editing, and publishing. He lives in Boston, Massachusetts.

Susan McAllister Swap (deceased) was Chair of the Department of Professional Studies and Professor of Education and Psychology at Wheelock College in Boston. Her published works include *Enhancing Parent Involvement in Schools* (1987), *Managing an Effective Staff Development Program* (1987), and *Building Home-School Partnerships with America's Changing Families* (with L. Braun, 1987).

Cornel West is Professor of Afro-American Studies, Faculty of Arts and Sciences, Harvard University, and Professor of the Philosophy of Religion at Harvard Divinity School. His current topics of academic interest include problems facing the Black urban underclass in the United States, and creating and maintaining an ongoing dialogue between African Americans and Jews. His many publications include *Race Matters* (1993) and *The Ethical Dimensions of Marxist Thought* (1991).

About the Editors

Ricardo Dobles is a doctoral student in Administration, Planning, and Social Policy at the Harvard Graduate School of Education. His research explores the socio-historical adjustment of urban school systems to cultural and economic changes in the communities they serve. He is particularly interested in those moments of struggle that defy the typical process of school policy and reconstruct school change as a process of negotiation between communities and schools.

José A. Segarra is a Puerto Rican doctoral student in the Teaching, Curriculum, and Learning Environments Program at the Harvard Graduate School of Education. He was born and raised in New York City.